AOL®
KEYWORDS
3rd Edition

AOL®

KEYWORDS

3rd Edition

Jennifer Watson

An International Data Group Company
Foster City, CA • Chicago, IL • Indianapolis, IN • New York, NY

AOL® Keywords, 3rd Edition

Published by

MIS:Press, an imprint of IDG Books Worldwide, Inc.

An International Data Group Company

919 E. Hillsdale Blvd., Suite 400

Foster City, CA 94404

www.idgbooks.com (IDG Books Worldwide Web site)

Library of Congress Catalog Card Number: 98-72474

ISBN: 0-7645-7502-3

Printed in the United States of America

10 9 8 7 6 5 4 3 2

3B/SY/QY/ZY/PC

Distributed in the United States by IDG Books Worldwide, Inc.

Distributed by Macmillan Canada for Canada; by Transworld Publishers Limited in the United Kingdom; by IDG Norge Books for Norway; by IDG Sweden Books for Sweden; by Woodslane Pty. Ltd. for Australia; by Woodslane (NZ) Ltd. for New Zealand; by Addison Wesley Longman Singapore Pte Ltd. for Singapore, Malaysia, Thailand, Indonesia, and Korea; by Norma Comunicaciones S.A. for Colombia; by Intersoft for South Africa; by International Thomson Publishing for Germany, Austria, and Switzerland; by Toppan Company Ltd. for Japan; by Distribuidora Cuspide for Argentina; by Livraria Cultura for Brazil; by Ediciencia S.A. for Ecuador; by Ediciones ZETA S.C.R. Lida. for Peru; by WS Computer Publishing Corporation, Inc., for the Philippines; by Unalis Corporation for Taiwan; by Contemporanea de Ediciones for Venezuela; by Computer Book & Magazine Store for Puerto Rico; by Express Computer Distributors for the Caribbean and West Indies. Authorized Sales Agent: Anthony Rudkin Associates for the Middle East and North Africa.

Trademarks: All brand names and product names used in this book are trade names, service marks, trademarks, or registered trademarks of their respective owners. IDG Books Worldwide is not associated with any product or vendor mentioned in this book.

is a trademark under exclusive license to IDG Books Worldwide, Inc., from International Data Group, Inc.

is a registered trademark of IDG Books Worldwide, Inc.

Credits

Acquisitions Editor
Juliana Aldous

Development Editor
Philip Wescott

Technical Editor
Teresa Deal

Copy Editor
Timothy Borek

Project Coordinator
Tom Debolski

Book Designers
Cátálin Dulfu
Kurt Krames

Graphics and Production Specialists
Renée Dunn
Linda Marousek
Dina F Quan

Quality Control Specialists
Mick Arellano
Mark Schumann

Proofreader
Mary Barnack

About the Author

Jennifer Watson is one of America Online's foremost teachers, sharing her knowledge with beginners and insiders alike. Her invaluable compilation of tips and tricks, prepared and shared with America Online's membership, became the top-selling *AOL Companion* by MIS:Press, Inc. (now in its second edition). As the founder of The VirtuaLeader Academy — an online training center for AOL's volunteers, partners, and employees — she teaches the leaders of the online community how to make AOL come alive. Jennifer lives in Ann Arbor, Michigan, with Kippi, her canine companion.

*To my mother, Carolyn Tody,
for long ago giving me the ultimate
"keyword" for my life: CONFIDENCE.
I can do anything worth doing.*

PREFACE

Hello and welcome to the third edition! If you made use of the first or second editions of this book, thank you! This incarnation of *AOL Keywords* includes over 4,500 more keywords than the last edition and has been entirely updated. If this is your first introduction to keywords, everything you need to know about them (and then some) is here at your fingertips.

Is This Book for You?

Don't expect me to tell you how this book will answer all your questions about America Online. No book can do that and, trust me, you wouldn't want one to. Some of the best parts of America Online are experienced up close and personal.

What I *will* tell you is that this book can help you decide if America Online is right for you, and if so, how to find what you need without a lot of fuss. In essence, *AOL Keywords* is a directory of what's on America Online. Many books explain *how* to use America Online, but none tells you *what* is available and *where* to find it as simply as the one you hold in your hands.

Using This Book

I debated even including this section. *AOL Keywords* is so easy to use, I don't think there is much that won't be obvious to you already. But for the sake of completeness, let me give you a few tips to help you get the most out of *AOL Keywords*.

- The listings and reviews in *AOL Keywords* are sorted into six chapters, organized in the order that I anticipate you prefer reading them. Even so, you're welcome to skip around as much as you like. Chapter 1, "Going Places with America Online," is an introduction to AOL in general, but more specifically, keywords. Chapter 2, "Key Chains," lists keywords that might apply to specific communities of members. Chapter 3, "Important Keywords," are just that — they are keywords everyone should know. Chapter 4, "New Keywords," obviously focuses on the keywords that have been added since the last edition of this book. Chapter 5, "Hot Keywords," are those considered favorites by many. Chapter 6 lists all keywords alphabetically, for easy reference.

- Every review is introduced by a RatingsBar. At the left end of each is the tip's title, with some useful symbols on the right. The symbols are explained at the beginning of each chapter.

- At the bottom of a keyword review, you may notice that I've indicated the name and screen name of the contributor. These are my own companions — community leaders from around America Online who represent years of combined experience. These folks are a wealth of information; adding their voices made the book much richer.

- At the back of this book, an appendix and a glossary describe keyboard shortcuts and a whole slew of America Online jargon and terms.

- Remember, the table of contents is great for finding exactly what you need!

- Your *AOL Keywords* is purposefully compact so that you can tuck it next to your monitor. It travels well, too!

America Online is the largest and fastest-growing online service in existence. Wandering about in search of what you need is no longer practical. Many folks have come away frustrated that they could not find something online only to later realize that what they sought was here all along — they just didn't know where to look.

You, however, are one step ahead. You've picked up this book. With it you can bypass the extra time spent not knowing what to do with America Online and go directly where you want to be. This book is the key that unlocks the doors to the many services, resources, and hidden treasures on America Online.

Even so, this isn't the kind of book you'd want to read in one sitting. Rather, treat this book as a reference. I recommend that you read Chapter 1 to gain a solid groundwork for the information that follows. After that, feel free to bounce around, look up your topic, and cruise the table of contents to find just what you need.

Good luck in your journeys ahead!

Jennifer O;>

P.S. I would love to hear from you when you get online. Send me e-mail at screen name: *Jennifer* and be sure to type *AOL Keywords* in the subject line so I don't miss it.

ACKNOWLEDGMENTS

This book is special for one important reason if no other. It is the embodiment of the support, knowledge, and community I am fortunate to have around me in my life. This takes the form of hundreds of friends, colleagues, and family members, most of whom I am pleased to report are on America Online. Just as with the first and second editions, they have each helped me in countless ways, and I am forever in their debt. So forgive me if I gush a bit here.

Although I cannot thank everyone who had a hand in bringing this book to you, I do want to express my appreciation to those who were most instrumental:

To the thousands of community leaders and partners who originally requested a keyword list so many years ago. Not only do you continue to appreciate my efforts, but you also give me valuable feedback. A very special thank you to the select group of community leaders who contributed keyword reviews to this edition: Sue Boettcher, Vicki DeVico, Valerie L. Downey, Becky Fowler, Ben Foxworth, Robert J. Hill, Genevieve Kazdin, Laura Kramarsky, Maria Therese Lehan, Linda Lindquist, George Louie, Dave Marx, Adrienne Quinn, Brendan Rice, Lauren Sebel, Eva Shaderowfsky, Gwen Smith, Brian Thomason, Kate Tipul, Bob Trautman, Kimberly Trautman, Stephen Urban, and Bradley Zimmer. Your words enrich this work beyond anything I could have done alone.

To Dave Marx, for practically co-authoring this edition with me. Your tireless efforts, valuable contributions, and expert advice really made a difference. A special thank you for your amazing SuperDooperSorter database.

To George Louie, for your much-appreciated-and-never-undervalued efforts and help with all those *C*s (classifieds, caring, camera, companionship, characters, carbohydrates, changes, calls — and so on).

To Ben Foxworth, for your unwavering support in my quest for keywords and everything else that lies before me.

To Tom Lichty, for being my role model and mentor.

To my families, offline and online: Carolyn Tody (my mother), Tom Anderson (my father), and Kim and Chad Larner (my sister and brother-in-law) for helping me offline, encouraging my work and doing your best to understand just what it is I do all the time on the computer; to Jeanne Beroza (my aunt) for your invaluable assistance with the keyword database and for Kippi; to the Watson family for your support in times of change; to the Bougher/DeGarmo family for your smiles; and to the Marx family for your open arms. Offline, my appreciation goes to the amazing VirtuaLeader Academy Cadre for helping with this book, but most of all for building an online community I am proud to call home. You each give me hope, inspiration, and a reason to continue in the face of uncertainty.

To the word-wonders at IDG Books Worldwide, Inc.: Chip Wescott, Juliana Aldous, Tim Borek, and all the behind-the-scenes folks I haven't yet had the pleasure of meeting. Thank you for adopting me and seating me in a place of honor at the family table.

To my colleagues and contacts at America Online, Inc.: Jane Bradshaw and all the knowledgeable folks in the ARC for your support and assistance; David Ehrlich and Lyn Cameron for believing in me; and Brad Schepp for your dedication to excellence.

To the many readers of the first and second editions who sent me e-mail overflowing with thanks and suggestions. You make it all worthwhile!

Last but not least, the millions of members who make America Online *the* place to be in cyberspace.

CONTENTS

CHAPTER 1

GOING PLACES WITH AMERICA ONLINE

I'll never forget my first visit to America Online. Back then, personal computers were usually one of two things — expensive toys or expensive office equipment. We had one at work, and it was both. During the day, it led a life of accounts receivable and desktop publishing. At night, it came alive with dragons and rogues.

One day, we received a free sign-on kit for something called America Online which, among other things, promised up-to-the-hour stock reports. That got my boss's attention and we installed it. He found his stock reports but unfortunately little else.

Knowing there must be more to this America Online, I returned in the evening to look around. With a few hours of aimless wandering, I discovered much more than dreary stock reports. I found more information to sponge, files to download, people to meet, and things to do than I'd ever imagined.

The next day I excitedly told my boss about the wonders I'd discovered during the night. I was met with a blank stare. I realized that what intrigued me was not necessarily what he was into. He liked money matters, which I've never had much of an eye for, and thus I was unable to show him all the financial services which I now know were there.

Looking back, I can see that my lack of experience with America Online cost him several opportunities and much invaluable information. Neither of us realized the extent of America Online's scope, which was significant even back then. We had the tools and the software, but no guides or references to help us find what we needed. In other words, we weren't going anywhere.

Nine years and six computers later, I practically live online. I've been to every area at least once and usually several times, if not hundreds. If there was a support group for America Online, I'd probably lead it. Thankfully, I've been able to make a living out of showing people how to do and find things online. America Online has really taken me places, and it can do the same for you.

America Online

America Online is no longer the small, intimate service it was when I discovered it years ago. It is growing up and coming into its own. As of this writing, there are more than 12 million members (six million more than the first edition of this book reported less than two years ago) and enough services and content for them all.

If you are not yet a member of America Online, details on how you can become one can be found by calling 1-800-827-6364. If you are a member, you may already have an idea of the sheer size that awaits you. To help both new and experienced members understand the scope and organization of America Online, let's take a quick tour of the features and content it offers.

"The More Windows You Open The Cooler It Gets," America Online's best-known slogan, describes only half the picture. Among other things, the e-mail gateways, chat rooms, and Internet doors are the framework upon which the service is built. Other features include Instant Messages, software file libraries, progressive artwork downloading, and more. All in all, America Online offers some of the best cutting-edge technology available over your modem.

America Online organizes their offerings into *channels* — think of it as your cable company on steroids. You can begin at the top with a menu of all channels by clicking the Channels button on your Welcome window or from the toolbar at the top of your screen. Each channel contains hundreds of individual forums and areas with more information than you would ever find on a television.

Channel Surfing

- AOL Today — Your one-stop guide to everything going on at America Online today (and tonight)! (keyword: AOL TODAY)

- News — Up-to-the-hour news, plus photos, discussion areas, and opinion polls, including your favorite magazines and newspapers. (keyword: NEWS)

- Sports — Every kind of sport, plus some you've yet to discover, along with stats, games, and events. (keyword: SPORTS)

- Influence — Move in the best society here with the inside scoop on people, media, and the good life. (keyword: INFLUENCE)

- Travel — Before you go, check here for information and then make all your reservations online. (keyword: TRAVEL)

- International — Explore countries, cities, and cultures around the world, including online forums in Germany, France, Japan, and the UK. (keyword: INTL)

- Personal Finance — Money matters for everyone, from information to investments to resources. (keyword: MONEY)

- Workplace — Find your ideal occupation, increase job satisfaction, and really network. (keyword: WORKPLACE)

- Computing — A mecca to all things computer-related, from forums to special-interest groups to company representatives to software file libraries. (keyword: COMPUTING)

- Research & Learn — The ultimate educational channel, with hundreds of searchable databases and thousands of ways to expand your mind. (keyword: RESEARCH)

Continued

- Entertainment — The stars really do come out on this channel, with movies, TV shows, and more! (keyword: E)

- Games — The ultimate toy chest with classics, trivia, adventures, and the latest interactive online games. (keyword: GAMES)

- Interests — Stop and smell the virtual flowers of cyberspace with a new pursuit or old hobby. (keyword: INTERESTS)

- Lifestyles — Special groups, communities, and associations to enhance happiness, love, and life. (keyword: LIFESTYLES)

- Shopping — A virtual marketplace with brand-name and specialty goods, plus online ordering. (keyword: SHOPPING)

- Health — A virtual health club with innovative ways to help you get in shape, stay healthy, and live well. (keyword: HEALTH)

- Families — Advice and information in a family-size helping, from growing to learning to relating. (keyword: FAMILIES)

- Kids Only — Kids have a place of their own, with everything from fun games to homework help. (keyword: KIDS)

- Local — Learn more about your community and visit cities around the country and overseas. (keyword: LOCAL)

Plus two more areas rich enough to qualify as channels in my book:

- Member Services — Step-by-step help on making the most out of your time on America Online. (keyword: HELP)

- People — The ultimate gathering place to chat with other members about any topic under the sun (not to mention ones on which the "sun don't shine"). (keyword: CHAT)

Behind Lock and Keyword

You may have noticed that after each channel, I give a *keyword* in parentheses. Keywords are one of the best-kept secrets to success with America Online. They are powerful and extraordinarily simple. In essence, they are shortcuts to all the places you want to go online. They allow you to bypass extra windows and avoid artwork you don't need. Keywords don't just get you places, they also help you find them. If you have a topic in mind, chances are it is a keyword and leads somewhere. Once you know keywords and how to use them, you can save considerable time. Besides, knowing keywords can really knock the socks off your friends and colleagues!

Many keywords are obvious, such as FINANCE for the Personal Finance channel or SAILING for the Boating & Sailing Forum. A great many are not as intuitive, such as EGG, which leads to the electronic Gourmet Guide, a haven for chefs and food lovers alike. Because of the vast number of services and resources online — many with overlapping topics — plenty of excellent areas have keywords you'd never think to try. If you are a writer or are interested in writing, you are sure to try keyword: WRITER (The Writers Club), but it may take a while to discover keyword: NOVEL, which goes to a popular writing forum called the Amazing Instant Novelist. And as frustrating as it may seem, there are keywords that are not published anywhere but are useful just the same.

With more than 10,000 keywords (currently), memorization is not an option. Luckily, you don't have to try. This book is a keyword directory to America Online's many services and resources. We will show you not only how to use keywords quickly, but also how to find them through tips, techniques, reviews, and lists of the keywords themselves. Just turn the page to get started!

Using Keywords

To use a keyword, begin by signing on to America Online. Once online, you can enter a keyword in one of two main ways. The first, and most obvious, is to type it directly into your toolbar at the top of your screen (see Figure 1.1) and then click the **Go** button or press the **Enter** or **Return** keys.

Figure 1.1 You can type any keyword into the toolbar's address field.

You can also bring up a special Keyword window (see Figure 1.2) that works much like the toolbar above.

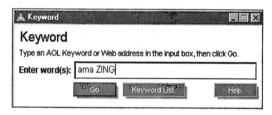

Figure 1.2 A window just for keywords.

There are three methods you can use to bring up the Keyword window:

- **Use the keyboard:** Press and hold down the **Ctrl** key (on the PC) or the **Command** key (on the Mac) and then press **K**.
- **Use the menus:** In Windows, click the **Favorites** icon on the toolbar and select **Go To Keyword**. On the Mac, select the **Window** menu, **AOL Shortcuts**, and then finally **Keywords**.
- **Use the button:** Click **Keyword** on the toolbar.

Once at the Keyword window, simply type your keyword in the box and click the **Go** button (or press the **Enter** or **Return** key). America Online instantly transports you to that keyword's area, closing the Keyword window behind you to keep things neat.

If the word you typed was not actually a keyword, you are immediately told so, and the keyword you tried to use is displayed. Should this happen, double-check that you spelled the keyword correctly. In some cases, especially when the keyword was only misspelled or was just a few letters off, America Online goes an extra step and displays a list of keywords which are close to what you entered (see Figure 1.3). If you find a match among the list of similar keywords, double-click it.

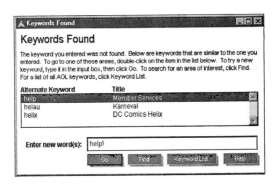

Figure 1.3 The Keywords Found window displays alternates when the keyword you entered doesn't work.

Keywords are neither case- nor space-sensitive, so you can type them any way that is convenient (as I did in Figure 1.2). You can also use URL addresses from the World Wide Web as keywords — they will take you directly to the referenced WWW page using America Online's browser. URL addresses tend to be long and complicated (for example, `http://members.aol.com/jennifer/` leads to my home page on the Web). We do not cover URL addresses in this book — there are plenty of WWW books out there — but do keep in mind that you can use either the Keyword window or the toolbar in America Online to access them.

If you look at Figure 1.2 again, you will notice two other buttons on the window: a Keyword List button and a Help button. The first button takes you to a simple list of keywords (described later). The Help button simply explains how to use a keyword.

Mousetraps: Using the Keyboard

The mouse (or trackball/trackpad) is a wonderful invention, but let's face it — it isn't always Mickey Mouse. Getting that tiny arrow in just the right spot with a mouse is not only downright challenging at times, it can be time-consuming and stressful for your wrist, as well. Rather than put undue strain on your body or sanity, try using keyboard shortcuts for repetitive tasks. **Ctrl+K** (or **Command+K** on the Mac) is a keyboard shortcut I've already introduced and one you will soon learn to do with your eyes closed. A complete list of keyboard shortcuts is available in Appendix A at the back of the book.

If you are using Windows, you can also use the keyboard to navigate the menus and menu items that may not have keyboard shortcuts assigned to them. To do this, press and hold down the **Alt** key and type the letter underlined in the menu title. The list drops down, allowing you to navigate the menu items with your arrow keys. To select an item, simply press **Enter**.

Where Are All the Keywords?

Now that you know how to use keywords, your next step is learning how to find them. As mentioned earlier, a number of obvious destinations are already keywords. If you have an idea of the kind of area you'd like to visit, type in a word that describes it. For example, keyword: AUTO takes you to the AOL Auto Center, which links to numerous auto-related areas online. In addition, if you know the name of the area you are seeking, often the name itself is a keyword. For example, keyword: ABC takes you directly to ABC Online. Beyond this, keywords tend to become collector's items — finding them is so challenging that it's natural to treasure those you have found. Up to now, that is.

Of all the techniques for finding keywords, the best is to simply use this book. In it are lists upon lists of not just the most useful or interesting keywords (although we have those, too), but all the keywords on America Online known at the time of writing. The keywords in this book represent over four years of research and work; they are all yours for the taking. America Online is growing so quickly, however, that by the time this book is printed there will be a slew of new keywords. To help you find the latest and greatest keywords, use the following techniques and ideas.

What's New on AOL

You can glean keywords to new online areas in the What's New on AOL area at keyword: NEW (see Figure 1.4). This window spotlights newly released forums and redesigned areas. The most convenient aspect of What's New is that it links to the areas themselves, allowing you to jump directly to an area with just a click of a mouse. If you take advantage of these links, make a note of the keyword so you can return again. Not all new areas make it into this list as space is limited — many of the smaller, low-profile forums just don't show up here at all. But this is a good place to get a general overview of the new areas online.

Figure 1.4 What's New on AOL regularly announces the most recent additions.

AOL Find

AOL Find is a good way to scout for undiscovered areas (see Figure 1.5). You can search it at keyword: AOL FIND. Each area you find includes a description, a keyword or two, and a way to access the area directly. As with keyword: NEW, be sure to make a note of the keyword if you choose to go directly to the area via the description. At the time of this writing, AOL Find did not include descriptions of all areas online, and the newest areas were noticeably absent.

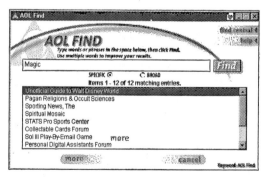

Figure 1.5 Search for areas with AOL Find.

AOL Channel Guide

Would you like to browse a list of every major area online rather than having to hunt through layers of windows? You can find just such a list at keyword: CHANNEL GUIDE (see Figure 1.6). All the big areas are listed here, organized into channels, so you don't have to wade through "banks" when you really just want to learn to "bake." Just choose the channel you're interested in from the button on the left — the list on the right will update with links to all the areas. Again, be sure to note the keyword when you arrive so you can return again later.

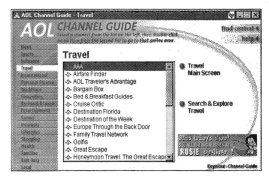

Figure 1.6 The Channel Guide compiles all major areas into simple lists.

Keyword List Online

If it is raw keywords you're after, America Online provides a simple list at keyword: KEYWORD (see Figure 1.7). You can list the keywords alphabetically or by channel using the buttons at the bottom of the window. Keep in mind that these are just lists and won't link you directly to the keywords — you need to manually type in the keyword. You may notice that the keywords listed here differ a bit from those in this book — I use my own database of keywords which I've carefully cultivated over the years. Still, keyword: KEYWORD is a good source of keywords, especially for newer ones.

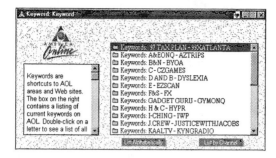

Keywords are shortcuts to AOL areas and Web sites. The box on the right contains a listing of current keywords on AOL. Double-click on a letter to see a list of all

Figure 1.7 The online keyword list.

Other Ways to Find Keywords

True keyword connoisseurs know that some of the best ways to find new areas online are more subtle. Here are some tricks I've discovered over the years:

- Read the Welcome window every time you sign on. The Welcome window is the second one that appears on your screen after you sign on (it follows the Channel window and has the words *Welcome* and your screen name at the top). New areas will sometimes show up here before they are officially announced. Special events and information frequently are highlighted here, as well.

- Check the corners of a window for keywords — they are usually placed in the lower left- or right-hand corners. If you notice a keyword and it seems as though it could be difficult to recall later, be sure to jot it down or grab the favorite place heart (Favorite Places are explained later in this chapter). This is particularly important if you found the area through the Welcome window, because the information there changes frequently.

- Use your toolbar History Trail — the list of areas you've visited recently that drops down when you click the down arrow to the right of the keyword field (see Figure 1.1 again). If you want to visit one of these places again, just select it from the list.

- Pay attention when reading articles, watching or listening to commercials, visiting trade shows, or talking to salespeople. Companies or associations with areas on America Online will often give their keyword and/or their World Wide Web (WWW) address. Once you realize this, you'll be surprised at how often this happens.

- Read the Goodbye window when signing off. Future events are often announced here along with their keywords. Again, be sure to note the keyword so you can visit when you sign on again.

Keyword Surfing

For those with wanderlust, keyword surfing is a satisfying (not to mention comfortable) adventure into the great unknown. Keyword surfing can be as simple as visiting keywords that catch your eye from one of my lists, or as challenging as trying to guess new or undiscovered keywords. And for the free-spirited surfer looking for new adventures, there is a special keyword just for you — keyword: RANDOM (see Figure 1.8). A virtual roulette wheel awaits you here. Spin the wheel (just click it) and a window to a randomly selected online area appears on your screen — where you go, no one knows!

Figure 1.8 Get lucky online with keyword: RANDOM.

Continued

One caveat: Some of the areas keyword: RAN-DOM will take you may seem strange (they may be uncompleted areas or "skeleton keywords") or, worse yet, take you to a window without a keyword displayed. If this happens and you wish to return to it later, grab the heart on the window and add it to your Favorite Places rather than try to guess the keyword later. Keyword surfers should also be prepared for massive artwork downloads as they visit new areas, causing slowdowns. But if you keep your wits about you and ride the modem carrier's wave in to shore, you will find more than you imagined. Surf's up!

A List of Your Own

Your discoveries on America Online will undoubtedly reward you with a collection of essential and frequently used keywords. You can and probably will memorize these keywords, but there is an easier way — use *shortcuts*. Your America Online software can be customized with up to ten shortcuts to your favorite keywords for quick access. Once a keyword shortcut is created in your software, you can go right to it by pressing the **Ctrl** key (or the **Command** key on the Mac) and a number between 0 and 9. It's fast and perfect if you're prone to forgetting directions (and keywords).

To customize your software with shortcuts, select **Edit Shortcuts** from the **My Shortcuts** submenu. You'll find **My Shortcuts** under the **Favorites** icon on the Windows AOL software (version 4.0) toolbar, and under the **Window** menu on the Mac AOL software (also version 4.0). **Edit Shortcuts** displays a window with two columns of boxes — the name of the area goes in the left column and the keyword goes in the right column (see Figure 1.9). You'll notice all your shortcuts are filled in when you open it for the first time. Feel free to change any or all of these "factory presets" as I have done. When you have finished, just click the **Save Changes** (on the PC) or the **OK** button (on the Mac). Your keywords now appear in the **My Shortcuts** menu along with the keyboard shortcut used to access them. You can update this menu at anytime, including while you are offline.

Edit Shortcut Keys		
Shortcut Title	Keyword/Internet Address	Key
What's New	NEW	Ctrl + 1
AOL Book Store	BOOK SHOP	Ctrl + 2
Movies	MOVIES	Ctrl + 3
		Ctrl + 4
AOL Keyword Book Web Site	http://members.aol.com/keylist/index.htm	Ctrl + 5
AOL Companion Book Web Site	http://members.aol.com/jennifer/aolc/inde	Ctrl + 6
		Ctrl + 7
Amazing Instant Novelist	AMAZING	Ctrl + 8
The Writer's Club	WRITER	Ctrl + 9
Random Keyword	RANDOM	Ctrl + 0
Save Changes	Cancel Help	

Figure 1.9 Create your own keyword list.

Getting to the Heart of the Matter: Favorite Places

Sometimes, where you want to be isn't directly accessible through a keyword. Winding your way down a twisting path of windows and prompts can be fun at first, but a real drag after that. But never fear — help is here! A feature called Favorite Places can get you there quicker. Favorite Places allow you to "bookmark" a window so that you can return to it later.

To mark a window, look for a small heart in the upper right-hand corner of the window (look at Figure 1.6 again to see what I mean). If you see a heart, click it once. A small window appears asking you were you want to insert your Favorite Place — choose the first option to store it in your list of Favorites (see Figure 1.10). Once stored, you can reference it again (and again) under the Favorites icon in your toolbar. Most all windows have this little heart on them, but if your window is unadorned, back up one level and look for a heart there.

Continued

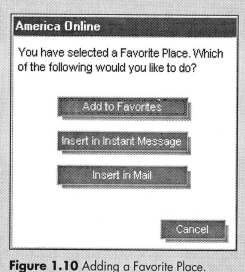

Figure 1.10 Adding a Favorite Place.

Elusive Keywords

If you just can't find what you are looking for and think you've exhausted all your resources, don't give up. Your next step is to ask someone who may know. First, try a friend or colleague who uses America Online, especially if their interests are similar to yours. Next, ask one of the many community leaders across the service, such as a Guide, an MHMS leader, a forum leader or assistant, a chat host, and so on. You can spot community leaders by their helpful natures and their screen names, which often carry a prefix of some sort such as *Guide, Host, Rngr, MHMS,* or something indicative of the forum you are visiting You can also post a message at keyword: MHM and let your fellow members help you.

Keyword: DEAD END

You've just typed in a keyword and the word *Invalid* glares back at you in that harsh, unearthly glow. It may have been a keyword that worked last week, or worse yet, one that appears here. Before you hit that wall, consider this: America Online is growing so quickly that sometimes they need to put up a wall to build a bigger building.

Don't be overly discouraged by invalid keywords. First of all, be certain you spelled the keyword correctly. If that checks out, scan the keyword lists to see if an alternate keyword exists — this is often the case, especially if the original keyword was general in nature. Also check for other areas that may be similar — they may contain a link to the area you are seeking.

Sometimes keywords aren't invalid but rather lead to areas that are off limits. These areas are usually construction areas for America Online staff and wouldn't be of much interest anyway. America Online does have an open door policy for their content online, but keep in mind that someone has to create those doors in the first place.

The Key to This Book

The keyword lists in this book are organized in several different ways to help you find what you need quickly. In most cases, I try to give you all of a keyword's synonyms so you can choose the keyword that is easiest to type or remember. Alternate yet similar keyword spellings are indicated by parentheses — for example, BEGINNER(S) means that both keywords: BEGINNER and BEGINNERS work. Also, note that I always give keywords in all capital letters so you can recognize them as such. You do not need to input a keyword in "all caps" — keywords are not case sensitive.

America Online is a living, growing being, particularly when it comes to keywords. It is important to understand that keywords are added and deleted daily. You should expect to encounter keywords in this book that no longer work. This is where the online keyword list at keyword: KEYWORD comes in helpful. Still, the vast majority of keywords in this book will be valid for a long while.

With that said, feel free to explore each and every keyword listed in this book. Your journey is just beginning. The following paragraphs provide an overview of what this book offers. Any chapter serves as an excellent starting point for your America Online explorations.

- Chapter 2, "Key Chains," sports a collection of keyword lists based on specific topics, from the essential to the offbeat. There is a list for everyone!

- Chapter 3, "Important Keywords," contains concise and informative descriptions of the most basic keywords online, listed in alphabetical order. Above each description is a quick-reference RatingsBar that tells you what to expect (see Figure 1.11). The symbols on the RatingsBar are explained at the beginning of the chapter.

SAMPLE BAR □ 🕸 🗐 🌐 *W* ✧ Q 🕮 📲 **PG** ▬

Figure 1.11 The RatingsBar gives you a quick overview of important information.

- Chapter 4, "New Keywords," describes and rates the most recently introduced areas and their keywords. Like Chapter 3, we include our RatingsBar with each description.

- Chapter 5, "Hot Keywords," lists and classifies the most exceptional and interesting areas online. Again, the RatingsBar prefaces each description.

- Chapter 6, "Keywords from A-Z," lists more than 10,000 keywords in alphabetical order, along with the area they lead to and any special notes. Begin here if you would like to browse or find out where a keyword leads before using it.

- At the end of this book are two appendices. A list of keyboard shortcuts helps you navigate the online terrain quickly and easily. And a glossary of key terms deciphers AOL-speak and explains important terms you should know for good keyword surfing.

What Do You Think?

Like America Online, keywords are in a state of constant flux. I encourage your suggestions on ways to improve future editions of this book. Please send your e-mail about this book to screen name: *Jennifer* and mention the title of the book in the subject line. I may not be able to reply to every piece of e-mail, but you can bet it will be read!

America Online's greatest strength lies in its communities. They come in all shapes and sizes and may be as binding as blood or as fleeting as the seasons. To help you find your own community, we compiled lists of keywords tailored for the individual. From kids to parents, book lovers to romantics, there is something here for everyone. Think of these lists as sets of keys on a ring, much like key chains, only instead of a lucky rabbit's foot, we're attaching those free America Online floppy disks everyone gets to the key rings. We wouldn't want you to misplace your keys!

Each key chain in this chapter lists the keywords in alphabetical order. The actual keyword is given first, followed by the name of the area. Things we would like to call to your attention are noted in parentheses and brackets. Keywords in bold letters are rated and described in detail within Chapters 3, 4, and 5.

AOLoholics

800 NUMBER — Traveling With AOL
ACCESS — Accessing America Online (Local Access Numbers)
ANNUAL PLANS — Annual Subscription Plans
ANNUAL REPORTS — AOL Annual Reports [Web site]
AOL CHORUS — AOL Chorus
AOL CRUISE — AOL Member Cruise
AOL DIAG — AOL Diagnostic Tool [Windows AOL only]
AOL FIND — AOL Find
AOL GIFT — AOL Gift Certificates
AOL GLOBALNET — International Access
AOL INSIDER — AOL Insider Tips
AOL IR — AOL Full Disclosure

AOL LINK — Using AOL Link [Mac AOL only]
AOL NETFIND — AOL NetFind
AOL ON TV — AOL on TV (commercials)
AOL REWARDS — AOL Rewards
AOL SECRETS — AOL Secrets
AOL SOUND — AOL Sounds
AOL STORE — The America Online Store
AOL TODAY — AOL Today
AOL VISA — AOL Visa Card
AOL WEATHER — Weather at AOL Headquarters
AOL WORLD — International channel
AOL.COM — America Online's Web Site
ASK AOL — AOL Member Services
AUTODIALER — AOL Autodialer [Windows AOL 3.0 and below only]
BEST OF AOL — The Best of AOL
BILLING — Billing Information
CALL AOL — AOL Telephone Support Numbers
CHANNEL GUIDE — AOL Channel Guide
CHANNELS — AOL Channels
CREDIT — Credit Request
FIND — Find Central
FIND EVENTS — Find Events on AOL
FIND PEOPLE — Find People on AOL
FIND SOFTWARE — Find Software on AOL
FUTURE — Can You Believe What's Possible These Days?
GALLERY — AOL Portrait Gallery
GET 25 — Download AOL 2.5 for Windows
GET 27 — Download AOL 2.7 for the Mac
GET 30 — Download AOL 3.0
GLOSSARY — The America Online Glossary
HOW TO CONNECT — Connecting to AOL
HOW TO DOWNLOAD — Downloading Files & Attachments on AOL
HOW TO GET AROUND — Getting Around & Using AOL
HOW TO MEET PEOPLE — Chatting on AOL
HOW TO SEARCH — Using Search & Find on AOL
INTEREST PROFILES — AOL Interest Profiles
NOTIFY AOL — Report a Violation
KEYWORD — Keyword List
LEARN ACCESS — Connecting to AOL
LEARN CHAT — Chatting on AOL
LEARN DOWNLOAD — Downloading on AOL
LEARN EMAIL — E-mail on AOL
LEARN FIND — Finding Things on AOL
LEARN GAMES — Playing Games on AOL
LEARN IMS — Sending Instant Messages on AOL
LEARN INTERNET — Using the Internet on AOL

LEARN KEYWORDS — Using Keywords on AOL
LEARN KID SAFETY — Using Parental Controls on AOL
LEARN MESSAGE BOARDS — Using Message Boards on AOL
LEARN NAVIGATION — Navigating on AOL
LEARN NEWS PROFILES — News Profiling on AOL
LEARN PP — Personal Publishing on AOL
LEARN QUOTES — Getting Investment Quotes on AOL
LEARN RICH TEXT — Using Rich Text on AOL
LEARN SECURITY — Online Safety on AOL
LETTER — Community Updates from Steve Case
MATCH YOUR INTERESTS — Match Your Interests
MEMBERS — AOL Member Directory
MEMBERS CHOICE — AOL Members' Choice
MHM — Members Helping Members
MY AOL — My AOL
NEIGHBORHOOD WATCH — AOL Neighborhood Watch
NETMAIL — AOL NetMail
NEW — What's New on AOL
PERKS — AOL Member Perks
PRESS — AOL Press Releases
PREVIEW — AOL Software Preview
PULSE OF AOL — Pulse of AOL
QUICKSTART — QuickStart
SHORTHANDS — AOL Shorthands
SHOW ME — Show Me How to Use People Connection
SLIDESHOWS — AOL Slideshows
TOS — Terms of Service
UPGRADE — Upgrade to Latest Version of AOL Software
VISUAL HELP — Visual AOL Help

Explorers of Sea and Sky

AERONAUTICS — Aviation and Aeronautics
AIRFORCE — Military City Online
AIR WARRIOR — Air Warrior
ASTRONOMY — The Astronomy Club
AVFORUM — Aviation Forum
BAY AREA BOATING — Rather Be Boating
BIRDING — Bird Watching and Info
BOAT DEALERS — Boat & Yachts Professional Forum
BOAT US — Boat Owners Association of the United States
BOATING — Boating & Sailing
BOATING ONLINE — Boating Online
BOSTON BOATING — Boating & Fishing (Boston)
BOSTON SAILING — Sailing (Boston)
CASSINI — Cassini Space Mission to Saturn

CHICAGO OUTDOORS — Great Outdoors Online (Chicago)
FBN — Fishing Broadcast Network
FFBN — Fly-Fishing Broadcast Network
FISHING — Fishing Selections
FLORIDA KEYS — The Florida Keys
FLYING — Flying Magazine
GORP SF — Great Outdoor Recreation Pages (San Francisco)
GS SWIMMING — Grandstand Swimming & Water Sports
INSIDEFLYER — InsideFlyer Online
MARS PATHFINDER — Mars Pathfinder Mission Center
OAO — Outdoor Adventures Online
OUTDOOR FUN — Outdoor Fun (Water Sports & Activities Board)
OUTDOORS — AOL Sports Outdoors
PP AVIATION — Aviation and Aeronautics Member Web Pages
RSD — Rodales's Scuba Diving
SCUBA — AOL Scuba
SN SPACE — Space and Astronomy
SPACE — Space Exploration Online
STAR TREK — Star Trek Club
SURF — SurfLink
THRIVE@OUTDOORS — Thrive@Outdoors
VGA PLANETS — VGA Planets
WEATHER — Weather

Friends

BUDDY — Edit Buddy Lists
BV — View Buddy Lists
CHAT — People Connection
CHATTER — People Connection Newsletter
FIND FRIENDS — Find Friends Online
FIND PEOPLE — Find People
HOW TO MEET PEOPLE — Chatting Online
MEMBERS — AOL Member Directory
PEOPLE FINDER — AOL NetFind: Find a Person
TEEN FRIENDS — AOL Teens: Friends

JennerationX

ALTERNATIVE — Alternative Music
ALUMNI HALL — Alumni Hall
APARTMENTS — Real Estate: Renting
COMMUNITIES — Communities (Generation X/The Twenties)
COUNTDOWN 2000 — Countdown the Minutes to the Millenium
DAFFY — Happy Birthday, Daffy Duck!

DILBERT — Dilbert Comics
ELECTRA — Electra: Real Women, Real Life
GENX — Ages & Stages
GRAD SCHOOL — Graduate & Professional
INSOMNIACS — Insomniacs Asylum
JENX — The Voice of JenX
JOBS — Finding a Job
KNOT — The Knot: Weddings For The Real World
LIFESTAGES MARRIAGE — Marriage & Money
LIFESTAGES SINGLE — On Your Own
LOCAL MOVIE GUIDE — Digital City Movie Guide
MAD MAGAZINE — Mad Magazine Online
MONEYWHIZ — MoneyWhiz: Bust Your Budget
MTV — MTV Online
NICK AT NITE — Nick at Nite: TV Land Online
NTN — NTN Games Studio
OLP STRESS DOC — Online Psych: Ask the Stress Doc
WDW — Walt Disney World

Kidwords

BEANIES — Beanie Babies
BLACKBERRY — Blackberry Creek
CARTOON NETWORK — Cartoon Network
CO KIDS — Christianity Online: Kids of the Kingdom
COMICS — Comic Books
DC COMICS FOR KIDS — DC Comics for Kids
DISNEYSOFT — Disney Interactive (demos, hints, and more)
ENCYCLOPEDIAS — Encyclopedias
FAO — FAO Schwarz
GAMES — Games channel
HH KIDS — Homework Help for Kids
HIGHLIGHTS — Highlights Online for Children
JEWISH YOUTH — Jewish Youth
KID TRAVEL — Family Travel Network
KIDS FIND — AOL NetFind for Kids [Web site]
KIDS — Kids Only channel
KIDS & INVESTING — Kids & Investing
KIDS DICTIONARY — Kids Dictionary from Merriam-Webster
KIDS KICKS — Kid's Kicks
KIDS' WB — Kids WB (Warner Brothers) Online
KIDS WEB — Top Internet Sites for Kids [Web site]
KIDZINE — ABC Kidzine
KO CENTRAL — Kids Only Central
KO CHAT — Kids Only Chat and Safety Tips
KO CLUBS — Kids Only Clubs

KO CREATE — Kids Only Create
KO FAME — Kids Only Hall of Fame
KO GAMES — Kids Only Games
KO GET INVOLVED — Kids Only Get Involved
KO HELP — I Need Help! (for kids)
KO HOT — Kids Only What's Hot
KO NEWS — Kids Only News
KO SERVICE — Kids Only Member Service
KO SPEAK — Kids Only Speak Out
KO SPORTS — Kids Only Sports
KO SS — Kids Only Shows + Stars
MARVEL — Marvel Comics Online
NICKELODEON — Nickelodeon Online
NTN TRIVIA — NTN Games Trivia (Kid's Trivia)
PENPAL — Find a Pen Pal
SCOUTING — Scouting Forum
VGS — Video Games Forum
YT — Youth Tech

LOL! (Laughers On Line)

AOOL — America Out of Line
BACK PAGE — The Back Page
BOSTON JOKES — Boston Joke of the Day
BUZZSAW — Buzzsaw
CAPITOL LAUGHTER — Capitol Laughter
CARTOON NETWORK — Cartoon Network
CHEAP LUNCH — Cheap Lunch:Trailer Park Wisdom
COMEDY CLINIC — The Comedy Clinic
COMICS — Comic Books
DAILY CHUCKLE — Buzzsaw's Daily Chuckle
DILBERT — Dilbert [Web site]
FUNNIES — The Funny Pages
HECKLERS — Hecklers Online
HUMOR THERAPY — Humor Therapy
HUMORWRITE — Humorwrite Online
IA — Insomniacs Asylum
INTOON — InToon with the News
JOKES — Joke Areas
JUST JOKING — Just Joking in Dallas-Fort Worth
LA JOKE BOX — Los Angeles Joke Box
LATE SHOW — David Letterman's Late Show
LUNCHBYTES — Lunchbytes by Jim Ayers
MAD MAGAZINE — Mad Magazine
MADWORLD — Mad, Mad World!
ROSIE — Rosie O'Donnell Online

SD COMICS — San Diego Comics
STRAIGHT DOPE — The Straight Dope
THE STRIP — The Strip [WWW page]
TV SPOOFS — TV Spoofs!

Can I Have My Own Keyword?

While this is one of the most frequently made requests concerning keywords, the answer is no. It is not possible to request your own keyword unless you are a contracted partner with America Online and charged with building an online area. Not only would it be impractical to allow individuals to have their own keywords (to what would the keyword lead?), it would be confusing, as well — keywords would probably lead to unexpected places not designed for general consumption. As America Online grows larger, keywords will become a commodity and something to be managed carefully lest we fall into chaos.

Even so, there is one way to have your own keyword of sorts. As mentioned in Chapter 1, World Wide Web addresses (URLs) can be input as keywords. As every member has the option of creating a World Wide Web page (which has URLs), you could have your own keyword to your page. It would probably look something like this: `http://members.aol.com/jennifer/`, which is the URL keyword to my own Web page. For more information on creating your own World Wide Web page, see keyword: MY HOME PAGE or keyword: MY PLACE.

Men

CO MEN — Christian Brother to Brother
FATHER — AOL Families
MEN'S HEALTH — Men's Health Forum
MEN'S HEALTH WEB — Men's Health Internet Sites
PEN — Personal Empowerment Network (Men's Health)
PS FATHERS DAY — Father's Day at Parent Soup
THRIVE — Thrive@AOL (The Men's Club)

Nature Lovers

ABE — American Birdwatchers Exchange
ASTRONOMY — The Astronomy Club
BACKPACKER — Backpacker Magazine
BETTER LIVING — Ideas for Better Living (Gardening)
BIRDING — Bird Watching and Info
CHICAGO OUTDOORS — Great Outdoors Online
ENVIROLINK — The EnviroLink Network
FBN — Fishing Broadcast Network
GARDEN — Gardening
GARDEN.COM — Garden.com [Web site] +
GORP SF — Great Outdoor Recreation Pages
GREEN FINGERS — Green Fingers: Gardening Tips
GS OUTDOOR — Grandstand: Outdoor Sports
HR GARDEN — Hampton Roads Gardening
LANDSCAPER — Landscaping & Gardening Community
NATURE — The Environment and Nature
NYT GARDEN — Gardening @ The New York Times
OAO — Outdoor Adventure Online
OUTDOOR FUN — Hobby Central: Outdoor Fun
OUTDOORS — AOL Sports Outdoors
PARKS — America's Parks Forum
RON'S TRAILS — Denver Trail Guide
SD GARDEN — San Diego Online Gardener
SD HIKE — San Diego Trail Guy [Web site]
SCI AM — Scientific American [Web site]
SCIENCE — Science
SPACE — Space Exploration Online
SURVIVAL WORLD — Survival World
TEXAS WILDLIFE — Texas Parks and Wildlife Department
THRIVE@OUTDOORS — Thrive@AOL: Outdoors
TNC — The Nature Conservancy
VOLCANO — Volcano Resources
WEATHER — Weather News

WALKING — AOL Fitness
ZOO — Zoos and Aquariums

Parents

ADOPTION — Adoption Forum
BABIES — Babies
BABY NAMES — A to Z Baby Name Finder
CAREGIVING — Parenting & Caregiving
CHICAGO EDUCATION — Digital City Chicago Education Forum
CHILD CARE — The Child & Elder Care Community
CHILD SAFETY — Neighborhood Watch
CHILDREN'S HEALTH — Children's Health Forum
CO FAMILY — Christianity Online: Family Forum
CONNECTED FAMILY — Connected Family [Web site]
DIS — DisABILITIES Community Forum
EDUCATION — AOL Research & Learn: Education
FAM HOT — AOL Families: What's Hot!
FAMILIES — AOL Families
FAMILY COMPUTING — Family Computing Software Resources
FAMILY FEED — Family Feed: A News Feed For Moms and Dads
FAMILY FINANCES — Lifestages: Advice & Planning
FAMILY LIFE — Family Life Online
FAMILY REFERENCE — Home & Family Reference
FAMILY TIES — Family Ties
FAMILY TIMESAVERS — Family Timesavers
FAMILY TRAVEL — Family Travel Network
GRANT A WISH — Grant-a-Wish Foundation
HEM — Home Education Magazine
HOMESCHOOL — Homeschooling Forum
IMH — Issues in Mental Health (Parenting Boards)
INFOSOURCE — The Family InfoSource
INSURANCE — AOL Insurance Center
JEWISH FAMILY — Jewish Family
KIDS & INVESTING — Kids & Investing
KIDS AND TEENS — Kids And Teens
KIDS READS — A Grown Up Guide to Kids Reading
KO PARENT — Send Feedback to Kids Only channel
LEARN KID SAFETY — Learn Parental Controls
LIFESTAGES DIAPERS — Diapers & Dollars
LIFESTAGES KIDS — Kids & Cash
LIFESTAGES SCHOOL — Saving for School
MIL FAM — Military Family Center
MISSING KIDS — The National Center for Missing & Exploited Children
MOMS ONLINE — Moms Online
NEMOURS — KidsHealth.Org

NF FAMILY — AOL NetFind Time Savers: Family [Web site]
NPC — The National Parenting Center [Web site]
ONLINE PSYCH — Online Psych
PARENT SOUP — Parent Soup
PARENTAL CONTROL — Parental Controls
PARENTING — AOL Families: Parenting
PARENTS CLUB — Parents Club
PHS — Practical Homeschooling
POLAROID — Polaroid & Parenting
PS AMERICAN BABY — Parent Soup: American Baby
PS BABIES — Parent Soup: Babies
PS DRUG FREE — Parent Soup: Drug-Free Kids Quiz
PS EXPECTING — Parent Soup: Expecting Parents
PS EXPERTS — Parent Soup: Ask the Experts
PS FAMILY COUNSELOR — Parent Soup: Ask the Family Counselor
PS FATHER — Parent Soup: Learning From Dad
PS FUN — Parent Soup: Fun & Games
PS GRADE — Parent Soup: Making the Grade
PS HE SHE — Parent Soup: He Says, She Says
PS JOIN — Parent Soup: Your Family Profile
PS LA LECHE LEAGUE — Parent Soup: Ask La Leche League
PS MESSAGES — Parent Soup: Message Boards
PS NEWSFLASH — Parent Soup: Newsflash
PS PARENTS CONNECT — Parent Soup: Connect with Parents
PS SCHOOL SPIRIT — Parent Soup: School Spirit
PS SCHOOL YEARS — Parent Soup: Parents of School-Age Children
PS SOFTWARE — Parent Soup: Software Library
PS TEENS — Parent Soup: Parents of Teens
PS TODDLERS — Parent Soup: Parents of Toddlers and Preschoolers
PP FAMILY — Family Member Web Sites
TC FAMILY — Twin Cities Family
THRIVE — Thrive@AOL (Kid's Health & Development)
WOMANS DAY — Woman's Day Online
WOMEN — Women's Network

Professionals

ABOUTWORK — AboutWork
ATT — AT&T Products & Services
BIZ HOURLY — Business News Summary
BIZ NEWS — Business News Center
BIZ RESEARCH — Business Research
BIZ TIP — Today's Business Tip
BUSINESS CHAT — Business Chat and Message Boards
BUSINESS DIRECTORY — America Online Business Directory
BUSINESS FIND — Find a Business [Web site]

BUSINESS ONQ — onQ: Business Center
BUSINESS FORUM — Computing Applications Forum
BUSINESS PERK — Business Perk of the Week
BUSINESS SCHOOL — Business School Test Prep Areas
BUSINESS TRAVEL — Business Travel Center
BW — Business Week Online
CAREER CENTER — Gonyea Online Career Center
CCH — CCH Business Owner's Toolkit
CLASSIFIEDS — AOL Classifieds
COUREUR — AOL Canada Business & Finance Web Reviews
CRAIN'S SMALL BIZ — Crain's Small Business
HOC — Home Office Computing Online
INC — Inc. Online [Web site]
MARKETING YOUR BUSINESS — Sales & Marketing
MONEYWHIZ — Money Whiz
NBR — Nightly Business Report
NOLO — Nolo Press Self-Help Law Center [Web site]
OFFICE MAX — Office Max Online
OFFICE SHOP — Home Office
ONLINE BUSINESS — Doing Business Online
PERSONAL FINANCE — Personal Finance channel
SBA — U.S. Small Business Administration
STRATEGIES — The Business Know-How Forum
TAX — Tax Planning
VJF — Virtual Job Fair
WHITE PAGES — Switchboard Directory [Web site]
WORKPLACE — AOL WorkPlace
YOUR CAREER — Your Career

Readers and Writers

AUDIO BOOK CLUB — Audio Book Club [Web site]
AUTHORS@AOL — AOL Live: Authors@AOL Events
BARNES AND NOBLE — Barnes and Noble Bookseller
BOOKACCINO — The Book Report: Chat Room
BOOKBAG — The Book Bag for Teens
BOOK CENTRAL — Book Central
BOOKNOTES — Barron's Booknotes
BOOK REPORT — The Book Report
BOOK SHELF — The AOL Book Shelf
BOOKS — Books & Writing
BOOKS & MUSIC SHOP — AOL Shopping: Books
BOOKS COMMUNITY — Books Community
COBC — Christianity Online: Books & Culture
DENVER BOOK — Denver Books
DFW WRITERS CORNER — Writer's Corner

DIGITAL WORLDS — Digital Worlds Interactive Online
ELECTRA — Electra (E-Book Club under Time-Off)
ETEXT — PDA Forum: Palmtop Paperbacks
EW — Entertainment Weekly [Web site]
JEWISH BOOKS — Jewish Books
MAGAZINE OUTLET — Magazine Outlet
NN BOOKS — NetNoir: Books
NOVEL — Amazing Instant Novelist
OPRAH — Oprah Online (Oprah's Book Club)
POETRY PLACE — Poetry Place
READING — Writing & Reading
REFERENCE BOOKSHELF — Reference Bookshelf
ROMANCE GROUP — Romance Writers & Readers
SN LIT GAME — Bookwoman's Literature Game
TC BOOK EM — Twin Cities Book 'Em Review
TEEN WRITERS — Teen Writers
TIMES BOOKS — The New York Times: Books of The Times
UK WRITERS — UK Writers Club
WORD OF MOUTH — Word of Mouth
WRITERS — The Writers Club
WRITERS RESOURCES — Grammar & Style

Keyword Trivia

Think you know your keywords? This trivia quiz tests your knowledge of America Online and, of course, keywords. The answers can be found within the keyword lists themselves. A score of 3 or above — without peeking at the lists — qualifies you as a bona fide Keyword Kollector. E-mail your answers to screen name: *Jennifer* and I'll e-mail you a nifty virtual certificate in return!

1. What is the longest keyword?

2. What area has the most keywords to it?

3. Where does keyword: :) lead?

4. What keyword gives you the current time?

5. Where does keyword: FREE lead?

Romantics

1ST SITE — Love@1st Site
2ND CHANCE — Second Chance at Love
ASK DELILAH — Thrive@AOL: Love and Relationships Expert
ASK DR. LOVE — Online Psych: Ask Dr. Love
ASTROMATES — ASTRONET: ASTROMates
ATLANTA PERSONALS — Digital City Atlanta: Personals
BAY AREA PERSONALS — Digital City San Francisco: Personals
CHICAGO PERSONALS — Digital City Chicago: Personals
COACH STEPHEN — Digital City New York: Love Advisor
DALLAS PERSONALS — Digital City Dallas: Personals
DATE DOC — The Date Doctor
DATE PLANS — Dr. Date's Date Plans
DC PERSONALS — Digital City Personals
DENVER PERSONALS — Digital City Denver: Personals
DOCTOR KATE — Love@AOL: Answers by Dr. Kate
DR. LOVE — Philadelphia StarSites
ELECTRA — Electra (Relationships)
FLIRT! — Love@AOL: Flirt Game
FLOWERS — 1-800-Flowers
FREE LOVE — Love@AOL Newsletter
GALLERY — AOL Portrait Gallery
GREET STREET — Greet Street Greeting Cards
HALLMARK — Hallmark Connections [Web site]
HEART TO HEART — onQ: Relationships (gay, lesbian, and bisexual)
HM RELATIONSHIPS — Health Magazine Relationships
HOT BED — Love@AOL: Hot Bed Chat
IMH — Issues in Mental Health (Relationships message board)
INSTAKISS — Love@AOL: Insta-Kiss
IVILLAGE — iVillage (Relationships)
JEWISH SINGLES — Jewish Singles
LIFESTAGES MARRIAGE — Marriage & Money
LIFESTAGES SINGLES — On Your Own
LOVE@AOL — Love@AOL
LOVE@AOL PERSONALS — Love@AOL: Personals
LOVE FILES — The Love Files
LOVE SHACK — The Love Shack (United Kingdom)
LOVE SHOP — The Love Shop
NETGIRL — NetGirl: Personal Guide to Online Relationships
NY LOVE — Digital City New York: Love Advice
NY PERSONALS — Digital City New York: Personals
OLPMYND — Online Psych: MyndTalk on Relationships
ONLINE PSYCH — Online Psych (Relationship Forum)
ONLINE WEDDING — CyberVows
PEOPLE — People Connection
PERS CLASSIFIEDS — AOL Classifieds: Personals

PHILLY PERSONALS — Digital City Philadelphia: Personals
PHOTO PERSONALS — Love@AOL: Photo Personals
PPL — Passport to Love
RELATIONSHIPS — Relationships & Sexuality
ROMANCE — Romance channel
ROMANCE CONNECTION — Romance Connection
SINGLESMINDED — Singles-Minded: Love Advice Online
SWOON — Swoon-O-Matic
THE COUCH — The Couch for Advice, Dates & Romance
THRIVE@LOVE — Thrive@Love [Web site]
THRIVE@SEX — Thrive@Sex
TWIL — This Week In Love
UTOPIA LOVE — Utopia: The Love Shack
VALENTINE VACATIONS — Top Ten Romantic Getaways
WEDDING — The Knot

Teens

17 — Seventeen Magazine Online
ASTROTEENS — ASTRONET: AstroTeens
BACK TO SCHOOL — Back to School
BLACK TEENS — NetNoir: Black Teens
BOOKBAG — The Book Bag for Teens
CLUELESS — Cher's Clueless Site
CO HANGOUT — Christianity Online: Teen Hangout
COLLEGE ONLINE — College Online
DC TEENS — Digital City Washington: The Underground
DFW TEENS — Digital City Dallas Ft. Worth: The Metro Underground
DO SOMETHING — Do Something!
EA TEEN — Entertainment Asylum: Teen Asylum
GAY TEEN — onQ: Communities
GEN X — AOL Lifetyles: Ages & Stages
HOMEWORK — Homework Help (Jr. High and High School)
LA TEENS — Digital City Los Angeles: Teen Zone
MTV — MTV Online
OLP TEEN — Online Psych: The Teen Scene
OUTPROUD — !OutProud!
PHILLY TEENS — Digital City Philadelphia: The Hot Zone
PLUG IN — Plug In
STAR TRACKS — Teen People Online: Stars & Stuff
TEEN BUZZ SF — Teen Buzz
TEEN FRIENDS — AOL Teens: Friends
TEEN FUN — AOL Teens: Fun
TEEN HANGOUT — Teen Scene
TEEN LIFE — AOL Teens: Life
TEEN PEOPLE — Teen People Online
TEEN PEOPLE HOROSCOPES — Teen People Online: Horoscopes

TEEN PEOPLE SEARCH — Teen People Online: Search
TEEN PEOPLE STYLEGRRL — Teen People Online: Ask Stylegrrl
TEEN SEARCH — Search the Web [Web site]
TEEN STYLE — AOL Teens: Style
TEENS — AOL Teens
TEEN WRITERS — Teen Writers
TOE — The Outer Edge
TP BOARDS — Teen People Online: Message Boards
TP DAILY DISH — Teen People Online: Daily Dish
TP LIVE — Teen People Online: Live
TP LOVE — Teen People Online: Looks & Love
TP HOST — Teen People Online: Chat Host Profiles
TP REALITY CHECK — Teen People Online: Reality Check
TP SARI SAYS — Teen People Online: Sari Says
TRENDSPOTTERS — Teen People: Trendspotters
YOUTH TECH — Youth Tech

The Keyword Bizarre

With the sheer number of keywords out there, you would expect there to be some oddball keywords. And sure enough, there are. For some comic relief, check out the following keywords. Can you guess where they go? You may be surprised. (No peeking in the back!)

<><	MENSCH FINDER
:-)	OBJECTS OF DESIRE
2000	RAW
ANT HILL	SCOUNDREL
BUTTHEAD	SEND A KISS
DON'T CLICK HERE	SEX
EGGHEAD	SHHHH
G IS IN THE HOUSE	SHOW ME THE MONEY
GRANDMA MARGO	TWANG THIS!
HEAVEN	UNCENSORED
HEY BUDDY	VIEWERS TAKE CONTROL
JESUS FREAKS	WAY TO GO
KICK BUTT	ZEN

Women

ABC WOMEN — ABC Women's Sports
ASK DR. RASKIN — Online Psych: Ask Dr. Raskin about Women's Health
AVON CRUSADE — Avon's Awareness Crusade Online
BETTER LIVING — Woman's Day: Ideas for Better Living
CO WOMEN — Christianity Online: Women to Women
ELECTRA WOMAN — Electra: Woman
ELLE — Elle Magazine Online
EWE — Evenings with Eva
JEWISH NEWS — Jewish Community News (LILITH)
LIFETIME — Lifetime Online: Television for Women [WWW page]
MOMS ONLINE — Moms Online
NANCY FRIDAY — Online Psych: Online with Nancy Friday
SF WOMEN — Digital City San Francisco: A Woman's Place
TALKWOMEN — TalkWomen
TAPESTRY OF WOMEN — Online Psych: Tapestry of Women
TCW — Today's Christian Woman Magazine
TWN CHAT — The Women's Network: Chat
WICS — Women in Community Service
WOMANS DAY — Woman's Day Magazine Online
WOMEN — Women's Network
WOMEN & INVESTING — Women & Investing
WOMEN'S HEALTH WEB — Women's Internet Sites
WOMEN CLASS — Women's Network: Courses
WOMEN TODAY — Women Today
WOMENS HEALTH — Women's Health Forum
WOMENS SPACE — onQ: Communities (lesbian issues)
WSF — Women's Sports
UTOPIA WOMEN — Utopia: Women
VIRTUE — The Women's Network: Fitness & Beauty

List Lovers

Have you compiled your own list of keywords for a certain topic? Tell me and I may include it in future editions. Just e-mail your list to screen name: *Jennifer* along with a description and why you think others would find it useful.

CHAPTER 3

IMPORTANT KEYWORDS

Like phone numbers, there are important keywords everyone should know. And like a phone book, I've put them near the front for quick reference. This chapter describes and rates each of these essential keywords. I introduce each keyword with a *RatingsBar* (see Figure 3.1) that gives you a general overview of the area, as well as important information to help you decide if it is worth a look.

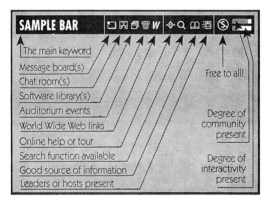

Figure 3.1 The RatingsBar explained.

A group of experienced community leaders chose and reviewed every keyword in this chapter. They each reviewed an area with which they were familiar, but never an area to which they had an official connection. Their chorus of voices is much more harmonious than anything I could have done on my own.

ACCESS

If you can't connect to America Online, you can't use keywords at all. But if you can connect, keyword: ACCESS is the place for the lowdown on upgraded connections. Find and/or request new access numbers. Report trouble with your current number. Learn to connect via TCP/IP. Traveling or moving? Domestic and international access numbers are available here. A helpful tip: if your region has new area codes, be sure to search on both the old and the new codes — sometimes numbers seem to fall through the cracks. Keyword: HIGH SPEED (MODEM) is another area that provides help in the same vein (see review later in this chapter). ACCESS is biased in favor of your phone connection, while keyword: HIGH SPEED is biased in favor of modem problems. What if you choose the wrong area? Don't worry; they're connected to each other! Be sure to also check out the review on keyword: PULSE OF AOL in Chapter 4.

Alternate keywords: ACCESS NUMBERS, AOLNET, CONNECT, CONNECTING, CONNECTION, NUMBERS, PHONE HELP, PHONE NUMBER(S), TELEPHONE, TELEPHONE NUMBERS.

Reviewed by Dave Marx (screen name: Dave Marx).

BILLING

Designed for easy use, keyword: BILLING allows you to change your billing information, name, address, and pricing plan, as well as view the billing terms of your account. Want to know all the details of the time you've spent online? Click **Display Your Detailed Bill**. Want to know when you'll be billed each month? Click **Display Your Billing Terms** and check the date at the top. BILLING also offers information on surcharge pricing, pricing plan changes, and access numbers that carry an additional fee (both U.S. and international). Answers to other billing questions are found within the **Frequently Asked Questions** section. If you can't find the answers you're looking for online, write to the staff with all the details of your situation, or talk to a billing representative online.

Alternate keywords: ADDRESS, BILING, BILL, BILLLING.

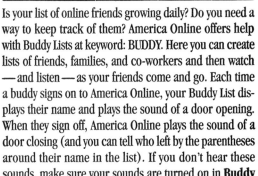

BUDDY

Is your list of online friends growing daily? Do you need a way to keep track of them? America Online offers help with Buddy Lists at keyword: BUDDY. Here you can create lists of friends, families, and co-workers and then watch — and listen — as your friends come and go. Each time a buddy signs on to America Online, your Buddy List displays their name and plays the sound of a door opening. When they sign off, America Online plays the sound of a door closing (and you can tell who left by the parentheses around their name in the list). If you don't hear these sounds, make sure your sounds are turned on in **Buddy List Preferences**. If you don't want a certain someone to know you're online or to send you Instant Messages, block them under **Privacy Preferences**. You can also use **Privacy Preferences** to block everyone and become invisible — a good tactic when you don't want to be disrupted. You can even invite one or all of your buddies who are online to a **Buddy Chat**. If you get stuck, just click **Help** to find out how to set up your Buddy Lists and Buddy Preferences. Then click **View** to see your Buddy List (or use keyword: BUDDY VIEW).

Alternate keywords: BL, BUDDIES, BUDDY LIST(S), BUDDY MAIN, (BUDDY VIEW, BV, HEY BUDDY).

Reviewed by Vicki DeVico (screen name: CmishVicki).

CLOCK

Hey, what time is it? It's the day we change our clocks. Is it an hour forward or an hour back? Spring forward, fall back — or the other way around? You were to meet someone online at 7 p.m. sharp. Is your clock or watch accurate? The last time you signed up for a class online you were 15 minutes late, but your clock said it was the right time. Aargghhhhh! Never fear. The online clock is always here! Think of it as the clock on the town square tower, keeping all America Online members in synch with one another. And it is always within view at keyword: CLOCK.

Alternate keyword: ONLINE CLOCK.

Reviewed by Eva Shaderoufsky (screen name: EvaS).

CREDIT

Yes, it happens every so often: you'll start downloading that interactive multimedia presentation of Proust's masterworks and get bumped offline right when you hit the "less than a minute" mark. Or it won't run because the file is somehow corrupted. Or perhaps your bill says you were online for 72 hours last night. What can you do? Try keyword: CREDIT! This handy credit request form lets you inform America Online of problems due to system slowness, interrupted/corrupted downloads, "host failed to respond" notices, and billing errors. Be prepared to type in the date and time the problem occurred, as well as the number of minutes lost. The credit request area even has information on America Online's Access Refund Policy, a must-see if you have had problems connecting to America Online!

Alternate keywords: CREDIT REQUEST, DOWNLOAD CREDIT.

Reviewed by Gwen Smith (screen name: Gwen Smith).

DICTIONARY

Surprise or *suprise*? *Truely* or *truly*? How *do* you spell it? Before you guess while talking to that special someone or writing to a business colleague, visit keyword: DICTIONARY for the answer. Wondering how to look up a word if you can't spell it? Type in the first few letters of the word followed by an asterisk (*) and click **Look Up** (or just press the **Enter** key). All matches are displayed along with their full definitions. Need help with all those complex Wall Street or fancy Internet terms? There are dictionaries for those as well! The area has recently added a cultural dictionary, as well as World Wide Web links to many sites for additional help and reference. Only a click away are a medical dictionary, kids' dictionary, rhyming dictionary, several foreign-language dictionaries, and much more!

Alternate keywords: COLLEGIATE, DICT, M-W DICTIONARY, MW DICT(IONARY), WEBSTER(S).

Reviewed by Kimberly Trautman
(screen name: KTrautman).

DOWNLOAD 101

What is this downloading stuff, and how do I do it? The answers to these questions are exactly what you'll find at keyword: DOWNLOAD 101. If you haven't downloaded yet, go there. Even veteran downloaders are amazed by how much well-written, well-organized information is available. There is a superb step-by-step demonstration of file searching in Lesson 2 and a free download library for your practicing pleasure. Download 101 covers the bases, from "What is Downloading?" to "Troubleshooting, Tips and Tricks." If you're at all intererested in moving software, sounds, or images from AOL's computers to your hard disk, keyword: DOWNLOAD 101 is the place to go to get started and the place to return to again and again for in-depth knowledge.

Alternate keyword: None.

Reviewed by Dave Marx (screen name: Dave Marx).

FILE SEARCH

America Online is one of the best places to get shareware, and keyword: FILE SEARCH assists you in finding just what you are looking for! Want a game to help you procrastinate? A word-processing program to work on that paper for school? A benchmark program to see the speed of your new hardware purchase? Just head over to keyword: FILE SEARCH, click the shareware option, and enter a description of what you need. Although the database does not include the company-run libraries (where you find updates for your commercial software), it does list the software that has been uploaded to America Online computing forums by members and staff. For your protection, all files are virus checked before they are released. Please note that keyword: FILE SEARCH presents you with only the software for the computer system you are using to access it; if you are using a Mac you will only see Mac software, and vice versa with the PC. There is a button at the bottom of the window that will take you to the other system's search engine, however.

Alternate keywords: SEARCH SHAREWARE, SEARCH SOFTWARE, SHAREWARE SEARCH, SOFTWARE SEARCH.

Reviewed by Laura Kramarsky
(screen name: AdeptMagic).

FIND

Oh where, oh where has my little dog gone? Keyword: AOL FIND may not be able to track down Rover, but it sure helps you rove around America Online. Type in a word or phrase, click **Search**, and a list of online areas that fit your needs appears. Double-click one of those listings and you'll receive a detailed description of the area. Click again to **Go There!** And click the **Find Central** button to fetch a collection of tools for finding members, software, and Internet sites. Another button helps you search America Online channel by channel, and **Find Help** guides you on your quest! Dare I say it? Once you were lost, but now you FIND. Happy finding!

Alternate keywords: AOL SEARCH, FIND CENTRAL.

Reviewed by Dave Marx (screen name: Dave Marx).

HELP

HELP!!! This is the keyword for America Online Customer Service and Technical Support. This is an online reference manual, troubleshooting guide, and gateway to live technical support all in one! Select a Help topic, find your subject within that topic, and read the article(s). Each window includes an **Ask the Staff** button, guiding you to further help — tech support phone numbers, message boards, e-mail, and even live help from an expert. Keep your eyes peeled for "5 Minute Guides" — easy, informative lessons scattered throughout the area. A visit to HELP also provides links to Accounts and Billing, and to Members Helping Members, which are reviewed in this chapter. There's even a **Search** tool to help you find whatever you need. This area doesn't answer your general computing questions (see keyword: HELP DESK for this). But for comprehensive, authoritative assistance with your AOL experience, there's no place else like it.

Alternate keywords: ANSWER(S), ASK AOL, ASK AMERICA ONLINE, CUSTOMER SERVICE, HOW TO, INFO SHOP, INFORMATION, MEMBER SERVICES, MEMBER SUPPORT, ONLINE SUPPORT, QUESTIONS, SERVICE, SUPPORT, SYSOP, TECH (HELP) LIVE, TECH(NICAL) SUPPORT.

Reviewed by Dave Marx (screen name: Dave Marx).

HELP DESK

What's a WAV file? What's an extension? How do you download and upload? What's a library? What do you mean my file is compressed? Computing is difficult, and now that you're online it may get even more complicated. Thankfully, the Help Desk is here. Whether you have a PC or a Mac, this platform-specific forum offers tips and hints, directions, answers frequently asked questions (FAQs), and more to help even the most novice user. I found their Visual Help on the PC an outstanding resource (get there quick with keyword: VISUAL HELP). The Help Desk also helps you use your computer and America Online. The instructions and information are straightforward and easy to comprehend. To see how easy, check out Download 101 (also reviewed in this chapter). Worried about viruses? The Help Desk gives you the lowdown on the latest virus news (see also keyword: VIRUS, reviewed in this chapter).

Alternate keywords: BEGINNER(S), COMPUTER HELP, MAC HELP, PC HELP.

Reviewed by J. Brian Thomason
(screen name: JBThomason).

HIGH SPEED

Keyword: HIGH SPEED leads to High Speed Access, an area intended to help you resolve America Online-related modem and connection problems, as well as get you connected at the highest possible speed. The help here is a treasure trove for technical do-it-yourselfers but is remarkably novice friendly. You'll find instructions, troubleshooting aids, modem profiles, answers to frequently asked questions, access numbers, the lowdown on Internet service providers, LAN, 56K and cable access, and links to the America Online Store's Modem Shop and modem manufacturers. Keyword: HIGH SPEED is a close cousin to keyword: ACCESS, which is also reviewed in this chapter.

Alternate keywords: 9600, MODEM, MODEM HELP.

Reviewed by Dave Marx (screen name: Dave Marx).

HOLIDAY

Do you need Easter recipes or a way to write to Santa? Keyword: HOLIDAY wraps the best of many forums into one neat package and whatever forum provided that neat little tip you can't live without is never more than a click away. Not content with just the major holidays, HOLIDAY also brings you back-to-school and wedding areas! The forms are beautifully designed but be prepared to wait a while for them to render the first time. As it gets close to *your* favorite holiday, try out keyword: HOLIDAY or the name of the holiday itself (usually also a keyword).

Alternate keywords: HOLIDAYS (others vary with holiday).

Reviewed by Kimberly Trautman
(screen name: KTrautman).

INSIDER

"Your backstage pass to the online experience," as they say. It's true! Meg, the AOL Insider, gives you the must-know information in the America Online world. The Insider offers you a daily tip on using America Online, plus archives of all past tips. Meg also offers a look at America Online traffic — find out when the system is going down for maintenance and when upgrades happen!

Alternate keywords: AOL INSIDER, AOL TIPS, BEST TIPS, HOT TIP(S), INSIDER (TIPS), MEG, ONLINE TIPS, TIP(S), TOP TIPS.

MAIL CENTER

In the world of e-mail, America Online is big. Really big. The biggest e-mail address on the Internet! And the Mail Center is the Grand Central Post Office. Come to keyword MAIL CENTER to read and compose e-mail, learn to use each and every e-mail feature, search for e-mail addresses, send a greeting card, and use e-mail for fun and at your place of business. Click the **Let's Get Started** button to learn the basics. Click **Mail Features** to learn how to control your mailbox and stop junk mail (read the next review).

Alternate keywords: E-MAIL, EMAIL, MAIL, MAIL GATEWAY, NEW MAIL, POST OFFICE.

Reviewed by Dave Marx (screen name: Dave Marx).

MAIL CONTROLS

Everyone hates *spam*! Ok, well maybe not e-mail advertisers or Hormel, but for the majority of us it's simply a pain. What's spam, you ask? It's a cute term for that not-so-cute, unsolicited, unrequested, and unwanted junk advertising e-mail that keeps filling up your mailbox. What can you do about it? America Online is already handling the matter! Hourly, AOL updates its system to prevent spam from reaching your e-mail box. If that isn't enough, you can also control your e-mail at keyword: MAIL CONTROLS. Available options are to block all mail coming from the Internet, block e-mail from specific individuals, or even allow mail from only a select group. If that's still not enough, you'll find more features and other controls (see the review on Parental Controls later in this chapter). Give MAIL CONTROLS a try today and give your mailbox a break!

Alternate keywords: EMAIL CONTROLS, MAIL CONTROL.

Reviewed by Bradley Zimmer
(screen name: Bradley476).

MEMBERS

When it comes to finding another America Online member, the Member Directory is one-stop shopping at its best. Search member profiles by name, location, and language on the first page and select **Advanced Search** if you'd like to try a more exacting search. The Member Directory accepts Boolean (*AND*, *OR*, and *NOT*) and wildcard (*) searches so you can widen and narrow your search. The latest versions of America Online also let you search for only those members who are online at the time — the older versions of the software will show a red arrow next to the people who're online instead. Select the **My Profile** button to create or modify your own profile. Not all members have profiles but this is the best place to start your search for that long-lost friend or new pal.

Alternate keywords: MEMBER DIRECTORY, DIRECTORY.

Reviewed by Kimberly Trautman
(screen name: KTrautman).

MHM

Finding the online experience a little overwhelming? Not sure just where to find the answers to those "How do I do that?" and "Where do I find this?" questions? Whether you're young or old, beginner or expert, Members Helping Members at keyword: MHM is the place to look for answers to your America Online questions. All questions are from America Online members, as are all answers. Nowhere else on the service is there such a vast base of knowledge to draw from. Message boards are at the heart of Members Helping Members, each organized by subject matter. Billing, access, add-ons, and help with upgrading are just a few of the topics covered. Have a question? Scan the message boards to see if your question has already been answered. If you don't see it, just post your question on the message board! With the millions of America Online members out there, helpful feedback to your question is usually posted within hours! And you're welcome to contribute your own help and tips here, too. This is a one-of-a-kind, grassroots resource.

Alternate keyword: MEMBERS HELPING MEMBERS.

Reviewed by Robert J. Hill (screen name: MudCatMax).

MY HOME PAGE

Doesn't it seem like everybody you know suddenly has their own Web page? It *must* be easy, but where do you start? Check out keyword: MY HOMEPAGE. This is the perfect spot for beginners and advanced web-weavers, alike. If the thought of coding in HTML (HyperText Markup Language) terrifies you, rest assured that you'll never have to touch the stuff—unless you want to. For the beginner, this area offers much in the way of tutorials and many very easy-to-use, preformatted, Web page templates and tools. For the more advanced, the sky is the limit. Web pages may be authored entirely in free-form HTML code, using Java applets, and other advanced features, or with a mixture of as much, or as little coding as you'd like, to achieve a functional, effective, and polished Web site.

Alternate keywords: HOMEPAGE, PERSONAL PUBLISHER.

Reviewed by Bob Trautman (screen name: PhotogBT).

NAMES

Do you have a great idea for a new screen name? Want to restore an old screen name or delete one? The screen name you choose is very important — other members identify you with it on America Online. You can use your real name, a nickname, or something that reveals something about your interests. A well-chosen screen name enables you to stand out from the crowd in a chat room or a message board, so be as creative as you would like to be when creating screen names! Your America Online account allows you to create up to four screen names in addition to the first screen name you created on your account (which can not be deleted). Naturally America Online offers control over these screen names, and you'll find it at keyword: NAMES. Whether you wish to create a new screen name, delete a screen name, restore a screen name, update the screen names on your computer, or set up different access levels for each screen name on an account using the Parental Controls, keyword: NAMES can help you manage it all. Note that you need to be signed on with your master screen name to effectively use keyword: NAMES.

Alternate keywords: HANDLE, NAME(S), SCREENAME(S), SCREEN NAME, USERNAME.

Reviewed by Maria Therese Lehan
(screen name: Sioux Mac).

NEW

Do you like to stay on top of things? At keyword: NEW, the latest and greatest services and areas offered on America Online are on display. Clicking a listing or icon takes you directly to that area. The keywords aren't always obvious, so once you arrive check the window for the keyword or add it to your Favorite Places if you want to return later. Also note that some of the areas at keyword: NEW aren't always new, but just updated. Even so, this is a great place to keep up with the new areas and offerings online. Don't be the last to know! Visit keyword: NEW regularly and be among the first to discover America Online's newest features!

Alternate keywords: FIVE, HOT (5), HOT FIVE, HOT TODAY, LATEST, THE LATEST, WHAT(I)S HOT, WHAT(I)S NEW.

NOTIFY AOL

There are a handful of keywords of such importance that they merit a sticky-note on the edge of the monitor. Keyword: NOTIFY AOL is one of these. Its easy-to-follow instructions make this an easy and fast way to contact the Community Action Team, the group of folks at America Online who assist you when there is a problem with another member. Click **Chat** when someone insists on disrupting a chat, click **E-mail & Attachments** when you've received something offensive in e-mail, click **Instant Message Notes** when something offensive comes by way of an IM, click **Message Boards** when you stumble across something wrong in a board, click **Web**

Pages when you discover an inappropriate Web page, and click **Screen Names & Profiles** when you see a screen name or profile that violates the Terms of Service. The Terms of Service are found at keyword: TOS (reviewed later in this chapter). If you aren't sure where to report a problem, click **Write to Staff** at the bottom. Oh, and by the way, America Online will never ask you for your password, credit card number, or other personal information online. Anyone who does ask you for those things is violating the Terms of Service and should be reported immediately at keyword: NOTIFY AOL.

Alternate keywords: I NEED HELP, NOTIFY AOL.

PARENTAL CONTROLS

Empower yourself with America Online's Parental Controls! With millions of members online, who knows what type of people your children can come across. In order to help you protect them from these various bad elements, and the more *mature* sites online, America Online developed a set of tools at keyword: PARENTAL CONTROLS. Many different kinds of controls are available, including my personal favorite: preset general controls. These simple controls allow you to designate a setting of **General**, **Mature Teen**, **Young Teen**, or **Child Access** for each screen name on your account. With just the click of a mouse, you can have access restricted to select child- or teen-oriented Internet sites and America Online forums, along with safer communication settings for other America Online features. For greater customization, the remainder of the tools let you selectively block or unblock areas of the service, such as chat rooms, Instant Messages, Internet newsgroups, and surcharged premium services (the latter of which are by default blocked on all screen names). Are your children safe online? Spend some time learning and customizing these controls to ensure just that! (See the review of Mail Controls earlier in this chapter for further details on e-mail preferences.)

Alternate keyword: PARENTAL CONTROL.

Reviewed by Bradley Zimmer
(screen name: Bradley476).

PASSWORD

Security in cyberspace is extremely important if you want to protect yourself and your checkbook. Your password is the key to your account, and it's important to change that key regularly in case it's compromised without your knowledge. The Change Password area at keyword: PASSWORD on America Online gives you the power to instantly change your account password, thus protecting yourself from thieves, scoundrels, and con artists who would cause you harm. We recommend you change your password frequently — once a month works for most people — and choose carefully. Read the rules, tips, and cautions in the VirtuaLingo Glossary before selecting a password. When you're ready, go to keyword: PASSWORD, click **Change Password**, make your choice, and then confirm it! It is important to note that your password is yours, and yours alone. Do not reveal it to anyone. America Online employees and staff will never ask you for your password for any reason. Never. If someone asks you for your password or account information online, use keyword: NOTIFY AOL to report it to the proper authorities immediately. If you forget your password, just call America Online at 1-800-827-6364.

Alternate keywords: CHANGE PASSWORD, PASSWORDS, (PASSWORD TIPS).

Reviewed by Bradley Zimmer
(screen name: Bradley476).

PRESS

Have you ever wanted more information about those joint ventures between America Online and other conglomerates? Wouldn't you like to know about a new area online *before* it launches? It's all waiting for you at keyword: PRESS, where you can read the latest America Online press releases as well as search past news articles from the archives. This is definitely news you can use, so visit this area often, get informed, and give your broker a call.

Alternate keyword: PRESS RELEASE.

Reviewed by Kate Tipul (screen name: KMTipul).

QUICKSTART

Ready to launch into cyberspace? Keyword: QUICKSTART is one of your first stops. AOL QuickStart helps you quickly get up to speed on America Online and make the most of your time. Start your learning experience with **Five Minutes to AOL**, a tour of some of the treats America Online has to offer. Move on to the **Best of AOL**, highlighting many of the features which makes America Online unique, including Buddy Lists, Instant Messages, and Find Central. **Match Your Interests** helps you find the areas that are best suited to your own hobbies and lifestyle, and leads you to new adventures too. **Meg's Insider Tips** are included here as well, helping you learn shortcuts and many how-to's for making your online time as rich as you want it to be (see the review of keyword: INSIDER also in this chapter). A whole new area of learning opens up with a click of the **More Help** button. The **New Member Help Room** is hosted by guides, trained and helpful AOL members who are eager to answer your questions. **Message Boards** are full of information and questions from new members (also available at keyword: MHM, and reviewed earlier in this chapter). QUICKSTART gets you started in nothing flat!

Alternate keywords: ?, AMERICA (ONLINE), AOL BEGINNERS, DISCOVER (AOL), DISCOVER AOL NEW MEMBER, NEWBIE, NEW MEMBER, NOVICE, ORIENTATION.

Reviewed by Becky Fowler (screen name: BeckyFowlr).

REMINDER

Did you forget your anniversary or your boss's birthday? Need a little help remembering all the important dates in your life? Take heart — keyword: REMINDER gives you a gentle nudge! Just go to keyword: REMINDER, fill in the names and dates you need to remember, and 14 days before a special date you are sent a reminder message. You also have the option receive another reminder message four days before a date and you can edit your reminders at any time. While you can't change the number of days before an event a reminder is sent, you can fudge it using a different date. Use keyword: REMINDER today and stay out of the doghouse next month.

Alternate keywords: GIFT REMINDER, GIFT VALET.

Reviewed by Maria Therese Lehan
(screen name: Sioux Mac).

TOS

If you love "fine print," this is the place! America Online's Terms of Service (TOS) are the rules of the road and service agreement for America Online's members. If you or your family can't abide by these rules you can be "tossed" offline, so it pays to review. On the flip side, when others misbehave, come here to check the rules and report to America Online's Community Action Team — the folks who enforce TOS. Three big buttons lead to the **Terms of Service** ("fine print"at its finest), **Rules of the Road** (straightforward rules on accessing and using America Online), and **Online Conduct** (dos and don'ts for good virtual citizens). These three texts are collectively known as *TOS*, a term used colloquially by members. The fourth button is for reporting TOS violations (see keyword: NOTIFY AOL reviewed earlier in this chapter).

Alternate keywords: TERMS, TERMS OF SERVICE, TOS ADVISOR.

Reviewed by Dave Marx (screen name: Dave Marx).

UPGRADE

Are you driving yesterday's America Online software? America Online upgrades its programs at least once a year, adding nifty, new features and (usually) improving technical performance. This is the place for the latest AOL software and much, much more. After witnessing and experiencing the pain of AOL software upgrades for many years, I can say they've finally gotten it right! You'll find extensive help resources, live chats, auditorium events, and message boards devoted to helping you prepare and survive your upgrade, and get the most out of the software once it is working. But that's not all — there's a glitzy guided tour of the new software's features and an

Upgrade Shop to help prepare your computer for the newest features. Bravo!

Alternate keywords: 4.0, AOL40, AOL 4.0, NEW AOL.

Reviewed by Dave Marx (screen name: Dave Marx).

VIRUS

With the popularity of the Internet booming, the volume of data passed between computers is at an all-time high. Do you know what is being placed on your computer when browsing the Web? Any idea what is in that file you just downloaded? If not, then the Virus Information Center (keyword: VIRUS) is the place for you. This area is filled with resources, giving precious information that every computer user needs to know. Here you will find: message boards, software libraries, informative articles, and links to other virus-related forums and Internet sites. Just the tools you need to educate yourself on viruses and their detection, elimination, and prevention.

Alternate keywords: MAC VIRUS, PC SECURITY, VIC, VIRUS UPDATE.

Reviewed by Robert J. Hill, Jr.
(screen name: MudCatMax).

CHAPTER 4

NEW KEYWORDS

New keywords are special. Some are announced with great fanfare, while others steal quietly onto the scene. More often than not, members exchange them with pride and excitement, heralding a new "place" with wonders yet unknown. I am pleased to present a broad cross-section of new keywords in this chapter — both the not-to-be-missed and the missed-the-mark. Like Chapter 3, each keyword's description is introduced by a *RatingsBar*, giving a general overview of the area (see Figure 4.1).

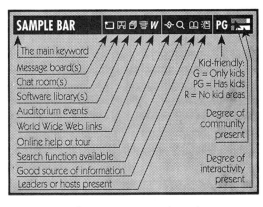

Figure 4.1 The RatingsBar explained.

AOL TODAY

Every hour of every day, keyword: AOL TODAY offers the hottest happenings on America Online. Serving as the *TV Guide* for the AOL service, AOL Today lists live events, the latest news, and timely features from forums and channels throughout the service. It's a bit like the Welcome window on steroids. AOL Today changes several times a day, offering morning, midday, prime-time, and late-night editions, and you'll always find a sneak peek at AOL Today on your Welcome window. Be forewarned that the links you find at AOL Today may take you on the scenic and winding path to your destination, but you do get there sooner or later. With the staggering number of areas on America Online, AOL Today is an essential tool for today's members.

Alternate keyword: TODAY.

*Reviewed by Bradley Zimmer
(screen name: Bradley476).*

ASYLUM 　　　　　　🖵 📠 🖃 🦢 *W* ⊹ Q 📖 🗒 **PG**

Seeking asylum from the stress and cruelty of the world? There's a place for you — the Entertainment Asylum at keyword: ASYLUM. Escape to a world of fun and frivolity, where movies and television rule supreme and good-natured gossip is the order of the day. The Entertainment Asylum is a new and surprisingly comprehensive entertainment community on America Online. It steals the scene with opportunities to interact with celebrities, the latest Tinsel Town gossip, up-to-the-minute news and commentary on entertainment escapades, and down-to-earth information on your favorite genres. The Entertainment Asylum plays host to smaller areas with personalities and keywords of their own — my favorite is keyword: CLUB SINATRA, dedicated to "Ol' Blue Eyes," Frank Sinatra. If the sheer size of the place feels overwhelming at first, try the **Search** button at the bottom to narrow in on what you want. Their search window is state of the art, offering lots of ways to find just what you need. Take a bow, Entertainment Asylum!

Alternate keywords: ASYLUM, EAMC, ENT ASYLUM, ENTERTAINMENT ASYLUM, SOL ASYLUM, THE ASYLUM.

CENTURY 21 　　　　　 *W* 　 Q 📖 　 **R**

Searching for a community? The real estate titan Century 21 invites members to search for their next offline community at keyword: CENTURY 21. Upon arrival you're invited to find a location — if your choice is listed (not a slam-dunk proposition), you receive extensive information on your chosen community. Search directly for properties or a Century 21 broker, and browse an extensive collection of real estate articles. Century 21 packs a lot of information behind its simple front page. Even so, with an entire world to cover you still may not find what you need.

Alternate keyword: None.

Reviewed by Dave Marx (screen name: Dave Marx).

CHANNEL GUIDE

America Online organizes its content into channels, much like cable TV. Yet sometimes going directly to the channel is as effective as flipping to channel 56 at 9 p.m.. You only get a sampling. If you want a clearer picture, use keyword: CHANNEL GUIDE. All channel content is listed by name here — just browse the channel list you're interested in, choose the "program" you want, and presto!

Alternate keyword: None.

CLOSED FUNDS

America Online's Personal Finance channel is a rich resource for the rich and rich at heart, and here's proof: keyword: CLOSED FUNDS. There are fewer than 500 of these closed-end funds — a drop in the mutual fund bucket. A fixed number of shares are issued, which are bought and sold like stocks. Still, it delivers a beginner's guide, a message board, and links to valuable information at keywords: BUSINESS WEEK, WORTH, and AAII (the American Association of Individual Investors). The *Business Week* and *Worth* materials are based on magazine articles and will become dated.

Alternate keyword: CLOSED-ENDFUNDS.

Reviewed by Dave Marx (screen name: Dave Marx).

COUNTDOWN 2000

Admit it — you're awaiting the turn of the century with bated breath. (Actually, I hope you aren't, because if you don't breathe normally you may miss it altogether.) But seriously, if the flip of the temporal odometer fascinates you, America Online has a nifty little clock counting down the minutes to the millennium at keyword: COUNTDOWN 2000. As I write this, it is flashing *853053* minutes (Greenwich Mean Time) to that fateful date: January 1, 2000. There are some that argue the new millennium starts on January 1 in 2001 (why does that date seem so familiar?). Regardless, I hope I'm not sitting here staring at a computer screen when it drops to zero.

Alternate keywords: 2000, MIL 2000, MILLENNIUM TICKER.

ELECTRA

From the moment you enter keyword: ELECTRA one thing is certain: this is a place for women, real women. Electra organizes itself into six main themes — Career, Money, Mind & Body, Relationships, Style, and Time-Off — with several smaller areas such as Travel, Horoscopes, and Shopping rounding out the picture. Yet I found myself questioning their choice of topics on the day I visited: choosing low-fat foods, protecting your skin, and getting through the day with a smile. Good things to know, yes, but is this really all real women care about? I know I have more on my mind than looking good, figuring out if he loves me, and getting my horoscope for the day. To be fair, I did discover more admirable stuff when I delved a bit deeper. There is an excellent forum on turning 40, and I was really impressed with the entire career section with its Career Advisor, resume help, mentoring information, and tip of the day. And all stressed-out, over-worked, burden-laden Superwomen can use a little Time-Off, with a woman's look at travel, entertainment, music, books, and games. You won't want to miss the crossword puzzle, which you can do *online* — no paper and pencil needed. Interestingly, the crossword puzzle was created by a man.

Alternate keywords: ELCTRA, ELECTRACITY.

FINANCIAL AID 🖵 🗐 W 🕮 PG ▬

Does the price of a good education ever go down? Find the keys to paying your way at keyword: FINANCIAL AID. Whether it's scholarships for undergrads, funding for research, or advice on making the tuition "nut," the value of FINANCIAL AID rests in the resources it has assembled. The College Board, National Association of Student Financial Aid Advisors, and U.S. Department of Education World Wide Web sites weigh in alongside a handsome group of America Online-grown resources. Polaris and RSP Funding publish funding, grant, and scholarship information, and Saving for School is a real gem, offering save-for-college wisdom from Motley Fool (keyword: FOOL), Parent Soup (keyword: PARENT SOUP), American Association of Individual Investors (keyword: AAII), and more. Here's a keyword that pays off in a big way!

Alternate keywords: GRANT(S), SCHOLARSHIPS.

Reviewed by Dave Marx (screen name: Dave Marx).

HISPANIC ONLINE 🖵 🖾 🗐 W ✧ Q 🕮 🧾 PG ▬

¿Que pasa? There's finally a dedicated area for the Hispanic and Latino community! Keyword: HISPANIC ONLINE is a rich tapestry of up-to-date information on social, cultural, and economic issues. The majority of the text found here is in English, though several labels and titles appear in the native tongue. Mundo leads to news and politics, Ritmo to arts & entertainment, Vida to lifestyles, Mercado to shopping, and Dialogo to chat rooms. And if you are still wondering what's happening, click **¿Que Pasa?** for the calendar of special events. Don't overlook the Daily Sorpresa — a closer look at important news stories — hidden at the very bottom of the main window. Note that keyword: HISPANIC leads to the AOL Ethnicity page, not Hispanic Online — use your Favorite Places or one of the shorter keywords below to get there quicker.

Alternate keywords: HISPANIC MAGAZINE, LATINA, LATINO.

INFLUENCE 　　　🖵 🎞 　≋W 🔍 📖 　R ▬

Keyword: INFLUENCE is for the rubber-neckers of the world. This brand new channel offers the skinny on celebrities, movers and shakers, media and the arts, trends and fads, and the good life. Yet, I feel Influence is more for those who want to *be influenced* than for those who want to *influence others*. You decide.

Alternate keywords: COMMENTARY, INTELLECTUAL, MOVERS & SHAKERS, PRESTIGE, SOCIETY, TREND(S), TRENDY, WEALTH.

KNOT 　　　🖵 🎞 　　W 🔍 📖 🖳 　R ▬

"Only six months until my wedding and I haven't a clue where to start!" If this sounds like you, drop by keyword: KNOT. Subtitled "weddings for the real world," The Knot is the be-all and end-all of wedding sites. America Online forums and Internet sites mesh smoothly here, from finding the perfect dress to registering for a free honeymoon. Message boards and articles cover subjects both serious and hilarious. Be prepared for lots of ads and shopping potential. But hey, that's to be expected from anything having to do with weddings these days.

Alternate keywords: BRIDE, GROOM, HONEYMOON, THE KNOT, WEDDINGS.

Reviewed by Kimberly Trautman
(screen name: KTrautman).

MAD WORLD 　　　🖵 　　W 🔍 📖 　PG ▬

"Parrot Saves Owner From Fire," "When Clothing Attacks," "AT&T Microwaves Checks." Yes, these are real news headlines, and keyword: MAD WORLD serves them up for you every Friday. From the curious to the crazy, it's all here in the self-proclaimed "Weird News from the Wires" headquarters. Straight from Reuters and The Associated Press, the weirdest thing about these stories is that they're all true! Besides offering a week's worth of odd news, Mad World provides the best pictures of the week along with links to similar sites on America Online. Truth is stranger than fiction — it's a mad, mad world out there!

Alternate keyword: MAD.

Reviewed by Bradley Zimmer
(screen name: Bradley476).

| **MUSIC BLVD** | | *W* | Q ▥ | **PG** |

Can't get that tune out of your head? If you can't beat it, buy it at keyword: MUSIC BLVD. Music Boulevard, a service of the ambitious music purveyor N2K, is a comprehensive music store with over 200,000 selections ranging from classical to country to rap and beyond. The user-friendly layout means you don't have to scroll past the entire Bob Dylan catalog to find that Spice Girls CD you've been wanting, and special features like VH-1 Online and *Billboard* Charts make it easy to find the freshest new music. On the downside, most of the buttons here point to sites on the World Wide Web. Even so, they are well designed and well integrated with one another and the pages on America Online, and they do take advantage of Web-based technologies to the fullest. Music Boulevard is just like your corner music store, only a lot bigger. And best of all, you can shop in your pajamas!

Alternate keywords: MB, MBCD, MUSIC BOULEVARD.

Reviewed by Adrienne Quinn (screen name: AAQuinn).

| **NYC** | ▭ ▨ | *W* | Q ▥ ▨ | **PG** |

The Big Apple. A scary unknown or a happening place to be? Keyword: NYC has the answers for the traveler and local alike. Organized into two main areas, Things to Do and People to Meet, the area is easy to navigate and simple to understand. Be sure to check out Your Neighbors in the Virtual Neighborhood — a collection of World Wide Web pages from New York City sites and members living in the various neighborhoods of New York City. Want to move in? Anyone online is welcome to join and set up a "home" page. When you register, they create a very basic home page for you, which can later be built upon. And you can have a chat room of your own in your home page. Even Ted Leonsis, President and CEO of AOL Studios, has a "home" in Silicon Alley. The drawbacks?

Graphic-intensive pages require patience — ads, ads, and more ads await each time you visit the site.

Alternate keywords: DCNY(C), NEW YORK (CITY).

*Reviewed by Kimberly Trautman
(screen name: KTrautman).*

PEOPLE

Imagine yourself arriving at a party. Instead of being greeted graciously by the host, getting directions to the munchies, and being introduced to your fellow partiers, you are unceremoniously thrust into the middle of a heated discussion as soon as you open the door. Not for me! Yet this is precisely what using keyword: PEOPLE did to members in the past (in a virtual sense, of course). I'm pleased to report that America Online has updated the keyword to take you to a virtual "foyer" first. Keyword: PEOPLE leads to the People Connection, America Online's chat room headquarters. You're greeted by a bouquet of "talk" balloons (like the kind that cartoon characters sport) that you can click. The Community Center is a warm and fuzzy collection of information for chatters, including a list of chat host biographies, a field guide (chat netiquette tips), and a member's journal (where members share their experiences). Find a Chat displays lists of the hundreds of chats going on at the time — click a category to update the list. Show Me How presents information about the tools and services you can use to communicate with others online. Chat Now is for those who really *do* want to be thrust unceremoniously into a chat room — clicking it dumps you into a Lobby. All in all, the new People Connection is just what was needed. I wish we had it when I was a host!

Alternate keywords: CHAT, LOBBY, PC, TALK.

PERKS

The name Member Perks really says it all — benefits just for being a member! America Online uses the buying power of over 12 million members to negotiate deals on everything from long-distance phone service to magazine subscriptions to travel. They also offer ways to earn points good for purchasing merchandise or even $20 for getting a friend to join America Online The rules and restrictions (you knew there had to be some) are stated plainly in each of the perk areas — be sure to read them.

Alternate keywords: MEMBEREXCLUSIVES, MEMBERPERKS.

Reviewed by Kimberly Trautman
(screen name: KTrautman).

PIX OF THE WEEK

Click, click, click! Camera shutters capture the news, and now your mouse can capture the best news photos! Keyword: PICTURES OF THE WEEK presents a gallery of the week's best color photos from the lenses of the Associated Press. It's like flipping through the pages of *LIFE Magazine*. Pictures of the Week offers three portfolios of from five to ten photos each, covering US & World News, Sports, and Entertainment. Each portfolio also offers useful links back to the AOL News channel. Navigation within each portfolio is limited to the "next" and "previous" buttons — your selections are limited, but the vistas are striking. Give PICTURES OF THE WEEK a click!

Alternate keywords: EDITORS CHOICE, PICTURES OF THE WEEK.

Reviewed by Dave Marx (screen name: Dave Marx).

PORTFOLIO DIRECT

Stock market maniacs can never get enough news (especially when the bull market is roaring) and America Online keeps finding new ways to feed them news. Do you want proof? Visit keyword: PORTFOLIO DIRECT. For no extra charge, every evening America Online sends you e-mail with closing quotations on up to 20 stocks, a market news summary, and Reuters news pertaining to the stocks you selected. The mail even includes hypertext links that lead to further in-depth information. Although AOL's online portfolios offer even more, PORTFOLIO DIRECT is well designed, convenient, and if you save your e-mail it's a good way to keep historic records.

Alternate keywords: DIRECT PORTFOLIO, PDC, PORT DIR.

Reviewed by Dave Marx (screen name: Dave Marx).

PROFESSIONS

So you want an area with more substance? Share advice and ideas with communities in your line of work at keyword: PROFESSIONS. Get help with your business and careers from A to V (that's "accounting" to "veterinarians") — over 48 communities at the time of writing. Each professional community has its own message board, scheduled chat, library, and links to related areas on America Online and the World Wide Web. Scheduled chats cover tax advice, marketing solutions, investing, business travel, and many more Business Know-How topics. For those of you with a jam-packed appointment book, this forum offers a "chat reminder" service to enable you to attend your choice of career enhancing topics. Explore other professions and careers in the Professional Forums Message Boards. Join the gathering at Water Cooler Conversations for opinions on the workplace in the '90s.

Alternate keywords: INDUSTRIES & NICHES, NICHES, PROFESSION, PROFESSIONAL FORUMS, YOUR INDUSTRY.

Reviewed by Linda Lindquist (screen name: NordiKat).

PULSE OF AOL

Have you taken your pulse lately? Not the one on your wrist, the one on your modem. Keyword: PULSE OF AOL checks the current status of America Online and provides an extremely valuable service for members. Though one of the simplest keywords you'll find, it is one of the best. Pulse of AOL displays the current system information on a daily basis. If a system like e-mail, downloading, message boards, or Instant Messages is down or is going down in the next few days for regular maintenance, it is noted here. If you are experiencing a problem, check here first for an explanation. Better yet, the latest cities receiving local access numbers or additional capacity on existing numbers are announced here regularly. The day I checked, several cities were receiving their very first local access number. Make it a point to check the pulse of America Online often at keyword: PULSE OF AOL.

Alternate keyword: POA.

SCOREBOARD

You don't know the score? AOL Sports wins points by posting the big scores at keyword: SCOREBOARD. Though only the largest sports are played here — football, basketball, hockey, and baseball — when that's what you need, keyword: SCOREBOARD is a hit. The interface is simple: click the button for your sport and get a mini-scoreboard for every game. Want to go deep? Click the buttons labeled **S** (game summary), **P** (game preview), or **B** (box score) to net all the details. You can also catch Top Stories and a listing of the best performances in the game. If you're a sports nut or just trying to avoid going nutty looking for your favorite sports scores, make SCOREBOARD your goal!

Alternate keyword: SCOREBOARDS.

Reviewed by Dave Marx (screen name: Dave Marx).

SCRAPBOOK

Scrapbooking is taking the hobby world by storm, and the thriving crafts community on America Online is no exception. Keyword: SCRAPBOOK is a fun and informative place to indulge in this creative hobby. More importantly, the folks here are friendly and really involved in the community. The message boards are packed with tips, hints, answers, and places to shop. Members even share sale information with each other! Swap supplies or participate in the secret pal program. Links to shopping and layout designs on the World Wide Web help you fill that blank spot on your page or get involved with a contest. There are also regular chats held in the People Connection Member Rooms area. This is a simple area, but one rich in community and information. So whether you're looking to memorialize your family vacation or your favorite team's championship, take a peek at keyword: SCRAP-BOOK and get some ideas!

Alternate keyword: CREATIVE SCRAPBOOKING.

Reviewed by Kimberly Trautman
(screen name: KTrautman).

TEENS `□ ⋈ 🗐 ≋ W` `□ 🗐 PG`

Need an upFront and inSide look at the teen life? Look no further than keyword: TEENS. upFront spotlights current gossip and live events just for teens, while inSide is a more in-depth look at Life, Friends, Fashion, and Fun. Keyword: TEEN is best described as a collection of special areas from other forums around America Online that aren't readily reachable by keyword. Featured here is Teen People (yep, like the magazine) with topics of particular interest to teens, like boys/girls, school, clothes, and TV. (And for teens that only care about boys/girls, school, clothes, and TV, click the **Reality Check** button for a dose of real life). Keyword: TEEN is really a channel unto itself — with an attitude.

Alternate keywords: TEEN, TEENS CHANNEL, TEENAGERS.

WORLDPLAY `□ ⋈ 🗐` `◇` `🗐 PG`

Do you like to play games? If you don't mind paying a bit extra, keyword: WORLDPLAY is an online gamer's paradise. The diversity of games available here is remarkable, ranging from Bridge to BattleTech to Backgammon. There are over 30 different games currently, and new offerings are in development. Each WorldPlay game tacks a surcharge on top of your regular online fees for America Online. At the time of writing, the surcharge is an additional $2 an hour. For your money, you get top-quality games — you won't find the text-based games of the past. The WorldPlay games have full-motion graphics and sound, with the realism of any computer game found in a store. The best thing about these games, and what makes them worth the extra bucks, is the opportunity to play with or against real people online. WorldPlay also offers live online classes to teach you how to play the games, along with tips and tricks from the experts. Even if you don't consider yourself a computer game aficionado, take a peek at WorldPlay to see if it is right for you.

Alternate keywords: INN, WORLDPLAY MAIN.

Reviewed by Bradley Zimmer
(screen name: Bradley476).

CHAPTER 5

HOT KEYWORDS

Remember Saturday morning cartoons? We all had our favorite cartoons, and we'd regale anyone who would listen to their plots and hijinks. Like those old favorites, these keywords are tried and true. We don't think you can miss with any of them. Each of the "hot" keywords descriptions are introduced by a *RatingsBar*, which gives a general overview of the area as well as other important information (see Figure 5.1).

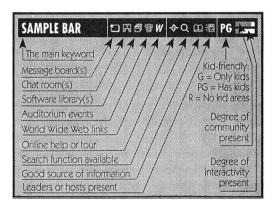

SAMPLE BAR

The main keyword
Message board(s)
Chat room(s)
Software library(s)
Auditorium events
World Wide Web links
Online help or tour
Search function available
Good source of information
Leaders or hosts present

Kid-friendly:
G = Only kids
PG = Has kids
R = No kid areas

Degree of community present

Degree of interactivity present

Figure 5.1 The RatingsBar explained.

ADOPTION

Adoption touches millions of lives. And they are each welcome at keyword: ADOPTION. Serving all arms of the adoption triad with knowledgeable community leaders, the Adoption Forum offers scheduled, hosted chats and message boards dealing with every aspect of the adoption experience. An unusual resource area lists informational links and addresses to help with virtually any situation a member may have (though there are no children's services in this area). One can explore international adoption, legal and political issues, plus learn how to parent an adopted child, search for a birth parent or child, and find the most up-to-date sources of information. Conversing with others who are dealing with the same issues adds a ready source of support and encouragement to the experience. This keyword has heart!

Alternate keyword: None.

Reviewed by Genevieve Kazdin (screen name: GenK).

AOL LIVE   🗐 ≋   ⟡Q   🗐   PG▰▰

Rosie O'Donnell, President Clinton, Oprah Winfrey, and Aerosmith are just a few of the guests who have appeared in AOL Live, your one-stop link to America Online's live events. Wouldn't it be great if you could get even one chance to sit down and just chat with your favorite celebrity? You can do just that by heading to keyword: AOL LIVE. You'll discover categorized lists of auditorium chat events featuring several celebrities *every day*! Can't make it to one of the scheduled events? No problem! Transcripts are kept for each event in searchable archives. This is your chance to rub elbows with the people making the headlines in a lively, open forum. You never know who might show up! So comb your hair, splash on some cologne, and head out for a night on the town in AOL Live. You won't be disappointed!

Alternate keywords: AUDITORIUM, BOWL, CENTER STAGE, COLISEUM, GLOBE, LIVE(!), LIVE TONIGHT, ODEON.

Reviewed by Bob Trautman (screen name: PhotogBT).

APPLE   🖼🗐   *W*   Q🕮🗐   R▰▰

Looking for a system update or other software direct from Apple Computer? Need a quick question answered? Keyword: APPLE is the place to go! Apple Computer's home on America Online is stocked with press releases and product information, Tech Support FAQs (Frequently

Asked Questions), links to Apple's Tech Info Library on the Web, developer information, and all software updates that Apple releases for both Macs and PCs. At Apple on AOL, informative conferences are sponsored, along with a cafe for unstructured chat with other Mac aficionados. There are also links to Apple-run World Wide Web sites, information for Apple/Mac professionals, and even QuickTime movies of Apple's unique TV ads. Take keyword: APPLE once a day to keep the Mac doctor away!

Alternate keyword: None.

Reviewed by Laura Kramarsky
(screen name: AdeptMagic).

ASTRONET 　　□戌団　*W*　◇　　□凋 PG

In need of answers about life and love? They're written in the stars at keyword: ASTRONET. A far cry from the Magic 8 Ball of old, ASTRONET boasts more cosmic information than you could absorb in all of Shirley MacLaine's lifetimes. From tarot to numerology, I-Ching to horoscopes, learn about your past, present, and future in relationships, health and wellness, money matters, and family life. There's even a special area for teens, guaranteeing a rush of girls desperate to know if Leonardo DiCaprio is their *true* soulmate. One of the more unique services is AstroMates, where you can browse profiles of fellow astrology lovers and post your own — you can find it under Love on the main window. Most services are free, but if your inner voice tells you to dig deeper, you can schedule live online one-on-one readings, e-mail readings, or printed reports (prices range from $14.95–$90.00). The crystal ball says you will be entertained and enlightened at keyword: ASTRONET.

Alternate keyword: None.

Reviewed by Adrienne Quinn (screen name: AAQuinn).

BISTRO 　　□戌団　　　　□凋 PG

Dreaming of taking a coffee break at a cafe on the Champs Elysées? Need to brush up on your foreign language skills? Or perhaps you prefer to have a discussion about world affairs with someone from abroad? If so, keyword: BISTRO is *the* place to be. This international cafe brings people from a variety of cultural and ethnic backgrounds together to speak in their native language, discuss global concerns, and develop friendships across the seas. A potpourri of language chat rooms is available from African to Vietnamese. Or simply join the International Chat room, in which all languages are welcome. Tired of chatting? Check out the Bistro Software Library or the Bistro World Boards to enhance your global experience.

Alternate keywords: GERMAN, INTERNATIONAL CAFE, LANGUAGE, SPANISH.

Reviewed by Linda Lindquist (screen name: NordiKat).

BLACKBERRY

By kids and for kids, keyword: BLACKBERRY is a haven for kids looking for a place to display their artistic talents or just have a good time. Staffed primarily by kids who volunteer their time, there's plenty to talk about and plenty to do at Blackberry Creek. Click **Join the Club** first to read the rules, get your Blackberry Creek membership card via e-mail, and sign up for the monthly *Blackberry Creek Gazette*. Then head over to the **Club** for story starters, scrapbooks, comics, poems, artwork, and a display case you won't find on the average refrigerator. Just like home, there are some rules, but they're easy to follow and help your kids learn to be safe online. Blackberry Creek is a graphics-intensive area — be prepared for a bit of a wait on your first visit. This place is better than a secret clubhouse in the backyard, and nobody has to clean up before they can go home!

Alternate keywords: BCREEK, BLACKBERRY CREEK, CREEKER.

*Reviewed by Kimberly Trautman
(screen name: Ktrautman).*

CAMPUS

Do you want to learn how to create a World Wide Web site for your growing business? Take a French class to surprise the new friend you just met in an America Online chat room? Or learn how to better organize your life and home? You can do it all — online — at keyword: CAMPUS! It's easy, it's fun, and best of all, you don't have to worry about getting stuck in traffic or finding a babysitter. America Online offers it's members a virtual campus where they can choose from a variety of courses taught by qualified instructors. There's an easy-to-follow step-by-step registration process, and do note there is a reasonable registration fee for some of the classes. Once your registration is processed, the instructor e-mails a confirmation of your order, welcomes you to the class, provides information needed for the class itself, and gives you access to the course library and message board. What could be better than taking a class and learning a new skill or hobby in the comfort of your own home?

Alternate keyword: ONLINE CAMPUS.

Reviewed by Maria Therese Lehan
(screen name: Sioux Mac).

COL   🖵 🕅 🗃 🗢 *W*   ✧ Q ▭ 🗐 **PG**▮▬

Voted an America Online Members' Choice forum year after year, Christianity Online (get there faster with keyword: COL) is a sanctuary for members of the online Christian community. Sun-streaked stained glass in the background of their welcome page is your first indication of the positive attitudes and affirming beliefs represented by the staff and fellow members. They have a delightfully comprehensive introduction for new members (look under the tiny **Help &Info** button at the very bottom). Christianity Online is a large, multifaceted forum, offering everything from Bible study to Christian rock. With all the content in Christianity Online, it is a bit too easy to get lost here. Use the help resources to navigate the forum, and the information you discover to navigate your life. Amen!

Alternate keywords: <><, CO, COL.

CLASSIFIEDS   🖵 🕅 🗃   ✧ Q ▭ 🗐 **PG**▮▬

Need a place to dispose of your childhood toys, or do you need to buy a new toy like a Power Macintosh? America Online fills these needs with keyword: CLASSIFIEDS.

More than just a 24-hour flea market, Classifieds Online features practical advice for buyers and sellers along with thousands of "Premier Ads." All the ads are searchable and can be viewed by region or category. Ads range in price from about $6.95 for two weeks to $159.95 per year depending upon the category. Unfortunately, the ads only allow text so you can't include the picture of that hula girl lamp you're selling, but it is likely that the ads will gain improved formatting and graphics in the near future. There are also message boards, chat rooms, and a newsletter buried within the area (check the **Welcome to AOLClassifieds!** document for links). So if you have something to sell, need to find a particular item, or just like looking over other people's offerings, visit Classifieds Online.

Alternate keywords: AOL CLASSIFIED(S), CLASSIFIED, CLASSIFIEDS ONLINE.

Reviewed by George Louie (screen name: NumbersMan).

CONTESTS ◆ ▭ PG

Congratulations! You just won $25,000 and a year's worth of free time on America Online. Sounds good, doesn't it? This is just one of the prizes given out in the past at keyword: CONTESTS. Whether you enjoy trivia contests, photo contests, or a great scavenger hunt, you will love America Online's Contest area. You could win anything from cold, hard cash to free online hours to the getaway vacation of your dreams. With so many different contests available, you are bound to win something. Be sure to click the gold seal for the latest Hot Contest. Contest legalities are found under the "return address" of The Legal Guys in the upper left-hand corner of the "envelope." Could you be the next big winner? Come to keyword: CONTESTS and find out.

Alternate keywords: CONTEST, CONTEST AREA, WINNER.

CRUISE ▭▯▤ *W* ◆ Q ▭▤ PG

As much as I enjoy writing keyword reviews, exploring keyword: CRUISE made me want to ditch it all and run off to the Cayman Islands. To say I need a vacation is an understatement. If you're in the same boat, surf on over to The Cruise Critic and plan your next cruise. They have lots of reviews, an interactive Cruise Selector, and tips on bargains! When can I start packing?

Alternate keywords: CRUISE(S), CRUISE CRITICS, SHIP CRITIC(S).

DEAD

You may be surprised to learn that keyword: DEAD leads to an America Online Member's Choice award-winner, but it does! The Grateful Dead Forum keeps the Dead alive with its psychedelic background, original artwork, and hot merchandise. Downloading art and sound files, keeping up with past Dead members' new groups tour dates, sharing your thoughts with fellow travelers, and buying merchandise are just a small representation of what this forum offers. People come to share the music, and stay to enjoy the community. Jerry Garcia lives!

Alternate keywords: :), GDF, GRATEFUL DEAD, THE DEAD.

Reviewed by J. Brian Thomason (screen name: JBThomason).

DIGITAL CITY

Are you ready to leave your keyboard? DIGITAL CITY is for people who go online and go out, too! DIGITAL CITY is actually Digital Cities — more than 60 city forums at last count. Created in partnership with local newspapers and broadcasters, each DIGITAL CITY provides a rich mix of local news, movie listings, entertainment and cultural guides, restaurant reviews, personal and classified ads, message boards, chats, real estate listings, and more for AOL members in their own backyards. Keyword: DIGITAL CITY is the gateway to all these communities. Once you've found yours, there's also a direct keyword back home.

Alternate keywords: CITIES, CITY, DCI, DCN, DIGITAL CITY.

Reviewed by Dave Marx (screen name: Dave Marx).

DIS

Keyword: DIS, as its name implies, concentrates both on empowering the disabled and on changing society's view of disabilities in general. Every possible resource is available in the forum, including legal information, medical databases, support groups, software, Internet links, and organizations serving the disabled community offline, as well as online. The term *disability* covers a lot: more than 100 discussion boards have topics ranging from Accessible Vacation Spots to Women With DisAbilities; the forum hosts deal with a variety of health issues and concerns such as attention deficit disorder, epilepsy, chemical sensitivities, blindness, chronic pain, depression, amputations, muscular dystrophy, and more. The Disabilities Community Forum is for members to discuss disorders, get information on assistive technologies and medications, and debate the political, sociological, and sexual implications. If you have a disability, find your *abilities* here!

Alternate keywords: BLIND, PHYSICALLY DISABLED.

*Reviewed by Laura Kramarsky
(screen name: AdeptMagic).*

EGG

Here's a keyword hot from the oven: EGG — the electronic Gourmet Guide. If you have a passion for great food and live to cook, you won't find a tastier online feast than the eGG. Everywhere you click you'll find beautifully presented recipes and background information from great chefs and fellow foodies. The Global Gourmet is to die for — more than 40 nations and cuisines are deliciously profiled. Recipe Finder, a top-notch collection of search tools, will delight the inveterate recipe hunter. But eGG isn't all browsing and salivating. Share your passion in regularly scheduled chats, swap tips and recipes on their message boards, play food trivia games, post your profile at the Food Lovers Directory, shop in the Global Gourmet Shops, and much more! You'll keep coming back for one more helping. It's rare to find the medium as well done as it is at eGG.

Alternate keyword: EGGSTERS.

Reviewed by Dave Marx (screen name: Dave Marx).

FDN   `⌧ 📠 🗊    W ⌖ Q 📖 📇   R ▤`

"Good eats, good drinks, good smokes" could be the Food & Drink Network's motto (keyword: FDN), but if the ingredients were listed in order, it would be the Drink & Food Network. The strengths of FDN are Wine, Beer, Spirits, and Cigars & Pipes. If you're a home brewer, this is the place to be! There's plenty of useful information at FDN, but it's a bit well aged. Although aging doesn't hurt wine, the Food area is stale — most restaurant reviews are three years old. If you love food and cooking, you'll be far better served at the electronic Gourmet Guide (see the preceding review).

Alternate keyword: FOOD & DRINK NETWORK.

Reviewed by Dave Marx (screen name: Dave Marx).

FOOL   `⌧ 📠 🗊    W ⌖ Q 📖 📇   R ▤`

Fools, ahoy! If you're not a fool, you can become one easily at The Motley Fool, an unconventional but successful approach to investing. Attend Fool's School and learn the 13 steps to investing foolishly and foolish job hunting tips! Motley Fool works to help you obtain financial information and learn the techniques of investing — foolishly, of course! You also have the opportunity to win prizes as you learn, and have fun as you play the daily investment game, the portfolios, or other games. Make sure to visit Fooldom, where the biggest fool wins!

Alternate keywords: FOOLS, MOTLEY FOOL, THE MOTLEY FOOL.

FULL DISCLOSURE   `W    Q 📖   R ▤`

Have you ever considered buying America Online? No, not the whole company, but maybe 100 shares of stock? In order to better serve its current stockholders and those who wish to research the company's performance before investing, America Online created keyword: FULL DIS-CLOSURE, an online investor relations area for the company. This forum has detailed information about America Online, Inc. — both current and archived. Also included are reports and analyses from independent firms, press releases, and other information about America Online operations. Before you pick up the phone to call your broker, be sure to stop here.

Alternate keyword: AOL FULL DISCLOSURE, AOL IR, INVESTOR RELATIONS, IR, FULL DISCLOSURE.

Reviewed by Bradley Zimmer
(screen name: Bradley476).

GENEALOGY   □ 🎬 🗐 ·W ✧ Q ⊞ 🖼 | PG ▰▰

"Genealogy. *G - E - N - E - A - L - O - G - Y*. Genealogy." Are you proud that great-grandma won the Kansas State Spelling Bee? Then you'll be right at home at keyword: GENEALOGY. Whether you've just begun to dig for your familial roots or are the official clan historian, the friendly folks at the Genealogy Forum enrich your history. They share all their tips, tricks, tools, and techniques for finding long-lost cousins, birth parents, famous ancestors, and that black sheep about whom grandma never talked. A Members' Choice award winner, keyword: GENEALOGY offers a fabulous Beginners Guide and links to hundreds of family histories in the Surname Center. Excavate a world of information from the Internet. The forum's warm, active volunteer community aids your research with message boards dedicated to information about names, places, ethnic and special groups, hosted chats, seminars and family reunions, a voluminous collection of libraries, research resources, newsgroups . . . I can go on and on about this phenomenally well-organized, lovingly built forum. Your family tree will grow new branches here!

Alternate keywords: GENEALOGY CLUB, ROOTS.

Reviewed by Dave Marx (screen name: Dave Marx).

GRANDSTAND 🗔 🖾 🖨 🖀 *W* | ✧ | 🕮 🗐 | PG ▰▰▰

Are you a sports fanatic? Whether you're an active participant or a loyal spectator, keyword: GRANDSTAND is a classic! The AOL Sports Grandstand is a special collection of forums built by fans for fans with one goal in mind: fun! Keep current on your favorite sports here and find fellow fans to discuss them with. It doesn't matter whether your favorite takes place on a field, court, rink, ring, or track; you can find it in The Grandstand. And you're not limited to reading or talking about sports — you can play them here as well! You can even become a star in one of the fantasy or simulation games. You'll find both competition and the opportunity for prizes in the Cyber Sports Tournaments at The Grandstand. So don your gear, take your place, and let the games begin!

Alternate keywords: GS, THE GRANDSTAND.

Reviewed by Valerie L. Downey
(screen name: KEYValerie).

HIGHLIGHTS 🖾 🖨 | ✧ | 🕮 | G ▰▰▰

Remember when you were a kid and the best part about going to the doctor was knowing you could read *Highlights* magazine while you waited? Well, now you can read it right here online at keyword: HIGHLIGHTS. And like the paper magazine, Highlights Online is a feast for the eyes! Click **Our Own Place** to discover art, poetry and stories by kids. Move to **Boredom Busters** for crafts, mindteasers, picture puzzles, and more. There's a library here too, full of articles and pictures. The blinking Special Features star leads you to nonfiction, short stories, science exploration, questions, and answers. Even the tried-and-true Goofus and Gallant and Timbertoes & More have a home in cyberspace. Be sure to sign your kids up for the Highlights Newsletter and leave a message for other kids in the Post It section. One of the best features is Ask Highlights, where you can get safety tips from Goofus and Gallant, find technical help, meet the editors, or get advice. Highlights Online remains fun with a purpose.

Alternate keyword: HFC, HIGHLITES.

Reviewed by Lauren Sebel (screen name: Lauren).

HOMESCHOOL   ☐ 🖾 🗐   📖 🔁 G ▬▬

Whether you're an experienced homeschooler or just curious about the concept, the homeschooling forum is the place for you! Here you can take a workshop, join a kids club in The Hangout, get the latest legal information, and link to two of the hottest homeschooling magazines. New to homeschooling? There's a beginner's file library just for you. Community leaders are friendly and knowledgeable, and be sure to sign up for your copy of the weekly newsletter, *Connections*. The homeschooling community is as incredibly diverse online as it is offline, so the conversation is always lively and informative. Where else would you find the best comebacks to the dreaded S-word question?

Alternate keyword: HOMESCHOOLING.

Reviewed by Kimberly Trautman
(screen name: Ktrautman).

HOMEWORK   ☐ 🖾 🗐   *W* ⟡ Q 📖 🔁 PG ▬▬

Ever been stumped by a homework assignment? Help is only a mouse click away at keyword: HOMEWORK. Specialists in many subject areas volunteer their time to provide assistance, live and via e-mail, to students of all ages. The help is tailored to your education level: Elementary, Jr. High and High School, and College and Beyond. Each of these categories has its own specialized resources: you can Look Up Answers with links to encyclopedias or the Knowledge Base. Or Post a Question and get answers from teachers and fellow members. Live teacher help offers five classrooms staffed by teachers: English, Math, Science, History, and the Main room for general questions, all open from 4:00 p.m. to midnight Eastern Time. Email a Teacher is the online equivalent of a "teacher pager" — just write your question, pick your subject, and send it off. More help is available under About Ask-A-Teacher — you can even sign up for one-on-one tutoring here. It is important to note that the online teachers don't do the work for you; rather they guide and assist you in finding the answer yourself.

Alternate keywords: AAC, ASK-A-TEACHER, HH ADULT, HOMEWORK HELP, TEACHER PAGER, TUTORING.

INTERNATIONAL 🖵 📺 🗐 🦢 ✛ Q 📖 🎮 PG ▬▬

Ever wanted to travel overseas but couldn't afford it? Now you can travel around the world at the touch of a button with keyword: INTERNATIONAL! This is your nonstop, virtual flight to the United Kingdom, France, Japan, Germany, Canada, the USA, South America, Africa, the Middle East, Sweden, Switzerland, Austria, Asia, Australia, and Oceania. Discover International News, Business, Cultures, Fun and Games, Travel, Classifieds, Country Information, and a Global Chat area that offers everything from a Bistro with foreign-language chat to Special Delivery that helps you find a pen pal. You can even get exotic recipes from the Global Gourmet! Where do you think you'll end up today?

Alternate keyword: AOL FRANCE, AOL INTERNATIONAL, AOL WORLD, INTERNATIONAL US, INTL, PARIS, WORLD.

Reviewed by Lauren Sebel (screen name: Lauren).

JEWISH 🖵 📺 🗐 🦢 *W* ✛ Q 📖 🎮 PG ▬▬

Whether you're Jewish or not, you're bound to feel welcome here. If you're looking for answers about Judaism, a chat (including scheduled youth chats and singles activities for all ages), information on Israel, travel, education, family, food, or holidays and spirituality, you'll find it. There are a variety of resources, message boards, chat activities, and even a mailing list to keep members in touch. Be sure to check out **This Day**, where you can find a short quote, a Torah reading, a historical event, a trivia question, and a new joke every day. Jewish Community just keeps getting better and better! It deserves its ranking as an America Online Members' Choice area.

Alternate keywords: JCOL, JEWISH COM(M), JEWISH COMMUNITY, SHALOM.

Reviewed by Sue Boettcher (screen name: SueBD).

LATE SHOW

Are you a fan of David Letterman and can't get enough of *The Late Show with David Letterman*? Want to find out what happened on last night's show? Meet and chat with other fans? Request an autograph or tickets to see the show? Visit keyword: LATE SHOW because it's almost as fun as the show itself, and it's guaranteed to make you laugh! Read Top Ten lists from past shows such as "Top Ten People I Would Thank If I Won an Academy Award," view slide shows of Dave working at a Taco Bell drive through, chat with other fans in a hosted chat room, and introduce yourself on the message boards. You can even participate in contests such as "Top Ten Lightning Round" where you compete with aspiring comedians by creating clever and witty Top Ten items. A visit to Late Show Online is as enjoyable as a bowl of popcorn and the remote control!

Alternate keywords: DAVE, LETTERMAN.

Reviewed by Maria Therese Lehan
(screen name: Sioux Mac).

LOVE@AOL

Don't have a date tonight? Lonely blues have you feeling down? Look no further because you can set your social life on fire at Love@AOL! Packed with advice, steamy message boards, social games, online love shopping, and daily live chat, Love@AOL can turn your quiet love life into a fountain of plenty. Come to exchange photos with other America Online members looking for that special soulmate or jump into **The Hot Bed** and chat the night away. Even special guests drop by to give you some great love pointers. Hey, why not become a success story? You can do it all at Love@AOL. Make sure you get your daily dose of Love@AOL. Love Doctor's orders! See you there!

Alternate keywords: LOVE AT AOL.

Reviewed by Stephen Urban (screen name: Stephen).

MOMS ONLINE

Are you an expectant mother trying to decide between breastfeeding or formula? Or a new mom looking for ways to help soothe a colicky infant? Trying to encourage your two-year-old's creativity but tired of scrubbing finger paint off the refrigerator? How do you talk to your teenager about sex? Keyword: MOMS ONLINE is a haven just for moms that has *the answers* to all these questions! Moms Online is a community-rich area run by moms with children of all ages, where you can meet, talk, and share in their hosted chat rooms and message boards. If you're stressed out, make a beeline to Mom's Time Out for tips on taking care of yourself. Show off your little angel in the Kid Of The Day area and get tips on breastfeeding, sibling rivalry, and everything in between. With keyword: MOMS ONLINE, mother's helper is just a keyword away!

Alternate keywords: MO, MOM ONLINE, MOTHER-HOOD.

Reviewed by Maria Therese Lehan
(screen name: Sioux Mac).

NEW YORK TIMES

The New York Times Online is like having a newspaper delivered to your front door every morning! Outfitted with a catchy name, @Times has all of the excellent articles, in-depth reviews, insightful editorials, and well-written pieces that you have come to expect from the top newspaper — and it's all online! @Times is divided into several sections — Today's News, Computers & Technology, Arts & Entertainment, Classifieds, and Education — just like its ink-and-paper sibling. The area is intuitively designed and updated the instant that new news comes out. This is your ultimate online companion — get the news as it happens with @Times online!

Alternate keywords: @TIMES, NY TIMES, NYT, TIMES, TIMES NEWS.

NETNOIR

Hearts are ripe for the taking everywhere on America Online, but where do you find the soul of cyberspace? Keyword: NETNOIR claims that distinction as the premier purveyor of Afrocentric entertainment and culture for the Afro-Caribbean, Afro-European, Afro-Latin, continental African, and African-American online communities. Newcomers can click the narrow bar at the top of the window for an introduction, or immediately immerse themselves in the news plus reviews on people, culture, business, and more. Need something wilder? Head for Black Erotica — the name speaks for itself.

Alternate keywords: AFRICANAMERICAN(S), AFRO-CENTRIC, BLACK, BLM, KWANZAA, NET_NOIR(E), NETNOIRE, NOIRNET.

NOVEL

How would you like to be the main character in a novel about *you*? Dan Hurley, the Amazing INSTANT Novelist and founder of this area, will write an Amazing Instant Novel to order! The fee is small and each is totally original! Don't want to pay for a novel? That's okay, too! This area is filled with "instant novels" written daily by Mr. Hurley, as well as by fellow America Online members. You can write one, too! The message boards are filled with funny, sad, and wild instant novels, and even poems. You can also chat about writing in a hosted chat. Unleash the creative writer in yourself!

Alternate keywords: DAN HURLEY, INSTANT NOVELIST.

NTN

Have you ever been to a bar or restaurant that offers interactive trivia to its patrons? If so, it was probably NTN Trivia, and you can play it to your heart's content right here on America Online at keyword: NTN. At last count, there were over 45 distinct trivia games — every one of them fun, interactive, and competitive. To get a complete list, look for the Trivia Games Index under Help & Game

Information. My favorite? Trekkie Trivia. Games are playing around the clock. Can you make the top 20?

Alternate keyword: NTN TRIVIA.

ONLINE PSYCH 　□⚙🖾⚙　*W*　✧Q 📖🗃 PG▓▓

If you like to lurk in the self-help section of the bookstore, hanging at keyword: ONLINE PSYCH is the cyberspace equivalent. Covering every imaginable popular psychology topic, from attention deficit disorder to suicide prevention, Online Psych offers articles, experts, and places to discuss the issues with your fellow members. I particularly like their collection of personality and relationship quizzes. And if you are a psychology professional, there's even a special surcharged forum. So head on over to Online Psych before you lose your head.

Alternate keywords: OLP, PSYCHONLINE.

ONQ 　□🖾⚙🕏*W*　✧Q 📖🗃 PG▓▓

Keyword:ONQ is America Online's community for the alternative lifestyle: gay, lesbian, bisexual, and transgendered. Previously known as the Gay & Lesbian Community Forum (GLCF), onQ's chats and conferences, online games, personal ad space, support resources, AIDS/HIV help and support, and message boards for every conceivable topic are only the beginning! The onQ staff is supportive, friendly, open, and caring — and they're some of the greatest folks you'll ever meet online. Welcome home!

Alternate keyword: GLCF.

PARASCOPE 　□🖾⚙　*W*　✧Q 📖🗃 PG▓▓

You can admit it to me. You watch television shows such as *In Search Of . . .* and read more than just the headlines on some of those checkout lane tabloids — and in Parascope, that's okay! Parascope is the answer for the "alien abduction" and "black helicopter" crowd, providing four main areas dedicated to conspiracies, UFOs, unexplained phenomena, and so-called "documented evidence." While in Parascope, don't forget to visit their chat room, The Grassy Knoll, or take part in the daily

ParaPoll. Even if you've scoffed at all the theories before, you may believe that the truth is "out there" after visiting keyword: PARASCOPE.

Alternate keywords: PERISCOPE, PSCP, SCOPE.

Reviewed by Gwen Smith (screen name: Gwen Smith).

PET CARE ☐ 🖾 🗐 ◆ ९ ⌨ 🖭 PG ▭

Have the kids recently talked you into buying a kitten, puppy, lizard, ferret, or bunny? Need information on the proper care a sick or older pet? Keyword: PET CARE is the one-stop information center for all your pet needs. In this area you can find a wealth of information on your pet and its care. Ask a veterinarian, meet other pet-loving America Online members, and trade advice in the chat rooms, as well as the message boards. Shop at an online pet store, participate in polls, and even enter your adored pet in a contest in which the winner's photo is displayed online for all to see. Pets are welcome, too! No leashes needed, but you might want a keyboard cover first.

Alternate keyword: PET CARE FORUM.

Reviewed by Maria Therese Lehan
(screen name: Sioux Mac).

PHOTOGRAPHY ☐ 🖾 🗐 *W* 🖭 PG ▭

Everybody takes pictures these days. Sometimes they're great, sometimes they're, well, not so great. Do not fret, help is but a keyword away! Go to keyword: PHOTOGRA-PHY. Here you'll find myriad resources, including message boards, hosted by Kodak's own Ron Baird, on nearly any subject even remotely related to photography. They're populated with messages from people just like you, and, oh yes, experts abound! They'll eagerly offer advice on any dilemma within their substantial abilities. You'll also find links to *Popular Photography*'s online presence, Kodak's World Wide Web site, and many other useful areas. There are numerous image libraries, classified ad boards, and a chat room. So if you snap pictures; pose for pictures; create artistic photography; need advice on buying new equipment; want to sell old equipment; are curious about electronic imaging; trying to locate a reputable camera dealer; or you'd just like to share your ideas, head to keyword: PHOTOGRAPHY. I'll see you there!

Alternate keywords: AOLPICTURES, CAMERA, DIGITALIMAGING, IMAGES, IMAGING, PHOTO, PHOTOGRAPH(S), PICTURE(S).

Reviewed by Bob Trautman (screen name: PhotogBT).

ROSIE `PG`

Are you a fan of Rosie O' Donnell and her show, *Rosie*? Want to learn more about her and meet other fans of the show? Want to find out if your favorite celebrity will be making an appearance on *Rosie* this week or download some sound or video clips from the show? Visit The Rosie O' Donnell Show at keyword: ROSIE, and you can join in the fun with fellow fans! Talk about Rosie and her show in one of the hosted chat rooms or on the message boards. Download one of Rosie's favorite television themes from the '70s such as *The Partridge Family* or *Nanny and The Professor*. Relive great moments from the show — such as Tom Cruise's guest spot — by downloading a photo or sound file. You can even join her fan club online. If you're a parent (like Rosie), there's a special area where you can find information on everything from choosing a name to feeding a fussy toddler who won't eat meat, and more. Plus, there's a place just for kids where they can play games, share jokes, and become a "Star of the Week"! The Rosie O'Donnell Show area on America Online definitely has something for everybody!

Alternate keywords: ODONNELL, O'DONNELL, ROSIE ODONNELL.

Reviewed by Maria Therese Lehan
(screen name: Sioux Mac).

SPACE `W` `PG`

Have you ever wanted to talk to an astronaut? You can do it here, at Space Exploration Online from The National Space Society, where there is an Astronaut of the Month on hand to answer questions. Space Online also provides information on current and past space exploration activities including political action alerts, detailed information about each Space Shuttle-Mir mission, and planetary probe. You can attend any of the five-times-weekly space chats. The libraries are stuffed with space photos, and a collection of space news from pro-space organizations rounds out the collection. Space Exploration Online is the next best thing to being there yourself!

Alternate keywords: NSS, NASA.

Reviewed by Sue Boettcher (screen name: SueBD).

THRIVE

Are you looking for a dose of healthy, vibrant living? Are you searching for some fresh new recipes, or a partner for your weight loss program? Need the latest medical information? At keyword: THRIVE you can find all of the above and much more! Thrive@AOL is all about living well, feeling good, and *thriving* in Passion, Shape, Eats, and Outdoors. Each of these four areas contains information on a variety of topics, an Ask an Expert feature, chat rooms, live events, message boards, contests, and more. You may come to Thrive looking for specific information, but chances are you will stay to explore once you start clicking each of the colorful inviting sub areas and the wealth of the resources available here. There is something for everyone whether you need the latest information on cancer treatments, herb supplements, how to combine sports and dating, weight loss, and more. The best part about Thrive@AOL is the caring community you find in chat rooms and message boards.

Alternate keywords: THRIVE@, THRIVEONLINE.

Reviewed by Maria Theresa Lehan
(screen name: Sioux Mac).

TREK

Space, the final frontier. These are the voyages of the Star Trek Club. Its continuing mission is to keep you entertained on America Online. Okay, so that isn't quite how the story goes. But if you are a Star Trek fan you should check out the Star Trek Club at keyword: TREK. The Star Trek Club has everything a Trekkie could ever want. It has a great message board, where you can discuss everything from the classic Star Trek episodes and The Next Generation shows, to the new adventures aboard Deep Space Nine and Voyager. There are even message boards that discuss the Star Trek movies. Another great thing the Star Trek Club has, and this is one of my favorites, are their Record Banks. Here you will find files that you can download — everything from pictures of your favorite Star Trek characters to stories written by other America Online members. And there is also a chat room called The Bridge where you can chat with fellow Trekkers. There are also trivia games every Friday and Saturday evening. So beam up to the Star Trek Club now at keyword: TREK.

Alternate keywords: STAR TREK CLUB, TREK, TREK-CLUB, USS ENTERPRISE.

WOMEN

Do you feel like your life has become one continuous juggling act? Need advice on finances, relationships, health matters? Find support for your concerns in at keyword: WOMEN, America Online's Women's Network. Rejuvenate your spirit and health in Body/Soul. Enlighten yourself at Work, Play, Relationships, and Family. The hosts are friendly and are carefully trained to ensure that the Women's Network is one of the safest chat environments around. Online cyber-safety tips are available in the "Street Smarts" program, enabling women to surf online wisely and happily. Explore posts from all the wonderful women (and men!) in the message boards at Women's Connection. This is the virtual pantheon for online goddesses.

Alternate keywords: WOMEN'S, WOMENS, WOMEN MAIN, WOMENS NETWORK.

Reviewed by Linda Lindquist (screen name: NordiKat).

WRITERS

Welcome to the Writers Club, the certified cure for writer's block and all other writer's blues! Sound too good to be true? Come on in and do the research. With authors both published and unpublished, agents, editors, and publishers all in residence, the Writers Club is the perfect place to get advice on every aspect of writing. Here you can find support and critique groups for every genre as well as software to download, conferences to attend, and articles and columns on every topic. Wherever you may be in your writing career, you will find companions in the Writers Club. You can even get away from the hustle and bustle of most online chatter and relax with some intelligent conversation in the Writers Cafe or the Writers Grill. Stop in soon!

Alternate keywords: WRITER, WRITER'S (CLUB), WRITERS CLUB.

Reviewed by Laura Kramarsky
(screen name: AdeptMagic).

YOUTH TECH

Calling all technically oriented teens! Youth Tech is America Online's place for kids interested in computers and technology and who know how to have a good time! Youth Tech was created by kids and teens *for* kids and teens. There are chats, conferences, games, contests, surveys, hot Web sites, resources of all kinds, and even a Techie Penpal program! You don't even have to like computers to be there!

Alternate keywords: SMART KIDS, SMART TEENS, YT.

CHAPTER 6

KEYWORDS FROM A TO Z

Looking for the definitive source of keywords? The following list includes every known keyword on America Online at the time of writing, organized alphabetically by keyword first. In fact, this list has over 550 keywords that weren't even mentioned in the online list at keyword: KEYWORD at the time of compilation — I've indicated these bonus keywords in bold print for you. Those keywords with odd spellings or names are underlined to call your attention to their spelling for correct keyword entry. All keywords work on version 4.0 of the AOL software, and special comments are given in brackets.

JOHNS HOPKINS INTELIHEALTH — InteliHealth [Web site]
.NET — AOL UK: Internet Magazine
.NET MAGAZINE — AOL UK: Internet Magazine
:) — Grateful Dead Forum
:-) — The Friendly Face@AOL
;) — Hecklers Online
;-D — Christianity Online: Contests & Fun Stuff
? — AOL Member Services: QuickStart
@ACTIVE SPORTS — Thrive@Healthy Living: Outdoors
@AOL LIVE — AOL Live: The AOL LIVE Auditorium
@AOL LIVE CHAT CAFE — Digital City Plaza Auditorium
@AOL SPORTS DOME — AOL Sports Dome Auditorium
@BARBELLS — Michael Harris @ BarBells
@BOWL — AOL Live: The Bowl Auditorium
@CAFE — Digital City Plaza Auditorium
@CHAT CAFE — Digital City Plaza Auditorium
@COLISEUM — AOL Live: The AOL Sports Dome Auditorium
@CYBER RAP — AOL Live: The Cyber Rap Auditorium
@CYBERPLEX — CyberPlex Auditorium
@DC RELIGION — Digital City Washington: Religion
@DOME — AOL Live: The AOL Sports Dome Auditorium
@EATS — Thrive@Healthy Living: Eats

@EATS EXPERTS — Thrive@Healthy Living: Ask The Experts

@EATS TALK — Thrive@Healthy Living: Thrive Guide

@EXCERCISE — Thrive@Healthy Living: Shape

@FITNESS — Thrive@Healthy Living: Shape

@FOOD — Thrive@Healthy Living: Eats

@GLOBE — AOL Live: The Globe Auditorium

@HEALTH — Thrive@Healthy Living: Health

@HEALTH EXPERTS — Thrive@Healthy Living: Ask The Experts

@HEALTH LIVE — Thrive@Healthy Living: Thrive Guide to What's Hot

@HEALTH TALK — Thrive@Healthy Living: Thrive Guide

@HEALTHY — Thrive@Healthy Living: Health

@INC LIVE — Inc. Online: Chat Room

@LOVE — Thrive@Healthy Living: Love [Web site]

@MARKETPLACE — Thrive@Healthy Living: Marketplace

@NEW YORK — Digital City New York

@NEWS ROOM — AOL Live: The News Room Auditorium

@NY — Digital City New York

@ODEON — AOL Live: The Odeon Auditorium

@OUTDOORS — Thrive@Healthy Living: Outdoors

@PASSION — Thrive@Healthy Living: Passion

@RELATIONSHIPS — Thrive@Healthy Living: Passion

@ROTUNDA — AOL Computing: The Computing Rotunda Auditorium

@SEX — Thrive@Healthy Living: Passion

@SEX EXPERTS — Thrive@Healthy Living: Ask the Experts

@SEX TALK — Thrive@Healthy Living: Thrive Guide

@SEXUALITY — Thrive@Healthy Living: Passion

@SHAPE — Thrive@Healthy Living: Shape

@SHAPE EXPERTS — Thrive@Healthy Living: Ask The Experts

@SHAPE LIVE — Thrive@Healthy Living: Thrive Guide to What's Hot

@SHAPE TALK — Thrive@Healthy Living: Thrive Guide

@SPORTSFAN — SportsFan Radio

@THE NEWS ROOM — AOL Live: The News Room Auditorium

@TIMES — The New York Times

@TIMES — The New York Times on America Online

@TIMES CHAT — The New York Times: Chat & Live Events

@TOWER — Tower Records

@TRAINING — Thrive@Healthy Living: Shape

@WASH RELIGION — Digital City Washington: Religion

'97 TAX PLAN — 1997 Tax Plan

<>< — Christianity Online

OS8 — Apple Computer. Inc.
1 800 FLOWERS — 1-800-FLOWERS
10 NEWS — Digital City San Diego: KGTV Channel 10
106 JAMZ — Digital City Chicago: V103 Online 106 JAMZ
12 1 97 — Happy Birthday HAL 9000
128 BROWSER — Enhanced 128-bit SSL Web Browser
1310 THE TICKET — Digital City Dallas-Fort Worth: KTCK 1310 AM
    Sports Radio
17 — Seventeen Online
1-800 FLOWERS — 1-800-FLOWERS
1-800-98-PERFUME — Brands for Less [Web site]
1987 CRASH — AOL Personal Finance: Special Report
1997 TAX PLAN — AOL Personal Finance: The '97 Tax Plan
1ST SIGHT — Digital City Los Angeles: Love@1st-Site
1ST SITE — Digital City Lost Angeles: Love@1st-Site
20/20 — ABC NEWS.com: 20/20 [Web site]
2000 — Millennium Countdown
2001 — Happy Birthday HAL 9000
2ND CHANCE — Digital City Philadelphia: Your Second Chance
2ND CHANCES — Digital City Philadelphia: Your Second Chance
3A — American Automobile Association (AAA) Online
3COM — 3Com/U.S. Robotics
3-D — AOL Computing: 3D Rendering
3D — AOL Computing: 3D Rendering
3-D RENDERING — 3D Rendering
3D RENDERING — AOL Computing: 3D Rendering
3D SIG — AOL Computing: 3D Rendering
3D-RENDERING — AOL Computing: 3D Rendering
4 STAR — Chef's Catalog Store: 4-Star Sale
4.0 — Upgrade to the Latest AOL Software
40 BROWSER — Enhanced 40-bit Web Browser
4TH — Independence Day@AOL [seasonal]
4TH OF JULY — Independence Day@AOL [seasonal]
5 STAR BOSTON — Digital City Boston: Five-Star Boston
50 STATES — The Fifty States
7 ONLINE — Digital City New York: Local TV News
76ERS — Philadelphia 76ers
777-FILM — MovieLink [Web site]
800 — AT&T Toll-Free Internet Directory [Web site]
800 BLOOM — 1-800-FLOWERS
800 DIRECTORY — AT&T Toll-Free Internet Directory [Web site]
800 FLOWERS — 1-800-FLOWERS
800 FRESH — 1-800-FLOWERS
800 NUMBER — Traveling with AOL
800 NUMBERS — AT&T Toll-Free Internet Directory [Web site]
800-98-PERFUME — Brands for Less [Web site]
800-FLOWERS — 1-800-FLOWERS

888 NUMBER — Traveling with AOL
9 — AOL Long Distance Savings Plan
90210 — AOL Entertainment: 90210 Wednesdays Fan Forum
90210 WEDNESDAYS — AOL Entertainment: 90210 Wednesdays Fan Forum
911 GIFT — AOL Shopping: 911 Gifts
911 GIFTS — AOL Shopping: 911 Gifts
91X — Digital City San Diego: 91x FM
91X FM — Digital City San Diego: 91x FM
94 CHAMPS — Real Fans: Montreal Expos Team Club
95 APPLY — Beta Test Application
96 ROCK — Digital City Atlanta: WKLS 96 Rock
96 ROCK GOLF — Digital City Atlanta: Golf Trivia Game
9600 — Modems and Connections
97 TAX FORMS — Tax Forms & Schedules
98 PERFUME — Brands for Less [Web site]
99X — Digital City Atlanta: WNNX 99.7 FM
99X ATLANTA — Digital City Atlanta: WNNX 99.7 FM
A WOMAN'S PLACE — Digital City San Francisco: A Woman's Place
A&A — Axies and Allies Club
A&E ONQ — onQ: Arts and Entertainment
A&R — Addiction & Recovery Forum
A&R BOARDS — Addiction & Recovery Forum: Message Boards
A&R CHAT — Addiction & Recovery Forum: Chat
A&R HOT — Addiction & Recovery Forum: What's Hot
A&R NEWS — Addiction & Recovery Forum: News Center
A&V — AOL Computing: Animation & Video Forum
A&V FORUM — AOL Computing: Animation & Video Forum
A/C CONTRATOR — AOL WorkPlace: Contractors' Community
AA MEET — Alcoholics Anonymous Online: Meetings
AA MEETING — Alcoholics Anonymous Online: Meetings
AA ONLINE — Alcoholics Anonymous Online
AA ONLINE MEETING — Alcoholics Anonymous Online: Meetings
AA PHILLY — Digital City Philadelphia
AAA — American Automobile Association (AAA) Online
AAA ONLINE — American Automobile Association (AAA) Online
AAA STORE — American Automobile Association: Store
AAC — AOL Research & Learn: Ask-A-Teacher
AAII — American Association of Individual Investors
AAO — Alcoholics Anonymous Online
AARDVARK — Aardvark Pet Store
AARDY'S SPECIALS — Aardvark Pet Store: Aardy's Specials
AARDYS SPECIALS — Aardvark Pet Store: Aardy's Specials
AARP — American Association of Retired People
AARP INSURANCE — AARP Insurance Program from The Hartford [Web site]
AAY — All About You

ABBCI — American Business Brokers and Consultants Group
ABC — ABC Online
ABC ARCH — ABC News: Slideshow Archives
ABC ARCHIVE — ABC News: Slideshow Archives
ABC AUDITORIUM — ABC Online: Auditorium
ABC AUTO — ABC Sports: Auto Racing
ABC CBB — ABC Sports: College Hoops
ABC CFB — ABC Sports: College Football
ABC CLASS — ABC Online: Classroom Newsletter
ABC CLASSROOM — ABC Online: Classroom Newsletter
ABC COLLEGE BASKETBALL — ABC Sports: College Hoops
ABC COLLEGE FOOTBALL — ABC Sports: College Football
ABC DANGEROUS MINDS — ABC Online: Dangerous Minds
ABC DAYTIME — ABC Online: Daytime
ABC DOSE — ABC Daily Dose
ABC ENTERTAINMENT — ABC Online: TV
ABC EVENTS — ABC Online: Auditorium
ABC EXCLUSIVES — ABC News: Live on AOL
ABC FIGURE SKATING — ABC Sports: Figure Skating
ABC FOOTBALL — ABC Sports: College Football
ABC GMA — ABC Online: Good Morning America [Web site]
ABC GOLF — ABC Sports: Golf
ABC GUESTS — ABC Online: Auditorium
ABC HOOPS — ABC Sports: College Hoops
ABC INDY — ABC Sports: Indianapolis 500
ABC INDY 500 — ABC Sports: Indianapolis 500
ABC KIDS — ABC Online: Kidzine
ABC KIDZINE — ABC Online: Kidzine
ABC LIVE — ABC Online
ABC NEWS — ABC NEWS.com [Web site]
ABC NEWS LIVE — ABC News: Live on AOL
ABC NEWS POLLS — ABC News: Polls
ABC NEWS SPECIALS — ABC Online: Specials [Web site]
ABC NEWS.COM — ABC NEWS.com
ABC POLLS — ABC News: Polls
ABC PREAKNESS — ABC Sports: Preakness Stakes
ABC PRIMETIME — ABC Online: TV
ABC PTL - ABC Online: Prime Time Live [Web site]
ABC RACING — ABC Sports: Auto Racing
ABC SATURDAY NIGHT — ABC Online: Saturday Night [Web site]
ABC SHOW — ABC News: Slideshows
ABC SHOWS — ABC Online: Stars & Shows
ABC SLIDE — ABC News: Slideshows
ABC SLIDESHOW — ABC News: Slideshows
ABC SLIDESHOW ARCHIVE — ABC News: Slideshow Archives
ABC SOAPS — ABC Online: Daytime
ABC SOCCER — ABC Sports: Soccer

ABC SPORTS — ABC Sports
ABC SPORTS STORE — ABC Sports: Store
ABC STARS — ABC Online: Stars & Shows
ABC STATION — ABC Online: Local Stations
ABC STATIONS — ABC Online: Local Stations
ABC THIS WEEK — ABC Online: This Week [Web site]
ABC TOOLBOX — ABC Online: Tool Box
ABC TRACK — ABC Sports: Track
ABC TRANSCRIPTS — ABC Online: Auditorium
ABC TV — ABC Online: TV
ABC TW — ABC Online: This Week [Web site]
ABC VIDEO — ABC News: Slideshows
ABC WNT — ABC Online: World News Tonight [Web site]
ABC WNTM — ABC Online: World News This Morning [Web site]
ABC WOMEN — ABC Sports: Women's Sports
ABC WOMEN'S — ABC Sports: Women's Sports
ABC WORLD CUP — ABC Sports: World Cup Soccer
ABCDS — ABCD's of Learning [Web site]
ABE — ABE Birdwatchers
ABE ONLINE — ABE Birdwatchers
ABERDEEN — AOL UK: Local Life
ABI — ABI Yellow Pages
ABI YELLOW PAGES — ABI Yellow Pages
ABL — AOL Sports: Pro Basketball
ABM — Adventures By Mail
ABOUTWORK — AOL Workplace: AboutWork!
ABOVE THE RIM — NESN: New England Basketball
ABT — Auto-By-Tel: Online Car Shopping
ACCESS — Accessing America Online
ACCESS CAMERA — Access Discount Camera [Web site]
ACCESS DISCOUNT CAMERA — Access Discount Camera [Web Site]
ACCESS EXCELLENCE — Access Excellence [Web Pointer]
ACCESS NUMBERS — Accessing America Online
ACCESSORIES — Third Party and Offline Applications
ACCORDING TO BOB — According to Bob
ACCOUNT — AOL Rewards
ACCOUNT ACTIVITY — AOL Rewards
ACCOUNT HISTORY — AOL Rewards
ACCOUNTANT — AOL Workplace: Accounting Community
ACCOUNTANTS — AOL Workplace: Accounting Community
ACCUTRADE — Accutrade
ACLU — American Civil Liberties Union
ACNE — AOL Health: Acne
ACOC — Metro Atlanta Chamber of Commerce
ACS — American Cancer Society
ACS NATL — American Cancer Society
ACTING — The Casting Zone

ACTION EXPLOSION — Entertainment Asylum: Action Explosion
ACTION GAMES — Antagonist, Inc.
ACTION HQ — Entertainment Asylum: Action Explosion
ACTIVISION — Activision Inc.
ACUPUNCTURE — AOL Health: Acupuncture & Acupressure
AD — Athlete Direct
AD AR — Athlete Direct: Athlete Direct Auto Racing
AD AUTO RACING — Athlete Direct: Auto Racing
AD BASE — Athlete Direct: Baseball
AD BASEBALL — Athlete Direct: Baseball
AD BASKETBALL — Athlete Direct: Hoops
AD BOXING — Athlete Direct: Boxing
AD FOOD — Athlete Direct: Food
AD FOOTBALL — Athlete Direct: Football
AD HOCKEY — Athlete Direct: Hockey
AD HOOPS — Athlete Direct: Hoops
AD HORSE — Athlete Direct: Jockeys
AD HORSES — Athlete Direct: Jockeys
AD JOCKEY — Athlete Direct: Jockeys
AD JOCKEYS — Athlete Direct: Jockeys
AD KARROS — Athlete Direct: Eric Karros
AD LIFESTYLES — Athlete Direct: Lifestyles
AD MOVIES — Athlete Direct: Movies
AD MUSIC — Athlete Direct: Music
AD NASCAR — Athlete Direct: NASCAR Family Community Area
AD PLAYOFFS — Athlete Direct: Playoffs
AD POTPOURRI — Athlete Direct: Potpourri
AD RACING — Athlete Direct: Auto Racing
AD SIG — AOL Workplace: Advertising
AD SOCCER — Athlete Direct: Soccer
AD TENNIS — Athlete Direct: Tennis
AD TRAVEL — Athlete Direct: Travel
AD&D — AD&D Online: Neverwinter Nights
ADAMS — Cindy Adams: Queen of Gourmet Gossip
ADD — AD&D Online: Neverwinter Nights
ADD ONS — Third Party and Offline Applications
ADDICTION — AOL Health: Addictions
ADDICTIONS — AOL Health: Addictions
ADDRESS — Billing Information and Changes
ADF — Athlete Direct: Football Area
ADHD — AOL Health: Attention Deficit Disorder
ADOPTION — AOL Families: Adoption Forum
ADP — Athlete Direct: NFL Playoffs
ADSL — Connecting to AOL: xDSL Information
ADV COMP — Digital City Los Angeles: Advanced Computers & Technology
ADVANCE IN YOUR CAREER — AOL Workplace: Advancing Your Career

ADVANCED COMPUTERS & TECHNOLOGY — Digital City Los Angeles: Advanced Computers & Technology
ADVANCED COMPUTERS — Digital City Los Angeles: Advanced Computers & Technology
ADVANCING YOUR CAREER — AOL Workplace: Advancing Your Career
ADVANTAGE — AOL Shoppers Advantage
ADVANTAGE STORE — AOL Shoppers Advantage
ADVENTURE TRAVEL — AOL Travel: Adventure and Outdoor Travel
ADVENTURES BY MAIL — Adventures By Mail
ADVERTISE WITH US — AOL NetFind: Advertising Link [Web site]
ADVERTISING SIG — AOL Workplace: Advertising
ADVICE & PLANNING — AOL Personal Finance: Advice & Planning
ADVICE — Love@AOL: Advice
AE — Entertainment Asylum
AECSIG — AOL Workplace: Professional Forums
AEFD — American Express: Financial Direct
AEGIS — onQ: Transgender Organizations
AEROBICS — AOL Sports: Fitness
AERONAUTICS — AOL Interests: Aviation & Aeronautics
AF.COM — Atlantic Financial [Web site]
AFFILIATE — AOL Studio Affiliates Program
AFFILIATE PROGRAM — AOL Studio Affiliates Program
AFFILIATES — AOL Studio Affiliates Program
AFGHANISTAN — AOL International: Afghanistan
AFRICA — AOL International: Africa
AFRICAN AMERICAN — Ethnicity
AFRICAN AMERICANS — NetNoir
AFRICAN-AMERICAN — NetNoir
AFRICAN-AMERICANS — NetNoir
AFRO AMERIC@ — Afro-Americ@ Newspapers
AFRO AMERICA — Afro-Americ@ Newspapers
AFROCENTRIC — NetNoir
AFT — American Federation of Teachers
AG CARDS — American Greetings
AGES & STAGES — AOL Lifestyles: Ages & Stages
AGES — AOL Lifestyles: Ages & Stages
AGGIE JOKES — Digital City Dallas-Fort Worth: Just Joking
AGGRESSIVE SKATING — AOL Sports: Aggressive Inline MiniForum
AGGROSKATE — AOL Sports: Aggressive Inline MiniForum
AGGROSKATING — AOL Sports: Aggressive Inline MiniForum
AGNOSTIC — AOL Lifestyles: Atheism/Agnosticism
AGNOSTICISM — AOL Lifestyles: Atheism/Agnosticism
AGOL — Christianity Online: Assemblies of God
AHH — Alternative Medical Forum
AHH BOARDS — Alternative Medical Forum: Message Center
AHH CHAT — Alternative Medical Forum: Chat Center
AHH! — Alternative Medical Forum

AIDS & HIV — AIDs/HIV
AIDS — AOL Health: AIDS & HIV
AIDS LINE — AIDS Line
AIDS ONQ — onQ: Positive Living with HIV/AIDS
AIDS QUILT — AIDS Memorial
AIM — AOL Instant Messenger
AINTREE — AOL UK: The Martell British Grand National
AIR SHOWS — AOL Interests: Aviation & Aeronautics
AIR WARRIOR — Air Warrior
AIRCRAFT — AOL Interests: Aviation & Aeronautics
AIRCRAFTS — AOL Interests: Aviation & Aeronautics
AIRFARE — Preview Travel
AIRFARE FINDER — Preview Travel: FareFinder
AIRFORCE — Military City Online
AIRPLANE — AOL Interests: Aviation & Aeronautics
AIRPORT — AOL Interests: Aviation & Aeronautics
AIRW EVENTS — Air Warrior: Events
AJGA — American Junior Golf Association
AKA EDDIE BAUER — Eddie Bauer
AL — AOL Sports: Baseball
AL SCOREBOARD — American League Scoreboard
AL SCORES — American League Scoreboard
ALA — American Lung Association
ALARM — AOL Computing: Products 2000
ALBANIA — AOL International: Albania
ALBANY — Digital City Albany: NewsGuide
ALBANY LOCAL NEWS — Digital City Albany: Local News
ALBANY NEWS — Digital City Albany: Local News
ALBUQUERQUE — Digital City Albuquerque: Local News
ALBUQUERQUE LOCAL NEWS — Digital City Albuquerque: Local News
ALBUQUERQUE NEWS — Digital City Albuquerque: Local News
ALCOHOL — AOL Health: Alcoholism
ALCOHOLIC — AOL Health: Alcoholism
ALCOHOLICS — AOL Health: Alcoholism
ALCOHOLICS ANONYMOUS ONLINE — Alcoholics Anonymous Online
ALCOHOLISM — AOL Health: Alcoholism
ALGERIA — AOL International: Algeria
ALL ABOUT YOU — All About You
ALL APARTMENTS — All Apartments [Web site]
ALL MY CHILDREN — ABC Online: Daytime
ALLE JEWELRY — Allé Fine Jewelry
ALLERGIES — AOL Health: Allergy & Respiratory Disorders
ALLERGY — AOL Health: Allergy & Respiratory Disorders
ALLIANCE ART — Digital City New York: Alliance Arts
ALLIANCE ARTS — Digital City New York: Alliance Arts
ALLSTATE — Allstate: Lincoln Benefit Life [Web site]
ALLY — Electra: Ally McBeal

ALLY MCBEAL — Electra: Ally McBeal
ALLYN & BACON — Simon & Schuster's College Online
ALOHA BOWL — College Bowls Fan Central
ALPT — The Grandstand: Simulation Golf
ALT MED — Alternatives Medicine Forum
ALT MED AIDS — Alternative Medical Forum: AIDS and HIV
ALT MED BOARDS — Alternative Medical Forum: Message Center
ALT MED CAN — AOL Canada: Alternative Medical Forum
ALT MED CANADA — AOL Canada: Alternative Medical Forum
ALT MED CDN — AOL Canada: Alternative Medical Forum
ALT MED CHAT — Alternative Medical Forum: Chat Center
ALT MED US — Alternative Medical Forum
ALTAMIRA — AOL Canada: Altamira Mutual Funds
ALTERNATIVE — AOL Entertainment: Alternative Music
ALTERNATIVE MEDICINE — AOL Health: Alternative & Complementary
    Medicine
ALTERNATIVES — Alternative Medical Forum
ALUMNAE RESOURCES — Digital City San Francisco: Career Advice
ALUMNI — AOL Lifestyles: Alumni Hall
ALUMNI HALL — AOL Lifestyles: Alumni Hall
ALUMNI RESOURCES — Digital City San Francisco: Career Advice
ALZHEIMER'S — AOL Health: Alzheimer's Disease
ALZHEIMERS — AOL Health: Alzheimer's Disease
ALZHEIMER'S DISEASE — AOL Health: Alzheimer's Disease
ALZHEIMERS DISEASE — AOL Health: Alzheimer's Disease
AM ASSEMBLY — American Assembly [Web site]
AMAZING — Amazing Instant Novelist: Trivia Game
AMELIA ISLAND — Destination Florida: Amelia Island
AMERICA — AOL Member Services: QuickStart
AMERICA DESUD — AOL International: South America
AMERICA ONLINE — AOL Member Services: QuickStart
AMERICA ONLINE STORE — AOL Store
AMERICA OUT OF LINE — ABC Online: America(n) Out of Line
AMERICAN — American Airlines [Web site]
AMERICAN AIR — American Airlines [Web site]
AMERICAN AIRLINE — American Airlines [Web site]
AMERICAN AIRLINES — American Airlines [Web site]
AMERICAN ASSEMBLY — American Assembly [Web site]
AMERICAN EXPRESS — American Express
AMERICAN GREETINGS — American Greetings
AMERICAN HEART @ BETTER HEALTH — American Heart Association
AMERICAN HEART ASSOCIATION @ BETTER HEALTH — American Heart
    Association
AMERICAN LEAGUE SCORES — American League Scoreboard
AMERICAN LUNG — American Lung Association
AMERICAN LUNG ASSOC — American Lung Association
AMERICAN OUT OF LINE — ABC Online: America(n) Out of Line

AMERICAN SMOKEOUT — AOL Health: Great American Smokeout
AMERICAN WHOLE HEALTH — Digital City Washington: American Whole Health
AMERICAN WOODWORKER — American Woodworker Online
AMERICA'S PARKS — AOL Sports: America's Parks
AMERICON — America Online Gaming Conference
AMERITRADE — Ameritrade Investing
AMEX — American Express
AMEX CARD — American Express: Cards
AMEX CARDS — American Express: Cards
AMEX SEW — American Express: SE Workstation [Web site]
AMSTERDAM — Time Out Guide: Amsterdam [Web site]
AMY AMATANGELO — Digital City Boston: TV Gal
AMY GRANT — Christianity Online: Friends Of Amy Grant
ANAHEIM ANGELS — California Angels
ANAWAVE — AnaWave Web Hosting [Web site]
ANAWAVE.COM — AnaWave Web Hosting [Web site]
ANDERS — Anders CD-ROM Guide
ANDERSEN — Digital City San Diego: Walter Andersen Nursery
ANDORRA — AOL International: Andorra
ANDY B — Digital City Philadelphia: Andy Belmont Racing
ANDY BELMONT — Digital City Philadelphia: Andy Belmont Racing
ANDY PARGH — The Gadget Guru Online
ANEMIA — AOL Health: Anemia
ANGELFIRE — Angelfire Communications [Web site]
ANGELS — California Angels
ANGLER — AOL Interests: Fishing
ANGLING — AOL Interests: Fishing
ANGOLA — AOL International: Angola
ANIMAL — AOL Interests: Pets
ANIMALS — AOL Interests: Pets
ANIME — Wizard World -or- Japanimation Station
ANNUAL PLAN — AOL Member Services: Accounts & Billing
ANNUAL PLANS — AOL Member Services: Accounts & Billing
ANNUAL REPORTS — AOL Annual Reports [Web site]
ANOREXIA — Eating Disorders
ANS — ANS: Corporate Wide-Area Networking Solutions [Web site]
ANSWER — Member Services
ANSWERS — Member Services
ANT — Antagonist, Inc.
ANT CELLAR — Antagonist, Inc.: Prize Cellar
ANT HILL — Antagonist, Inc.: ANT Hill News
ANT PC — Antagonist, Inc.: PC Games
ANT PRIZES — Antagonist, Inc.: Prize Cellar
ANT TRIVIA — Antagonist, Inc.

ANTAG — Antagonist, Inc.
ANTAGONIST — Antagonist, Inc.
ANTAGONISTS — Antagonist, Inc.
ANTHEM — AOL International: National Anthems of the World
ANTHEMS — AOL International: National Anthems of the World
ANTIGUA & BARBUDA — AOL International: Antigua and Barbuda
ANTIGUA — AOL International: Antigua and Barbuda
ANTIQUE — AOL Interests: Antiques
ANTIQUES — AOL Interests: Antiques
ANTONYMS — Merriam-Webster Thesaurus
ANXIETY — AOL Health: Anxiety & Panic Disorders
AOL 4 — Upgrade to the Latest AOL Software
AOL 4.0 — Upgrade to the Latest AOL Software
AOL 40 — Upgrade to the Latest AOL Software
AOL ANNUAL PLAN — AOL Annual Pricing Plans
AOL ANNUAL PLANS — AOL Annual Pricing Plans
AOL AUTO CENTER — AOL Auto Center
AOL AUTODIALER — AOL Autodialer
AOL BIKE — Bicycling on AOL
AOL BOOK SHOP — AOL Store: Book Shop
AOL BUSINESS DIRECTORY — AOL Business Directory [Web site]
AOL CA — AOL Canada [Web site]
AOL CANADA — AOL Canada
AOL CHORUS — CultureFinder: AOL Chorus
AOL CLASSIFIED — AOL Classifieds
AOL CLASSIFIEDS — AOL Classifieds
AOL COM NETHELP — AOL.com: NetHelp [Web site]
AOL CREDIT ALERT — AOL Credit Alert
AOL CRUISE — AOL Member Cruise
AOL DIAG — AOL Diagnostic Tool
AOL DIGITAL SHOP — AOL Store: Digital Shop
AOL EDUCATION — AOL Education Initiative
AOL ELSEWHERE — International Access
AOL FAMILIES — AOL Families channel
AOL FIND — AOL Find
AOL FRANCE — AOL International channel
AOL FULL DISCLOSURE — AOL Full Disclosure
AOL GAMES NEWSSTAND — AOL Games: Newsstand
AOL GIFT — AOL Gift Certificates
AOL GIFT CERTIFICATES — AOL Gift Certificates
AOL GLOBALNET — International Access
AOL GLOSSARY — AOL Glossary
AOL GUARANTEE — AOL Shopping: Our Guarantee
AOL HARDWARE SHOP — AOL Store: Computer Shop
AOL HOME PAGE — AOL.com [Web site]
AOL I — AOL Insider Tips

AOL INSIDER — AOL Insider Tips
AOL INSIDER TALENT SEARCH — AOL Insider Talent Search
AOL INTERNATIONAL — AOL International channel
AOL IR — AOL FullDisclosure
AOL ISRAEL — AOL International: Israel
AOL ISREAL — AOL International: Israel
AOL JAPAN — AOL Japan Software
AOL JAPAN DISK — AOL Japan Software
AOL LD — AOL Long Distance Savings Plan
AOL LINK — Winsock Central
AOL LIVE — AOL Live
AOL LIVE QUICK START — AOL Live: QuickStart
AOL LIVE! — AOL Live
AOL LOGO — AOL Store: Logo Shop
AOL LOGO SHOP — AOL Store: Logo Shop
AOL LONG DISTANCE — AOL Long Distance Savings Plan
AOL MARKETDAY — AOL Personal Finance: Market Day
AOL MEMBER CRUISE — AOL Member Cruise
AOL MERCHANDISE — AOL Store: Logo Shop
AOL MFC — Mutual Fund Center
AOL MODEM SHOP — AOL Store: Modem Shop
AOL MUTUAL FUND CENTER — Mutual Fund Center
AOL NEIGHBORHOOD WATCH — AOL Neighborhood Watch
AOL NETFIND — AOL NetFind [Web site]
AOL NETFIND TIPS — AOL NetFind: NetFind Tips [Web site]
AOL NETHELP — AOL.com: NetHelp [Web site]
AOL NETMAIL — AOL NetMail
AOL ON TV — AOL on TV
AOL PICTURES — AOL Interests: Pictures
AOL PLUG INS — AOL Multimedia Showcase [Web site]
AOL POINTS — AOL Rewards
AOL PREVIEW — AOL Software Preview
AOL PRODUCTS — AOL Store
AOL R — AOL Rewards
AOL REDIALER — AOL Autodialer
AOL REWARDS — AOL Rewards
AOL SA — AOL Shoppers Advantage
AOL SAVINGS CLUB — AOL Savings Clubs
AOL SAVINGS CLUBS — AOL Savings Clubs
AOL SCUBA — AOL Sports: Scuba Forum
AOL SEARCH — AOL Find
AOL SECRETS — AOL Secrets
AOL SHOPPING CLUB — AOL Shoppers Advantage
AOL SOFTWARE SHOP — AOL Store: Software Shop
AOL SPECIAL SAVINGS CLUBS — AOL Savings Clubs
AOL SPORTS — AOL Sports channel
AOL SPORTS LIVE — AOL Sports: Live Events

AOL STORE — AOL Store
AOL STORIES — AOL Stories
AOL STORY — AOL Stories
AOL STUDIOS — AOL Studios [Web page]
AOL SUPERSTORE — AOL Shoppers Advantage
AOL TALENT SEARCH — AOL Insider: Talent Search
AOL TICKER — AOL News
AOL TIPS — AOL Insider Tips
AOL TODAY — AOL Today
AOL TRAVELERS ADVANTAGE — AOL Travelers Advantage
AOL UPDATE — A Letter From Steve Case
AOL VISA — AOL Visa Card
AOL VISA CARD — AOL Visa Card
AOL W — AOL Headquarters Weather
AOL WEATH — AOL Headquarters Weather
AOL WEATHER — AOL Headquarters Weather
AOL WEB — AOL.com [Web site]
<u>AOL WEBOPAEDIA</u> — AOL Computing: Webopædia [Web site]
AOL WEBOPEDIA — AOL Computing: Webopædia [Web site]
AOL WORLD — AOL International
AOL.CA — AOL Canada [Web site]
AOL.COM — AOL.com [Web site]
AOLNET — Accessing America Online
AOL'S HOME PAGE — AOL.com [Web site]
AOL'S WEB PAGE — AOL.com [Web site]
AOOL — ABC Online: America(n) Out of Line
AOP — Association of Online Professionals
AOTW — AOL Computing: Computer Paint Artists
APARTMENT LOCATOR — Southern Management Corporation
APARTMENT LOCATORS — Southern Management Corporation
APARTMENTS PLUS — Apartments.com
APARTMENTS.COM — Apartments.com
APPAREL — AOL Shopping: Apparel & Accessories
APPAREL BIZ — AOL Workplace: Apparel Professionals Forum
APPAREL SHOP — AOL Shopping: Apparel & Accessories
APPLE — Apple Computer, Inc.
APPLE BIZ — Apple Business Consortium
APPLE CAFE — Apple Computer: Cafe Chat Room
APPLE COMMUNITY — Apple Computer: Community Live
APPLE COMPUTER — Apple Computer, Inc.
APPLE DIRECTORY — Apple Computer: Apple Directory
APPLE GUIDE — AOL Computing: AppleScript Development
APPLE INFO — Apple Computer: Apple Info Center
APPLE INFO CENTER — Apple Computer: Apple Info Center
APPLE UPDATE — Macintosh Apple Software Update
APPLESCRIPT — AOL Computing: AppleScript Development
APPLESCRIPT SIG — AOL Computing: AppleScript Development

APPLESCRIPTS — AOL Computing: AppleScript Development
APPLIANCE REPAIR — AOL Workplace: Appliance Sales & Service
APPLIANCE SALES PROS — AOL Workplace: Appliance Sales & Service
APPLIANCE SERVICE PROS — AOL Workplace: Appliance Sales &
    Service
APPLIANCE SUPERSTORE — AOL Shoppers Advantage: Appliance Store
APPLIANCES — AOL Workplace: Appliance Sales & Service
APPLICATIONS — AOL Computing: Applications Forums
APPLICATIONS FORUM — AOL Computing: Applications Forums
APPS — AOL Computing: Applications Forums
APRIL 1 — April Fool's Day @ AOL [seasonal]
APRIL 15 — AOL International: Tax Information [seasonal]
APRIL FOOL — April Fool's Day @ AOL [seasonal]
APRIL FOOLS — April Fool's Day @ AOL [seasonal]
AQUARIUS — Horoscope Selections
ARABIC — AOL International: Middle East
ARCHAEOLOGY — Archaeology Forum
ARCHEOLOGY — Archaeology Forum
ARCHIE — Internet Connection: Gopher
ARCHITECT — AOL Workplace: Architects & Architecture
ARCHITECTURE — AOL Interests: Home & Garden
ARCHIVE PHOTOS — Archive Photos [Web pointer]
ARCHY — Archaeology Forum
ARCTIC — Arctic Journal Polar Expeditions
ARCTIC JOURNAL — Arctic Journal Polar Expeditions
ARDYS SPECIALS — Aardvark Aardy: Specials
ARENA — Online Gaming Forum: The Arena and Parthenon
ARFA — American Running and Fitness Association
ARGENTINA — AOL International: Argentina
ARGONAUT — Digital City Denver: Argonaut Wine and Liquor
ARGONAUT WINE AND LIQUOR — Digital City Denver: Argonaut Wine
    and Liquor
ARIES — Horoscope Selections
ARIZONA — Arizona Central
ARIZONA CENTRAL — Arizona Central
ARLINGTON HEIGHTS — Digital City Arlington Heights [Web site]
ARM QB — Real Fans: Armchair Quarterback
ARMCHAIR — Real Fans: Armchair Quarterback
ARMCHAIR QB — Real Fans: Armchair Quarterback
ARMENIA — AOL International: Armenia
ARMY — Military City Online
AROMATHERAPY — AOL Health: Aromatherapy
AROUND THE HORN — NESN Around the Horn
ART — AOL Influence: Arts and Leisure
ART BELL — ParaScope: Art Bell
ART LARRY — Digital City San Francisco: Larry's Art O Rama
ART SHOPPING — Image Exchange: Marketplace

ART SKATE — Artistic Roller Skating MiniForum
ART SKATING — Artistic Roller Skating MiniForum
ARTHRITIS MONTH — Arthritis Relief
ARTHRITIS PAIN — AOL Health: Arthritis Pain
ARTISTIC SKATING — Artistic Roller Skating MiniForum
ARTISTS & GALLERIES — AOL Workplace: Artists & Galleries
    Community
ARTS & CRAFT — Arts & Crafts
ARTS & CRAFTS — Arts & Crafts
ARTS — AOL Influence: Arts and Leisure
ARTS AND CRAFT — Arts & Crafts
ARTS AND CRAFTS — Arts & Crafts
ARTS AND LEISURE — AOL Influence: Arts and Leisure
ARTS FEST ATLANTA — Digital City Atlanta: Arts Festival
ARTS ONQ — onQ: Arts
ARUBA — AOL International: Aruba
ARVADA NEWS — Digital City Denver: Jefferson Sentinel Online
A'S — Oakland Athletics
ASAP — AOL Studio Affiliates Program
ASCD — Association for Supervision & Curriculum Development [Web
    pointer]
ASF MAG — Atlanta Sports and Fitness Magazine
ASF MAGAZINE — Atlanta Sports and Fitness Magazine
ASFL — The Grandstand: Simulation Football
ASFM — Atlanta Sports and Fitness Magazine
ASG — Automotive Service Garage [Web site]
ASG INC — Automotive Service Garage [Web site]
ASHTON-DRAKE — Collectibles Today [Web site]
ASIA — AOL International: Asia
ASIAN — AOL Lifestyles: Ethnicity
ASIAN AMERICAN — Channel A: Modern Asian Living
ASIANMERICAN — Channel A: Modern Asian Living
ASK A TEACHER — AOL Research & Learn: Ask-A-Teacher
ASK AMERICA ONLINE — AOL Member Services
ASK AOL — AOL Member Services
ASK ARNIE — Travel Corner: Ask Arnie
ASK DELILAH — Thrive@Healthy Living: Meet Delilah
ASK DR. LOVE — Online Psych: Ask Dr. Love
ASK DR. RASKIN — Online Psych: Ask Dr. Raskin
ASK ERIK — Wheels: Ask the Expert
ASK GAYE — Online Psych: Ask Gaye
ASK MICHELE — Online Psych: Ask Michele
ASK MPD — Online Psych: Ask MPD
ASK PEGGY — Online Psych: Ask Peggy
ASK THE EXPERT — Wheels: Ask the Expert
ASK THE PRO — Wheels: Ask the Expert
ASK TODD — Image Exchange: Ask Todd Art

ASK TODD ART — Image Exchange: Ask Todd Art
ASK-A-TEACHER — AOL Research & Learn: Ask-A-Teacher
ASP — Association of Shareware Professionals [Web site]
ASSEMBLIES OF GOD — Christianity Online: Assemblies of God
ASSEMBLY — AOL Computing: Development Forum
ASSEMBLY OF GOD — Christianity Online: Assemblies of God
ASSESS YOUR HEALTH — AOL Health: Assess Your Health
ASSN ONLINE PROF — Association of Online Professionals
AST — AST Computer Support Forum
ASTHMA — AOL Health: Asthma
ASTHMA@THRIVE — Thrive@Healthy Living: Asthma
ASTROBYTES — Astrobytes Daily Horoscopes
ASTROLOGY — Horoscope Selections
ASTRONET — Astronet
ASTRONOMY — Astronomy Club
ASTROS — Houston Astros
ASYLUM — Entertainment Asylum
ASYLUM CHAT — Entertainment Asylum
ASYLUM FEEDBACK — Entertainment Asylum: Feedback
ASYLUM HELP — Entertainment Asylum: Help
ASYLUM NEWS — Entertainment Asylum: Weekly News
ASYLUM TEEN — Entertainment Asylum: Teen Asylum
ASYLUM TEEN CHAT — Entertainment Asylum: Teen Asylum Chat
ASYLUM X FILES — Entertainment Asylum: The X Files
AT — Antagonist, Inc.
AT HOME NN — NetNoir: Out & At Home
AT MUSIC MIDTOWN — Digital City Atlanta: Music Midtown
AT RELIGION — Digital City: Religion
AT&T — AT&T Wireless Service
ATHEISM — AOL Lifestyles: Atheism/Agnosticism
ATHEIST — AOL Lifestyles: Atheism/Agnosticism
ATHLETE DIRECT — Athlete Direct
ATHLETE DIRECT FOOTBALL — Athlete Direct: Football
ATHLETE DIRECT TENNIS — Athlete Direct: Tennis
ATHLETES DIRECT — Athlete Direct
ATHLETICS — Oakland Athletics
ATL ANTIQUES — Digital City Atlanta: Antiques
ATL ART — Digital City Atlanta: Museums and Galleries
ATL CHAMBER — Digital City Atlanta: Chamber of Commerce
ATL CHAT — Digital City Atlanta: Chat
ATL CLASSIFIEDS — Digital City Atlanta: Classifieds
ATL DINES — Digital City Atlanta: Dining
ATL DINING — Digital City Atlanta: Dining
ATL GALLERIES — Digital City Atlanta: Museums and Galleries
ATL HEALTH — Digital City Atlanta: Health
ATL M4M — PlanetOut: FantasyMan Island For Atlanta
ATL MOVIE — Digital City Atlanta: Movies

ATL MOVIES — Digital City Atlanta: Movies
ATL MUSEUMS — Digital City Atlanta: Museums and Galleries
ATL PERSONALS — Digital City Atlanta: Personals
ATL TOP BROKERS — Digital City Atlanta: Real Estate Ticket
ATL TRAVEL — Digital City Atlanta: Traveler
ATLANTA — Digital City Atlanta
ATLANTA 99X — Digital City Atlanta: WNNX 99.7 FM
ATLANTA ANTIQUES — Digital City Atlanta: Antiques
ATLANTA ART — Digital City Atlanta: Museums and Galleries
ATLANTA ARTS FESTIVAL — Digital City Atlanta: Arts Festival
ATLANTA BEER — Digital City Atlanta: Beer Haus
ATLANTA BEER HAUS — Digital City Atlanta: Beer Haus
ATLANTA BRAVES — Atlanta Braves
ATLANTA BREW — Digital City Atlanta: Beer Haus
ATLANTA CAR — Digital City Atlanta: Auto Mart
ATLANTA CAREERS — Digital City Atlanta: Employment Classifieds
ATLANTA CARS — Digital City Atlanta: Auto Mart
ATLANTA CBS — Digital City Atlanta: WGNX-TV Channel 46
ATLANTA CHAMBER — Digital City Atlanta: Chamber of Commerce
ATLANTA CHAT — Digital City Atlanta: Chat
ATLANTA CLASSIFIEDS — Digital City Atlanta: Classifieds
ATLANTA DINES — Digital City Atlanta: Dining
ATLANTA DINING — Digital City Atlanta: Dining
ATLANTA DINING GUIDE — Digital City Atlanta: Dining
ATLANTA EMPLOYMENT — Digital City Atlanta: Employment Classifieds
ATLANTA FITNESS — Digital City Atlanta: Sports and Fitness Magazine
ATLANTA GALLERIES — Digital City Atlanta: Museums and Galleries
ATLANTA HEALTH — Digital City Atlanta: Health
ATLANTA HOMES — Digital City Atlanta: Real Estate
ATLANTA HOUSES — Digital City Atlanta: Real Estate
ATLANTA JOBS — Digital City Atlanta: Employment Classifieds
ATLANTA KID — Digital City Atlanta: Safest Kid in Atlanta
ATLANTA KIDS — Digital City Atlanta: Kids Safe
ATLANTA KIDS SAFE — Digital City Atlanta: Kids Safe
ATLANTA LOCAL NEWS — Digital City Atlanta: Local News
ATLANTA M4M — PlanetOut: FantasyMan Island For Atlanta
ATLANTA MOVIE — Digital City Atlanta: Movies
ATLANTA MOVIES — Digital City Atlanta: Movies
ATLANTA MOVING — Digital City Atlanta: Relocation Guide
ATLANTA MUSEUM — Digital City Atlanta: Museums and Galleries
ATLANTA MUSEUMS — Digital City Atlanta: Museums and Galleries
ATLANTA NEWS — Digital City Atlanta: Local News
ATLANTA OMNI — Digital City Atlanta: The Omni
ATLANTA PERSONALS — Digital City Atlanta: Personals
ATLANTA REAL ESTATE — Digital City Atlanta: Real Estate
ATLANTA RELO — Digital City Atlanta: Relocation Guide
ATLANTA RELOCATION — Digital City Atlanta: Relocation Guide

ATLANTA SINGLES — Digital City Atlanta: Personals
ATLANTA SOAP — Digital City Atlanta: Soap Opera Now
ATLANTA SOAPS — Digital City Atlanta: Soap Opera Now
ATLANTA SPORTS MAG — Digital City Atlanta: Sports and Fitness Magazine
ATLANTA TOP BROKERS — Digital City Atlanta: Real Estate Ticket
ATLANTA TRANSFER — Digital City Atlanta: Relocation Guide
ATLANTA TRAVEL — Digital City Atlanta: Traveler
ATLANTA TRAVELER — Digital City Atlanta: Traveler
ATLANTA WGST — Digital City Atlanta: PlanetRadio WGST
ATLANTIC — Virtual Atlantic Canada
ATLANTIC CITY — Digital City Philadelphia
ATLANTIC FINANCIAL — Atlantic Financial [Web site]
ATLAS — Virtual Planet
ATLUS — Atlus Software
ATT — AT&T Wireless Services
ATT WIRELESS — AT&T Wireless Services
ATTENTION DEFICIT DISORDER — AOL Health: Attention Deficit Disorder
ATTORNEY — AOL Workplace: Legal Professionals
ATTORNEYS — AOL Workplace: Legal Professionals
AU.CHILDREN — AOL Australia: Kids channel
AU.COMMUNITY — AOL Australia: Lifestyles channel
AU.COMP — AOL Australia: Computing channel
AU.COMPUTING — AOL Australia: Computing channel
AU.FINANCE — AOL Australia: Money channel
AU.GAMES — AOL Australia: Games channel
AU.INT — AOL Australia: International channel
AU.INTERNATIONAL — AOL Australia: International channel
AU.INTERNET — AOL Australia: Internet channel
AU.KIDS — AOL Australia: Internet channel
AU.LEARNING — AOL Australia: Learning channel
AU.MONEY — AOL Australia: Money channel
AU.NEWS — AOL Australia: News channel
AU.NEWSPAPER — AOL Australia: News channel
AU.PEOPLE — AOL Australia: Lifestyles channel
AU.PLAY — AOL Australia: Games channel
AU.SCHOOL — AOL Australia: Learning channel
AU.SPORT — AOL Australia: Sport channel
AU.SPORTS — AOL Australia: Sport channel
AU.TRAVEL — AOL Australia: Travel channel
AU.WEATHER — AOL Australia: Weather Station
AU.WEB — AOL Australia: Internet channel
AUCTION SUPERSITE — Onsale Online Auction Supersite [Web site]
AUDIO A — Audio Adrenaline
AUDIO ADRENALINE — Audio Adrenaline
AUDIONET — Digital City Dallas-Fort Worth: Broadcast.com

AUDITORIUM — AOL Live: Today's Events
AUG — User Groups Network [Web site]
AUSTIN — Digital City Austin
AUSTIN LOCAL NEWS — Digital City Austin: Local News
AUSTIN NEWS — Digital City Austin: Local News
AUSTRALIA — AOL International: Australia and Oceania
AUSTRIA — AOL International: Austria
AUTHOR @ AOL — Barnes & Noble: Author Series
AUTHORS @ AOL — Barnes & Noble: Author Series
AUTISM — AOL Health: Autism
AUTO — AOL Auto Center
AUTO BUYING — AOL Auto Center: Buying Guide
AUTO BUYING GUIDE — AOL Auto Center: Buying Guide
AUTO CENTER — AOL Auto Center
AUTO CLASSIFIEDS — AOL Classifieds: Automobiles
AUTO DISCOUNTS — AOL Auto Center
AUTO FINDER — Digital City Hampton Roads: Autofinder
AUTO GUIDE — Personal Finance: Auto Guide
AUTO GUY — Digital City Boston: Auto Guy
AUTO HELP — Wheels: Ask the Expert
AUTO RACING — AOL Sports: Auto Racing
AUTO RACING STARS — AOL Sports: Auto Racing Stars
AUTO SHOP — AOL Shopping: Auto & Travel
AUTO SOUND — AOL Computing: Products 2000
AUTO SPORT — Autosport Magazine
AUTO SUPERSTORE — AOL Shoppers Advantage: Car Stereo &
    Accessories
AUTOCAD — AOL Computing: Computer Aided Drafting
AUTODIALER — AOL Autodialer
AUTOMOBILE — AOL Auto Center
AUTOMOBILES — AOL Auto Center
AUTOMOTIVE — AOL Auto Center
AUTOMOTIVE SERVICE GARAGE — Automotive Service Garage
    [Web site]
AUTOS — AOL Auto Center
AUTOVANTAGE — AOL AutoVantage: New Car
AUTUMN SALE — AOL Shopping: Fall Spectacular Sale [seasonal]
AV — AOL AutoVantage: New Car
AV FORUM — AOL Interests: Aviation Forum
AV NEW CAR — AutoVantage New Cars
AVALAN EVENTS — Digital City Los Angeles: Avalon Events
AVALANCHE — Colorado Avalanche
AVALON — Digital City Los Angeles: Avalon Events
AVALON CONCERTS — Digital City Los Angeles: Avalon Events
AVALON L.A. — Digital City Los Angeles: Avalon Events
AVEDA SALON — Digital City Denver: Oxford/Aveda Spa at Oxford
    Hotel

AVEDA SPA — Digital City Denver: Oxford/Aveda Spa at Oxford Hotel
AVIATION — AOL Interests: Aviation & Aeronautics
AVIATION FORUM — AOL Interests: Aviation Forum
AVON — Avon
AVON CRUSADE — Avon: Breast Awareness Crusade Online
AVON PREFERRED — Avon: Preferred
AW — AOL WorkPlace: AboutWork
AW ENTREPRENEUR — AboutWork
AW GUT INSTINCT — AboutWork: Gut Instinct
AWRT — American Women in Radio & Television
AXIS — Axies and Allies Club
AZ ALT — Arizona Central: ALT.
AZ ALT. — Arizona Central: ALT.
AZ ASU — Arizona Central: Sports
AZ BENSON — Arizona Central: Opinions
AZ BEST — Arizona Central: Best
AZ BUSINESS — Arizona Central: Money
AZ CACTUS — Arizona Central: Cactus League
AZ CARDINALS — Arizona Central: Sports
AZ CARDS — Arizona Central: Sports
AZ CAROUSING — Arizona Central: Getting Out
AZ CARTOON — Arizona Central: Opinions
AZ CENTRAL — Arizona Central
AZ COLUMNS — Arizona Central: Opinions
AZ COMMUNITY — Arizona Central: Community
AZ COMPUTERS — Arizona Central: Computers
AZ CONCERTS — Arizona Central: Getting Out
AZ COUCHING — Arizona Central: Getting Out
AZ DESTINATIONS — Arizona Central: Destinations
AZ DIAMONDBACKS — Arizona Central: Sports
AZ DINING — Arizona Central: Dining
AZ EATS — Arizona Central: Dining Out and Entertainment
AZ EDITORIALS — Arizona Central: Opinions
AZ FUN — Arizona Central: Fun
AZ GARDENING — Arizona Central: Home
AZ GOLF — Arizona Central: Golf
AZ HIGH SCHOOLS — Arizona Central: High School Sports
AZ HOME — Arizona Central: Home and Garden
AZ HOUSE — Arizona Central: Home
AZ KTAR — Arizona Central: KTAR Talk Radio Online
AZ LIFE — Arizona Central: Life
AZ MONEY — Arizona Central: Money
AZ NEWS — Arizona Central: News
AZ NEWSLINE — Arizona Central: News
AZ OPINIONS — Arizona Central: Opinions
AZ PHOTOS — Arizona Central: Photo Album
AZ PREPS — Arizona Central: High School Sports

AZ SCHOOLS — Arizona Central: School Life
AZ SCOREBOARD — Arizona Central: Scoreboard
AZ SCORES — Arizona Central: Scoreboard
AZ SOUND OFF — Arizona Central: Opinions
AZ SPORTS — Arizona Central: Sports
AZ SPORTS CALENDARS — Arizona Central: Sports Calendars
AZ SPORTS SCHEDULE — Arizona Central: Sports Calendars
AZ STARDUST — Arizona Central: The Arts
AZ SUNS — Arizona Central: Sports
AZ THEATER — Arizona Central: The Arts
AZ THEATRE — Arizona Central: The Arts
AZ TRAVEL — Arizona Central: Destinations
AZ TRIPS — Arizona Central: Destinations
AZ TV — Arizona Central: Television
AZ U OF A — Arizona Central: Sports
AZ VOLUNTEERS — Arizona Central: Volunteers
AZERBAIJAN — AOL International: Azerbaijan
B A HOMES — Digital City San Francisco: Real Estate
B OF A — Bank of America
B&B — Pamela Lanier's Bed and Breakfast Guide
B&C — Christianity Online: Books & Culture
B&C STORE — Christianity Online: Books & Culture Store [Web site]
B5 — Babylon 5
BA — Bank of America
BA RENTALS — Digital City San Francisco: Rental Solutions
BABIES — AOL Families: Babies
BABY — AOL Families: Babies
BABY BOOMER — Ages & Stages Communities: Baby Boomers
BABY BOOMERS — Ages & Stages Communities: Baby Boomers
BABY NAME — Parent Soup: Baby Names
BABY NAMES — Parent Soup: Baby Names
BABYLON — Babylon 5
BABYLON 5 — Babylon 5
BAC — Bay Area California
BAC BLAST — Bay Area California: Blast Youth Forum
BAC CHAT — Bay Area California Chat Room
BAC PARTY CENTRAL — Bay Area California: Party Central
BACK — Pain Relief Center: Back Pain
BACK BACON — AOL Canada: The Back Bacon Caf-eh Chat Room
BACK PAGE — InToon: Daily Cartoon
BACK PAIN — AOL Health: Back Pain
BACK STREET HEROES — Motorcycle Magazine
BACK TO SCHOOL — Back To School [seasonal]
BACK TO SCHOOL SALE — AOL Shopping: Back To School Sale
BACKBEAT — Digital City Denver: Westword News & Arts Weekly
BACKGAMMON — WorldPlay: Backgammon
<u>BACKGAMON</u> — WorldPlay: Backgammon

BACKPACK — Backpacker Magazine
BACKPACKER — Backpacker Magazine
BACKROOM ONQ — onQ: Backroom
BAHA'I — Spirituality: Baha'i Faith Area
BAHAI — Spirituality: Baha'i Faith Area
BAHA'I FAITH — Spirituality: Baha'i Faith Area
BAHAMAS — AOL International: Bahamas
BAHRAIN — AOL International: Bahrain
BAJA — Digital City San Francisco: The Latina Tag Team
BALANCE — AOL Rewards
BALANCE SHEET — Disclosure: Financial Statements
BALD — AOL Health: Baldness & Hair Loss
BALDNESS — AOL Health: Baldness & Hair Loss
BALI — One Hanes Place
BALLOON — 1-800-FLOWERS: Balloon Boutique
BALLOON DECORATING — AOL WorkPlace: Gift Baskets & Balloon
    Decorating Forum
BALLOONS — 1-800-FLOWERS: Balloon Boutique
BALLOTIN — Godiva Chocolatier
BALTIMORE — Digital City Baltimore
BALTIMORE DC — Digital City Baltimore
BALTIMORE DCITY — Digital City Baltimore
BALTIMORE LOCAL NEWS — Digital City Baltimore: Local News
BALTIMORE MD — Digital City Baltimore
BALTIMORE NEWS — Digital City Baltimore: Local News
BALTIMORE ORIOLES — Baltimore Orioles
BANGLADESH — AOL International: Bangladesh
BANK — AOL Personal Finance: Banking Center
BANK AMERICA — Bank of America
BANK OF AMERICA — Bank of America
BANK OF MONTREAL — Mbanx: Bank of Montreal Electronic Banking
BANK RATE — Bank Rate Monitor
BANK RATE MONITOR — Bank Rate Monitor
BANKING — AOL Personal Finance: Banking Center
BANKING CENTER — AOL Personal Finance: Banking Center
BANKING CENTRE — Canadian Banking Centre
BANKS — AOL Personal Finance: Banking Center
BAR — AOL WorkPlace: Taverns & Bars Community
BARB — Buzzsaw: Daily Chuckle
BARBADOS — AOL International: Barbados
BARBUDA — AOL International: Antigua Barbuda
BARGAIN — AOL Shopping: Bargain Basement
BARGAIN BASEMENT — AOL Shopping: Bargain Basement
BARGAIN BOX — The Independent Traveler: Bargain Box
BARGAINS — Washington Consumers' Checkbook Magazine: Bargains
BARNES — Barnes & Noble Booksellers
BARNES AND NOBLE — Barnes & Noble Booksellers

BARRINGTON — Digital City Chicago: Barrington
BARRON'S — Barron's Booknotes
BARRONS — Barron's Booknotes
BARRON'S BOOK NOTES — Barron's Booknotes
BARRONS BOOK NOTES — Barron's Booknotes
BARRYMORE — Love@AOL: Jaid Barrymore Uncensored
BASCOMBS — Planning Your Golf Vacation with Mr. Bascombs
BASEBALL — AOL Sports: Baseball
BASEBALL DAILY — Real Fans Sports Network: Baseball Daily
BASEBALL DAILY CHAT — Real Fans Sports Network: Baseball Daily Chat
BASEBALL PHILLY — Digital City Philadelphia: Baseball
BASEBALL STARS — AOL Sports: Baseball Stars
BASEBALL WORKSHOP — Motley Fool Sports: The Fool Dome
BASEBALL-ITIS — Andy Strasberg's Baseball-Itis
BASEBALLITIS — Andy Strasberg's Baseball-Itis
BASIC — AOL Computing: Development Forum
BASKETBALL — AOL Sports: Pro Basketball
BASKETBALL STARS — AOL Sports: Pro Basketball Stars
BASKETBALL TRIVIA — NTN Trivia: Basketball Trivia
BATH — AOL UK: Digital City Bath
BATMAN — DC Comics
BATTLETECH — Engage: BattleTech
BAY AREA AUTOS — Digital City San Francisco: AutoGuide
BAY AREA BOATING — Rather Be Boating
BAY AREA CALIFORNIA — Bay Area California
BAY AREA CARS — Digital City San Francisco: AutoGuide
BAY AREA DINING — Digital City San Francisco: Dining Guide
BAY AREA HANGOUT — Digital City San Francisco: Hangout
BAY AREA HOMES — Digital City San Francisco: Real Estate
BAY AREA LOVE — Digital City San Francisco: Personals
BAY AREA PERSONALS — Digital City San Francisco: Personals
BAY AREA REAL ESTATE — Digital City San Francisco: Real Estate
BAY AREA RENTALS — Rental Solutions
BAY AREA RESTAURANTS — Digital City San Francisco: Dining Guide
BAY AREA WEATHER — Digital City San Francisco: Weather
BAY WATCH FRAGRANCE — The Fragrance Counter: Baywatch Collection
BAYOU — Antagonist, Inc.: Black Bayou Game
BAYWATERS — Digital City San Francisco: Waters Celebrity Chats
BB — Antagonist, Inc.: Black Bayou Game
BBACON — AOL Canada: The Back Bacon Caf-eh Chat Room
BBS — AOL Computing: BBS Corner
BBS CORNER — AOL Computing: BBS Corner
BC — Book Central: Book and Author Information and Discussion
BCENTRE — Canadian Banking Centre

BCREEK — Blackberry Creek
BCTS — Christianity Online: Bethel Theological Seminary
BD — Real Fans: Baseball Daily
BDCHAT — Real Fans Sports Network: Baseball Daily Chat
BEAN BAGS — AOL Interests: Beanbag Collectibles
BEANIE BABIES — AOL Interests: Beanbag Collectibles
BEANIES — AOL Hobby Central: Beanbag Collectibles
BEANTOWN CIGAR — Digital City Boston: The Cigar Guy
BEANTOWN STYLE — Digital City Boston: Style Eye
BEANTOWN THEATER GUY — Digital City Boston: Theater Guy
BEANY BABY — AOL Hobby Central: Beanbag Collectibles
BEARS — Chicago Bears Football
BEAT CO — AOL Canada: Beaty & Company
BEATY & CO — AOL Canada: Beaty & Company
BEATY — AOL Canada: Beaty & Company
BEAUTY SHOP — AOL Shopping: Beauty & Jewelry
BEAVIS & BUTTHEAD — MTV Online
BEAVIS — MTV Online
BEAVIS AND BUTTHEAD — MTV Online
**BED & BREAKFAST — Pamela Lanier's Bed and Breakfast
    Guide**
BED — Pamela Lanier's Bed and Breakfast Guide
BED AND BATH — AOL Shopping: Home, Kitchen & Garden
BEEF — Omaha Steaks International
BEEPER — AOL Computing: Products 2000
BEER GUY — Digital City Boston: Beer Guy
BEGINNER — AOL Computing: Help Desk
BEGINNERS — AOL Computing: Help Desk
BEHIND THE SCENES — NetGuide: Behind the Scenes
BELARUS — AOL International: Belarus
BELFAST — AOL UK: Local Life in Belfast
BELFAST EOL — AOL UK: Local Life in Belfast
BELFORT — Digital City Washington: Belfort Furniture
BELFORT FURNITURE — Digital City Washington: Belfort Furniture
<u>BELGIE</u> — AOL International: Belgium
<u>BELGIQUE</u> — AOL International: Belgium
BELGIUM — AOL International: Belgium
BELIZE — AOL International: Belize
BELMONT STAKES — AOL Sports: Triple Crown
BENIN — AOL International: Benin
BERK SYS — Bezerk Online: The Free Online Entertainment Network
    [Web site]
BERK SYS WIN — Bezerk Online: The Free Online Entertainment
    Network [Web site]
BERKELEY — Bezerk Online -or- Digital City San Francisco
BERMUDA — AOL International: Bermuda
BEST FUNDS — Best Mutual Funds

BEST MUTUAL FUNDS — Best Mutual Funds
BEST NEWS — AOL News: What's Hot in News
BEST OF AOL — AOL Member Services: QuickStart
BEST OF BOSTON — Digital City Boston: Bests & Worsts
BEST OF INFLUENCE — AOL Influence: Best of AOL Influence
BEST OF LA — Digital City Los Angeles: Best of LA
BEST OF LIFESTYLES — AOL Lifestyles: Best of AOL Lifestyles
BEST TIPS — AOL Insider Tips
BESTSELLING HOME PLANS — Home Magazine Online: Bestselling
    Home Plans
BETA APPLY — Beta Test Application
BETHEL — Christianity Online: Bethel Theological Seminary
BETTER CANCER HEALTH — Glenna's Garden: Cancer Support Forum
BETTER HEALTH — Better Health & Medical Network
BETTER HEALTH BOOKS — Better Health: Bookstore
BETTER HEALTH CANCER — Glenna's Garden: Cancer Support Forum
BETTER HEALTH DIABETES — Better Health: Diabetes
BETTER HEALTH HEART — Better Health: Heart Health
BETTER HEART — Better Health: Heart Health
BETTER HEART HEALTH — Better Health: Heart Health
BETTER LIVING — Woman's Day: Better Living
BEVERAGES — AOL Interests: Drinks
BEVERLY HILLS 90210 — AOL Entertainment: 90210 Wednesdays
BEVERLY HILLS REAL ESTATE — Digital City Los Angeles: Beverly Hills
    Real Estate Broker
BG — AOL Computing: Buyer's Guide
BH — Better Health & Medical Network
BH ADVICE — Better Health: Experts
BH AMERICAN HEART ASSOCIATION — Better Health: American Heart
    Association
BH CONFERENCE — Better Health: Conference Center
BH DEAF — Better Health: Deaf & Hard of Hearing Community
BH DIABETES — Better Health: Diabetes
BH EVENT — Better Health: Conference Center
BH EXPERT — Better Health: Experts
BH EXPERTS — Better Health: Readers
BH HEART — Better Heart: Heart Health
BH HOH — Better Health: Deaf & Hard of Hearing Community
BH LIVE — Better Health: Conference Center
BH PHARMACISTS — Better Health: Pharmacists Network
BH REFERENCE — AOL Research & Learn: Black History Reference
BH SLEEP — Better Health: Sleep & Related Concerns
BHH — Better Heart Health
BHUTAN — AOL International: Bhutan
BI — AOL Lifestyles: Gay & Lesbian
BI CHAT — onQ: Chat and Conferences
BI DEMAND — PlanetOut: Bisexual Community

BI ONQ — onQ: Bisexual
BIBLE — AOL Spirituality: Christianity
BIBLELAND SOFTWARE — Christianity Online: Bibleland Software
BIBLICAL EQUALITY — Christianity Online: Christians for Biblical Equality
BIC MAG — Bicycling Magazine
BICYCLE — AOL Sports: Bicycling
BICYCLE DEALERS — AOL WorkPlace: Bicycle Dealers Community
BICYCLE REPAIR — AOL WorkPlace: Bicycle Dealers Community
BICYCLES — AOL Sports: Bicycling
BICYCLING — Bicycling Magazine
BICYCLING MAG — Bicycling Magazine
BICYCLING MAGAZINE — Bicycling Magazine
BIDDLE — Christianity Online: Brother Biddle
BIG AND TALL — JCPenney: Plus & Tall store
BIG BUCKS — AOL News: Lottery Results & State
BIG HORN — Bighorn Computer Services [Web site]
BIG TENT — Christianity Online: Big Tent Revival from Forefront Records
BIG TENT REVIVAL — Christianity Online: Big Tent Revival from Forefront Records
BIG TWIN — Cycle World: Big Twin All Harley Magazine
BIKE BRATS — onQ: Bike Brats [Web site]
BIKENET — The Bicycle Network
BILING — Accounts and Billing
BILL — Accounts and Billing
BILL CLINTON — AOL News: Bill Clinton News Special
BILL SIMMONS — Digital City Boston: Sports Guy
BILLING — Accounts and Billing
BILLLING — Accounts and Billing
BINGO — RabbitJack's Casino
BINGO ZONE — Bingo Zone [Web site]
BINGO ZONE.COM — Bingo Zone [Web site]
BIOBYTE — OWL Magazine: Mighty Mites Animals
BIOBYTES — OWL Magazine: Mighty Mites Animals
BIONET — OWL Magazine: Mighty Mites Animals
BIOTECH — AOL WorkPlace: Biotechnology Community
BIOTECHNOLOGY — AOL WorkPlace: Biotechnology Community
BIPOLAR — AOL Health: Bipolar Disorder/Manic Depression
BIPOLAR DISORDER — AOL Health: Bipolar Disorder/Manic Depression
BIRD — AOL Interests: Pets
BIRD WATCHER — AOL Interests: Bird Watching & Info
BIRD WATCHERS — AOL Interests: Bird Watching & Info
BIRDERS — AOL Interests: Bird Watching & Info
BIRDING — AOL Interests: Bird Watching & Info

BIRDS — AOL Interests: Pets
BIRDS ONQ — onQ: Pets
BIRTH CONTROL — AOL Health: Birth Control
BIS ONQ — onQ: Bisexual
BISEXUAL — AOL Lifestyles: Gay & Lesbian
BISEXUAL CHAT — onQ: Chat and Conferences
BISEXUAL ONQ — onQ: Bisexual
BISSAU — AOL International: Guinea-Bissau
BISTRO — AOL International: The Bistro
BITECASTER — AOL Canada: Eventcasters Media Production
BITECASTERS — AOL Canada: Eventcasters Media Production
BIZ — AOL Entertainment: The Biz
BIZ FUNDS — Fund Focus
BIZ HOURLY — AOL News: Business News Summary
BIZ NEWS — Business News Center
BIZ PRESS — Digital City Dallas: The Business Press
BIZ TALK — AOL WorkPlace: Business Talk
BIZ TIP — AOL WorkPlace: Today's Business Tips
BIZ UPDATE — AOL News: Business News Summary
BIZ WEEK — Business Week Online
BK — AOL International: Bosnia Herzegovina
BL — Buddy Lists: Setup
BLACK — NetNoir
BLACK AMERICAN — NetNoir
BLACK BAYOU — Antagonist, Inc.: Black Bayou
BLACK EROTICA — NetNoir: Black Erotica
BLACK HISTORY REFERENCE — AOL Research & Learn: Black History
    Reference
BLACK LIBERATION MONTH — NetNoir
BLACK REFERENCE — AOL Research & Learn: Black History Reference
BLACK TEENS — NetNoir: Black Teens
BLACK VOICES — Orlando Sentinel Online: Black Voices
BLACK VOICES CHICAGO — Digital City Chicago: Black Voices
BLACK VOICES HAMPTON ROADS — Digital City Hampton Roads: Black
    Voices
BLACK VOICES HR — Digital City Hampton Roads: Black Voices
BLACK-AMERICAN — NetNoir
BLACKBERRY — Blackberry Creek
BLACKBERRY CREEK — Blackberry Creek
BLACKHAWKS — Chicago Blackhawks
BLACKSBURG — Digital City Roanoke [Web site]
BLAIR — Digital City San Diego: Columnist Tom Blair
BLAZERS — Portland Trailblazers
BLEACH — Christianity Online: Bleach by Forefront Records
BLIND — DisABILITIES Community Forum
BLIZZARD — Today's Weather
BLM — NetNoir

BLOCKBUSTER — Blockbuster Music Store
BLOCKBUSTER MUSIC — Blockbuster Music Store
BLOOD DISORDERS — Better Health: Blood Disorders
BLOOD PRESSURE — AOL Health: Hypertension/High Blood Pressure
BLOOMBERG — Bloomberg Financial Markets
BLOOMBERG NEWS — Bloomberg Financial Markets
BLS — Christianity Online: Bibleland Software
BLUE EYES — Entertainment Asylum: Club Sinatra
BLUE JAYS — Toronto Blue Jays
BMG — BMG Records
BMXTRA — BMXtra Online Magazine [Web site]
BOARDS ONQ — onQ: Message Boards
BOAT — AOL Interests: Boating & Sailing
BOAT DEALERS — AOL WorkPlace: Boat & Yacht Dealers Community
BOAT US — Boat Owners Association of the U.S.
BOATING — AOL Interests: Boating & Sailing
BOATING MAGAZINE — Boating Magazine Online
BOATS — AOL Interests: Boating & Sailing
BOB B — AOL Canada: Beaty & Company
BOB BEATY — AOL Canada: Beaty & Company
BOB DYLAN — Bob Dylan: Celebrating 35 Years of Inspiration
BOB WALDRON — Digital City Los Angeles: Bob Waldron's Real Estate
BODY BUILDING — AOL Sports: Fitness
BODY SHOP — The Body Shop: Skin and Hair Care Products
BOGLE — Vanguard Group Mutual Funds [Web site]
BOLIVIA — AOL International: Bolivia
BOMB TRIAL — Digital City Denver: McVeigh Trial Coverage [Web site]
BON JOVI — AOL MusicSpace: Jon Bon Jovi
BOND FUNDS — Mutual Funds Center: Bond Funds
BONDAGE ONQ — onQ: Leather Community
BONES — AOL Health: Bones, Joints & Muscles
BONJOUR — AOL International: Bonjour Paris
BONJOUR PARIS — AOL International: Bonjour Paris
BONNIE — Find Bonnie: Lost Dog [Web site]
BOOK — AOL Entertainment: Books
BOOK BAG — AOL Teens: The Book Bag
BOOK CENTRAL — Book Central
BOOK LIVE — QuickStart: Learn About AOL Live
BOOK OF THE DAY — AOL Book of the Day
BOOK REPORT — The Book Report
BOOK REPORTER — The Book Report
BOOK REVIEW — The Book Report
BOOK SHELF — AOL Store: Book Shop
BOOK SHOP — AOL Store: Book Shop
BOOKACCINO — The Book Report: Chat Rooms
BOOKKEEPING — AOL WorkPlace: Desktop Publishing, Word
    Processing & Office Services

BOOKNOTES — Barron's Booknotes
BOOKS & CULTURE STORE — Christianity Online: Books & Culture
  [Web site]
BOOKS & MUSIC SHOP — AOL Shopping: Books, Music & Video
BOOMERS — Ages & Stages: Baby Boomers
BOS MARKETPLACE — Digital City Boston: Marketplace
BOSNA — AOL International: Bosnia Herzegovina
BOSNIA — AOL International: Bosnia Herzegovina
BOSOX — Boston Red Sox
BOSTON — Digital City Boston
BOSTON 5 STAR — Digital City Boston: High Style Living
BOSTON AUTO — Digital City Boston: AutoGuide
BOSTON AUTO GUY — Digital City Boston: Auto Guy
BOSTON AUTOGUIDE — Digital City Boston: AutoGuide
BOSTON AUTOMART — Digital City Boston: AutoGuide
BOSTON AUTOS — Digital City Boston: AutoGuide
BOSTON BARS — Digital City Boston: Spirits of Massachusetts
BOSTON BEER — Digital City Boston: Beer
BOSTON BEER GUY — Digital City Boston: Beer Guy
BOSTON BEST & WORST — Digital City Boston: Bests & Worsts
BOSTON BEST — Digital City Boston: Bests & Worsts
BOSTON BISEXUAL — Digital City Boston: Gay & Lesbian
BOSTON BLUES — Digital City Boston: Music
BOSTON BOATING — Digital City Boston: Boating & Fishing
BOSTON BOOZE — Digital City Boston: Spirits of Massachusetts
BOSTON BREW — Digital City Boston: Beer
BOSTON BREW PUBS — Digital City Boston: Beer
BOSTON BRUINS — Boston Bruins
BOSTON BUSINESS — Digital City Boston: Directory [Web site]
BOSTON BUSINESS DIRECTORY — Digital City Boston: Directory
  [Web site]
BOSTON BUSINESSES — Digital City Boston: Directory [Web site]
BOSTON CAR — Digital City Boston: AutoGuide
BOSTON CAREERS — Digital City Boston: Employment Classifieds
BOSTON CARS — Digital City Boston: AutoGuide
BOSTON CELTICS — Boston Celtics
BOSTON CIGAR GUY — Digital City Boston: Cigar Guy
BOSTON CLASSICAL — Digital City Boston: Music
BOSTON CLASSIFIEDS — Digital City Boston: Classifieds [Web site]
BOSTON CONTEST — Digital City Boston: Contests
BOSTON CONTESTS — Digital City Boston: Contests
BOSTON CROSSWORD — Digital City Boston: Crossword Puzzles
BOSTON CROSSWORD PUZZLES — Digital City Boston: Crossword
  Puzzles
BOSTON CROSSWORDS — Digital City Boston: Crossword Puzzles!
BOSTON CRUISING — Digital City Boston: Sailing
BOSTON DINING — Digital City Boston: Dining

BOSTON DIRECTORY — Digital City Boston: Directory [Web site]
BOSTON DRINKS — Digital City Boston: Spirits of Massachusetts
BOSTON EMPLOYERS — Digital City Boston: Employers
BOSTON EMPLOYMENT — Digital City Boston: Employment Classifieds
BOSTON FISHING — Digital City Boston: Boating & Fishing
BOSTON FLICKS — Digital City Boston: Movies
BOSTON FLIX — Digital City Boston: Movies
BOSTON FOLK — Digital City Boston: Music
BOSTON GAY — Digital City Boston: Gay & Lesbian
BOSTON GLOBE — Boston Globe [Web site]
BOSTON GOLF — Digital City Boston: Golf
BOSTON HERALD — Digital City Boston: Boston Herald Newspaper
BOSTON JAZZ — Digital City Boston: Music
BOSTON JOBS — Digital City Boston: Employment Classifieds
BOSTON JOKE OF THE DAY — Digital City Boston: Joke of the Day
BOSTON JOKES — Digital City Boston: Joke of the Day
BOSTON KIDS — Digital City Boston: Kid Safe
BOSTON KIDS SAFE — Digital City Boston: Kid Safe
BOSTON LESBIAN — Digital City Boston: Gay & Lesbian
BOSTON LINKS — Digital City Boston: Golf
BOSTON LOCAL NEWS — Digital City Boston: Local News
BOSTON MARKET — Digital City Boston: Marketplace
BOSTON MARKETPLACE — Digital City Boston: Marketplace
BOSTON MOVIE GUY — Digital City Boston: Movie Guy
BOSTON MOVIES — Digital City Boston: Movies
BOSTON MUSIC — Digital City Boston: Music
BOSTON NEIGHBORHOOD GUY — Digital City Boston: Neighborhood
   Guy
BOSTON NEIGHBORHOODS — Digital City Boston: Neighborhood Guy
BOSTON OFF BEAT — Digital City Boston: Offbeat Boston
BOSTON ONLINE — Digital City Boston
BOSTON RED SOX — Boston Red Sox
BOSTON RELO — Digital City Boston: Relocation Guide
BOSTON RELOCATE — Digital City Boston: Relocation Guide
BOSTON RELOCATION — Digital City Boston: Relocation Guide
BOSTON ROCK — Digital City Boston: Music
BOSTON SAIL — Digital City Boston: Sailing
BOSTON SAILING — Digital City Boston: Sailing
BOSTON SHOPPING — Digital City Boston: Marketplace
BOSTON SKIING — Digital City Boston: Snow Sports
BOSTON SOAPBOX — Digital City Boston: Opinion Area
BOSTON SPIRITS — Digital City Boston: Spirits and Fancy Drinks
BOSTON SPORTS GUY — Digital City Boston: Sports Guy
BOSTON STATE HOUSE NEWS — Digital City Boston: Politics Today
BOSTON STYLE — Digital City Boston: Style Eye
BOSTON SUDS — Digital City Boston: Beer
BOSTON THEATER GUY — Digital City Boston: Theater Guy

BOSTON TRANSFER — Digital City Boston: Relocation Guide
BOSTON TRAVEL GUY — Digital City Boston: Travel Guy
BOSTON TV — Digital City Boston: TV Gal
BOSTON VINEYARDS — Digital City Boston: Wine
BOSTON WANT ADS — Digital City Boston: Classifieds [Web site]
BOSTON WINE — Digital City Boston: Wine
BOSTON WINE GUY — Digital City Boston: Wine Guy
BOSTON WORST — Digital City Boston: Bests & Worsts
BOSTON YELLOW PAGES — Digital City Boston: Directory [Web site]
BOTSWANA — AOL International: Botswana
BOULDER — Digital City Denver
BOULDER BYTES — Digital City Denver: Boulder Forum
BOW HUNTING — Hunting Broadcast Network
BOWL — AOL Live
BOWL WATCH — Real Fans College Football: Bowls
BOWLING — AOL Sports: Bowling
BOXER JAM — Boxer*Jam Game Shows
BOXER*JAM — Boxer*Jam Game Shows
BOXING — AOL Sports: Boxing
BOYS 2 MEN — Boyz to Men [Web site]
BOYS II MEN — Boyz to Men [Web site]
BOYS TORQUE — AOL UK: Car Channel Gallery
BOYZ 2 MEN — Boyz to Men [Web site]
BOYZ II MEN — Boyz to Men [Web site]
BP MARKETPLACE — Backpacker Magazine: Marketplace
BPS — BPS Software
BPS SOFTWARE — BPS Software
BRADFORD — AOL UK: Local Life in Bradford
BRADFORD EOL — AOL UK: Local Life in Bradford
BRADFORD X — Collectibles Today Net: Bradford Exchange [Web site]
BRAIN — AOL Health: Brain & Nervous System Disorders
BRAINBUSTER — NTN Online: Brainbuster Trivia
BRAINSTORMS — Brainstorm Products
BRANDS FOR LESS — Brands For Less [Web site]
BRAVES — Atlanta Braves
BRAZIL — AOL International: Brazil
BREAST CANCER — AOL Health: Breast Cancer
BREAST CANCER AWARE — Better Health: Breast Cancer
BREAST CANCER AWARENESS — Better Health: Breast Cancer
BREASTFEEDING — AOL Families: Babies
BREIFING — Briefing.com Business Commentary [Web site]
BREW GUY — Digital City Boston: Beer Guy
BREWERS — Milwaukee Brewers
BRICKYARD — ABC Sports: Brickyard 400
BRICKYARD 400 — ABC Sports: Brickyard 400
BRIDE — The Knot: Weddings for the Real World
BRIDGE — Bridge Games

BRIDGES — Digital City San Francisco: WWWomen
BRIEFING — Briefing.com Business Commentary [Web site]
BRIEFING COM — Briefing.com Business Commentary [Web site]
BRIEFING.COM — Briefing.com Business Commentary [Web site]
BRIEFINGS — Briefing.com Business Commentary [Web site]
BRIGHTON — AOL UK: Local Life
BRING YOUR OWN ACCESS — Accessing AOL: Bring Your Own Access
BRISTOL — AOL UK: Local Life
BRISTOL EOL — AOL UK: Bristol Events Online
BRIT AWARDS — AOL UK: British Music Awards
BRITISH SCHOOL — AOL UK: Forum for UK Secondary Schools
BRITISH SCHOOLS — AOL UK: Forum for UK Secondary Schools
BRITS — AOL UK: British Music Awards
BRM — Bank Rate Monitor
BROADBAND — AOL Cable Center: Cable Modems
BROADWAY — BuyBroadway Theatrical Events, Souvenirs & Weblinks
   [Web site]
BRODERBUND — Broderbund Software Online
BROKER — AOL Brokerage Center
BROKERAGE — AOL Brokerage Center
BROKERAGE CENTRE — AOL Canada: Brokerage Centre
BRONCOS — Denver Broncos
BRONSON PINCHOT — Warner Brothers Online: Meego
BROTHER BIDDLE — Christianity Online: Brother Biddle
BROWARD BLACK VOICES — Black Voices: South Florida
BROWSER — Microsoft Internet Explorer Browser Software
BROWSER AM — Thrive@Healthy Living: Amazon.com Books
   [Web site]
BROWSER HF — Thrive@Healthy Living: Healthfront.com [Web site]
BRUINS — Boston Bruins
BRUINS HOCKEY — Boston Bruins
BRUTES — Military City Online: Villains of Fact and Fiction
BSH — Back Street Heroes Motorcycle Magazine
BTC — Business Travel Center
BUCHALTER'S RECRUITING — Digital City Orlando Sports: College
   Recruiting [Web site]
BUCKS — Milwaukee Bucks
BUCKY — AOL Sports: Newsletter
BUDAPEST — Time Out: Travel Guide to Budapest [Web site]
BUDDHA — AOL Spirituality: Buddhism
BUDDHISM — AOL Spirituality: Buddhism
BUDDHIST — AOL Spirituality: Buddhism
BUDDIES — Buddy Lists
BUDDIES ONLINE — Learn AOL: Buddy Lists
BUDDY — Buddy Lists
BUDDY INVITE — Learn AOL: Buddy Lists Invite
BUDDY LIST — Buddy Lists

BUDDY LISTS — Buddy Lists
BUDDY MAIN — Buddy Lists
BUDDY ONLINE — Learn AOL: Buddy Lists
BUDDY VIEW — Buddy Lists: Buddy View
BUFFALO — Digital City Buffalo: Local News
BUFFALO GROVE — Digital City Chicago: Buffalo Grove [Web site]
BUFFALO LOCAL NEWS — Digital City Buffalo: Local News
BUFFALO NEWS — Digital City Buffalo: Local News
BUGJUICE — BMG Records: BUGjuice [Web site]
BUILDERS — AOL WorkPlace: Contractor's Community
BUILDING CONTRACTOR — AOL WorkPlace: Contractor's Community
BUJUMBURA — AOL International: Burundi
BULGARIA — AOL International: Bulgaria
BULIMIA — AOL Health: Eating Disorders
BULLETS — Washington Wizards
BULLS — Chicago Bulls
BURKINA FASO — AOL International: Burkina Faso
BURT — Digital City Denver: Burt Automotive Network
BURUNDI — AOL International: Burundi
BUS HOURLY — AOL News: Hourly Business News Summary
BUS KNOW HOW — AOL WorkPlace: Business Know-How Forum
BUS NEWS — AOL Business News Center
BUS NEWS CENTER — AOL Business News Center
BUS UPDATE — AOL News: Business News Summary
BUSINESS — AOL WorkPlace channel
BUSINESS CHAT — AOL WorkPlace: Business Chats
BUSINESS CHAT — AOL WorkPlace: Business Talk
BUSINESS CLASSIFIEDS — AOL Classifieds: Business
BUSINESS DIRECTORY — AOL Business Directory [Web site]
BUSINESS FIND — AOL NetFind: Find a Business
BUSINESS FORUM — AOL Computing: Applications Forum
BUSINESS INSIDER — Herb Greenberg's Bizinsider Column [Web site]
BUSINESS KNOW HOW — AOL WorkPlace: Business Know-How Forum
BUSINESS KNOW-HOW — AOL WorkPlace: Business Know-How Forum
BUSINESS LISTINGS — AOL Business Directory [Web site]
BUSINESS NEWS — AOL Business News Center
BUSINESS ONQ — onQ: Business Center
BUSINESS OWNERS TOOLS — CCH Business Owner's Toolkit [Web site]
BUSINESS PERK — AOL WorkPlace: Business Perks
BUSINESS PERKS — AOL WorkPlace: Business Perks
BUSINESS PRESS — Digital City Dallas: The Business Press Online
BUSINESS PRODUCTS — AOL WorkPlace: Business Services
BUSINESS REFERENCE — AOL WorkPlace: Tools & Reference
BUSINESS SCHOOL — Kaplan Online -or- The Princeton Review
BUSINESS SEARCH — AOL NetFind: Find a Business
BUSINESS SENSE — Business Sense Software
BUSINESS SERVCIES — AOL WorkPlace: Business Services

BUSINESS SERVICES — AOL WorkPlace: Business Services
BUSINESS STORE — AOL WorkPlace: Business Services
BUSINESS STRATEGIES — AOL WorkPlace: Business Know-How Forum
BUSINESS SUMMARY — AOL News: Business News Summary
BUSINESS TALK — AOL WorkPlace: Business Chat
BUSINESS TALK — AOL WorkPlace: Business Talk
BUSINESS TAX — AOL WorkPlace: Business Tax Center
BUSINESS TAXES — AOL WorkPlace: Business Tax Center
BUSINESS TIP — AOL WorkPlace: Today's Business Tips
BUSINESS TIPS — AOL WorkPlace: Today's Business Tips
BUSINESS TOOLKIT — CCH Business Owner's Toolkit [Web site]
BUSINESS TOOLS — AOL WorkPlace: Tools & Reference
BUSINESS TRAVEL CENTER — AOL Travel: Business Travel Center
BUSINESS TRAVELER — AOL Travel: Business Travel Center
<u>BUSINESS TRAVELLER</u> — AOL Travel: Business Travel Center
BUSINESS UPDATE — AOL News: Business News Summary
BUSINESS WEEK — Business Week Magazine
BUTTHEAD — MTV Online
BUY — AOL Shopping channel
BUY COMPUTER — AOL Classifieds: Computing
BUYBROADWAY — BuyBroadway Theatrical Events, Souvenirs &
    Weblinks [Web site]
BUYER'S GUIDE — AOL Computing: Buyer's Guide
BUYERS GUIDE — AOL Computing: Buyer's Guide
BUYING GUIDE — AOL Computing: Buyer's Guide
BUZZ — Buzzsaw
BUZZSAW — Buzzsaw
BV — Buddy Lists: Buddy View
BV CHAT — Black Voices: Chat
BV CHICAGO — Digital City Chicago: Black Voices
BV CLUBS — Black Voices: Club and Interests
BV GAY — Black Voices: Gay and Lesbian
BV HAMPTON ROADS — Black Voices: Hampton Roads
BV HR — Black Voices: Hampton Roads
BV SOUTH FLORIDA — Black Voices: South Florida
BW — Business Week Magazine
BW ONLINE — Business Week Magazine
BW SEARCH — Business Week Magazine: Search & Downloads
BWOL — Motley Fool: Baseball Workshop Online
BYOA — Accessing AOL: Bring Your Own Access
C — AOL Computing: Development Forum
C CABIN — AOL Canada: The Country Cabin
C! — AOL Computing channel
C&S — AOL Computing channel
C&S GRAD — AOL Computing: Graduation [seasonal]
C&S GREETINGS — AOL Computing: Easter Greetings [seasonal]
C&S LIVE — AOL Computing: Events

C&S MAIL — AOL Computing: Suggestions and Comments
C&S NEWS — AOL Computing: The Weekly Byte
C/D CHAT — Car and Driver: Live!
CA — AOL Credit Alert
CA ELECTION — Digital City Los Angeles: Voting Guide
CA NET — Digital City Denver: Colorado Advisory Network
CA SWEEPS — AOL Credit Alert: Sweepstakes
CA VOTING — Digital City Los Angeles: Voting Guide
CABLE — AOL Cable Center
CABLE MODEM — Cable
CAD — AOL Computing: Computer Aided Drafting
CADD — AOL Computing: Computer Aided Drafting
CADILLAC — Cadillac [Web site]
CAESARS — Digital City Philadelphia: Boxing
CAF EH — AOL Canada: The Back Bacon Caf-eh Chat Room
CAFE — AOL Shopping: Gourmet Gifts
CAFE BOOKA — Book Central: Cafe Booka Reading Groups
CAFFE STARBUCKS — Starbucks Coffee
CALHOUN — Digital City Denver: Westword News & Arts Weekly
CALIFORNIA ANGELS — California Angels
CALL AOL — AOL Member Services: Telephone Support Numbers
CAMBODIA — AOL International: Cambodia
CAMBRIDGE — AOL UK: Local Life
CAMDEN — Digital City South Jersey
CAMERA — AOL Interests: Pictures
CAMEROON — AOL International: Cameroon
CAMPUS — AOL Research & Learn: Online Campus
CAMPUS LIFE — Christianity Online: Campus Life
CAN — Digital City Denver: Colorado Advisory Network
CAN THANKSGIVING — AOL Canada: Thanksgiving @ AOL [seasonal]
CAN'T TAKE IT — AOL LifeStages: Can't Take it With You
CAN'T TAKE IT WITH YOU — AOL LifeStages: Can't Take it With You
CANADA — AOL Canada
CANADA BOARDS — AOL Canada: Message Boards
CANADA CHAT — AOL Canada: Chat
CANADA ICE STORM — AOL Canada: The Great Ice Storm
CANADA INTERNET — AOL Canada: Internet
CANADA MESSAGE — AOL Canada: Message Boards
CANADA MESSAGE BOARDS — AOL Canada: Message Boards
CANADA MSG — AOL Canada: Message Boards
CANADA REFERENCE — AOL Canada: Reference Bookshelf
CANADA ROUND TABLE — AOL Canada: Chat
CANADA SHIRTHAND — AOL Canada: Smileys and Shorthand
CANADA SMILES — AOL Canada: Smileys and Shorthand
CANADA SMILEYS — AOL Canada: Smileys and Shorthand
CANADA SUMMER — AOL Canada: Spring into Summer
CANADA TOUR — AOL Canada: Guided Tour

CANADA TRUST — AOL Canada: Canada Trust
CANADIAN — AOL Canada
CANADIAN GEOGRAPHIC — AOL Canada: Canadian Geographic
CANADIAN ICE — AOL Canada: The Great Ice Storm
CANADIAN ICE STORM — AOL Canada: The Great Ice Storm
CANADIAN LIVING — AOL Canada: Canadian Living Magazine
CANADIAN SNOWBIRD — AOL Canada: Canadian Snowbird Association
CANADIAN SNOWBIRDS — AOL Canada: Canadian Snowbird
    Association
CANADIENS — Montreal Canadiens
CANCEL — AOL Member Services: Canceling Your AOL Membership
CANCER — AOL Health: Cancer
CANNON PRINTERS — Canon [Web site]
CANON PRINTERS — Canon [Web site]
CANON USA — Canon [Web site]
CANT TAKE IT WITH YOU — AOL LifeStages: Can't Take it With You
CANTERBURY — AOL UK: Local Life
CANUCKS — AOL Canada: Vancouver Canucks
CANUKS — AOL Canada: Vancouver Canucks
CAP LAF — Digital City Washington: Laughter
CAP LAUGH — Digital City Washington: Laughter
CAP RES — Digital City Washington: Discount Hotel Reservations
    [Web site]
CAPE VERDE — AOL International: Cape Verde
CAPITAL — AOL News: Political News
CAPITALS — The Washington Capitals
CAPITOL LAUGHTER — Digital City Washington: Capitol Laughter
CAPITOL RESERVATIONS — Digital City Washington: Discount Hotel
    Reservations [Web site]
CAPRICORN — Horoscope Selections
CAPS — The Washington Capitals
CAPTURED — AOL Australia: Great Sporting Moments on Film [Web
    site]
CAR — AOL Interests: Auto Center
CAR AND DRIVER — Car and Driver Online
CAR AND DRIVER CHAT — Car and Driver: Chat
CAR BUYING — AOL Interests: Auto Center
CAR CARE — AOL Interests: Car Care
CAR GURU — Wheels: Ask the Expert
CAR HELP — Wheels: Ask the Expert
CAR INFO — AOL Interests: Auto Center
CAR PHOTOS — Wheels: Photo Exchange
CAR RENTAL — AOL Travel: Car Rental Center
CAR SUMMARY — AOL Interests: Auto Center
CARD — Card Selections
CARD ONQ — onQ: Tzabaco
CARDIFF — AOL UK: Local Life

CARDIFF EOL — AOL UK: Wales Events Online
CARDINALS — St. Louis Cardinals
CARD-O-MATIC — American Greetings Online Greetings
CARDOMATIC — American Greetings Online Greetings
CARDS — Card Selections
CAREER — AOL WorkPlace: Your Career
CAREER ADVANCEMENT — AOL WorkPlace: Advancing Your Career
CAREER CHANGE — AOL WorkPlace: Changing Direction
CAREER RESEARCH — AOL WorkPlace: Career Research
CAREER STUDY — AOL WorkPlace: Career Research
CAREERPATH — CareerPath [Web site]
CAREERPATH.COM — CareerPath [Web site]
CAREERS — AOL WorkPlace: Your Career
CAREGIVER — AOL Health: Parenting & Caregiving
CAREGIVING — AOL Health: Parenting & Caregiving
CARLISLE — AOL UK: Local Life
CARLISLE EOL — AOL UK: Far North Events Online
CARMEN — Broderbund Software Online
CAROLINA HURRICANES — Carolina Hurricanes
CAROLINA PANTHERS — Carolina Panthers
CARPAL TUNNEL — AOL Health: Carpal Tunnel Syndrome
CARPETS — AOL WorkPlace: Carpet & Rug Dealers Community
CARS — AOL Interests: Auto Center
CARTOON — Cartoon Network World
CARTOON NETWORK — Cartoon Network World
CARTOONS — Cartoon Network World
CASE — A Letter From Steve Case
CASH CONVERTER — The Universal Currency Converter [Web site]
CASINO — Casino Poker Games
CASINO POKER — GameStorm: Online Casino
CASSINI — Space Exploration Online: Cassini Mission to Saturn
CASTING — The Casting Forum
CASTING ZONE — The Casting Forum
CAT ONQ — onQ: Pets
CATALINA — Digital City Los Angeles: Guide to Catalina
CATALINA ISLAND — Digital City Los Angeles: Guide to Catalina
CATALINA ISLAND SERVICES — Digital City Los Angeles: Guide to
    Catalina
CATALOG — AOL Shopping: Sale Catalog
CATALOGS — AOL Shopping: Sale Catalog
CATARACT — AOL Health: Cataracts
CATARACTS — AOL Health: Cataracts
CATCHWORD — GameStorm: CatchWord
CATERING — AOL WorkPlace: Catering Community
CATFISH — Digital City Denver: The Catfish Report
CATFISH REPORT — Digital City Denver: The Catfish Report
CATH NEWS — Catholic Community: News

CATHOLIC — AOL Lifestyles: Catholic Community
CATHOLIC NEWS — Christianity Online: Catholic News Service
CATHOLIC NEWS SERVICE — Christianity Online: Catholic News Service
CATS — AOL Interests: Pets
CAVITIES — AOL Health: Tooth Decay & Cavities
CAVS — Cleveland Cavaliers
CB — AOL Research & Learn : College Board [Web site]
CBD — Commerce Business Daily
CBE — Christianity Online: Christians for Biblical Equality
CBG — Christianity Online: Church Buyers Guide
CBS — CBS.com [Web site]
CBS ATLANTA — Digital City Atlanta: WGNX-TV Channel 46
CBS.COM — CBS.com [Web site]
CC BIZ — AOL Computing: Company Connection - Business
CC BUSINESS — AOL Computing: Company Connection -
  Business
CC CHATS — AOL Computing: Events
CC DEV — AOL Computing: Company Connection - Development
CC ED — AOL Computing: Company Connection - Education
CC GF — Collectable Cards
CC HARD — AOL Computing: Company Connection -
  Hardware
CC LIVE — AOL Computing: Events
CC MEDIA — AOL Computing: Company Connection - Multimedia
<u>CC MULTIMED</u> — AOL Computing: Company Connection - Mulitmedia
CC MULTIMEDIA — AOL Computing: Company Connection - Multimedia
CC MUSIC — AOL Computing: Company Connection - Music & Sound
CC PROGRAMMING — AOL Computing: Company Connection -
  Development
CC PROGS — AOL Computing: Company Connection - Development
CC SONGS — AOL Computing: Company Connection - Music & Sound
CC TELECOM — AOL Computing: Company Connection -
  Telecom/Networking
CC TOYOTA — Digital City Philadelphia: Central City Toyota
CC TUNES — AOL Computing: Company Connection - Music & Sound
CC UTIL — AOL Computing: Company Connection - Utilities
CC UTILITIES — AOL Computing: Company Connection - Utilities
CC UTILS — AOL Computing: Company Connection - Utilities
CCA — Crossman's Computer America [Web site]
CCC GAMES — AOL Computing: Company Connection -
  Games
CCE — Concise Columbia Encyclopedia
CCFL — AOL Grandstand: Simulation Football
CCG — Christianity Online: Christian College Guide
CCH — CCH Business Owner's Toolkit [Web site]
CCH TOOLKIT — CCH Business Owner's Toolkit [Web site]
CCH TOOLS — CCH Business Owner's Toolkit [Web site]

CD 94 — CD 94.7 Classic Rock
CD CHAT — Car and Driver: Chat
CDN — AOL Canada
CDN 40 — AOL Canada: Over 40 Chat
CDN AUTO TOUR — AOL Canada: Guided Tour
CDN BOARDS — AOL Canada: Message Boards
CDN CHAT — AOL Canada: Chat
CDN DISCLOSURE — AOL Canada: Disclosure Financial Services
CDN ELECTION CHAT — AOL Canada: Election Chat
CDN GEO — AOL Canada: Canadian Geographic
CDN GEO BOUTIQUE — AOL Canada: Canadian Geographic Boutique
CDN GEO STORE — AOL Canada: Canadian Geographic Boutique
CDN INTERNATIONAL — AOL Canada: International channel
CDN INTL — AOL Canada: International channel
CDN LIVING — AOL Canada: Canadian Living Magazine [Web site]
CDN MORE SPORT — AOL Canada: More Sports
CDN MORE SPORTS — AOL Canada: More Sports
CDN NTN — AOL Canada: NTN Trivia
CDN RECIPE — AOL Canada: Canadian Living Magazine
CDN REFERENCE — AOL Canada: Reference Bookshelf
CDN SHEENA — AOL Canada: It's Sheena the Shopping Queen
CDN SHORTHAND — AOL Canada: Smileys and Shorthand
CDN SMILES — AOL Canada: Smileys and Shorthand
CDN SMILEYS — AOL Canada: Smileys and Shorthand
CDN SUMMER — AOL Canada: Spring into Summer [seasonal]
CDN THANKSGIVING — AOL Canada: Thanksgiving @ AOL [seasonal]
CDN TOUR — AOL Canada: Guided Tour
CDN TRIVIA — AOL Canada: NTN Trivia
CDNOW — CDNow.com [Web site]
CDNOW.COM — CDNow.com [Web site]
CDOOR — Digital City Washington: Cellar Door Entertainment
CD-ROM — AOL Computing: Superstore
CE — AOL Computing: Products 2000
CEC — Christianity Online: Christian Education Center
CECIL — The Straight Dope
CECIL ADAMS — The Straight Dope
CEL — Japanimation Station!
CELEB — AOL Entertainment channel
CELEB CONTEST — AOL Celebrity "You've Got Mail" Voice Gallery
CELEB MAIL — AOL Celebrity "You've Got Mail" Voice Gallery
CELEB SWEEPS — AOL Celebrity "You've Got Mail" Voice Gallery
CELEBRITIES — AOL Entertainment channel
CELEBRITY — AOL Entertainment channel
CELEBRITY CONTEST — You've Got Mail Celebrity Contest
CELEBRITY CRUISE — Cruise Critic: Vacation Contest
CELEBRITY FIX — AOL Entertainment: Daily Fix
CELEBRITY GALLERY — You've Got Mail Celebrity Contest

CELEBRITY MAIL — You've Got Mail Celebrity Contest
CELEBRITY SWEEPSTAKES — You've Got Mail Celebrity Contest
CELEBRITY VOICES — You've Got Mail Celebrity Contest
CELEBS — AOL Entertainment channel
CELL DOOR — Digital City Washington: Cellar Door Entertainment
CELLAR DOOR — Digital City Washington: Cellar Door Entertainment
CELLAR DOOR ENTERTAINMENT — Digital City Washington: Cellar Door
    Entertainment
CELLULAR — AOL Computing: Products 2000
CELLULAR PHONE — AOL Computing: Products 2000
CELTICS — Boston Celtics
CELTICS BASKETBALL — Boston Celtics
CELTS — Boston Celtics
CENSUS — U.S. Census Bureau [Web site]
CENTER B.M.W — Digital City Los Angeles: Center BMW
CENTER BMW — Digital City Los Angeles: Center BMW
CENTER STAGE — AOL Live
**CENTRAL AFRICAN REPUBLIC — AOL International: Central
    African Republic**
CENTURA HEALTH — Centura Health
CENTURY 21 — Century 21 Communities
CEP — Council on Economic Priorities
CEREBRAL PALSY — AOL Health: Cerebral Palsy
CERES — Ameritrade
CERVICAL CANCER — AOL Health: Cervical Cancer
CESKA REPUBLIKA — AOL International: Czech Republic
CF GAME DAY — AOL College Football: Game Day Fan Central
CF GD — AOL College Football: Game Day Fan Central
CFB GAME DAY — AOL College Football: Game Day Fan Central
CFB GD — AOL College Football: Game Day Fan Central
CFU — CultureFinder: University
CG — AOL Canada: Canadian Geographic
CG STORE — AOL Canada: Canadian Geographic Boutique
CGEO — AOL Canada: Canadian Geographic
CH — Christianity Online: Christian History
CH MUSIC — Columbia House [Web site]
CH VIDEO — Columbia House [Web site]
CHAD — AOL International: Chad
CHAMPION — One Hanes Place
CHAMPIONS BUICK — Digital City Atlanta: Champion's Buick
CHANGE — Change Your Billing Information
CHANGE OF ADDRESS — Change Your Billing Information
CHANGE PASSWORD — Change Your Password
CHANGE PROFILE — AOL Member Directory
CHANGING CAREERS — AOL WorkPlace: Changing Direction
CHANGING DIRECTION — AOL WorkPlace: Changing Direction
CHANGING JOBS — AOL WorkPlace: Changing Direction

CHANGING WORKPLACE — AOL WorkPlace channel
CHANNEL — AOL Channels
CHANNEL 17 — Digital City Philadelphia: WPHL-TV
CHANNEL 17 SPORTS — Digital City Philadelphia: WB 17 Sports Radio
CHANNEL 46 — WGNX-TV Channel 46
CHANNEL 56 — Digital City Boston: WB 56
CHANNEL A — Channel A: Modern Asian Living
CHANNEL GUIDE — AOL Channel Guide
CHANNELS — AOL Channels
CHANUKAH — Jewish Community: Chanukah [seasonal]
CHARLES SCHWAB — Charles Schwab Online
CHARLOTTE — Digital City Charlotte
CHARLOTTE LOCAL NEWS — Digital City Charlotte: Local News
CHARLOTTE NEWS — Digital City Charlotte: Local News
CHARTER — Charter Schools
CHARTER SCHOOL — Charter Schools
CHARTER SCHOOLS — Charter Schools
CHARTOMATIC — AOL Personal Finance: Chart-O-Matic
CHASE — The Chase Manhattan Bank
CHASE 24 — The Chase Manhattan Bank
CHASE BANK — The Chase Manhattan Bank
CHASE MANHATTAN — The Chase Manhattan Bank
CHAT & MESSAGES — AOL Computing: Chat & Messages
CHAT — People Connection
CHAT AND MESSAGES — AOL Computing: Chat & Messages
CHAT BEACH — Digital City San Diego: Chat
CHAT DC — DC Comics: Chat
CHAT HELP — AOL Member Services: People Connection Help
CHAT ONQ — onQ: Chat
CHAT SEARCH — People Connection: Search Featured Chats
CHAT UK — AOL UK: Chat
CHATTER — People Connection: Chatter Newsletter
CHATTERS — People Connection: Chatter Newsletter
CHEAP LUNCH — Digital City Dallas-Fort Worth: CheapLunch
CHEAP SEATS — AOL UK: Planet Ealing Cheat Seats
CHEERLEADER — AOL Sports: Cheerleading Forum
CHEERLEADERS — AOL Sports: Cheerleading Forum
CHEERLEADING — AOL Sports: Cheerleading Forum
CHEF — Chef's Catalog Store
CHEF'S — Chef's Catalog Store
CHEFS — Chef's Catalog Store
CHEF'S CATALOG — Chef's Catalog Store
CHEFS CATALOG — Chef's Catalog Store
CHEFS CLOTHING — Professional Cutlery Direct
CHEM BANK — The Chase Manhattan Bank
CHEMICAL — The Chase Manhattan Bank
CHEMICAL BANK — The Chase Manhattan Bank

CHERRY — AOL Canada: Don Cherry Online
CHESROWN — Digital City Denver: Chesrown Autos
CHESROWN POSSE — Digital City Denver: Chesrown Autos
CHESS — The Chess Club
CHESTER — AOL UK: Local Life
CHESTER EOL — AOL UK: North West Events Online
CHICAGO — Digital City Chicago
CHICAGO BLACK VOICES — Black Voices: Chicago
CHICAGO BV — Black Voices: Chicago
CHICAGO CALENDAR — Digital City Chicago: Weather
CHICAGO COMPUTING — Digital City Chicago: Computing
CHICAGO CUBS — Chicago Cubs
CHICAGO ED — Digital City Chicago: Education Forum
CHICAGO EDUCATE — Digital City Chicago: Education Forum
CHICAGO EDUCATION — Digital City Chicago: Education Forum
CHICAGO FILES — Digital City Chicago: Download Libraries
CHICAGO FOOD — Digital City Chicago: Food
CHICAGO GOVERNMENT — Digital City Chicago: Government Guide
CHICAGO GOVT — Digital City Chicago: Government Guide
CHICAGO INDEX — Digital City Chicago: Index
CHICAGO KIDS — Digital City Chicago: KidSafe
CHICAGO KIDS SAFE — Digital City Chicago: KidSafe
CHICAGO LOCAL NEWS — Digital City Chicago: Local News
CHICAGO M4M — PlanetOut: FantasyMan Island in Chicago
CHICAGO MAGAZINE — Digital City Chicago: Chicago Magazine
CHICAGO MALL — Digital City Chicago: Mall
CHICAGO MARKETPLACE — Digital City Chicago: Marketplace
CHICAGO MEDIA — Digital City Chicago: Radio and TV
CHICAGO MESSAGES — Digital City Chicago: Message Boards
CHICAGO OUTDOORS — Digital City Chicago: Outdoors
CHICAGO PERSONALS — Digital City Chicago: Personals
CHICAGO PLANNER — Digital City Chicago: Plan Your Week
CHICAGO RADIO AND TV — Digital City Chicago: Radio and TV
CHICAGO SCIFI — Digital City Chicago: Sci Fi Forum
CHICAGO SUBURBS — Digital City Chicago: Suburbs
CHICAGO SYMPHONY — Digital City Chicago: Chicago Symphony
   Orchestra
CHICAGO TECH — Digital City Chicago: Computing
CHICAGO TICKET — Digital City Chicago: Ticketmaster
CHICAGO TONIGHT — Digital City Chicago: Chicago Tonight
CHICAGO TRAFFIC — Digital City Chicago: Traffic
CHICAGO TRIBUNE — Chicago Online: Chicago Tribune
CHICAGO WEATHER — Digital City Chicago: Weather
CHICKEN SOUP CONTEST — Chicken Soup for the Soul
CHILD CARE — AOL WorkPlace: Child & Elder Care
CHILD SAFETY — AOL Neighborhood Watch
CHILDREN — AOL Kids Only channel

CHILDREN HEALTH — AOL Health: Children's Health
CHILDREN'S DICTIONARY — Merriam-Webster's Kids Dictionary
CHILDRENS DICTIONARY — Merriam-Webster's Kids Dictionary
CHILDREN'S HEALTH — AOL Health: Children's Health
CHILDRENS HEALTH — AOL Health: Children's Health
CHILE — AOL International: Chile
CHINA — AOL International: China
CHIROPRACTIC — AOL Health: Chiropractic
CHIT CHAT — Digital City Washington: Chit Chat
CHLAMYDIA — AOL Health: Chlamydia
CHOCOLATIER — Godiva Chocolatier
CHOICE — Marketing Preferences
CHOICES — Marketing Preferences
CHOLESTEROL — AOL Health: High Cholesterol
CHOOSE PDA — AOL Computing: PDA Buyers Guide
CHOPARA — Deepak Chopra
CHOPRA — Deepak Chopra
CHORTLE — AOL News: Daily Chuckle
CHRIST — AOL Lifestyles: Christianity
CHRISTIAN — AOL Lifestyles: Christianity
CHRISTIAN CAREER CENTER — Christianity Online: Career Center
CHRISTIAN COLLEGES — Christianity Online: Colleges & Seminaries
CHRISTIAN CONNECTION — Christianity Online: Chat & Live Events
CHRISTIAN EDUCATION — Christian Education Center
CHRISTIAN EQUALITY — Christianity Online: Christians for Biblical
    Equality
CHRISTIAN FAMILIES — Christianity Online: Family
CHRISTIAN FAMILY — Christianity Online: Family
CHRISTIAN HISTORY — Christianity Online: Christian History
CHRISTIAN KID — Christianity Online: Kids
CHRISTIAN KIDS — Christianity Online: Kids
CHRISTIAN MAGAZINES — Christianity Online: Newsstand
CHRISTIAN MAN — Christianity Online: Men
CHRISTIAN MEDIA — Christianity Online: Christian Media Source
CHRISTIAN MEN — Christianity Online: Men
CHRISTIAN MUSIC — Christianity Online: Christian Music
CHRISTIAN PRODUCTS — Christianity Online: Christian Products Center
CHRISTIAN READER — Christianity Online: Christian Reader
CHRISTIAN SINGLE — Christianity Online: Singles
CHRISTIAN SINGLES — Christianity Online: Singles
CHRISTIAN STUDENTS — Christianity Online: Student Hangout
CHRISTIAN WOMAN — Christianity Online: Women
CHRISTIAN WOMEN — Christianity Online: Women
CHRISTIANITY — Christianity Area of Religion & Beliefs
CHRISTIANITY ONLINE — Christianity Online
CHRISTIANITY TODAY — Christianity Today
CHRISTIANS FOR BIBLICAL EQUALITY — Christians for Biblical Equality

CHRISTMAS — Holidays @ AOL [seasonal]
CHRISTOPHER HOMES — Digital City Los Angeles: Christopher Homes
CHRONIC BRONCHITIS — AOL Health: Chronic Bronchitis
CHRONIC FATIGUE — AOL Health: Chronic Fatigue Syndrome
CHRONIC PAIN — AOL Health: Chronic Pain
CHURCH IMPRESSIONS — Christianity Online: Church Impressions
CHURCH LEADERS — Christianity Online: Church Leaders Network
CHURCH LEADERS NETWORK — Christianity Online: Church Leaders
    Network
CHURCH LOCATOR — Christianity Online: Church Locator
CHURCH SUPPLIERS — Christianity Online: Church Buyers Guide
CHURCH SUPPLIES — Christianity Online: Church Buyers Guide
CI — Music Boulevard: Classical Insites [Web site]
CICC — AOL Grandstand: Simulation Auto Racing
CIE 98 UPDATES — Compton's Interactive Encyclopedia: Monthly
    Updater
CIGAR — AOL Influence: The Good Life
CIGAR AFICIONADO — Cigar Aficionado [Web site]
CIGAR BOSTON — Digital City Boston: Cigar Guy
CIGAR GUY — Digital City Boston: Cigar Guy
CIGARS — AOL Influence: The Good Life
CINCINNATI — Digital City Cincinnati
CINCINNATI LOCAL NEWS — Digital City Cincinnati: Local News
CINCINNATI NEWS — Digital City Cincinnati: Local News
CINCINNATI REDS — Cincinnati Reds
CINDY — Cindy Adams: Queen of Gourmet Gossip
CINDY ADAMS — Cindy Adams: Queen of Gourmet Gossip
CINDY CENTRAL — EXTRA Online: Cindy Margolis
CINDY MARGOLIS — EXTRA Online: Cindy Margolis
CINEMA CHAT — AOL Entertainment: Cinema Chat
CINEMAN — EXTRA Online: Film Reviews
CINEMATIQUE — Digital City Twin Cities: Movie Maven
CIRILLO — onQ: Business Center
CITI — Citibank
CITIBANK — Citibank
CITICORP — Citibank
CITIES — Digital City Online
CITRUS BOWL — AOL Sports: Citrus Bowl
CITY — Digital City Online
CITY LIMITS — Digital City Denver: Westword News & Arts Weekly
CITY WISE — Digital City New York: Citywise
CITY.NET — Excite Travel [Web site]
CIUDAD DIGITAL — Digital City Dallas-Fort Worth: Hispanic
CIUDAD DIGITAL DFW — Digital City Dallas-Fort Worth: Hispanic
CIVIL WAR — The Civil War Forum
**CIVIL WAR JOURNAL — The History Channel: Civil War
    Journal**

CJJ — Coalition for Juvenile Justice
CL — Christianity Online: Campus Life
CLAN — Gathering of the Clans
CLAN GATHER — Gathering of the Clans
CLANCY — The Book Report: Tom Clancy's Politika
CLANS — Gathering of the Clans
CLANS GATHER — Gathering of the Clans
CLARIS — FileMaker, Inc.
CLARK — Digital City Philadelphia: Digital DeLeon
CLARK DELEON — Digital City Philadelphia: Digital DeLeon
CLASS ACTION — AOL International: Swiss Banks and Nazi Plunder
CLASS SCHEDULE — AOL Computing: Class Schedule
CLASSES — AOL Computing: Class Schedule
CLASSIC CARDS — Classic Card Games
CLASSICAL — AOL Entertainment: Classical Music
CLASSICAL MUSIC — AOL Entertainment: Classical Music
CLASSIFIED — AOL Classifieds
CLASSIFIEDS — AOL Classifieds
CLASSIFIEDS ONLINE — AOL Classifieds
CLASSIFIEDS ONQ — onQ: Classifieds
CLASSROOM — AOL Computing: Online Classroom
CLAY PIPES — AOL Canada: Stephen Bray Clay Pipes
CLE — Christianity Online: Chat & Live Events
CLEANERS — AOL WorkPlace: Cleaning & Janitorial Services
CLEANING — AOL WorkPlace: Cleaning & Janitorial Services
CLEARANCE — Fragrance Counter: Clearance
CLEVELAND — Digital City Cleveland
CLEVELAND DIGC — Digital City Cleveland
CLEVELAND INDIANS — Cleveland Indians
CLEVELAND LOCAL NEWS — Digital City Cleveland: Local News
CLEVELAND NEWS — Digital City Cleveland: Local News
CLICK & GO 4.0 — AOL Click & Go
CLICK AND GO — AOL Click & Go
CLICK AND GO 4.0 — AOL Click & Go
CLICK ART — Broderbund: Click Art Collection
CLICKED ON — Digital City Twin Cities: Newsletter
CLINTON — AOL News: Bill Clinton News Special
CLIPPERS — Los Angeles Clippers
CLIPS — Los Angeles Clippers
CLN — Christianity Online: Church Leaders Network
CLOCK — Online Clock
CLOSED FUNDS — AOL Personal Finance: Wide World of Closed-End
    Funds
CLOSED-END FUNDS — AOL Personal Finance: Wide World of Closed-
    End Funds
CLUB BAJA — The Latina Tag Team
CLUB GLOBAL — Club.Global

CLUB SINATRA — Entertainment Asylum: Club Sinatra
CLUB SKIRTS — Digital City San Francisco: Lesbian Bars
CLUB.GLOBAl — Club.Global
CLUBCALL — AOL UK: Clubcall Football
CLUELESS — AOL Teens: Cher's Clueless Site
CMB — Chase Manhattan Bank
CMC — Creative Musicians Coalition
CMP — CMPNet For AOL [Web site]
CMPNET — CMPNet For AOL [Web site]
CMS — Christianity Online: Christian Media Source
CN SEARCH — Christianity Online: Christianity.net Web Search
    [Web site]
CN.NET — Christianity Online: Christianity.net [Web site]
CNMCD3 — Compton's Bible Connection
CNS — Christianity Online: Catholic News Service
CNW — Cartoon Network
CO — Christianity Online
CO A&I — Christianity Online: Associations & Interests
CO AI — Christianity Online: Associations & Interests
CO AMY — Christianity Online: Friends Of Amy
CO ASSOCIATIONS — Christianity Online: Associations
CO B&C — Christianity Online: Books and Culture
CO BC — Christianity Online: Books and Culture
CO BLEACH — Christianity Online: Bleach Main Page
CO BLS — Christianity Online: Bibleland Software
CO BOOKS & CULTURE — Christianity Online: Books and Culture
CO BOOKS — Christianity Online: Christian Media Source
CO BOOKS AND CULTURE — Christianity Online: Books and Culture
CO BRO — Christianity Online: Brother Biddle's Archives
CO BUYERS — Christianity Online: Church Buyers Guide
CO CAREER CENTER — Christianity Online: Career Center
CO CHRISTMAS — Christianity Online: Merry Christmas [seasonal]
CO CLASSIFIEDS — Christianity Online: Classifieds
CO CLS — Christianity Online: Classifieds
CO COLLEGES — Christianity Online: Colleges and Seminaries
CO COMMENTARIES — Christianity Online: News Commentaries
CO CONTEST — Christianity Online: Contests
CO CONTESTS — Christianity Online: Contests
CO DEVOS — Christianity Online: Spiritual Devotion
CO EASTER — Christianity Online: Easter [seasonal]
CO EDUCATION — Christianity Online: Christian Education Center
CO FAMILIES — Christianity Online: Family
CO FAMILY — Christianity Online: Family
CO FUN — Christianity Online: Contests
CO FUN STUFF — Christianity Online: Contests
CO HANGOUT — Christianity Online: Student Hangout
CO HELP — Christianity Online: Help & Info

CO HOLI — Christianity Online: Holidays & Special Events
CO HOLIDAY — Christianity Online: Holidays & Special Events
CO HOLIDAYS — Christianity Online: Holidays & Special Events
CO HOME SCHOOLING — Christianity Online: Home Schooling
CO HS — Christianity Online: Home Schooling
CO INFO — Christianity Online: Help & Info
CO INTERESTS — Christianity Online: Associations
CO KID — Christianity Online: Kids
CO KIDS — Christianity Online: Kids
CO LIVE — Christianity Online: Chat & Live Events
CO MAN — Christianity Online: Men
CO MC — Christianity Online: Merry Christmas [seasonal]
CO MEDIA — Christianity Online: Media
CO MEN — Christianity Online: Men
CO MERRY CHRISTMAS — Christianity Online: Merry Christmas
    [seasonal]
CO MUS — Christianity Online: Christian Music
CO MUSIC — Christianity Online: Christian Music
CO NEWS — Christianity Online: Newsstand
CO NEWSLETTERS — Christianity Online: Newsletters
CO NEWSLTRS — Christianity Online: Newsletters
CO NEWSSTAND — Christianity Online: Newsstand
CO PRODUCTS — Christianity Online: Christian Products Center
CO SENIOR — Christianity Online: Senior Citizens
CO SENIORS — Christianity Online: Senior Citizens
CO SINGLE — Christianity Online: Singles
CO SINGLES — Christianity Online: Singles
CO SKILLET — Christianity Online: Skillet
CO SMALLTOWN POETS — Christianity Online: Smalltown Poets
CO SOFTWARE — Christianity Online: Software Store
CO SPN — Christianity Online: Sponsor Hotlist
CO SPONSOR — Christianity Online: Sponsor Hotlist
CO SPONSORS — Christianity Online: Sponsor Hotlist
CO STEWARDSHIP — Christianity Online: Global Stewardship
CO STUDENT — Christianity Online: Students
CO SW — Christianity Online: Software Store
CO TEEN — Christianity Online: Students
CO TEENS — Christianity Online: Students
CO WOMAN — Christianity Online: Women
CO WOMEN — Christianity Online: Women
CO YOUTH — Christianity Online: Students
CO.NET — Christianity Online: Christianity.Net [Web site]
COACH HOLLY — Digital City New York: Love Coach
COACH STEPHEN — Digital City New York: Love Coach
COACH'S CORNER — AOL Sports: Coach Tom Bass
COAST GUARD — Military City Online
COBB — Digital City Philadelphia: Gary Cobb -or- Cobb Group Online

COBB GROUP — Cobb Group Online
COCC — Christianity Online: Career Center
COCO — Christianity Online: Community Connection
COCOA — AOL Shopping: Gourmet Gifts
COFFEE — Starbucks Coffee
COGS — Christianity Online: Global Stewardship
COIN OP — AOL WorkPlace: Vending and Coin-Op Machines
COIN-OP — AOL WorkPlace: Vending and Coin-Op Machines
COL — Christianity Online
COL ENTERTAINMENT — Chicago Tribune: Local Entertainment Guide
COL SON — Christianity Online: News Commentaries
COL TICKET — Digital City Chicago: Ticketmaster
COL TRAFFIC — Digital City Chicago: Traffic Updates
COLD — AOL Health: Common Cold
COLD SORE — AOL Health: Cold & Canker Sores & Fever Blisters
COLE — Christianity Online: News Commentaries
COLISEUM — AOL Live
COLITIS — AOL Health: Colitis
COLLECT CARDS — Collectable Cards
COLLECT CARDS — Collectable Cards
COLLEGE — AOL Research & Learn: College Education
COLLEGE ALOHA BOWL — AOL Sports: Aloha Bowl
COLLEGE BASKETBALL — AOL Sports: College Basketball
COLLEGE BOARD — College Board Online [Web site]
COLLEGE BOARDS — College Board Online [Web site]
COLLEGE CITRUS BOWL — AOL Sports: Citrus Bowl
COLLEGE COTTON BOWL — AOL Sports: Cotton Bowl
COLLEGE ENTRY EXAMS — College Board [Web site]
COLLEGE FIESTA BOWL — AOL Sports: Fiesta Bowl
COLLEGE HOOPS — AOL Sports: College Basketball
COLLEGE HOOPS SCORES — NCAA Basketball Scores [seasonal]
COLLEGE INSIGHTCOM BOWL — Real Fans: Insight.com Bowl
COLLEGE ONLINE — Simon & Schuster College Online
COLLEGE ORANGE BOWL — Orange Bowl
COLLEGE PREP — College Education Online [Web site]
COLLEGE ROSE BOWL — AOL Sports: Rose Bowl
COLLEGE SUGAR BOWL — AOL Sports: Sugar Bowl
COLLEGE SUN BOWL — AOL Sports: Sun Bowl
COLLEGE TESTS — College Board Online [Web site]
COLLEGIATE — Merriam-Webster Collegiate Dictionary
COLOGNE — Fragrance Counter
COLOMBIA — AOL International: Colombia
COLOR WEATHER MAPS — Today's Weather
COLORADO ADVISORY NETWORK — Colorado Advisory Network
COLORADO APARTMENTS — Digital City Denver: Real Estate
COLORADO BUILDERS — Digital City Denver: New Homes

COLORADO EMPLOYMENT — Digital City Denver: Employment Classifieds

COLORADO FAIRWAYS — Digital City Denver: Golfing

COLORADO GOLF — Digital City Denver: Golfing

COLORADO HISTORY — Digital City Denver: OutWest Online

COLORADO LINKS — Digital City Denver: Golfing

COLORADO LOTTERY — Digital City Denver: Lottery

COLORADO MORTGAGE RATES — Digital City Denver: Mortgage Information and Rates

COLORADO MORTGAGES — Digital City Denver: Mortgage Information and Rates

COLORADO MUSEUM — Digital City Denver: Museum of Natural History

COLORADO NEW HOMES — Digital City Denver: New Homes

COLORADO REAL ESTATE — Digital City Denver: Real Estate

COLORADO REAL ESTATE ADVICE — Digital City Denver: Real Estate

COLORADO REAL ESTATE INFO — Digital City Denver: Real Estate

COLORADO REALTORS — Digital City Denver: Real Estate

COLORADO RENTALS — Digital City Denver: Real Estate

COLORADO ROCKIES — Colorado Rockies

COLORADO SPECIAL NEEDS — Colorado Advisory Network

COLORADO TREKKING — Digital City Denver: Outdoors

COLORECTAL CANCER — AOL Health: Colorectal Cancer

COLORWORKS — The Knot: M&M Colorworks

COLOSSEUM — Online Gaming Forum: The Arena and Parthenon

COLUMBIA — Columbia Selections

COLUMBIA MUSIC — Columbia House: Music [Web site]

COLUMBIA VIDEO — Columbia House: Video [Web site]

COLUMBUS — Digital City Columbus: Local News

COLUMBUS LOCAL NEWS — Digital City Columbus: Local News

COLUMBUS NEWS — Digital City Columbus: Local News

COMEDY — AOL Entertainment: Etcetera

COMEDY CLINIC — Entertainment Asylum: Comedy Clinic

COMEDYSPORTZ — Digital City Washington: ComedySportz Fun Factory

COMIC BOOKS — Comic Books

COMICS — Comic Books

COMING ATTRACTIONS — AOL Live: Coming Attractions

COMING OUT — onQ: Coming Out

COMMENTARY — AOL Influence channel

COMMERCIAL WEB SITE — AOL PrimeHost

COMMON COLD — AOL Health: Common Cold

COMMUNICATIONS — AOL Computing: Telecom & Networking Forums

COMMUNITIES — AOL Lifestyles: Communities

COMMUNITIES INC — Communities, Inc. [Web site]

COMMUNITIES ONQ — onQ: Communities

COMMUNITY — AOL Lifestyles: Communities

COMMUNITY CENTER — People Connection: The Community Center
COMMUNITY CONNECTION — Christianity Online: Community Connection
COMMUNITY DCSD — Digital City San Diego: Community
COMMUNITY NEWS — Community News
COMMUNITY ONQ — onQ: Communities
COMMUNITY SD — Digital City San Diego Community
COMMUNITY UPDATE — Community Update
COMOROS — AOL International: Comoros
COMP CLASS — AOL Computing: Online Classroom
COMP LIVE — AOL Computing: Events
COMP TAX — AOL Computing: Tax Software
COMPANIES — AOL Computing: Companies
COMPANY CONNECTION — AOL Computing: Companies
COMPANY PROFILE — Hoover's Company Profiles
COMPANY PROFILES — Hoover's Company Profiles
COMPAQ — Compaq on AOL
COMPLETED SYSTEMS — Digital City Washington: Completed Systems
COMPOSER — The Composer's Coffeehouse
COMPOSER'S — The Composer's Coffeehouse
COMPOSERS — The Composer's Coffeehouse
COMPTON'S — Compton's Encyclopedia Online
COMPTONS — Compton's Encyclopedia Online [Web site]
COMPTONS ENCYCLOPEDIA — Compton's Encyclopedia Online [Web site]
COMPTON'S MAIN — Compton's Encyclopedia Online [Web site]
COMPTONS MAIN — Compton's Encyclopedia Online [Web site]
COMPTONS NEW MEDIA — Compton's Encyclopedia Online
COMPTONS SOFTWARE — Compton's Software Library
COMPTONS SOFTWARE LIB — Compton's Software Library [Web site]
COMPU FOURTH — AOL Computing: Independence Day Downloads [seasonal]
COMPU GRAD — AOL Computing: Graduation [seasonal]
COMPU LIVE — AOL Computing: Events
COMPU STORE — AOL Computer: Superstore
COMPU TAX — AOL Computing: Tax Software
COMPUTER — AOL Computing channel
COMPUTER AMERICA — Crossman's Computer America [Web site]
COMPUTER ARTIST — AOL Computing: Computer Paint Artists
COMPUTER ARTISTS — AOL Computing: Computer Paint Artists
COMPUTER ASSISTED — AOL Computing: Computer Aided Drafting
COMPUTER CHAT — AOL Computing: Chat & Messages
COMPUTER CLASS — AOL Computing: Online Classroom
COMPUTER CLASSES — AOL Computing: Online Classroom
COMPUTER CLASSIFIEDS — AOL Computing: Classifieds
COMPUTER COMPANIES — AOL Computing: Companies
COMPUTER CURRENTS — Computer Currents

COMPUTER EQUIPMENT — AOL Computing: Classifieds
COMPUTER FORUM — AOL Computing channel
COMPUTER GAMES — Computer Game Selections
COMPUTER GUIDE — AOL Computing: New Computer User's Guide
COMPUTER HARDWARE — AOL Shopping: Computer Hardware
COMPUTER HELP — AOL Computing: Help Desk
COMPUTER INSURANCE — Safeware Online: Computer Insurance
COMPUTER LAW — CyberLaw/CyberLex
COMPUTER LISTINGS — AOL Computing: Classifieds
COMPUTER MAGAZINES — AOL Computing: Newsstand
COMPUTER MAGS — AOL Computing: Newsstand
COMPUTER NEWS — AOL Computing: Newsstand
COMPUTER REFERENCE — AOL Research & Learn: Computing
    Reference
COMPUTER REVIEW — AOL Computing: Buyer's Guide
COMPUTER REVIEWS — AOL Computing: Buyer's Guide
COMPUTER SCHOOL — AOL Computing:: Online Classroom
COMPUTER SHOP — AOL Store: Computers
COMPUTER STORE — AOL Store: Computer
COMPUTER SUPERSTORE — AOL Computing: Superstore
COMPUTER TIPS — AOL Computing: Tips
COMPUTERS & SOFTWARE — AOL Computing channel
COMPUTERS — AOL Computing channel
COMPUTERS AND SOFTWARE — AOL Computing channel
COMPUTERS TIP — AOL Computing: Tips
COMPUTERVILLE — Digital City San Francisco: Computer Currents
COMPUTING & SOFTWARE — AOL Computing channel
COMPUTING — AOL Computing channel
COMPUTING CHAT — AOL Computing: Chat & Messages
COMPUTING CHATS — AOL Computing: Events
COMPUTING CLASSIFIEDS — AOL Computing: Classifieds
COMPUTING COMPANIES — AOL Computing: Companies
COMPUTING FORUMS — AOL Computing: Help Desk
COMPUTING HELP — AOL Computing: Help Selections
COMPUTING LIVE — AOL Computing: Events
COMPUTING MESSAGE BOARDS — AOL Computing: Chat & Messages
COMPUTING MESSAGES — AOL Computing: Chat & Messages
COMPUTING NEWS — AOL Computing: Newsstand
COMPUTING NEWSSTAND — AOL Computing: Newsstand
COMPUTING REFERENCE — AOL Research & Learn: Computing
    Reference
COMPUTING SEARCH — AOL Computing: Search and Explore
COMPUTING SEARCH AND EXPLORE — AOL Computing: Search and
    Explore
COMPUTING STORE — AOL Computing: Superstore
COMPUTING SUPERSTORE — AOL Computing: Superstore
COMPUTING T — Christianity Online: Computing Today Magazine

COMPUTING TIP — AOL Computing: Tips
COMPUTING TIPS — AOL Computing: Tips
COMPUTING TODAY — Christianity Online: Computing Today Magazine
CONAN — EXTRA Online: Conan
CONDITION OF SERVICE — AOL UK: Conditions of Service
CONDITIONS OF SERVICE — AOL UK: Conditions of Service
CONFERENCE — AOL Computing: Events
CONGO — AOL International: Congo
CONGRESS — AOL News: Politics
CONGRESSIONAL — Congressional Quarterly [Web site]
CONICELLI — Digital City Philadelphia: Conicelli AutoPlex
CONNECT — Accessing America Online
CONNECTED FAMILY — Connected Family [Web site]
CONNECTING — Accessing America Online
CONNECTION — Accessing America Online
CONNECTION HELP — AOL Member Services: Connecting to AOL
CONNECTIX — Connectix Corporation
CONRADO BONDOC — Digital City Boston: Style Eye
CONSIDERING LILY — Forefront Records: Considering Lily
CONSULTANT — AOL WorkPlace: Consultants
CONSULTING — AOL WorkPlace: Consulting
CONSUMER AP — AOL News: Consumer Briefs
CONSUMER BRIEFS — AOL News: Consumer Briefs
CONSUMER DIRECT — Consumer Direct [Web site]
CONSUMER ELECTRONICS — AOL Computing: Products 2000
CONSUMER INFO — AOL Research & Learn: Consumer & Money
    Matters
CONSUMER REPORTS — Consumer Reports
CONSUMER WIRES — AOL News: Consumer Briefs
CONTAGIOUS — AOL Health: Infectious & Contagious Diseases
CONTEST — Contest Area
CONTEST AREA — Contest Area
CONTEST WB — WB Online: Contest
CONTESTS — Contest Area
CONTESTS WB — WB Online: Contest
CONTICELLI — Digital City Philadelphia: Conicelli AutoPlex
CONTINENTAL — Continental Airlines [Web site]
CONTINENTAL AIRLINES — Continental Airlines [Web site]
CONTRACTORS — AOL WorkPlace: Contractor's Community
CONTRASTING WORDS — Merriam-Webster Thesaurus
CONVERTER — The Universal Currency Converter [Web site]
COOK — AOL Interests: Food
COOK ISLANDS — AOL International: Cook Islands
COOKBOOK — AOL Interests: Food
COOKBOOKS — AOL Interests: Food
COOKING — AOL Interests: Food
COOL NEWS — AOL News: What's Hot

CORBIS — Corbis Media
CORBIS MEDIA — Corbis Media
CORCODILOS — Motley Fool: Ask the Headhunter
CORCORAN — Corcoran School of Art Online
COREL — Corel Business Solutions
COREL WP — AOL Computing: Word Processing Applications
CORELDRAW — AOL Computing: CorelDRAW SIG
CORPORATE PROFILES — Hoover's Company Profiles
CORRECTION — AOL Personal Finance: Market Correction
COS — AOL UK: Conditions of Service
COS UK — AOL UK: Conditions of Service
COSM — Christianity Online: Christian Products Center
COSMETICS PLUS — Cosmetics Plus Store
COSMIC — AOL Studios [Web site]
COSTA RICA — AOL International: Costa Rica
<u>COTE D'LVORE</u> — AOL International: Ivory Coast
COTTON BOWL — AOL Sports: Cotton Bowl
COUNTDOWN — NTN Trivia: Countdown
COUNTDOWN 2000 — Millennium Countdown
COUNTRIES — AOL International: Country Information Search
COUNTRY — AOL Entertainment: Country Music
COUNTRY CABIN — AOL Canada: The Country Cabin
COUNTRY INFO — AOL International: Country Information Search
COUNTRY INFO SEARCH — AOL International: Country Information Search
COUNTRY MB — Music Boulevard: Country.com [Web site]
COUNTRY SEARCH — AOL International: Country Information Search
COUREUR — AOL Canada: Coureur de Business
COURSES — AOL Research & Learn: Courses Online
COURT TV — Court TV
COURTESY ACURA — Digital City Denver: Courtesy Acura and Isuzu
COURTESY ISUZU — Digital City Denver: Courtesy Acura and Isuzu
COURTROOM TELEVISION — Court TV Law Center
COURTSIDE — Real Fans: Courtside
COVENTRY — AOL UK: Local Life
COVER TO COVER — Thrive@Healthy Living: Shape
COWLES — Cowles Business Media [Web site]
COWLES SIMBA — Cowles Business Media [Web site]
COYOTES — Phoenix Coyotes
CP — AOL Health: Cerebral Palsy
CPM — Christianity Online: Computing Today Magazine
CQ — Congressional Quarterly [Web site]
CR — Christian Reader -or- Consumer Reports -or- Company Research
CRAFT MAG — Crafts Magazine
CRAFT MAGAZINE — Crafts Magazine
CRAFTS MAGAZINE — Crafts Magazine
CRAIG CROSSMAN — Crossman's Computer America [Web site]

CRAIN'S SMALL BIZ — Crain's Small Business
CRAINS SMALL BIZ — Crain's Small Business
CRAIN'S SMALL BUSINESS — Crain's Small Business
CRAINS SMALL BUSINESS — Crain's Small Business
CRAZY CREEK — Backpacker Magazine: Marketplace
CREATIVE ARTS — AOL WorkPlace: Creative Arts Forum
CREATIVE LOAFING — Digital City Atlanta: Creative Loafing
CREATIVE SCRAPBOOKING — Creative Scrapbooking
CREDIT — AOL Credit Request
CREDIT ALERT — AOL Credit Alert
CREDIT REQUEST — AOL Credit Request
CREEKER — AOL Kids Only: Blackberry Creek
CRESTAR — Crestar Bank
CRESTAR BANK — Crestar Bank
CRIBBAGE — WorldPlay: Cribbage
CRICKETER — AOL UK: The Cricketer Magazine
CRIMESWEEP — Digital City Philadelphia: CrimeSweep
CRITIC — Critics Inc.
CRITICAL MASS — Digital City San Francisco: News & Weather
CRITICAL MASS SF — Digital City San Francisco: News & Weather
CRITICS — Critics Inc.
CRITICS CHOICE — Critics Inc.
CROATIA — AOL International: Croatia
CROHN'S — AOL Health: Crohn's Disease
CROHNS — AOL Health: Crohn's Disease
CROHN'S DISEASE — AOL Health: Crohn's Disease
CROHNS DISEASE — AOL Health: Crohn's Disease
CROSS COUNTRY — AOL Travel: Planning a Cross Country Road Trip
CROSSMAN — Crossman's Computer America [Web site]
CROSSWORD — New York Times: Crossword Puzzles
CROSSWORDS — New York Times: Crossword Puzzles
CRUISE — Cruise Critic
CRUISE CONTEST — Cruise Critic: Vacation Contest
CRUISE CRITIC — Cruise Critic
CRUISE CRITICS — Cruise Critic
CRUISE HOLIDAYS — Digital City San Francisco: Cruise Holidays
CRUISES — Cruise Critic
CRUSADER — Digital City Philadelphia: Crime Sweep
CRUTCHFIELD — Crutchfield [Web site]
CRYSTAL — Crystal Dynamics
CRYSTAL BALL — Crystal Ball
CRYSTAL LAKE — Digital City Crystal Lake [Web site]
CS GREETING — AOL Computing: Easter Greetings [seasonal]
CS GREETINGS — AOL Computing: Easter Greetings [seasonal]
CS MAIL — AOL Computing: Suggestions and Comments
CS MARKETPLACE — AOL Computing: Superstore
CS ONQ — onQ: CyberShop

CS STORE — AOL Computing: Superstore
CS TIP — AOL Computing: Tips
CS TIPS — AOL Computing: Tips
CS@MO — Moms Online: CyberShop
CSB — Crain's Small Business
CSO — Digital City Chicago: Chicago Symphony Orchestra [Web site]
C-SPAN — C-SPAN Online
CSPAN — C-SPAN Online
CSPAN BUS — C-SPAN: In the Classroom
CSPAN CLASS — C-SPAN: In the Classroom
CSPAN CLASSROOM — C-SPAN: In the Classroom
CSPAN ONLINE — C-SPAN Online
CSPAN SCHOOLS — C-SPAN: In the Classroom
CSS — AOL Computing: Superstore
CSSL — Cyber Sports Strat League
CT — Christianity Online: Christianity Today
CTN — Collectibles Today [Web site]
CUBA — AOL International: Cuba
CUBA 2 — AOL International: Cuba
CUBBIES — Chicago Cubs
CUBS — Chicago Cubs
CUC AUTO — Credit Alert: Sweepstakes
CUC CREDIT — Credit Alert: Sweepstakes
CUC SHOP — Credit Alert: Sweepstakes
CUC TRAVEL — AOL Travel: Vacation Sweepstakes
CUISINE ONQ — onQ: Home & Garden
CULTURAL — AOL Influence: Arts and Leisure
CULTURE — AOL Influence: Arts and Leisure
CULTUREFINDER U — CultureFinder: University
CULTUREFINDER UNIVERSITY — CultureFinder: University
CUMBRIA EOL — AOL UK: Far North Events Online
CUPQUEST — Digital City Philadelphia: Flyers Cup Coverage
CURRENCY CONVERTER — The Universal Currency Converter
    [Web site]
CURRENT CONDITIONS — Today's Weather
CURRENT EVENTS — Today's News
CURRENTS — Computer Currents
CURRENTS LA — Digital City Los Angeles: Computer Currents
CURRENTS SF — Digital City San Francisco: Computer Currents
CUSTOMER SERVICE — AOL Member Services
CUTTING EDGE — NESN Cutting Edge
CW — Cycle World
CW STORE — Creative Wonders Store
CWUG — Claris Works Users Group [Web site]
CYBER COMIC — Marvel Comics
CYBER COMICS — Marvel Comics
CYBER SERIALS — Soap Opera Forum

CYBER SOAP — Soap Opera Forum
CYBER SOAPS — Soap Opera Forum
CYBER SPORTS — Cyber Sports Simulation Leagues
CYBER WEDDING — Love@AOL: CyberVows
CYBER WEDDINGS — Love@AOL: CyberVows
CYBERCON — Digital Words Online: CyberCon Chicago
CYBERCOUPLES — Love@AOL: Love~Links
CYBERIAN — Cyberian Outpost [Web site]
CYBERIAN OUTPOST — Cyberian Outpost [Web site]
CYBERLAW — CyberLaw/CyberLex
CYBERLEX — CyberLaw/CyberLex
CYBERMEDIA — CyberMedia [Web site]
CYBERSALON — Cybersalon
CYBERSHOP — CyberShop
CYBERSHOPPING — CyberShop
CYBERSTOCK — Hoover's Cyberstocks [Web site]
CYBERSTOCKS — Hoover's Cyberstocks [Web site]
CYBERVOW — Love@AOL: CyberVows
CYBERVOWS — Love@AOL: CyberVows
CYBERZINES — AOL Entertainment: Digizine Sites on the Web
CYCLE VIDEO — Cycle World: Cycle Video
CYCLE WORLD — Cycle World
CYCLING — AOL Sports: Bicycling
CYG — AOL Canada: Cygnet Travel
CYG TRAV — AOL Canada: Cygnet Travel
CYGNET — AOL Canada: Cygnet Travel
CYGNET TRAVEL — AOL Canada: Cygnet Travel
CYGNETTRAVEL — AOL Canada: Cygnet Travel
CYMRU — AOL UK: Virtual Wales Travel Area
CYPRUS — AOL International: Cyprus
CYSTIC FIBROSIS — AOL Health: Cystic Fibrosis
CYSTITIS — AOL Health: Cystitis
CZECH REPUBLIC — AOL International: Czech Republic
CZECHY — AOL International: Czech Republic
**D A LA CARD — Digital City Chicago: Dining a la Card
 [Web site]**
D AND B — Dun & Bradstreet@AOL [Web site]
D BUSINESS — Digital City South Florida: Business News from
 dbusiness.com
D CHERRY — AOL Canada: Don Cherry Online
D FALLS — Engage Games Online: Darkness Falls
D&B — Dun & Bradstreet@AOL [Web site]
DAD — AOL Families
DADE BLACK VOICES — Black Voices: South Florida
DADS — AOL Families
DADS AND GRADS — Digital City: Dads & Grads [seasonal]
DAFFY — WB Online: Daffy Duck Turns 60!

DAFFY DUCK — WB Online: Daffy Duck Turns 60!

DAILY BOOK — AOL Book of the Day

DAILY CHUCKLE — AOL News: Daily Chuckle

DAILY DISH — Teen People: Daily Dish

DAILY DOWNLOAD — AOL Computing: Daily Download

DAILY FACT — AOL Research & Learn: Fact-A-Day

DAILY FIX — AOL Entertainment: Daily Fix

DAILY JOKE — AOL News: Daily Chuckle

DAILY LIVING — AOL Health: Daily Living Forum

DAILY NEWS — Digital City Los Angeles: Daily News

DAILY NEWS LA — Digital City Los Angeles: Daily News

DAILY NEWS LOS ANGELES — Digital City Los Angeles: Daily News

DAILY PRESS — Digital City Hampton Roads: Daily Press

DAILY PRESS PHOTOS — Daily Press: Photo of the Month

DAILY SOFTWARE — AOL Computing: Daily Download

DALLAS — Digital City Dallas-Fort Worth

DALLAS 1963 — Digital City Dallas-Fort Worth: JFK Assassination

DALLAS CAREERS — Digital City Dallas-Fort Worth: Employment Classifieds

DALLAS CHAT — Digital City Dallas-Fort Worth: Chat

DALLAS CLASSIFIEDS — Digital City Dallas-Fort Worth: Employment Classifieds

DALLAS COPS — Digital City Dallas-Fort Worth: Police Department

DALLAS DINING — Digital City Dallas-Fort Worth: Culinary-Dining

DALLAS DINING GUIDE — Digital City Dallas-Fort Worth: Restaurant Search [Web site]

DALLAS EMPLOYMENT — Digital City Dallas-Fort Worth: Employment Classifieds

DALLAS FT WORTH LOCAL NEWS — Digital City Dallas-Fort Worth: Local News

DALLAS JOBS — Digital City Dallas-Fort Worth: Employment Classifieds

DALLAS KIDWATCH — Digital City Dallas-Fort Worth: Community KidWatch

DALLAS LOCAL NEWS — Digital City Dallas-Fort Worth: Local News

DALLAS MOVIES — Digital City Dallas-Fort Worth: MetroMovie

DALLAS PATROL — Digital City Dallas-Fort Worth: Police Department

DALLAS PERSONALS — Digital City Dallas-Fort Worth: Personals

DALLAS POLICE — Digital City Dallas-Fort Worth: Police Department

DALLAS POLICE DEPT — Digital City Dallas-Fort Worth: Police Department

DALLAS REAL ESTATE — Digital City Dallas-Fort Worth: Real Estate

DALLAS RELIGION — Digital City Dallas-Fort Worth: Religion

DALLAS SPORTS — Digital City Dallas-Fort Worth: Sports

DALLAS TV NAVIGATOR — Digital City Dallas-Fort Worth: TV Navigator

DALLAS WEB RUNNER — Digital City Dallas-Fort Worth: Web Runner

DALLAS WEBGUIDE — Digital City Dallas-Fort Worth: WebGuide [Web site]

DALLAS WHITE PAGES — Digital City Dallas-Fort Worth: White Pages [Web site]

DALLAS YELLOW PAGES — Digital City Dallas-Fort Worth: Yellow Pages [Web site]

DALLAS-FT. WORTH KIDS — Digital City Dallas-Fort Worth: KidSafe

DALLAS-FT. WORTH KIDSSAFE — Digital City Dallas-Fort Worth: KidSafe

DALLAS-FT. WORTH ROADS KIDS — Digital City Dallas-Fort Worth: KidSafe

DAMRON — onQ: Travel

DAN HURLEY — Amazing Instant Novelist

DANCE — AOL Interests: Dance

DANCE INSTRUCTOR — AOL WorkPlace: Sports & Recreation Industry Community

DANGER WILL ROBINSON — Entertainment Asylum: Lost In Space

DANGEROUS MINDS — ABC Online: Dangerous Minds

DANMARK — AOL International: Denmark

DANNY KRIFCHER — AOL Studios [Web site]

DARK SHADOWS — Digital City Chicago: Dark Shadows Online

DARKNESS — Engage Games Online: Darkness Falls

DARKNESS FALLS — Engage Games Online: Darkness Falls

DASHBOARD — Starfish Software [Web pointer]

DASTARDLY DOWNLOADS — AOL Computing: Dastardly Downloads [seasonal]

DATABASE — AOL Computing: Database Applications

DATABASE DEVELOPER — AOL Computing: Database Applications

DATABASE DEVELOPERS — AOL Computing: Database Applications

DATABASES — AOL Computing: Database Applications

DATE DOC — Digital City Los Angeles: The Date Doctor

DATE DOCTOR — Digital City Los Angeles: The Date Doctor

DATE PLANS — Digital City San Francisco: The Date's Date Plans

DATE SF — Digital City San Francisco: Bay Area Dating

DATING — Electra: Dating

DATING DIVA — Electra: The Dating Diva

DAVE — Late Show Online

DC — DC Selections

DC AGENTS — Digital City Washington: Real Estate Agents

DC APARTMENT — Digital City Washington: Apartments

DC APARTMENTS — Digital City Washington: Apartments

DC ATLANTA — Digital City Atlanta

DC AUDIONET — Digital City Dallas-Fort Worth: Broadcast.com

DC AUTO BY TEL — Digital City Los Angeles: Auto-By-Tel

DC AUTO HOT DEALS — Digital City Washington: Hot Deals

DC BACK TO SCHOOL — Digital City: Back to School [seasonal]

DC BALTIMORE — Digital City Baltimore
DC BEACH — Digital City Washington: Reach the Beach
DC BOARD — Digital City Washington: Message Boards
DC BOARDS — Digital City Washington: Message Boards
DC BOSTON — Digital City Boston
DC BUNNY — Digital City: Easter [seasonal]
DC CAREERS — Digital City Washington: Employment Classifieds
DC CHAT — Digital City Chat -or- DC Comics Chat
DC CHIT CHAT - Digital City Washington: Chat
DC CINCINNATI — Digital City Cincinnati
DC CLEVELAND — Digital City Cleveland
DC COMICS — DC Comics Online
DC COMICS ONLINE — DC Comics Online
DC COMICS.COM — DC Comics.com [Web site]
DC COMMUNITY SERVER — Digital City Washington: Kids Kicks
DC COTTON TAIL — Digital City: Easter [seasonal]
DC DAD — Digital City: Dads & Grads [seasonal]
DC DADS — Digital City: Dads & Grads [seasonal]
DC DALLAS — Digital City Dallas-Fort Worth
DC DC — Digital City Washington
DC DENVER — Digital City Denver
DC DETROIT — Digital City Detroit
DC DINING — Digital City: Dining Guide
DC EASTER — Digital City: Easter [seasonal]
DC FATHERS DAY — Digital City: Dads & Grads [seasonal]
DC FINANCE — Digital City Washington: Money Matters
DC FIT — Digital City Washington: Health & Fitness
DC FITNESS — Digital City Washington: Health & Fitness
DC FOOD — Digital City: Dining Guide
DC FOOTBALL — Digital City: NFL Football
DC FORT WORTH — Digital City Dallas-Fort Worth
DC GETAWAY - Digital City Washington: Local Day and Weekend Trips
DC GOLF — Digital City Washington: Golf
DC GRADS — Digital City: Dads & Grads [seasonal]
DC GRADUATION — Digital City: Dads & Grads [seasonal]
DC HALLOWEEN — Digital City: Halloween [seasonal]
DC HEALTH & FITNESS — Digital City Washington: Health & Fitness
DC HEALTH — Digital City Washington: Health & Fitness
DC HOMES — Digital City Washington: Real Estate
DC HOT DEALS — Digital City Washington: Hot Deals
DC HOTEL — Digital City Washington: Destination DC Hotels
DC HOTELS — Digital City Washington: Destination DC Hotels
DC HOTLANTA — Digital City Atlanta
DC HOUSTON — Digital City Houston
DC JOBS — Digital City Washington: Employment Classifieds
DC JOIN — Digital City: Become A Digital Citizen

DC KIDWATCH — Digital City Dallas-Fort Worth: KidWatch
DC LA — Digital City Los Angeles
DC LA ADVANCED COMPUTERS — Digital City Los Angeles: Advanced
Computers & Technology
DC LA TRAVEL AGENT — Digital City Los Angeles: Travel Agents
DC LOCAL NEWS — Digital City Washington: Local News
DC LOTTERY — Digital City Washington: Lottery Numbers
DC MALL — Digital City Washington: Shopping
DC MARKETPLACE — Digital City Washington: Shopping
**DC MIDATLANTIC — Digital City Philadelphia: Delaware
Interactive**
DC MINNEAPOLIS — Digital City Twin Cities
DC MOM — Digital City: Mother's Day [seasonal]
DC MOMS DAY — Digital City: Mother's Day [seasonal]
DC MONEY — Digital City Washington: Money Matters
DC MONEY MATTERS — Digital City Washington: Money Matters
DC MORTGAGE — Digital City Washington: Mortgage Financing
DC MORTGAGE FINANCING — Digital City Washington: Mortgage
Financing
DC MORTGAGE SERVICES — Digital City Washington: Mortgage
Financing
DC MOTHER'S DAY — Digital City: Mother's Day [seasonal]
DC MOTHERS DAY — Digital City: Mother's Day [seasonal]
DC MOTION — Digital City Washington: Active Sports & Recreation
DC MOVIE GUIDE — Digital City: Movie Guide [Web site]
DC NEW YEARS — Digital City: New Years [seasonal]
DC NEW YORK — Digital City New York
DC NEWS — Digital City Washington: Local News
DC NIGHTLIFE — Digital City Washington: Nightlife
**DC NORTHEAST — Digital City Philadelphia: South Jersey
Interactive**
DC NRB — Digital City Las Vegas: National Reservation Bureau
DC NY — Digital City New York
DC NYC — Digital City New York
DC OC — Digital City Orange County
DC OC COMMUNITY — Digital City Orange County: Community!
DC OC ENTERTAINMENT — Digital City Orange County: Entertainment!
DC OC NEWS — Digital City Orange County: News, Weather & Traffic!
DC OC PEOPLE — Digital City Orange County: People!
DC ORLANDO — Digital City Orlando
DC PEOPLE — Digital City Washington: People
DC PERSONALS — Digital City: Personals
DC PHILADELPHIA — Digital City Philadelphia
DC PHILLY — Digital City Philadelphia
DC PHILLY FLORIST — Digital City Philadelphia: Polites Florist
DC PORTLAND — Digital City Portland

DC RELIGION — Digital City Washington: Religion
DC RENTAL — Digital City Washington: Apartments
DC RENTALS — Digital City Washington: Apartments
DC SAN DIEGO — Digital City San Diego
DC SANTA — Digital City: Holidays
DC SCHOOL — Digital City: Back to School [seasonal]
DC SCOTLAND — AOL UK: Digital City Scotland
DC SEATTLE — Digital City Seattle
DC SKIING — Digital City: Skiing
DC SO FLA CHAT — Digital City South Florida: Interact
DC SO FLA INTERACT — Digital City South Florida: Interact
DC SOCCER — Digital City Washington: Soccer Moms
DC SOUTH JERSEY — Digital City South Jersey
DC SPORTS — Digital City Washington: Sports
DC ST PAUL — Digital City Twin Cities
DC ST PETERSBURG — Digital City Tampa Bay
DC SUMMER — Digital City: Summer [seasonal]
DC TALK ON CO — Christianity Online: Jesus Freaks
DC TAMPA — Digital City Tampa Bay
DC TC EMPLOYMENT — Digital City Twin Cities: Employment
DC TEENS — Digital City Washington: Teens
DC THANKS — Digital City: Thanksgiving [seasonal]
DC THANKSGIVING — Digital City: Thanksgiving [seasonal]
DC TORONTO — Digital City Toronto
DC TRANSPORT — AOL UK: Edinbirgh Transport
DC TURKEY — Digital City: Thanksgiving [seasonal]
DC TURKEY DAY — Digital City: Thanksgiving [seasonal]
DC TV LA — Digital City Los Angeles: TV Navigator
DC WALES — AOL UK: Digital City Wales
DC WHITE PAGES — Digital City: Directory [Web site]
DC WP — Digital City: Directory [Web site]
DC YELLOW PAGES — Digital City: Directory [Web site]
DC YP — Digital City: Directory [Web site]
DCA HEALTH — Digital City Atlanta: Health & Wellness
DCAA — Alcoholics Anonymous Online
DCC — Christianity Online: Colleges & Seminaries
DCC BARRINGTON — Digital City Chicago: Barrington [Web site]
DCC BUFFALO GROVE — Digital City Chicago: Buffalo Grove [Web site]
DCC DES PLAINES — Digital City Chicago: Des Plaines [Web site]
DCDS NEWS — Digital City San Diego: News
DCE ACCOMMODATION — AOL UK: Edinburgh Accommodation
DCE ACCOMODATION — AOL UK: Edinburgh Accommodation
DCE EVENTS — AOL UK: Edinburgh Major Events
DCE MUSEUMS — AOL UK: Edinburgh Museum & Galleries Guide
DCE VENUES — AOL UK: Edinburgh Venues
DCH — Don't Click Here

DCHR AUTO — Digital City Hampton Roads: Autofinder
DCHR CHAT — Digital City Hampton Roads: Chat
DCHR COMMUNITY — Digital City Hampton Roads: Community
DCHR DINING — Digital City Hampton Roads: Dining
DCHR ENTERTAINMENT — Digital City Hampton Roads: Ticket
DCHR EVENTS — Digital City Hampton Roads: Events
DCHR HOME — Digital City Hampton Roads: Home Guide
DCHR HOME GUIDE — Digital City Hampton Roads: Home Guide
DCHR MARKETPLACE — Digital City Hampton Roads: Marketplace
DCHR MOVIES — Digital City Hampton Roads: Movies
DCHR NEWS — Digital City Hampton Roads: News
DCHR PEOPLE — Digital City Hampton Roads: People
DCHR SHOP — Digital City Hampton Roads: Marketplace
DCHR SPORTS — Digital City Hampton Roads: Sports
DCHR TICKET — Digital City Hampton Roads: Ticket
DCHR YOU — Digital City Hampton Roads: People
DCI — Digital City Online
DCI AD AREA — Digital City: Ads
DCI AD AREAS — Digital City: Ads
DCI MOM — Digital City: Mothers Day Area [seasonal]
DCI MOTHERS DAY — Digital City: Mothers Day Area [seasonal]
DCI VALENTINE — Digital City: Valentine's Day [seasonal]
DCITY BALTIMORE — Digital City Baltimore [Web site]
DCITY LAS VEGAS — Digital City Las Vegas
DCL — Dictionary of Cultural Literacy
DCN — Digital City Online
DCO CHAT — Digital City Orlando: Chat Room
DCO HEALTH — Digital City Orlando: Healthy U.
DCO RECRUITING — Digital City Orlando: College Sports Recruiting
DCO THEME PARKS — Digital City Orlando: Go2Orlando Travel Service
DCP — Digital City Philadelphia
DCP BOXING — Digital City Philadelphia: Boxing
DCP DEALERS ONLY — Digital City Philadelphia: For Dealers Only!
DCP FLORIST — Digital City Philadelphia: Polites Florist
DCP FOOTBALL — Digital City Philadelphia: Pro Football
DCP HEALTH — Digital City Philadelphia: Health
DCP HOCKEY — Digital City Philadelphia: Hockey
DCP MOVIES — Digital City Philadelphia: Movies
DCP RELOCATION — Digital City Philadelphia: Relocation
DCP WEEKEND — Digital City Philadelphia: Philadelphia Weekend
DCSD — Digital City San Diego
DCSD CHATS — Digital City San Diego: Chat
DCSD COMMUNITY — Digital City San Diego: Community
DCSD ENTERTAINMENT — Digital City San Diego: Entertainment
DCSD FUN — Digital City San Diego: Entertainment
DCSD HOSTS — Digital City San Diego: Hosts

DCSD INDEX — Digital City San Diego: Index
DCSD LISA — Digital City San Diego: Dear Lisa
DCSD MARKET — Digital City San Diego: Marketplace
DCSD MOVIES — Digital City San Diego: MovieGuide [Web site]
DCSD NEWS — Digital City San Diego: KGTV Channel 10
DCSD PEOPLE — Digital City San Diego: People
DCSD PERSONALS — Digital City San Diego: Personals
DCSD SPORTS — Digital City San Diego: Sports
DCSD ZOOM — Digital City San Diego: Zoom
DCSF — Digital City San Francisco
DCSF AUTOGUIDE — Digital City Bay Area: AutoGuide
DCSF EVENTS — Digital City San Francisco: Community
DCSF MAP — Digital City South Florida: Map
DCSF STAGE — Digital City South Florida: Stage
DCW TEENS — Digital City Washington: Teens
DDC — Christianity Online: Colleges & Seminaries
DE FEEDBACK — Sun-Sentinel Digital Edition: Message Boards
DE HOMES — Digital City Philadelphia: Delaware Real Estate
DE PERSONALS — AOL UK: Edinburgh Personals
DEAD — The Grateful Dead Forum
DEADLINE — Dead Online [Web site]
DEAF — AOL Health: Deafness and Hearing Disorders
DEAF COMMUNITY — Deaf Community
DEAFNESS — AOL Health: Deafness and Hearing Disorders
DEAL — AOL Shopping: Bargain Basement
DEAL OF THE DAY — AOL Shopping: Deal of the Day
DEALS — AOL Shopping: Bargain Basement
DEAR LISA — Digital City San Diego: Dear Lisa
DEAR MYRTLE — Genealogy Forum: DearMYRTLE Daily Column
DEBATE ONQ — onQ: Debate It
DECISION POINT — Decision Point Timing & Charts
DECORATING — AOL Interests: House & Garden
DEEPAK — Deepak Chopra
DEEPAK CHOPRA — Deepak Chopra
DEEPAK CHOPRA@AOL — Deepak Chopra
DEEPAK@AOL — Deepak Chopra
DEER HUNTING — Hunting Broadcast Network
DEFENSE CONTRACTING — AOL WorkPlace: Defense
    Contractor's Community
DEJANEWS — AOL NetFind: Search Newsgroups [Web site]
DEJANEWS.COM — AOL NetFind: Search Newsgroups
    [Web site]
DELAWARE — Digital City Philadelphia: Delaware
    Interactive
DELAWARE CHAT — Digital City Philadelphia: Chat
DELAWARE HOMES — Digital City Philadelphia: Delaware Real Estate

DELAWARE REAL ESTATE — Digital City Philadelphia: Delaware Real Estate

DELEON — Digital City Philadelphia: Digital DeLeon

DELHI — AOL International: India

DELIGHTS — American Greetings: Daily Delights Postcards

DELILAH — Thrive@Healthy Living: Sex Expert

DELL — Dell Computer Corporation

DELPHI — Delphi Resource Center

DELRINA — Symantec Corporation

DEMA — AOL Scuba: DEMA Show

DEMOCRAT — Democratic National Committee [Web site]

DEMOCRATIC PARTY — Democratic National Committee [Web site]

DEMOCRATS — Democratic National Committee [Web site]

DEMS — Democratic National Committee [Web site]

DEN HEALTH — Digital City Denver: Health Care

DEN TREK — Digital City Denver: Outdoors

DENMARK — AOL International: Denmark

DENNIS RODMAN — Athlete Direct: Dennis Rodman

DENOMINATION — AOL Lifestyles: Spirituality

DENTAL — AOL Health: Dental & Oral Health

DENTAL BILLING — AOL WorkPlace: Medical Billing & Claims Processing

DENTAL CLAIMS — AOL WorkPlace: Medical Billing & Claims Processing

DENTON — Digital City Dallas-Fort Worth: Denton Record-Chronicle [Web site]

DENTON ENTERTAINMENT — Digital City Dallas-Fort Worth: Denton Record-Chronicle [Web site]

DENTON PUBLISHING — Digital City Dallas-Fort Worth: Denton Record-Chronicle [Web site]

DENTON RECORD — Digital City Dallas-Fort Worth: Denton Record-Chronicle [Web site]

DENVER — Digital City Denver

DENVER APARTMENTS — Digital City Denver: Real Estate Information

DENVER AUTO ADS — Digital City Denver: Auto Ads

DENVER AUTO CLASSIFIEDS — Digital City Denver: Auto Ads

DENVER AUTO DEALERS — Digital City Denver: Auto Dealers

DENVER AUTOGUIDE — Digital City Denver: Auto Dealers

DENVER AUTOMART — Digital City Denver: Autos Online

DENVER AUTOS — Digital City Denver: Autos Online

DENVER BOOK — Digital City Denver: Books

DENVER BOOKS — Digital City Denver: Books

DENVER BRONCOS — Digital City Denver: Sports

DENVER BUILDERS — Digital City Denver: Real Estate

DENVER CAR CLASSIFIEDS — Digital City Denver: Auto Ads

DENVER CAREERS — Digital City Denver: Employment Classifieds

DENVER CARS — Digital City Denver: Autos Online
DENVER CENTER — Digital City Denver: Center for the Performing Arts
DENVER CHARITY — Digital City Denver: Non Profits
DENVER CHAT — Digital City Denver: Chat
DENVER CLASSIFIEDS — Digital City Denver: Employment Classifieds
DENVER COMEDY — Digital City Denver: Humorwrite Online
DENVER COSTUME — Digital City Denver: Denver Costume Company
DENVER DIGC — Digital City Denver
DENVER DIGITAL CITY — Digital City Denver
DENVER DINING — Digital City Denver: Dining
DENVER DUMB FRIENDS — Digital City Denver: Denver Dumb Friends
    League
DENVER EMPLOYMENT — Digital City Denver: Employment Classifieds
DENVER ENT — Digital City Denver: Entertainment
DENVER ENTERTAINMENT — Digital City Denver: Entertainment
DENVER EXHIBITS — Digital City Denver: Museum of Natural History
DENVER EXPO — Digital City Denver: Business Expo
DENVER FILM SOCIETY — Digital City Denver: Movies
DENVER FILMS — Digital City Denver: Movies
DENVER FOOD — Digital City Denver: Dining
DENVER GAMES — Digital City Denver: The Wizard's Chest
DENVER GAY — Digital City Denver: Gay & Lesbian
DENVER GOLF — Digital City Denver: Golf
DENVER HEALTH — Digital City Denver: Health Care
DENVER HISTORY — Digital City Denver: OutWest Online
DENVER HOMES — Digital City Denver: Real Estate
DENVER JOBS — Digital City Denver: Employment Classifieds
DENVER KIDS — Digital City Denver: KidSafe
DENVER KIDS SAFE — Digital City Denver: KidSafe
DENVER LOCAL NEWS — Digital City Denver: Local News
DENVER MAGIC — Digital City Denver: Magic Fun and Games
DENVER MAGICIAN — Digital City Denver: Magic Fun and Games
DENVER MORTGAGES — Digital City Denver: Mortgage Information
    and Rates
DENVER MOVIES — Digital City Denver: Movies
DENVER MUSEUM — Digital City Denver: Museum of Natural History
DENVER MUSIC — Digital City Denver: Music
DENVER MUSIC SCENE — Digital City Denver: The Catfish Report
DENVER NEW HOMES — Digital City Denver: Real Estate
DENVER NIGHT LIFE — Digital City Denver: Entertainment
DENVER NUGGETS — Digital City Denver: Sports
DENVER PERSONALS — Digital City Denver: Personals
DENVER PHOTOS — Digital City Denver: Photo Booth
DENVER POST — Digital City Denver: Backpage
DENVER RADIO — Digital City Denver: TV & Radio
DENVER READING — Digital City Denver: Books

DENVER REAL ESTATE — Digital City Denver: Real Estate
DENVER REALTORS — Digital City Denver: Real Estate
DENVER RENTALS — Digital City Denver: Real Estate
DENVER RESTAURANTS — Digital City Denver: Dining
DENVER SHOWS — Digital City Denver: Entertainment
DENVER SOUNDS — Digital City Denver: The Catfish Report
DENVER SPORTS — Digital City Denver: Sports
DENVER STORIES — Digital City Denver: Humorwrite Online
DENVER TAROT — Digital City Denver: Mo's Mystical Metaphysical Tour
DENVER TELEVISION — Digital City Denver: TV & Radio
DENVER TV — Denver TV and Radio Listings — Stations and news
DENVER VOLUNTEERS — Digital City: Non Profits
DENVER WEBGUIDE — Digital City Denver: Web Guide [Web site]
DENVER WIZARD — Digital City Denver: The Wizard's Chest
DEPARTMENT 56 — AOL Shopping: Department 56 Collecting
DEPARTMENT STORE — AOL Shopping: Department Stores
DEPARTMENT STORES — AOL Shopping: Department Stores
DEPENDENCY — AOL Health: Addictions
DEPIXION — InToon with the News
DEPR CHAT — Depression Information Forum: Recovery Chat
DEPRESSION — AOL Health: Depression
DEPRESSION INFO — Depression Information Forum
DEPRESSION INFORMATION — Depression Information Forum
DEPRESSION RECOVERY — Depression Information Forum
DEPT 56 — AOL Shopping: Department 56 Collecting
DERBY — AOL UK: Local Life
DERBY EOL — AOL UK: Midlands Events Online
DERMATITIS — AOL Health: Dermatitis/Eczema
DERRY — AOL UK: Local Life
DES PLAINES — Digital City Chicago: Des Plaines [Web site]
DESIGNER — AOL WorkPlace: Designers' Community
DESKTOP PUBLISHING — AOL Computing: Desktop & Web Publishing
DESTINATION DC — Digital City Washington: Destination DC
DESTINATION DINING — Digital City New York: Dining
DESTINATION EUROPE — AOL Travel: Destination Europe!
DESTINATION FLORIDA — AOL Travel: Florida
DESTINATION FOCUS — AOL Travel: Decadent Delights
DESTINATION HOTELS & RESORTS — Digital City Washington:
    Destination DC
DESTINATIONS & INTERESTS — AOL Travel: Destination Guides
DESTINATIONS — AOL Travel: Destination Guides
DETROIT — Digital City Detroit
DETROIT DIGC — Digital City Detroit
DETROIT DIGITAL CITY — Digital City Detroit
DETROIT LOCAL NEWS — Digital City Detroit: Local News
DETROIT NEWS — Digital City Detroit: Local News

DETROIT TIGERS — Detroit Tigers
DEV — AOL Computing: Development Forum
DEV STUDIO — AOL Developers Studio
DEVELOPER — AOL Computing: Development Forum
DEVELOPER STUDIO — AOL Developers Studio
DEVELOPERS STUDIO — AOL Developers Studio
DEVELOPMENT — AOL Computing: Development Forum
DEVELOPMENT DISORDERS — AOL Health: Learning Disorders
DEVELOPMENT FORUM — AOL Computing: Development Forum
DEVELOPMENTAL DISORDERS — AOL Health: Learning Disorders
DEVIL RAYS — Tampa Bay Devil Rays
DEVIL RAYS BASEBALL — Tampa Bay Devil Rays
DEVILS — New Jersey Devils
DEVOTIONAL RESOURCES — Christianity Online: Spiritual Devotion
DEVOTIONAL RESOURCES — Christianity Online: Spiritual Devotion
DF — AOL Entertainment: Daily Fix
DFG — AOL Canada: Doug Forsythe Gallery
DFW — Digital City Dallas-Fort Worth
DFW AUTOGUIDE — Digital City Dallas-Fort Worth: AutoGuide
DFW BANDS — Digital City Dallas-Fort Worth: Music
DFW CHAT — Digital City DFW: Chat Area
DFW CITY HALL — Digital City Dallas-Fort Worth: City Hall
DFW CLUBS — Digital City Dallas-Fort Worth: Music
DFW DINES — Digital City Dallas-Fort Worth: Dining
DFW DINING GUIDE — Digital City Dallas-Fort Worth: Dining
DFW EMPLOYMENT — Digital City Dallas-Fort Worth: Employment
    Classifieds
DFW GAY FORUM — Digital City Dallas-Fort Worth: Gay & Lesbian
DFW LOCAL NEWS — Digital City Dallas-Fort Worth: Local News
DFW MUSIC — Digital City Dallas-Fort Worth: Music
DFW PERSONALS — Digital City Dallas-Fort Worth: Personals
DFW REAL ESTATE — Digital City Dallas-Fort Worth: Real Estate
DFW RELIGION — Digital City Dallas-Fort Worth: Religion
DFW SPORTS — Digital City Dallas-Fort Worth: Sports
DFW TEENS — Digital City Dallas-Fort Worth: Teens
DFW TODAY — Digital City Dallas-Fort Worth: City Hall
DFW TV NAVIGATOR — Digital City Dallas-Fort Worth: TV Navigator
DFW WEB RUNNER — Digital City Dallas-Fort Worth: Web Runner
DFW WEBGUIDE — Digital City Dallas-Fort Worth: WebGuide
    [Web site]
DFW WHITE PAGES — Digital City Dallas-Fort Worth: Directory
    [Web site]
DFW WRITERS CORNER — Digital City Dallas-Fort Worth: Writers
    Forum
DFW YELLOW PAGES — Digital City Dallas-Fort Worth: Directory
    [Web site]

DG — Hecklers Online: Digital Graffiti
DGATE — Dragon's Gate
DHR — Destination Hotels & Resorts!
DI — Disney Interactive
DIABETES — AOL Health: Diabetes
DIABETES, THYROID & ENDOCRINE — AOL Health: Diabetes, Thyroid &
    Endocrine Disorders
DIAMOND GUY — The Knot: Diamond Guy
DIAMOND REPORT — Digital City Philadelphia: Diamond Report
DIAMONDBACK GOLF — Diamondback Golf Course
DIAMONDBACKS — Arizona Diamondbacks
DIAMONDBACKS BASEBALL — Arizona Diamondbacks
DIAMONDBALL — NTN Trivia: Diamondball
DIANA — AOL International: Royalty Forum
DICT — Merriam-Webster Collegiate Dictionary
DICTIONARIES — AOL Research & Learn: Dictionaries
DICTIONARY — Merriam-Webster Collegiate Dictionary
DIET — AOL Health: Dieting & Weight Loss
DIETING — AOL Health: Dieting & Weight Loss
DIF CHAT — Depression Information Forum: Recovery Chat
DIG CITY VALENTINE — Digital City: Valentine's Day [seasonal]
DIG ED CHAT — Sun-Sentinel Digital Edition: Chat Schedule
DIG IT — Digital City Twin Cities: Dig the New Breed
DIGC CLEVELAND — Digital City Cleveland
DIGC DENVER — Digital City Denver
DIGC DETROIT — Digital City Detroit
DIGESTIVE — AOL Health: Digestive Disorders
DIGESTIVE DISORDERS — AOL Health: Digestive Disorders
DIGIDESIGN — DigiDesign On Line
DIGIQUEERS — onQ: Digital Queers [Web site]
DIGITAL CAMERA — AOL Computing: Digital Photography
DIGITAL CAMERAS — AOL Computing: Digital Photography
DIGITAL CITIES — Digital City Online
DIGITAL CITY — Digital City Online
DIGITAL CITY ATLANTA — Digital City Atlanta
DIGITAL CITY BOSTON — Digital City Boston
DIGITAL CITY BOSTON SKIING — Digital City Boston: Skiing
DIGITAL CITY CHICAGO — Digital City Chicago
DIGITAL CITY CINCINNATI — Digital City Cincinnati
DIGITAL CITY DALLAS — Digital City Dallas-Fort Worth
DIGITAL CITY DC — Digital City Washington
DIGITAL CITY DENVER — Digital City Denver
DIGITAL CITY DETROIT — Digital City Detroit
DIGITAL CITY EASTER — Digital City: Easter [seasonal]
DIGITAL CITY FOOTBALL — Digital City: NFL Football
DIGITAL CITY FT WORTH — Digital City Dallas-Fort Worth

DIGITAL CITY GREENSBORO — Digital City Greensboro
DIGITAL CITY HEALTH — Digital City Philadelphia: Health
DIGITAL CITY HIGH POINT — Digital City: High Point
DIGITAL CITY HOUSTON — Digital City Houston
DIGITAL CITY JOIN — Become A Digital Citizen
DIGITAL CITY LA — Digital City Los Angeles
DIGITAL CITY LA TEENS — Digital City Los Angeles: Teens
DIGITAL CITY MOM — Digital City: Mother's Day [seasonal]
DIGITAL CITY MOVIE GUIDE — Digital City: Movie Information
DIGITAL CITY NEW YEARS — Digital City: New Years [seasonal]
DIGITAL CITY NY — Digital City New York
DIGITAL CITY ORLANDO — Digital City Orlando
DIGITAL CITY PORTLAND — Digital City Portland
DIGITAL CITY RADIO — Digital City Dallas-Fort Worth: Broadcast.com
DIGITAL CITY ROANOKE — Digital City Roanoke
DIGITAL CITY SANTA FE — Digital City Santa Fe
DIGITAL CITY SCHOOL — Digital City: Back to School
DIGITAL CITY SD — Digital City San Diego
DIGITAL CITY SEATTLE — Digital City Seattle
DIGITAL CITY SF — Digital City San Francisco
DIGITAL CITY SKIING — Digital City: Skiing
DIGITAL CITY SOUTH — Digital City South
DIGITAL CITY ST PAUL — Digital City Minneapolis
DIGITAL CITY SUMMER — Digital City: Summer [seasonal]
DIGITAL CITY TACOMA — Digital City Seattle
DIGITAL CITY TAMPA — Digital City Tampa Bay
DIGITAL CITY TORONTO — Digital City Toronto
DIGITAL CITY UK — AOL UK: Digital City
DIGITAL CITY VALENTINE — Digital City: Valentine's Day [seasonal]
DIGITAL CITY WEST — Digital City West
DIGITAL CITY WINSTON SALEM — Digital City Winston Salem
DIGITAL CITY YELLOW PAGES — Digital City: Directory [Web site]
DIGITAL DELEON — Digital City Philadelphia: Digital DeLeon
DIGITAL EDITION — Sun Sentinel South Florida
DIGITAL GRAFFITI — Hecklers Online: Digital Graffiti
DIGITAL IMAGING — AOL Interests: Pictures
DIGITAL MAVICA — Sony Digital Mavica
DIGITAL MILK CARTON — National Center for Missing & Exploited
    Children
DIGITAL PHOTO — AOL Computing: Digital Photography
DIGITAL PHOTO SIG — AOL Computing: Digital Photography
DIGITAL PHOTOGRAPHY — AOL Computing: Digital Photography
DIGITAL SHOP — AOL Store: Digital Shop
DIGITAL STATION — Digital City San Francisco: High Tech Jobs & News
DIGITAL STATION SF — Digital City San Francisco: High Tech Jobs &
    News

DIGITAL WHITE — Digital City: Directory [Web site]
DIGITAL WHITE PAGES — Digital City: Directory [Web site]
**DIGITAL WORLDS — Digital City Chicago: Digital Words
    Interactive Online**
DIGITAL YELLOW — Digital City Directory
DIGITS — WebCounter [Web site]
DIGITS.COM — WebCounter [Web site]
DIGIZINES — AOL Entertainment: Digizine Sites on the Web
DILBERT — Dilbert Comics [Web site]
DILBERT COMICS — Dilbert Comics [Web site]
DILBOARD — Dilbert Comics [Web site]
DINING — AOL Interests: Food
**DINING A LA CARD — Digital City Chicago: Dining a la Card
    [Web site]**
DINING LA — Digital City Los Angeles: Dining
DINING SAN DIEGO — Digital City San Diego: Dining Guide
DINING SD — Digital City San Diego: Dining Guide
DINNER ON US — Dinner On Us Club
DINNERWARE — AOL Shopping: Department Stores
DIRECT ACCESS — Citibank: Direct Access
DIRECT PORTFOLIO — Direct Portfolio
DIRECTORY — AOL Member Directory
DIRTY LAUNDRY — Love@AOL: Dirty Laundry
DIS — DisABILITIES Community Forum
DISABILITIES — DisABILITIES Community Forum
DISABILITY — DisABILITIES Community Forum
DISCLOSURE — AOL Full Disclosure
DISCOUNT SHOPPING — AOL Shoppers Advantage
DISCOVER — AOL Member Services: QuickStart
DISCOVER AOL — AOL Member Services: QuickStart
DISCOVER AOL NEW MEMBER — AOL Member Services: QuickStart
DISCOVER BROKERAGE — Discover Brokerage
DISCOVERY.COM — Discovery Channel Online [Web site]
DISEASE PREVENTION — AOL Health: Wellness & Disease Prevention
DISNEY ADVENTURES — Disney Adventures
DISNEY INTERACTIVE — Disney Interactive
DISNEY JOBS — Disney Jobs
DISNEY MAGAZINE — Disney Adventures
DISNEY RESORTS — Walt Disney World Resorts
DISNEY SOFT — Disney Interactive
DISNEY SOFTWARE — Disney Interactive
DISNEY STORE — The Disney Store
DISNEY WORLD — Walt Disney World Resorts
DIVA — Soap Opera Digest Online
DJ INDUSTRY — Dow Jones Business Center
DJIBOUTI — AOL International: Djibouti

DJUNA — Digital City Philadelphia: DjunaVerse
DJUNA VERSE — Digital City Philadelphia: DjunaVerse
DL CITY — AOL UL: Local Life London
DLJ — DLJ Direct Brokers
DLJ DIRECT — DLJ Direct Brokers
DLJD — DLJ Direct Brokers
DMX — Reebok: DMX Series 2000
DMX 2000 — Reebok: DMX Series 2000
DNC — Democratic National Committee [Web site]
DO IT YOURSELF — AOL Interests: Do-It-Yourself
DOCL — Dictionary of Cultural Literacy
DOCTOR KATE — Love@AOL: Dr. Kate
DODGE — Dodge [Web site]
DODGELAND — Digital City Philadelphia: Metro Dealerships
DODGERS — Los Angeles Dodgers
DOG — AOL Interests: Pets
DOG ONQ — onQ: Pets
<u>DOGERS</u> — Los Angeles Dodgers
DOING BUSINESS ONLINE — AOL WorkPlace: Doing Business Online
DOM — Digital City Orlando: Downtown Orlando Monthly
DOM GIORDANO — Digital City Philadelphia: Crime Sweep with Dom
    Giordano
DOMESTIC ABUSE — Massachusetts Coalition of Battered Women
    Service Groups
DOMINICA — AOL International: Dominica
DOMINICAN REPUBLICAN — AOL International: Dominican
    Republican
DON — AOL Canada: Don Cherry Online
DON CHERRY — AOL Canada: Don Cherry Online
DONT CLICK HERE — Don't Click Here
DON'T CLICK HERE — Don't Click Here
DOPE — The Straight Dope
DOS 6 — AOL Computing: MS-DOS 6.0 Resource Center
DOS 60 — AOL Computing: MS-DOS 6.0 Resource Center
DOSSIER — Digital City Atlanta: Dossier Magazine [Web site]
DOSSIER ATLANTA — Digital City Atlanta: Dossier Magazine [Web site]
DOSSIER MAGAZINE — Digital City Atlanta: Dossier Magazine
    [Web site]
DOSSIER MAGAZINE ATLANTA — Digital City Atlanta: Dossier Magazine
    [Web site]
DOSSIER ONLINE — Digital City Atlanta: Dossier Magazine [Web site]
DOT NET — AOL UK: Internet Magazine
DOT NET MAGAZINE — AOL UK: Internet Magazine
DOU — Dinner On Us Club
DOUG FORSYTHE — AOL Canada: Doug Forsythe Gallery
DOUG FORSYTHE GALLERY — AOL Canada: Doug Forsythe Gallery

DOW 1987 — Personal Finance: Special Report
DOW CRASH — Personal Finance: Special Report
DOWN THE SHORE — Digital City Philadelphia: Down the Shore
DOWN UNDER — AOL International: Australia and Oceania
DOWNLOAD — AOL Computing: Daily Download
DOWNLOAD 101 — AOL Member Services: Download 101
DOWNLOAD CREDIT — AOL Member Services: Credit Request
DOWNLOAD HELP — AOL Member Services: Downloading Files &
    Attachments
DOWNLOAD NETSCAPE — Download Netscape for AOL
DOWNLOAD OF THE DAY — AOL Computing: Daily Download
DOWNLOAD SOFTWARE — AOL Computing: Download Software
DOWNLOAD STORE — AOL Computing: Superstore
DOWNLOADING — AOL Computing: Download Software
DOWNTOWN ORLANDO — Digital City Orlando: Downtown Orlando
    Monthly
DOWNTOWN ORLANDO MONTHLY — Digital City Orlando: Downtown
    Orlando Monthly
DOWNTURN — Personal Finance: Market Correction
DP — Decision Point Timing & Charts
DP PHOTOS — Daily Press: Photo of the Month
DPD — Digital City Dallas-Fort Worth: Police Department
DR D — AOL Health: Dr. D Talks
DR D TALKS — AOL Health: Dr. D Talks
DR D TALKS ABOUT — AOL Health: Dr. D Talks
DR DATE — Digital City San Francisco: Dr. Date's Date Plans
DR DATE'S DATE PLANS — Digital City San Francisco: Dr. Date's Date
    Plans
DR KATE — Love@AOL: Dr. Kate
DR LOVE — Digital City Philadelphia: Star Sites
DR SOLOMON — Safety Online with Dr Solomon
DR SOLOMONS — Safety Online with Dr Solomon
DR SOLOMON'S SOFTWARE — Safety Online with Dr Solomon
DR SOLOMONS SOFTWARE — Safety Online with Dr Solomon
DR. ADD — Online Psych: Ask Dr. ADD
DR. D — AOL Health: Dr. D Talks
DR. D TALKS — AOL Health: Dr. D Talks
DR. GLASS — Electra: Dr. Shirley Glass
DR. KATE — Love@AOL: Dr. Kate
DR. LOVE — Digital City Philadelphia: Star Sites
DR. SHIRLEY GLASS — Electra: Dr. Shirley Glass
DR. WANTMAN — Digital City Philadelphia: The Love Files
DRAFT — TeamNFL Draft
DRAFT CENTRAL — NFL Draft '97
DRAGON'S GATE — Dragon's Gate
DRAGONS GATE — Dragon's Gate

DRAMA DEN — Entertainment Asylum: Drama Den
DRESSAGE — AOL Sports: Dressage Mini Forum
DREW — WB Online: The Drew Carey Show
DREW BLEDSOE — Athlete Direct
DREW CAREY — WB Online: The Drew Carey Show
DREW CAREY ONLINE — WB Online: The Drew Carey Show
DREYFUS — Dreyfuss Online Investment Center
DREYFUSS — Dreyfuss Online Investment Center
DRINKS — AOL Interests: Drinks
DRIVE — AOL UK: Car channel
DRIVER NEWS — AOL UK: Car Channel News
DROBB ZONE — AOL Greenhouse
DRUDGE — AOL Influence: Drudge Report
DRUM CIRCLE — The Grateful Dead Forum: Drum Circle
DSL — xDSL Field Trial
DSL LITE — xDSL Field Trial
DTP — AOL Computing: Desktop & Web Publishing Forums
DUBLIN — AOL International: Irish Heritage
DUCK HUNTING — Hunting Broadcast Network
DUCKS — Anaheim Mighty Ducks
DUMP PHILLY — Digital City Philadelphia: Dumpadelphia
DUMPADELPHIA — Digital City Philadelphia: Dumpadelphia
DUN & BRADSTREET — Dun & Bradstreet@AOL [Web site]
DUN AND BRADSTREET — Dun & Bradstreet@AOL [Web site]
DUNDEE — AOL UK: Local Life
DUNDEE EOL — AOL UK: Scotland Events Online
DUNHAM & MILLER — Digital City Dallas-Fort Worth: KTCK 1310 AM
   Sports Radio
DURHAM — Digital City Raleigh-Durham [Web site]
DURHAM EOL — AOL UL: Far North Events Online
DVORAK — Software Hardtalk with John C. Dvorak
DWP — AOL Computing: Desktop & Web Publishing Forums
DYKESVILLE — PlanetOut: Women's Community
DYNOTECH — DynoTech Software Forum
DYSLEXIA — AOL Health: Dyslexia
E — AOL Entertainment channel
E BAUER — Eddie Bauer
E BEAUTY — Electra: Beauty
E CAREER — Electra: Careers
E CHAT — AOL Entertainment: Chat
E COMMERCE — AOL WorkPlace: Doing Business Online
E DATING — Electra: Dating
E FASHION — Electra: Fashion
E GODDESS — Electra: Goddess of the Week
E HELP — AOL Entertainment: Help Desk
E HELP DESK — AOL Entertainment: Help Desk

E HOME — Electra: Home
E HOROSCOPE — Electra: Horoscopes
E HOROSCOPES — Electra: Horoscopes
E LIBRARY — Electric Library@AOL
E LIVE — Entertainment Online
E LOVE LIFE — Electra: Love Life
E MIND & BODY — Electra: Mind & Body
E MIND AND BODY — Electra: Mind & Body
E MONEY — Electra: Money
E N & T — AOL Health: Ear, Nose & Throat
E PARTNERS — Electronic Partnerships
E RELATIONSHIP — Electra: Lifestyles
E RELATIONSHIPS — Electra: Lifestyles
E STORE — AOL Entertainment: Store
E STYLE — Electra: Lifestyles
E TIME OFF — Electra: Lifestyles
E TIME-OFF — Electra: Lifestyles
E TRADE — E*Trade Stock Brokerage
E WOMAN — Electra: Woman
E ZINES — AOL Entertainment: Digizine Sites on the Web
E! — E! Online [Web site]
E! ONLINE — E! Online [Web site]
E*TRADE — E*Trade Stock Brokerage
E.WIRE — AOL Entertainment: Newsletter Subscription
E3 — Antagonist Inc.
EA — Entertainment Asylum
EA ACTION — Entertainment Asylum: Action Explosion
EA AE — Entertainment Asylum: Action Explosion
EA ARCADE — Entertainment Asylum: Arcade
EA BIG SCREEN — Entertainment Asylum: The Big Screen
EA CC — Entertainment Asylum: Comedy Clinic
EA CHAT — Entertainment Asylum: Chat
EA COMEDY — Entertainment Asylum: Comedy Clinic
EA COMEDY CLINIC — Entertainment Asylum: Comedy Clinic
EA DD — Entertainment Asylum: Drama Den
EA DRAMA — Entertainment Asylum: Drama Den
EA EOL — AOL UK: East Anglia Events Online
EA FEEDBACK — Entertainment Asylum: Feedback
EA HELP — Entertainment Asylum: Help and Feedback
EA HIGHWAY — Entertainment Asylum: Pulp Cult Horror Highway
EA HOLLYWOOD — Entertainment Asylum: Hollywood Wire
EA HW — Entertainment Asylum: Hollywood Wire
EA INSIDER — Entertainment Asylum: Hollywood Wire
EA LIVE — Entertainment Asylum: Chat
EA MOVIE — Entertainment Asylum: The Big Screen
EA MOVIES — Entertainment Asylum: The Big Screen

EA NOW PLAYING — Entertainment Asylum: Movie Listings [Web site]
EA NP — Entertainment Asylum: Movie Listings [Web site]
EA PCH — Entertainment Asylum: Pulp Cult Horror Highway
EA SCI FI ZONE — Entertainment Asylum: Sci-Fi Zone
EA SCI-FI ZONE — Entertainment Asylum: Sci-Fi Zone
EA SCREEN TEAM — Entertainment Asylum: Screen Team
EA SF — Entertainment Asylum: Sci-Fi Zone
EA SF CHAT — Entertainment Asylum: Sci-Fi Zone Chat
EA SI — Entertainment Asylum: Chat
EA SILVER SCREEN — Entertainment Asylum: The Big Screen
EA SOAPS — Entertainment Asylum: Soaps Asylum
EA SOUTH PARK — Entertainment Asylum: South Park Chat
EA SP CHAT — Entertainment Asylum: South Park Chat
EA SPOTLIGHT — Entertainment Asylum: Weekly News
EA TEEN — Entertainment Asylum: Teen Asylum
EA TEEN CHAT — Entertainment Asylum: Teen Asylum Chat
EA TELE — Entertainment Asylum: Television
EA TELEVISION — Entertainment Asylum: Television
EA TITANIC — Entertainment Asylum: Titanic
EA TRIVIA — Entertainment Asylum: Inmate Trivia
EA TV — Entertainment Asylum: Television
EA WIRE — Entertainment Asylum: Hollywood Wire
EA WO — Entertainment Asylum: What's On TV
EAGLE — Eagle Automobile [Web site]
EAGLES — Philadelphia Eagles
EAGLES ONLINE — Digital City Philadelphia: Philadelphia Eagles
EAMC — Entertainment Asylum
EAMC CHAT — Entertainment Asylum: Chat
EAR ACHE — AOL Health: Otitis Media
EAR ACHES — AOL Health: Otitis Media
EARN POINTS — AOL Rewards
EARN POINTS NOW — AOL Rewards
EARS — AOL Health: Ear, Nose & Throat
EAST COUNTY HOMES — Digital City San Diego: Real Estate
EASTER — Easter@AOL [seasonal]
EASTER BUNNY — Letters to the Easter Bunny [seasonal]
EASTER MARKETPLACE — AOL Shopping: Easter [seasonal]
EASTER SHOP — AOL Shopping: Easter [seasonal]
EASTER SHOPPING — AOL Shopping: Easter [seasonal]
EASTER STORE — AOL Shopping: Easter [seasonal]
EASTER SUNDAY — Easter@AOL [seasonal]
EASTER@AOL — Easter@AOL [seasonal]
EASTERN BANK — Eastern Bank [Web site]
EASTLAKE — Digital City San Diego: EastLake Property Development
EASTLAKE GOLF — Digital City San Diego: EastLake Property Development

EASTLAKE HOMES — Digital City San Diego: EastLake Property
Development
EASTLAKE.NET — Digital City San Diego: EastLake Property
Development
EASY WEB — AOL Canada : Trust Online Bank System
EAT QUICHE — Upgrade to the Latest AOL Software
EATING DISORDERS — AOL Health: Eating Disorders
EATING WELL — AOL Health: Eating Well
EAX — Entertainment Asylum: The X Files
EB STORE — Eddie Bauer
EB TEK — Eddie Bauer
EBAY — eBay Auction Classifieds [Web site]
EBONY ZONE — NetNoir: Ebony
EBOOK — AOL Computing: PDA Palmtop Paperbacks
ECCLIPSE — Solar Eclipse
ECLIPSE — Solar Eclipse
ECOLOGY — Environmental Links
ECON AP — AOL News: Economics News
ECON FEED — AOL News: Economics News
ECON NEWS — AOL News: Economics News
ECON REUTERS — AOL News: Economics News
ECON WIRES — AOL News: Economics News
ECOTOURISM — Backpacker Magazine
ECUADOR — AOL International: Ecuador
ECZEMA — AOL Health: Dermatitis/Eczema
ED — Digital City: Emotion Detector
ED COMICS — AOL News: Backpage Daily Cartoon
ED LIBRARY — AOL Computing: Library Media Center SIG
ED TECH — Association of Supervision and Curriculum Development
Online
EDDIE — Eddie Bauer
EDDIE BAUER — Eddie Bauer
EDDIE BAUER HOME — Eddie Bauer
EDELSTEIN — AOL Sports: Fred Edelstein's Pro Football Insider
EDGAR — Disclosure's Edgar [Web site]
EDIBLE — AOL Interests: Recipes
EDINBURGH PERSONALS — AOL UK: Digital City Edinburgh: Personals
EDIT PROFILE — AOL Member Directory
EDITORIAL CARTOONS — InToon with the News
EDITORS CHOICE — AOL News: Pictures of the Week
EDMARK — IBM Edmark
EDMUNDS — Edmund's Automobile Buyer Guides [Web site]
EDUCATION — AOL Research & Learn: Education
EDUCATION LIBRARY — AOL Computing: Library Media Center SIG
EF — Real Fans Sports Network
EF 1908 — Real Fans: Chicago Cubs Team Club

EF 2131 — Real Fans: Baltimore Orioles Team Club
EF ALBERT — Real Fans: Chicago White Sox Team Clubs
EF ALLEN — Real Fans: Seattle Seahawks Team Clubs
EF ALOU — Real Fans: Montreal Expos
EF APPLE — Real Fans: Washington Team Club
EF ARCHIE — Real Fans: Ole Miss Team Club
EF BACK TO BACK — Real Fans: Kansas Team Club
EF BAGWELL — Real Fans: Houston Astros Team Club
EF BASEBALL — Real Fans: Baseball
EF BASH BROTHERS — Real Fans: Transactions
EF BD — Real Fans: Baseball
EF BEAR — Real Fans: Alabama Team Club
EF BEAU — Real Fans: Air Force Team Club
EF BEDNARIK — Real Fans: Philadelphia Team Club
EF BELLINO — Real Fans: Navy Team Club
EF BEVO — Real Fans: Texas Team Club
EF BIDWELL — Real Fans: Arizona Cardinals Team Club
EF BIG RED MACHINE — Real Fans: Reds Team Club
EF BIG UNIT — Real Fans: Seattle Mariners Team Club
EF BLEDSOE — Real Fans: England Patriots Team Club
EF BO — Real Fans: Auburn Team Club
EF BONDS — Real Fans: San Francisco Giants Team Club
EF BONFIRE — Real Fans: Texas A&M Team Club
EF BOOMER — Real Fans: Oklahoma Team Club
EF BRETT — Real Fans: Kansas City Royals Team Club
EF BREW CREW — Real Fans: Milwaukee Brewers Team Club
EF BREWERS — Real Fans: Milwaukee Brewers Team Club
EF BROWN — Real Fans: Cincinnati Bengals Team Club
EF BRUNELL — Real Fans: Jacksonville Jaguars Team Club
EF C HOOPS — Real Fans: College Hoops
EF CANES — Real Fans: Miami Team Club
EF CATS — Real Fans: Kansas State Team Club
EF CHAT — Real Fans: Chat Rooms and Message Boards
EF CHIEF WAHOO — Real Fans: Cleveland Indians Team Club
EF CLONG — Real Fans: Iowa Team Club
EF CLUB — Real Fans: Join Your Team Club
EF CLUBS — Real Fans: Join Your Team Club
EF COLLINS — Real Fans: Carolina Panthers Team Club
EF COOKE — Real Fans: Washington Redskins Team Club
EF COURTSIDE — Real Fans: Courtside
EF DAWSON — Real Fans: Kansas City Chiefs Team Club
EF DAYNE — Real Fans: Wisconsin Team Club
EF DILFER — Real Fans: Tampa Bay Buccaneers Team Club
EF DITKA — Real Fans: New Orleans Saints Team Club
EF DOC — Real Fans: Army Team Club
EF DOUG — Real Fans: Boston College Team Club

EF E DAVIS — Real Fans: Syracuse Team Club
EF ELWAY — Real Fans: Denver Broncos Team Club
EF FAB FIVE — Real Fans: Michigan Team Club
EF FERRY — Real Fans: Duke Team Club
EF FISHER — Real Fans: Tennessee Oilers Team Club
EF FISSEL — Real Fans: Kentucky Team Club
EF FRIARS — Real Fans: San Diego Padres Team Club
EF GAME ROOM — Real Fans: College Hoops Gameroom
EF GR — Real Fans: College Hoops Gameroom
EF GREEN MONSTER — Real Fans: Boston Red Sox Team Club
EF GRIESE — Real Fans: Purdue Team Club
EF HALAS — Real Fans: Chicago Bears Team Club
EF HALOS — Real Fans: Anaheim Angels Team Club
EF HARBAUGH — Real Fans: Indianapolis Colts Team Club
EF HERZOG — Real Fans: St. Louis Cardinals Team Club
EF HOCKEY — Real Fans: NHL Today
EF HOGS — Real Fans: Arkansas Team Club
EF HORSESHOE — Real Fans: Ohio State Team Club
EF HOWARDS ROCK — Real Fans: Clemson Team Club
EF HUMPHRIES — Real Fans: San Diego Chargers Team Club
EF HUNDLEY — Real Fans: New York Mets Team Club
EF JERSEY — Real Fans: Rutgers Team Club
EF LAMBEAU — Real Fans: Green Bay Packers Team Club
EF LANE — Real Fans: Virginia Tech Team Club
EF LAVELL — Real Fans: Brigham Young Team Club
EF LEAHY — Real Fans: Notre Dame Team Club
EF LEVY — Real Fans: Buffalo Bills Team Club
EF LEYLAND — Real Fans: Florida Marlins Team Club
EF LOBO — Real Fans: Connecticut Team Club
EF LUPPINO — Real Fans: Arizona Team Club
EF MAGIC — Real Fans: Michigan State Team Club
EF MAJOR — Real Fans: West Virginia Team Club
EF MANSTER — Real Fans: Maryland Team Club
EF MARA — Real Fans: New York Giants Team Club
EF MILE HIGH — Real Fans: Colorado Rockies Team Club
EF MO — Real Fans: Seton Hall Team Club
EF MOTOR CITY — Real Fans: Detroit Tigers Team Club
EF NBA — Real Fans: Pro Basketball
EF NHL — Real Fans: NHL Today
EF NOLAN — Real Fans: Arkansas Team Club
EF PAPA JOE — Real Fans: Penn State Team Club
EF PARCELLS — Real Fans: New York Jets Team Club
EF PIAZZA — Real Fans: Los Angeles Dodgers Team Club
EF PISTOL — Real Fans: LSU Tigers Team Club
EF PLUNKET — Real Fans: Stanford Team Club
EF POLLS — Real Fans: Polls

EF PRO — Real Fans: Pro Football
EF PRO HOOPS — Real Fans: Pro Basketball
EF PUDGE — Real Fans: Texas Rangers Team Club
EF RALPHIE — Real Fans: Colorado Team Club
EF RED — Real Fans: Nebraska Cornhuskers Team Club
EF REEVES — Real Fans: Atlanta Falcons Team Club
EF REGGIE — Real Fans: Arizona State Team Club
EF ROLEN — Real Fans: Philadelphia Phillies Team Club
EF ROLLIE — Real Fans: Villanova Team Club
EF ROONEY — Real Fans: Pittsburgh Steelers Team Club
EF RUTH — Real Fans: New York Yankees Team Club
EF SANDERS — Real Fans: Detroit Lions Team Club
EF SCOREBOARD — Real Fans: Score Ticker
EF SCORES — Real Fans: Score Ticker
EF SHULA — Real Fans: Miami Dolphins Team Club
EF SINGLETARY — Real Fans: Baylor Team Club
EF SKYDOME — Real Fans: Toronto Blue Jays Team Club
EF SMITH — Real Fans: Dallas Cowboys Team Club
EF SMOKEY — Real Fans: Tennessee Team Club
EF ST — Real Fans: Score Ticker
EF STABLER — Real Fans: Oakland Raiders Team Club
EF STARGELL — Real Fans: Pittsburgh Pirates Team Club
EF SWAMP — Real Fans: Florida Team Club
EF TAILBACK — Real Fans: USC Team Club
EF TARKENTON — Real Fans: Minnesota Vikings Team Club
EF TEAM CLUBS — Real Fans: Join Your Team Club
EF TEST AVERDE — Real Fans: Baltimore Ravens Team Club
EF TICKER — Real Fans: Score Ticker
EF TIM — Real Fans: Wake Forest Team Club
EF TLS — Real Fans: The Last Shot
EF TOMAHAWK — Real Fans: Atlanta Braves Team Club
EF TOP COACH — Real Fans: North Carolina Team Club
EF TRACKER — Real Fans: Score Ticker
EF TROY — Real Fans: UCLA Team Club
EF TWINKIES — Real Fans: Minnesota Twins Team Club
EF TWISTER — Real Fans: Iowa ST Team Club
EF VARITEK — Real Fans: Georgia Tech Team Club
EF VERMEIL — Real Fans: St. Louis Rams Team Club
EF VINCE — Real Fans: Georgia Team Club
EF WAHOOS — Real Fans: Virginia Team Club
EF WAR CHANT — Real Fans: Florida State Team Club
EF WILLIE — Real Fans: Northwestern Team Club
EF YOUNG — Real Fans: San Francisco 49ers Team Club
EFT — Real Fans: Score Ticker
EFTI — Real Fans: Tenth Inning
EGG — Electronic Gourmet Guide

EGG BASKET — Electronic Gourmet Guide: Global Gourmet Shops
EGG HEAD — Electronic Gourmet Guide: Trivia
EGG HEAD TRIVIA — Electronic Gourmet Guide: Trivia
EGG HUNT — Electric Gourmet Guide: Easter Hunt [seasonal]
EGG SF — Digital City San Francisco: Electronic Gourmet Guide
EGG TRIVIA — Electronic Gourmet Guide: Trivia
EGG-SF — Digital City San Francisco: Electronic Gourmet Guide
EGGSTERS — Electronic Gourmet Guide
EGYPT — AOL International: Egypt
EGYPTOLOGY — Archaeology Forum
EINDUSTRY — AOL Entertainment: The Industry
EIRE — AOL International: Ireland
EIU — The Economist Intelligence Unit
EL NINO SF — Digital City San Francisco: El Nino Guide
EL SALVADOR — AOL International: El Salvador
ELAN JEWELRY — Elan Allé Fine Jewelry
ELCTRA — Electra
ELECTION 97 — Election Coverage
ELECTRA — Electra
ELECTRA BEAUTY — Electra: Beauty
ELECTRA CAREER — Electra: Career
ELECTRA CHAT — Electra: Chat
ELECTRA CITY — Electra
ELECTRA DATING — Electra: Dating
ELECTRA FASHION — Electra: Fashion
ELECTRA GODDESS — Electra: Goddess of the Week
ELECTRA HOME — Electra: Home
ELECTRA HOROSCOPE — Electra: Horoscopes
ELECTRA HOROSCOPES — Electra: Horoscopes
ELECTRA LOVE LIFE — Electra: Love Life
ELECTRA MIND & BODY — Electra: Lifestyles
ELECTRA MIND AND BODY — Electra: Lifestyles
ELECTRA MONEY — Electra: Lifestyles
ELECTRA NEWS — Electra: News
ELECTRA RELATIONSHIP — Electra: Lifestyles
ELECTRA STYLE — Electra: Lifestyles
ELECTRA TIME OFF — Electra: Lifestyles
ELECTRA TIME-OFF — Electra: Lifestyles
ELECTRA WOMAN — Electra: Woman
ELECTRIC CONTRACTOR — AOL WorkPlace: Contractor's Community
ELECTRIC LIBRARY — Electric Library@AOL
ELECTRONIC GREETINGS — American Greetings: Online Greetings
ELECTRONIC NEWS — The Electronic Newsstand [Web site]
ELECTRONIC PARTNERS — Electronic Partnerships
ELECTRONIC POSTCARDS — American Greetings Online Greetings
ELECTRONICS SHOP — AOL Shopping: Electronics & Photo

ELECTRONICS SUPERSTORE — AOL Shoppers Advantage: Electronics and Cameras

ELI — Eli's Cheesecakes

ELI ON CO — Christianity Online: Eli

ELI'S — Eli's Cheesecakes

ELI'S CHEESECAKES — Eli's Cheesecakes

ELK GROVE VILLAGE — Digital City Chicago: Elk Grove Village [Web site]

ELLAS — AOL International: Greece

ELLE — Elle Online

ELM ST — AOL Canada: Subscribe to Elm Street Magazine!

ELM STREET — AOL Canada: Subscribe to Elm Street Magazine!

ELM STREET MAGAZINE — AOL Canada: Subscribe to Elm Street Magazine!

ELMER — Perkin Elmer Customer Service [Web Site]

ELVIS SHOP — AOL Shopping: Elvis Shop

E-MAIL — AOL Mail Center

EMAIL — AOL Mail Center

EMAIL CONTROLS — AOL Mail Center: Mail Controls

EMAIL EXTRA — AOL Mail Center: Mail Extras

EMAIL EXTRAS — AOL Mail Center: Mail Extras

EMAIL FILTER — AOL Mail Center: Junk Mail

EMAIL FINDER — AOL NetFind: Email Finder [Web site]

E-MAIL HELP — AOL Member Services: E-mail

EMAIL NEWS TO YOU — AOL Member Services: Get Only the News You Want

EMAIL SPICE UP — AOL Member Services: Spice Up Your E-mail

EMAIL WITH COLOR — AOL Member Services: Spice Up Your E-mail

EMAILED NEWS — AOL Member Services: Get Only the News You Want

EMATE — AOL Computing: eMate Portable Computing SIG

EMBASSY — Embassy Suites [Web site]

EMBASSY SUITE — Embassy Suites [Web site]

EMBASSY SUITES — Embassy Suites [Web site]

EMBROIDERY BUSINESS — AOL WorkPlace: Embroidery Community

EMERGENCY — Public Safety Center

EMIGRATION — Tell Us Your Story: Immigration Stories

EMOTION DETECTOR — Digital City: Emotion Detector

EMOTIONAL EATING — Thrive@Healthy Living: Food and Emotions

EMP CLASSIFIEDS — AOL Classifieds: Employment

EMPHYSEMA — AOL Health: Emphysema

EMPIRE STRIKES — Digital City Philadelphia: Star Wars

EMPLOYER CONTACTS — Employer Contacts Database

EMPLOYMENT — AOL WorkPlace channel

EMPLOYMENT AGENCIES — AOL WorkPlace: Employment Agencies & Services: Community

EMPLOYMENT CLASSIFIEDS — AOL Classifieds: Employment

EMPOWERMENT — Personal Empowerment Network
EN — American Express
ENCINO — Digital City Los Angeles: Carol Wolfe Real Estate
ENCINO HOMES — Digital City Los Angeles: Carol Wolfe Real Estate
ENCYCLOPEDIA — AOL Research & Learn: Encyclopedias
ENCYCLOPEDIAS — AOL Research & Learn: Encyclopedias
ENDOMETRIOSIS — AOL Health: Endometriosis
ENDOMETRIOSIS@THRIVE — Thrive@Healthy Living: Endometriosis
ENEWS & ISSUES — Electra: News
ENGAGE — Engage Games Online
ENGINEER — AOL WorkPlace: Engineering Community
ENGLAND — AOL UK (United Kingdom)
ENIGMA — Virgin Records: Enigma
ENT ASYLUM — Entertainment Asylum
ENT HELP — AOL Entertainment: Help Desk
ENT NEWSLETTER — AOL Entertainment: Newsletter Subscription
ENT STORE — AOL Entertainment: Store
ENTERTAIN — AOL Entertainment channel
ENTERTAINMENT — AOL Entertainment channel
ENTERTAINMENT ASYLUM — Entertainment Asylum
ENTERTAINMENT CHAT — AOL Entertainment: Chat
ENTERTAINMENT HELP DESK — AOL Entertainment: Help Desk
ENTERTAINMENT INDUSTRY — AOL Entertainment: The Industry
ENTERTAINMENT NEWSLETTER — AOL Entertainment: Newsletter
    Subscription
ENTERTAINMENT ONQ — onQ: Arts
ENTERTAINMENT REFERENCE — AOL Research & Learn: Entertainment
    and Leisure
ENTERTAINMENT SD — Digital City San Diego: Entertainment
ENTERTAINMENT SEARCH — AOL Entertainment: Search & Explore
ENTERTAINMENT SHOP — AOL Entertainment: Store
ENTERTAINMENT STORE — AOL Entertainment: Store
ENTERTAINMENT WEEKLY — Entertainment Weekly Online
ENTERTIANMENT HELP — AOL Entertainment: Help Desk
ENVIROLINK — The EnviroLink Network
ENVIRONMENTAL — Environmental Forum
ENVIRONMENTAL ED — Get Environmentally Educated
EOL BELFAST — AOL UK: Belfast Events Online
EOL BRISTOL — AOL UK: Bristol Events Online
EPCOT — Walt Disney World Resorts
EPICURIOUS — Epicurious Food and Travel [Web site]
EPICURIOUS.COM — Epicurious Food and Travel [Web site]
EPILEPSY — AOL Health: Epilepsy
EPSTEIN-BARR — AOL Health: Epstein-Barr Virus
EPSTEIN-BARRE — AOL Health: Epstein-Barr Virus
EPSTEIN-BARRE VIRUS — AOL Health: Epstein-Barr Virus

EQUATORIAL GUINEA — AOL International: Equatorial Guinea

EQUIBASE — ABC Sports: At The Track

EQUICHE — Upgrade to the Latest AOL Software

EQUITY REPORT — Morningstar: Stock Reports

EQUITY REPORTS — Morningstar: Stock Reports

ER — WB Online: ER

ERIC KARROS — Athlete Direct: Eric Karros

ERITREA — AOL International: Eritrea

ESCAPE DC — Digital City Washington: Local Day and Weekend Trips

ESEARCH — AOL Entertainment: Search & Explore

ESEARCH 97 — AOL Entertainment: Search & Explore

ESH — AOL Research & Learn: Electronic Schoolhouse

ESHOP — AOL Entertainment: Store

ESPANA — AOL International: Spain

ESPATRIATE TAXES — AOL International: Tax Information

ESPN — AOL Sports channel

ESPRESSO — Starbucks Coffee

ESTES PARK — Digital City Denver: Ponderosa Realty & Property

ESTONIA — AOL International: Estonia

ETEXT — AOL Computing: PDA Palmtop Paperbacks

ETEXTS — AOL Computing: PDA Palmtop Paperbacks

ETF — AOL Computing: Mac Education/Technology Forum

ETHIOPIA — AOL International: Ethiopia

ETHNICITY — AOL Lifestyles: Ethnicity

ETOY — EToys [Web site]

ETOYS — EToys [Web site]

E-TRADE — E*Trade Stock Brokerage

EURASIA — AOL International: Asia

EURO SKI REPS — AOL Sports: Skiing

EUROPE — AOL International: Europe

EVA — AOL International: Evita

EVA PERON — AOL International: Evita

EVANDER HOLYFIELD — Athlete Direct: Evander Holyfield

EVANSTON — Digital City Evanston [Web site]

EVENING STANDARD — AOL UK: Evening Standard Online [Web site]

EVENINGS WITH EVA — Women's Network: Evenings with Eva

EVENT — AOL Live

EVENT GUIDES — Digital City New York: Event Guide

EVENT PLANNING — AOL WorkPlace: Event Planning

EVENT SSF — Digital City San Francisco: Entertainment

EVENTCASTER — AOL Canada: Eventcasters

EVENTCASTERS — AOL Canada: Eventcasters

EVENTS — AOL Live

EVENTS ONQ — onQ: Chat and Conferences

EVERYTHING EDIBLE — AOL Entertainment: Recipes

EVITA — AOL International: Evita
EW — Entertainment Weekly Online
EWE — Women's Network: Evenings with Eva
EWIRE — AOL Entertainment: Newsletter Subscription
EXC — CultureFinder: Extreme Culture For Students
EXCEL — AOL Computing: Spreadsheet Applications
EXCITE — AOL NetFind [Web site]
EXCITE.COM — AOL NetFind [Web site]
EXERCISE — AOL Sports: Fitness
EXNET — American Express
EXPERT PAD — AOL Computing: PDA & Palmtop Forum
EXPLORE — AOL Canada: Arctic Journal
EXPLORE COMPUTING — AOL Computing: Search and Explore
EXPLORE LIFESTYLES — AOL Lifestyles: Search & Explore
EXPLORE PF — AOL Personal Finance: Search & Explore
EXPLORE PLACES — AOL Member Services: Places To Explore
EXPLORING YOUR HEALTH — Pfizer: Exploring Your Health
EXPOS — Montreal Expos
EXPRES RES — American Express: Travel
EXPRESS RESERVATION — American Express: Travel
EXPRESSNET — American Express
EXTRA — EXTRA Online
EXTRA STARS — EXTRA Online: Stars
EXTRA STARZ — EXTRA Online: Stars
EXTRA TV — EXTRA [Web site]
EXTRA TV.COM — EXTRA [Web site]
EXTREME — AOL Sports: Extreme Sports
EXTREME CULTURE — CultureFinder: Extreme Culture For Students
EXTREME FANS — Real Fans Sports Network
EXTREME SPORTS — AOL Sports: Extreme Sports
EXTREMISTS — AOL Sports: Extreme Sports
EYE ON INVESTMENTS — AOL Member Services: Keep an Eye on
    Investments
EYE ON SAN DIEGO — Digital City San Diego: Tom Blair
EYES — AOL Health: Eyes and Vision
EZINE — AOL Computing: PDA Palmtop Paperbacks
EZINES — AOL Entertainment: Digizine Sites on the Web
EZSCAN — Image Exchange: EZ Scan
F&S — Field & Stream Magazine
F4F — PlanetOut: Women's Community
FACE IT — Digital City Twin Cities: Face It with Summer & Suzi
FACT A DAY — AOL Research & Learn: Fact-A-Day
FACT-A-DAY — AOL Research & Learn: Fact-A-Day
FALL FOLIAGE — Fall Foliage [seasonal]
FALL GETAWAYS — AOL Travel: Great Fall Getaways
FALL SALE — AOL Shopping: Fall's Shop of Horrors [seasonal]

FALL SWEEPS — AOL Shopping: Sweepstakes [seasonal]

FALL SWEEPSTAKES — AOL Shopping: Sweepstakes [seasonal]

FALL TRAVEL — AOL Shopping: Sweepstakes [seasonal]

FALLS — Engage Games Online: Darkness Falls

FAMILIES — AOL Families channel

FAMILIES NEWSSTAND — AOL Families: NewsStand

FAMILIES SEARCH — AOL Families: Search & Explore

FAMILY — AOL Families channel

FAMILY AP — AOL News: Family Feed

FAMILY COMPUTING — AOL Computing: Family Computing

FAMILY DELUXE — AOL Store: Logo Shop

FAMILY DOCTOR — The Family Doctor

FAMILY DODGE — Digital City Philadelphia: Family Dodge

FAMILY FEED — AOL News: Family Feed

FAMILY FINANCES — Advice & Planning

FAMILY FOOD — AOL Interests: Family Food & Fun

FAMILY HISTORY — Tell Us Your Story: Immigration Stories

FAMILY INFOSOURCE — The Family Info Source

FAMILY LIFE — Family Life Online

FAMILY ONQ — onQ: Home & Family

FAMILY REFERENCE — AOL Research & Learn: Home and Family

FAMILY REUTERS — AOL News: Family Feed

FAMILY SOFTWARE — AOL Computing: Family Computing

FAMILY TIES — AOL Families: Extended Family

FAMILY TIMESAVERS — AOL NetFind: Family Timesavers

FAMILY TRAVEL — Family Travel Network

FAMILY TRAVEL NETWORK — Family Travel Network

FAMILY TREE — Family Tree Maker Online [Web site]

FAMILY VIOLENCE — Massachusetts Coalition of Battered Women
    Service Groups

FAMILY WIRES — AOL News: Family Feed

FAN CENTRAL — Fan Central Selections

FANCY — AOL Influence: The Good Life

FANCY DRINKS — Digital City Boston: Spirits and Fancy Drinks

FANS — Real Fans Sports Network

FANS CENTRAL — Fan Central Selections

FANTASY BASEBALL — AOL Grandstand: Fantasy Baseball

FANTASY BASEBALL PHILLY — Digital City Philadelphia: Fantasy
    Baseball

FANTASY BASKETBALL — AOL Grandstand: Fantasy Basketball

FANTASY HOCKEY — AOL Grandstand: Hockey

FANTASY HOOPS — AOL Grandstand: Fantasy Basketball

FANTASY LEAGUE — Cyber Sports Simulation Leagues

FANTASY LEAGUES — Cyber Sports Simulation Leagues

FANTASY MANHATTAN ISLAND — PlanetOut: FantasyMan Island Local

FANTASY ROCK — AOL UK: Fantasy Rock & Roll

FANTASYMAN — PlanetOut: FantasyMan Island
FANTASYMAN ISLAND — PlanetOut: FantasyMan Island for Chicago
FANTASYMAN ISLAND — PlanetOut: FantasyMan Island for Chicago
FANTASYMAN ISLAND BOSTON — PlanetOut: FantasyMan Island for Boston
FANTASYMAN ISLAND FLORIDA — PlanetOut: FantasyMan Island for Florida
FANTASYMAN ISLAND LOCAL — PlanetOut: FantasyMan Island
FANTASYMAN ISLAND WASHINGTON DC — PlanetOut: FantasyMan Island for
FAO — FAO Schwarz
FAO SCHWARZ — FAO Schwarz
FAO STORE — FAO Schwarz
FAQ FILES — Online Psych: FAQ Files
FAREFINDER — Preview Travel: FareFinder
FAREWAR — Preview Travel: Newswire
FAREWARS — Preview Travel: Newswire
FARGO — Wells Fargo Bank
FARM — AOL Interests: Pets
FARM ANIMAL — AOL Interests: Pets
FARM ANIMALS — AOL Interests: Pets
FARMER — AOL WorkPlace: Farming Community
FARMING — AOL WorkPlace: Farming Community
FARSIGHTED — AOL Health: Farsightedness
FARSIGHTEDNESS — AOL Health: Farsightedness
FASHION SUPERSTORE — AOL Shoppers Advantage: Fashion & Style
FAT OF THE LAND — British Bands: The Prodigy
FATHER — AOL Families channel
FATHER'S DAY — Father's Day @ AOL [seasonal]
FATHERS — AOL Families channel
FATHERS DAY — Father's Day @ AOL [seasonal]
FAVORITE PLACE — AOL Member Services: Favorite Places
FAVORITE PLACES — AOL Member Services: Favorite Places
FAVOURITE PLACES — AOL Member Services: Favorite Places
FB SCOREBOARD — STATS Football Scoreboard
FBI PARANORMAL SIM — AOL Entertainment: The X-Files
FBN — Fishing Broadcast Network
FC — AOL Computing: Family Computing
FC TIP — AOL Computing: Tips
FC TIPS — AOL Computing: Tips
FCF — AOL Computing: Family Computing
FD — AOL Full Disclosure
FDN — Food & Drink Network
FEB 14 — Valentine's Day @AOL [seasonal]
FED WATCH — Personal Finance: Fed Watch
FEEDBACK — AOL Member Services: Suggestion Boxes

FELLINI — Image Exchange: La Dolce Vita
FELLOWSHIP HALL — Christianity Online: Chat & Live Events
FEMALE — Formerly Employed Mothers at the Leading Edge
FEN — Family Education Network [Web site]
FERRIS — Digital City Denver: Magic Fun and Games
FFBN — Fly Fishing Broadcast Network
FFGF — Free-Form Gaming Forum
FFH — World Crisis Network
FIBROMYALGIA — AOL Health: Fibromyalgia
FID — Fidelity Investments
FID AT WORK — Fidelity Investments: Workplace Savings [Web site]
FID BROKER — Fidelity Investments
FID FUND — Fidelity Investments
FID FUNDS — Fidelity Investments
FID GUIDE — Fidelity Investments
FID NEW — Fidelity Investments
FID NEWS — Fidelity Investments
FID PLAN — Fidelity Investments
FIDELITY — Fidelity Investments
FIELD & STREAM — Field & Stream Magazine
FIESTA BOWL — AOL Sports: Fiesta Bowl
FIGURE SKATING — AOL Sports: Figure Skating
FIJI — AOL International: Fiji
FILE SEARCH — AOL Computing: File Search
FILEMAKER — Filemaker, Inc.
FILES — AOL Computing: File Search
FILM FORUM — AOL Entertainment: Movie Forums
FILM FORUMS — AOL Entertainment: Movie Forums
FILM INDUSTRY — AOL Entertainment: Etcetera
FILM REVIEW DATABASE — EXTRA: Film Reviews
FILM SEARCH — EXTRA: Film Reviews
FILM STUDIO — Film Studios
FILM STUDIOS — Film Studios
FILM TIMES — MovieLink [Web site]
FILMADELPHIA — Digital City Philadelphia: Movies
FIN WEB — AOL Personal Finance: Web Sites
FINANCE — AOL Personal Finance channel
FINANCE CENTER — AOL WorkPlace: Finance Center
FINANCE DC — Digital City Washington: Money Matters
FINANCIAL — AOL Personal Finance channel
FINANCIAL AID — AOL Research & Learn: Financial Aid
FINANCIAL NETWORK — DLJ Direct Brokers
FINANCIAL PLANNING — AOL Personal Finance: LifeStages Advice &
    Planning
FINANCIAL STATEMENT — Disclosure Financials
FINANCIALS — Disclosure Financials

FINANCING YOUR BUSINESS — AOL WorkPlace: Finance Center

FIND — AOL Find

FIND A BUSINESS — AOL NetFind: Yellow Pages [Web site]

FIND A JOB — AOL WorkPlace: Finding a Job

FIND A NEWSGROUP — AOL NetFind: Search Newsgroups [Web site]

FIND A PERSON — AOL NetFind: White Pages [Web site]

FIND BONNIE — Find Bonnie: Lost Dog [Web site]

FIND CENTRAL — AOL Find Central

FIND EMAIL — AOL NetFind: Email Finder [Web site]

FIND EVENTS — AOL Find: Online Events

FIND FOR KIDS — AOL NetFind: Kids [Web site]

FIND FRIENDS — AOL Member Services: Find Family and Friends
    Online

FIND GAME — AOL Games: Channel Guide

FIND GAMES — AOL Games: Channel Guide

FIND KIDS — AOL NetFind: Kids [Web site]

FIND PEOPLE — AOL Find: People

FIND SOFTWARE — AOL Find: Software

FINDING A JOB — AOL WorkPlace: Finding a Job

FINE DINING — AOL Interests: Fine Dining

FINLAND — AOL International: Finland

FINNAIR — FinnAir

FIREFIGHTING — Public Safety Center

FIRST PURCHASE — AOL Shopping: First Time Shopper Offer

FIRST TIME SHOPPER — AOL Shopping: First Time Shopper Offer

FIRST TRACKS — TransWorld Snowboarding

FIRST UNION — First Union National Bank

FIRST WIFE — Women's Network: The Club for First Wives

**FIRST WIVES — Women's Network: The Club for First
    Wives**

FIRSTFLOOR — Smart Bookmarks [Web site]

FISH — AOL Interests: Fishing

FISH ONQ — onQ: Pets

FISHIN — AOL Interests: Fishing

FISHING — AOL Interests: Fishing

FITNESS — AOL Sports: Fitness

FITNESS GEAR — The Fitness Store

FITNESS SHOP — Health & Fitness Shops

FITNESS SHOPPING — The Fitness Store

FITNESS STORE — Health & Fitness Shops

**FITZGERALD — Digital City Los Angeles: Valerie Fitzgerald
    Real Estate**

FITZGERALD REAL ESTATE BROKER — Digital City Los Angeles: Valerie
    Fitzgerald Real Estate

FIVE — What's New on AOL

FIVE STAR BOSTON — Digital City Boston: Style Eye

FIVE-STAR BOSTON — Digital City Boston: Style Eye
FIZER — Pfizer: Exploring Your Health
FLA BIZ REPORT — Digital City South Florida: Business news from
    dbusiness.com
FLIGHT — AOL Interests: Aviation & Aeronautics
FLIGHT SIM — Flight Simulations Resource Center
FLIGHT SIMS — Flight Simulations Resource Center
FLIGHT SIMULATIONS — Flight Simulations Resource Center
FLIRT! — Love@AOL: Flirt! Game
FLOODS — AOL News: Flood Coverage
FLOOR PLANS — Home Magazine Online: Build Your Own Home
FLORIDA BUSINESS — Digital City South Florida: Business news from
    dbusiness.com
FLORIDA M4M — PlanetOut: FantasyMan Island for Florida
FLORIDA MAP — Digital City South Florida: Map
FLORIDA MARLINS — Florida Marlins
FLORIDA TURKEY — Digital City Orlando: Let's Talk Turkey!
FLORIST — 1-800-FLOWERS
FLORISTS — 1-800-FLOWERS
FLOWER — 1-800-FLOWERS
FLOWER PRO — AOL WorkPlace: Florists Community
FLOWER PROFESSIONAL — AOL WorkPlace: Florists Community
FLOWER PROFESSIONALS — AOL WorkPlace: Florists Community
FLOWER PROS — AOL WorkPlace: Florists Community
FLOWERS & CARDS — AOL Shopping: Flowers, Cards & Candy
FLOWERS & CARDS SHOP — AOL Shopping: Flowers, Cards & Candy
FLOWERS — 1-800-FLOWERS
FLOWERS AND CARDS — AOL Shopping: Flowers, Cards & Candy
FLU — AOL Health: Influenza
FLY — AOL Interests: Aviation & Aeronautics
FLY FISH — Fly Fishing Broadcast Network
FLY FISHING — Fly Fishing Broadcast Network
FLY-FISHING — Fly Fishing Broadcast Network
FLYING — Flying Magazine Online
FLYING MAG — Flying Magazine Online
FLYING MAGAZINE — Flying Magazine Online
FMI — PlanetOut: FantasyMan Island
FMI ATL — PlanetOut: FantasyMan Island for Atlanta
FMI ATLANTA — PlanetOut: FantasyMan Island for Atlanta
FMI BARRACKS — PlanetOut: Military M4M
FMI BOSTON — PlanetOut: FantasyMan Island for Boston
FMI CHICAGO — PlanetOut: FantasyMan Island for Chicago
FMI DC — PlanetOut: FantasyMan Island for Washington DC
FMI FLORIDA — PlanetOut: FantasyMan Island for Florida
FMI LA — PlanetOut: FantasyMan Island for Los Angeles
FMI LOCAL — PlanetOut FantasyMan Island

FMI LOS ANGELES — PlanetOut: FantasyMan Island for Los Angeles
FMI MILITARY — PlanetOut: Military M4M
FMI NEW YORK — PlanetOut: FantasyMan Island for New York
FMI NYC — PlanetOut: FantasyMan Island for New York
FMI SAN FRANCISCO — PlanetOut: FantasyMan Island for San Francisco
FMI SF — PlanetOut: FantasyMan Island for San Francisco
FN EOL — AOL UK: Far North Events Online
FOA — Christianity Online: Friends Of Amy
FOCUS — AOL Research & Learn: Photography
FOCUS ON ART — AOL Research & Learn: Focus on Art
FOG — The Fellowship of Online Gamers
FOLIAGE — Fall Foliage [seasonal]
FOMC — AOL Personal Finance: Fed Watch
FOOD & DRINK NETWORK — Food & Drink Network
FOOD — AOL Interests: Food
FOOD ADDICTION — AOL Health: Food Addiction
FOOD ALLERGIES — AOL Health: Food Allergies
FOOD FOR THE HUNGRY — World Crisis Network
FOOD LOVER — Electronic Gourmet Guide: Food Lovers Main Directory
FOOD LOVERS — Electronic Gourmet Guide: Food Lovers Main Directory
FOOD NETWORK — The Food Network's CyberKitchen [Web site]
FOOD SERVICE — AOL WorkPlace: Food & Beverage
FOOL — Motley Fool
FOOL BALL — Motley Fool: Foolball
FOOL CAFE — Motley Fool: Fool Cafe
FOOL DTV — Motley Fool: Video
FOOL HEALTH — Motley Fool: Health
FOOL MART — Motley Fool: FoolMart!
FOOL REIT — Motley Fool: Real Estate
FOOL SPECIAL — Motley Fool: Special Offer
FOOL SPORTS — Motley Fool: Foolball
FOOL STORE — Motley Fool: FoolMart!
FOOL TRIVIA — The Motley Fool Trivia
FOOL UK — AOL UK: The Motley Fool
FOOL VID — Motley Fool: Video
FOOLBOWL — Motley Fool: College FoolBowl
FOOLS — Motley Fool
FOOTBALL — AOL Sports: Pro Football
FOOTBALL PHILLY — Digital City Philadelphia: Pro Football
FOOTBALL SCOREBOARD — STATS Football Scoreboard
FOOTBALL STARS — AOL Sports: Pro Football Stars
FOR — Christianity Online: ForeFront Records
FOREFRONT — Christianity Online: ForeFront Records

FOREIGN — AOL Research & Learn: International

FOREIGN DICTIONARY — AOL International: Language Dictionaries & Resources

FOREIGN EXCHANGE — The Universal Currency Converter [Web site]

FOREIGN LANGUAGE — AOL International: Language Dictionaries & Resources

FOREIGN NATIONALS TAXES — AOL International: Tax Information

FORMAT — Digital City Twin Cities: Format Magazine

FORSYTHE — AOL Canada: Doug Forsythe Gallery

FORSYTHE GALLERY — AOL Canada: Doug Forsythe Gallery

FORT LAUDERDALE BLACK VOICES — Black Voices: South Florida

FORUM — AOL Computing: Help Desk

FORUMS — AOL Computing: Help Desk

FOSSIL — Fossil Watches [Web site]

FOSSIL WATCHES — Fossil Watches [Web site]

FOTO FORUM — Digital City Philadelphia: Photo Galleries

FOTO PHILLY — Digital City Philadelphia: Photo Galleries

FOURTH OF JULY — Independence Day@AOL [seasonal]

FRAGRANCE — The Fragrance Counter

FRAGRANCE COUNTER — The Fragrance Counter

FRANCE — AOL International: France

FRANCHISE — AOL WorkPlace: Franchising

FRANK — Goodbye, Blue Eyes [special]

FRANK SINATRA — Entertainment Asylum: Club Sinatra

FRASIER — AOL Entertainment: Frasier Tuesdays Fan Forum

FRASIER TUESDAYS — AOL Entertainment: Frasier Tuesdays Fan Forum

FREE CARDS — Digital City San Francisco: Electronic Cards

FREE POSTCARDS — Digital City San Francisco: Electronic Cards

FREEDOM LIFTS — Digital City Washington: Freedom Lifts

FREEHAND — AOL Computing: Vector Artists SIG

FREELANCE — AOL WorkPlace: Illustration

FREELOVE — Love@AOL: Free Love Newsletter

FREEWARE — AOL Computing: Download Software

FRENCH POLYNESIA — AOL International: French Polynesia

FRENCH TEST — Sign On A Friend in France

FRENCH WORDS — AOL International: Language Games

FREQUENT FLYER — InsideFlyer Online

FRESH AIR CAFE — Fresh Air Cafe: Smokefree Party

FRESNO LOCAL NEWS — Digital City Fresno: Local News

FRESNO NEWS — Digital City Fresno: Local News

FRIEND IN FRANCE — Sign on a Friend in France

FRIENDS OF AMY — Christianity Online: Friends Of Amy Grant

FRIENDS ONLINE — AOL Member Services: Find Family and Friends Online

FROM THE CHEAP SEATS — AOL UK: Planet Ealing: In The Cheap Seats [Web site]

FRONTIERS — Scientific American: Frontiers

FSFCA — Digital City San Francisco: Fantasy and Science Fiction Creative Artists Forum

FSRC — Flight Simulations Resource Center

FSS — AOL Shopping: Fall Shop of Horrors [seasonal]

FT LAUD LOCAL NEWS — Digital City Fort Lauderdale: Local News

FT LAUDERDALE LOCAL NEWS — Local News for South Florida

FT WORTH — Digital City Dallas-Forth Worth

FT WORTH CHAT — Digital City Dallas-Forth Worth: Chat

FT WORTH DINING GUIDE — Digital City Dallas-Forth Worth: Dining Guide

FT WORTH LOCAL NEWS — Digital City Dallas-Forth Worth: Local News

FT WORTH MOVIES — Digital City Dallas-Forth Worth: Movie Guide

FT WORTH PERSONALS — Digital City Dallas-Forth Worth: Personals

FT WORTH REAL ESTATE — Digital City Dallas-Forth Worth: Real Estate

FT WORTH RELIGION — Digital City Dallas-Forth Worth: Religion

FT WORTH SPORTS — Digital City Dallas-Forth Worth: Sports

FT WORTH TV NAVIGATOR — Digital City Dallas-Forth Worth: TV Navigator

FT WORTH WEBGUIDE — Digital City Dallas-Forth Worth: WebGuide

FT WORTH WHITE PAGES — Digital City Dallas-Forth Worth: Directory [Web site]

FT WORTH YELLOW PAGES — Digital City Dallas-Forth Worth: Directory [Web site]

FTM — Genealogy Forum: Family Tree Maker Online

FTN — Family Travel Network

FTP — File Transfer Protocol (FTP)

FTP HELP — AOL Member Services: Internet & World Wide Web

FULL DISCLOSURE — AOL Full Disclosure

FUN GAMES — AOL Member Services: Play Games Online

FUN NEWS — AOL News: The Back Page

FUN SD — Digital City San Diego: Entertainment

FUNB — First Union National Bank

FUND — AOL Personal Finance: Mutual Fund Center

FUND BRIEF — Mutual Fund Center: Brief

FUND NEWS — Mutual Fund Center: Brief

FUND NEWS DAILY — Mutual Fund Center: Brief

FUND PORTFOLIO — Mutual Fund Center: Building Your Fund Portfolio

FUND VAULT — Mutual Fund Center: Vault

FUNDATA — AOL Canada: Fundata Mutual Fund Updates and Interest

FUNDING FOCUS — RSP Funding Focus

FUNDS & RETIREMENT — Mutual Fund Center: Retirement Investment Strategies

FUNDS — AOL Personal Finance: Mutual Fund Center

FUNDS LIVE — Mutual Fund Center: Live

FUNDWORKS — Mutual Fund Center: Fundworks

FUNERAL — AOL WorkPlace: Funeral Directors' Community
FUNERAL DIRECTOR — AOL WorkPlace: Funeral Directors' Community
FUNERAL PARLOR — AOL WorkPlace: Funeral Directors' Community
FUNNIES — The Funny Pages
FURNISHINGS — AOL Interests: Home & Garden
FURNITURE — Furniture Selections
FURRY SCURRY — Digital City Denver: Dumb Friends League
FUTURE — Can You Believe What's Possible These Days?
FUTURE CONNECT — Future Connectivity Options
FUTURE CONNECTIVITY — Future Connectivity Options
FW — Mutual Fund Center: Fundworks
FW STORE — Fossil Watches [Web site]
FX — The Universal Currency Converter [Web site]
G IS IN THE HOUSE — Garry Cobb's Sports Notebook
GABON — AOL International: Gabon
GADGET — The Gadget Guru Online
GADGET GURU — The Gadget Guru Online
GALAXY — Digital City Los Angeles: Galaxy
GALLERY — AOL Gallery
GALLSTONES — AOL Health: Gallstones
GALPIN — Digital City Los Angeles: Galpin Motor Cars
GALPIN FORD — Digital City Los Angeles: Galpin Ford
GALPIN JAGUAR — Digital City Los Angeles: Galpin Jaguar
GALPIN JAGUAR LA — Digital City Los Angeles: Galpin Jaguar
GALPIN LINCOLN — Digital City Los Angeles: Galpin Lincoln-Mercury
GALPIN LINCOLN-MERCURY — Digital City Los Angeles: Galpin Lincoln-
    Mercury
GALPIN MOTOR CARS — Digital City Los Angeles: Galpin Motor Cars
GAMBIA — AOL International: The Gambia
GAME — AOL Games channel
GAME CELEBRITY — Game Show: Celebrity Connection
GAME DAY — Pro and College Football Game Day Selections
GAME DEMOS — AOL Games: Download Game Demos [Web site]
GAME DESIGN — Game Designers Forum
GAME DESIGNER — Game Designers Forum
GAME DESIGNERS — Game Designers Forum
GAME DOWNLOADS — AOL Games: Download Game Demos
    [Web site]
GAME FIND — AOL Games: Channel Guide
GAME HELP — Online Games Technical Support
GAME ON — AOL UK: Games channel
GAME PICKS — AOL Games: Top Games Picks
GAME SHOP — AOL Shopping: Toys & Collectibles
GAME SHOW — AOL Games: Game Shows
GAME SHOWS — AOL Games: Game Shows
GAME SHOWS CHAT — Game Shows: Chat

GAMEROOM — Real Fans: Gameroom
GAMERZ PIT — PlugIn: The GAMERz Pit
GAMES — AOL Games channel
GAMES BY WORLDPLAY — WorldPlay: Games
GAMES CELEB — Game Shows: Celebrity Connection
GAMES CENTRAL — AOL Games: Games Central
GAMES CHANNEL — AOL Games channel
GAMES CHANNEL FIND — AOL Games: Channel Guide
GAMES COMMUNITY — AOL Games: Community
GAMES COOL LINKS — AOL Games: Cool Links
GAMES DOWNLOADS — AOL Games: Download Game Demos
    [Web site]
GAMES FIND — AOL Games: Channel Guide
GAMES FORUM — AOL Games: PC Games
GAMES GUIDE — AOL Games: Games Guide
GAMES HELP — AOL Games: Online Games Technical Support
GAMES HOME PAGES — AOL Games: Official Game Sites [Web site]
GAMES HOT — AOL Games: Top Games Picks
GAMES INSIDER — AOL Games: Games Insider
GAMES INTERN — AOL UK: Local Life Newsletter
GAMES NEWSSTAND — AOL Games: Newsstand
GAMES PLAY — AOL Member Services: Play Games Online
GAMES SEARCH — AOL Games: Search & Explore
GAMESPOT UK — AOL UK: GameSpot
GAMESTORM — GameStorm Corporation
GAMING — AOL Games: Online Gaming Forums
GAP — The Gap [Web site]
GARDEN — AOL Interests: Gardening
GARDEN ESCAPE — Garden.com [Web site]
GARDEN ONQ — onQ: Home & Garden
GARDEN SPOT — AOL Interests: Gardening
GARDEN.COM — Garden.com [Web site]
GARDENER — AOL Interests: Gardening
GARDENING — AOL Interests: Gardening
GARDENS — AOL Interests: Gardening
GARRY COBB — Garry Cobb's Sports Notebook
<u>GARY COBB</u> — Garry Cobb's Sports Notebook
GASO — Great American Smokeout
GATEWAY — Gateway 2000
GATEWAY 2000 — Gateway 2000
GATHER CLAN — Gathering of the Clans
GATHER CLANS — Gathering of the Clans
GATHERING OF CLAN — Gathering of the Clans
GATHERING OF CLANS — Gathering of the Clans
GAY — AOL Interests: Gay & Lesbian
GAY AFRO — NetNoir: Gay & Lesbian

GAY ART — onQ: Image
GAY BLACKS — NetNoir: Gay & Lesbian
GAY BOARDS — onQ: Message Boards
GAY BOOKS — Lambda Rising Bookstore Online
GAY BUSSINESS — onQ: Business
GAY CAFE — Digital City Dallas-Fort Worth: Metro Gay & Lesbian
   Forum
GAY CARDS — onQ: Tzabaco
GAY CHAT — onQ: Chat and Conferences
GAY ENTERTAINMENT — onQ: Arts
GAY HOMES — onQ: Home & Garden
GAY LIBRARY — onQ: Libraries
GAY MARRIAGE — onQ: Marriage
GAY MESSAGE — onQ: Message Boards
GAY NEWS — onQ: News
GAY NN — NetNoir: Gay & Lesbian
GAY ONQ — onQ: Men
GAY ORG — onQ: Organizations
GAY ORGS — onQ: Organizations
GAY PHILLY — Digital City Philadelphia: Gay & Lesbian Links
GAY PRIDE SF — Digital City San Francisco: Gay Pride
GAY SF CHAT — Digital City San Francisco: Gay & Lesbian Chat
GAY SOFTWARE — onQ: Libraries
GAY TEEN — onQ: Youth
GAY TRIVIA — onQ: Gaymeland
GAY UK — AOL UK: Utopia Gay & Lesbian Forum
GAY VET — onQ: Military
GAY YOUTH — onQ: Youth
GAYLE FEE — Boston Herald: Gossip Gals
GAYME — onQ: Gaymeland
GAYMELAND — onQ: Gaymeland
GAYMES — onQ: Gaymeland
GAZEBO — onQ: Transgender Community Chats
GBL — AOL Grandstand: Simulation Baseball
GC CENTRAL — AOL Games: Games Central
GC COOL — AOL Games: Cool Links
GC COOL LINKS — AOL Games: Cool Links
GC DIRECTX — AOL Games: DirectX Information
GC FIND — AOL Games: Channel Guide
GC FL — AOL Grandstand: Simulation Football
GC FUN — AOL Games: Game Shows
GC HOT — AOL Games: Top Games Picks
GC INFO — AOL Games: Video Games Forum
GC INSIDER — AOL Games: Games Insider
GC NEWSSTAND — AOL Games: Newsstand
GC VOICE — AOL Games: Games Insider

GCS — AOL Games: Gaming Company Support
GD STORE — The Grateful Dead Forum: Store
GDF — The Grateful Dead Forum
GDF BUS DRIVER — The Grateful Dead Forum: Chat Rules Area
GDF BUS DRVIER — The Grateful Dead Forum: Chat Rules Area
GEICO — Geico Insurance
GEICO INSURANCE — Geico Insurance
GEMINI — Horoscope Selections
GENEALOGY — Genealogy Forum
GENEALOGY CLUB — Genealogy Forum
GENERAL AVIATION — AOL Interests: Aviation & Aeronautics
GENERAL HOSPITAL — ABC Online: Daytime
GENERAL REFERENCE — AOL Research & Learn: More References
GENERATION — Generation Next
GENESIS — AOL Games: Video Games Forum
GENX — AOL Lifestyles: Ages & Stages
GEO BOUTIQUE — AOL Canada: Canadian Geographic Boutique
GEO STORE — AOL Canada: Canadian Geographic Boutique
GEOFF MOORE — Christianity Online: Geoff Moore & the Distance
GEOFF MOORE — Forefront Records: Geoff Moore & The Distance
GEOGRAPHIC RESEARCH — Regional Resources
GEOGRAPHY — AOL Research & Learn: Geography & Maps
GEOGRAPHY REFERENCE — AOL Research & Learn: Geography &
    Maps
GEORGE — George Magazine
GEORGE HOBICA — Digital City Boston: Travel Guy
GEORGE MAG — George Magazine
GEORGE MAGAZINE — George Magazine
GEORGE ONLINE — George Magazine
GEORGES PERRIER — Digital City Philadelphia: Dining Guide
GEORGETOWN MED — Georgetown University Medical Center
    [Web site]
GEORGIA EMPLOYMENT — Digital City Atlanta: Employment Classifieds
GERMAN — AOL International: The Bistro
GERMAN DICTIONARY — AOL International: Language Dictionary &
    Resources
GERMAN WORDS — AOL International: Language Games
GERMANY — AOL International: Germany
GERTIE SF — Digital City San Francisco: Triviana
GET 2.7 — Download Mac AOL v.2.7 Software
GET 25 — Download Windows AOL v.2.5 for Windows
GET 27 — Download Mac AOL v.2.7 Software
GET 3.0 — Download Windows AOL v.3.0 for Windows
GET 30 — Download Windows AOL v.3.0 for Windows
GET 95 — Download Windows AOL v.3.0 for Windows 95
GET MAC 27 — Download Mac AOL v.27 Software

GET NETSCAPE — Download Netscape Navigator for AOL
GETSMART — GetSmart Loan Center
GETTING AHEAD — AOL WorkPlace: Advancing Your Career
GETTING AROUND HELP — AOL Member Services: Getting Around & Using AOL
GETTING STARTED — AOL WorkPlace: Getting Started
GF BASE — AOL Grandstand: Fantasy Baseball
GF BASEBALL — AOL Grandstand: Fantasy Baseball
GFB — AOL Grandstand: Fantasy Basketball
GFBL — AOL Grandstand: Fantasy Baseball
GFH — AOL Grandstand: Fantasy Hockey
GFPBL — AOL Grandstand: Simulation Baseball
GG TODAY — Global Gourmet: Today
GGL — AOL Grandstand: Simulation Golf
GGS — Global Gourmet: Shops
GGT — Global Gourmet: Today
GHANA — AOL International: Ghana
GHG — Good Hotel Guide to Great Britain & Ireland [Web site]
GHN — The AOL Greenhouse
GI JANE — EXTRA: G.I. Jane
GIANTS — San Francisco Giants -or- New York Giants
GIFT — Gifts Screen
GIFT BASKET MAKER — AOL WorkPlace: Gift Baskets Professional Forum
GIFT BASKET PRO — AOL WorkPlace: Gift Baskets Professional Forum
GIFT CERTIFICATE — AOL Shopping: Gifts and Gadgets
GIFT CERTIFICATES — AOL Shopping: Gifts and Gadgets
GIFT FIND — AOL Shopping: Message Boards
GIFT FINDER — AOL Shopping: Message Boards
GIFT REMINDER — AOL Reminder Service
GIFT SENDER — AOL Shopping: Message Boards
GIFT SERVICE — AOL Shopping: May We Help You?
GIFT SERVICES — AOL Shopping: May We Help You?
GIFT SHOP — AOL Shopping: Gifts & Gadgets
GIFT VALET — AOL Reminder Service
GIFT WORK — 911 Gifts Online Store
GIFT WORKS — 911 Gifts Online Store
GIFTS — AOL Shopping: Gifts & Gadgets
GIFTS 911 — 911 Gifts Online Store
GIL SPORTS — Digital City Denver: Gil Sports
GIN — WorldPlay: Gin
GIRL POWER — Virgin Records: The SPICE Girls
GIRL SPOT — Digital City San Francisco: Lesbian Bars [Web site]
GIRLJOCK — onQ: GirlJock Magazine
GIRLJOCK MAGAZINE — onQ: GirlJock Magazine
GIRLJOCK ONQ — onQ: GirlJock Magazine

GIX — AOL Games: Gaming Information Exchange
GJ — onQ: GirlJock Magazine
GL — AOL Influence: The Good Life
GLASGOW — AOL UK: Local Life
GLASGOW PERSONALS — AOL UK: The Love Shack
GLAUCOMA — AOL Health: Glaucoma
GLCF — onQ: Gay & Lesbian Community
GLCF BOARDS — onQ: Message Boards
GLCF CARDS — onQ: Tzabaco
GLCF CHAT — onQ: Chat and Conferences
GLCF H2H — onQ: Relationships
GLCF LIBRARIES — onQ: Libraries
GLCF LIBRARY — onQ: Library
GLCF NEWS — onQ: News
GLCF ORGS — onQ: Organizations
GLCF QUILT — AIDS Memorial
GLCF SF — onQ: San Francisco
GLCF SOFTWARE — onQ: Library
GLCF WOMAN — onQ: Women's Space
GLCF WOMEN — onQ: Women's Space
GLCF YOUTH — onQ: Youth
GLENNA — Glenna's Garden: Cancer Support Forum
GLENNA'S — Glenna's Garden: Cancer Support Forum
GLENNA'S GARDEN — Glenna's Garden: Cancer Support Forum
GLOBAL — Global Village
GLOBAL ACCESS — International Access
GLOBAL DINER — The Global Gourmet: Diner
GLOBAL GOURMET SHOP — The Global Gourmet: Shops
GLOBAL GOURMET TODAY — The Global Gourmet: Today
GLOBAL LINK — Globalink Store
GLOBAL MEDIC — AOL UK: Global Medic Health Center
GLOBAL MEETING — AOL International: Global Meeting Place
GLOBAL MEETING PLACE — AOL International: Global Meeting Place
GLOBAL STEWARDSHIP — Christianity Online: Global Stewardship
GLOBALINK — Globalink Store
GLOBALNET — International Access
GLOBE — AOL Live
GLOSSARY — AOL Glossary
GLOUCESTER — Digital City Philadelphia: South Jersey Interactive
GLSF — Digital City San Francisco: Gay Community
GLSF CHAT — Digital City San Francisco: Gay & Lesbian Chat
GM — General Motors [Web site]
GM CABLE — Digital City Philadelphia: Greater Media Cable Company
GM CC — Digital City Twin Cities: Greater Minneapolis Chamber of Commerce
GM FORUM — Guerrilla Marketing Forum

GMA — ABC Online: Good Morning America
GMAT — KAPLAN Online -or- The Princeton Review
GMD — Forefront Records: Geoff Moore & The Distance Main Page
GMEDIC — AOL UK: Global Medic Health Center
GMFL — AOL Grandstand: Simulation Football
GN — GrittySoft Newsletters
GO 2 ORLANDO — Digital City Orlando: Go2Orlando Travel Service
GO DC — Digital City Washington: Business and Tourist Travel
    Information
GO DEACS — Real Fans: Wake Forest Team Club
GO DODGE — Digital City Philadelphia: Family Dodge
GO EXPOS — Real Fans: Montreal Expos Team Club
GO OS — Omaha Steaks International
GO SCUBA — AOL Scuba
GODIVA — Godiva Chocolatier
GODIVA CHOCLATIER — Godiva Chocolatier
GOING ON — Digital City New York: What's Going On
GOLD MEDALLION — Christianity Online: Gold Medallion Winners
GOLDEN — Molson's [Web site]
GOLDEN GATE — Digital City San Francisco: Golden Gate Forum
GOLF — AOL Sports: Golf
GOLF AMERICA — iGolf
GOLF ATLAS — Golf Atlas
GOLF COURSE — iGolf: golfcourse.com
GOLF COURSE.COM — iGolf
GOLF PRO SHOP — iGolf: Golf Pro Shop
GOLF SHOPPING — iGolf: Golf Pro Shop
GOLF STORE — iGolf: Golf Pro Shop
GOLFDATA — GolfData Information Center
GOLFER — AOL Sports: Golf
GOLFIS — Golfis Forum
GOLFWEB — GolfWeb [Web site]
GONORRHEA — AOL Health: Gonorrhea
GONYEA — AOL WorkPlace: Gonyea Online Career Center
GOOD HOTEL — Good Hotel Guide to Great Britain & Ireland
    [Web site]
GOOD HOTEL GUIDE — Good Hotel Guide to Great Britain & Ireland
    [Web site]
GOOD HOTELS — Good Hotel Guide to Great Britain & Ireland
    [Web site]
GOOD LIFE — AOL Influence: The Good Life
GOOD LIVING — AOL Influence: The Good Life
GOOD MORNING AMERICA — ABC Online: Good Morning America
GOOD TASTE — AOL UK: Good Taste
GOP — Republican National Committee [Web site]
GOPHER — Internet Connection: Gopher

GOPHER HELP — AOL Member Services: Internet & World Wide Web
GORILLAS — Saving Gorillas in the Mist
<u>GORLIER'S</u> — The Grolier Multimedia Encyclopedia [Web site]
GORP SF — Digital City San Francisco: Outdoor Recreation
GOSSIP GALS — Digital City Boston: Gossip Gals
GOTC — Gathering of the Clans
GOURMET FOOD — AOL Shopping: Gourmet Gifts
GOURMET GARAGE — AOL Australia: Gourmet Garage
GOURMET GIFTS — AOL Shopping: Gourmet Gifts
GOURMET SUPERSTORE — AOL Shoppers Advantage: The Perfect Table
GPFL — AOL Grandstand: Simulation Football
GRAD SCHOOL — AOL Research & Learn: Graduate & Professional
    Schools
GRADS — Graduation@AOL [seasonal]
GRADUATE SCHOOL — Graduate School
GRADUATION — Graduation@AOL [seasonal]
GRADUATION@AOL — Graduation@AOL [seasonal]
GRAFFITI — Hecklers Online: Digital Graffiti
GRAMMAR — AOL Research & Learn: Grammar and Style
GRAMMATRAIN — Forefront Records: Grammatrain Main Page
GRAND NATIONAL — AOL UK: The Martell British Grand National
GRAND OLD PARTY — Republican National Committee [Web site]
GRAND OLE PARTY — Republican National Committee [Web site]
GRAND PRIX — AOL UK: Motor Sport Area
GRAND RAPIDS LOCAL NEWS — Digital City Grand Rapids: Local News
GRAND RAPIDS NEWS — Digital City Grand Rapids: Local News
GRANDMA MARGO — AOL Shopping: Virtual Fruitcake
GRANDSTAND — AOL Sports: Grandstand
GRANDSTAND FANTASY BASEBALL — AOL Grandstand: Fantasy
    Baseball
GRANDSTAND FANTASY BASKETBALL — AOL Grandstand: Basketball
GRANDSTAND FANTASY HOCKEY — AOL Grandstand: Fantasy Hockey
GRANDSTAND FANTASY HOOPS — AOL Grandstand: Fantasy
    Basketball
GRANDSTAND TRIVIA — AOL Grandstand: Trivia
GRANT — AOL Research & Learn: Financial Aid
GRANT A WISH — Grant-A-Wish Foundation
GRANT FUNDING — AOL Computing: Education/Technology Polaris
    Grants Center
GRANT WRITING — AOL Computing: Education/Technology Polaris
    Grants Center
GRANTS — AOL Research & Learn: Financial Aid
GRAPEFRUIT LEAGUE — Digital City Philadelphia: Phillies Spring
    Training
GRAPHIC DESIGN — AOL WorkPlace: Designers
GRAPHIC SUITE — AOL Store: GraphicSuite

GRAPHIC TOOLS — AOL Computing: Graphic Tools
GRAPHICS TOOLS — AOL Computing: Graphic Tools
GRAPHSUITE — AOL Store: GraphicSuite
GRATEFUL DEAD — The Grateful Dead Forum
GRE — AOL Research & Learn: Graduate & Professional Schools
GREAT CANADA ICE STORM — AOL Canada: The Great Ice Storm
GREAT ESCAPE — AOL Travel: Great Escape Newsletter
GREATER CABLE — Digital City Philadelphia: Greater Media Cable
    Company
GREATER MEDIA — Digital City Philadelphia: Greater Media Cable
    Company
GREECE — AOL International: Greece
GREEN BEER — AOL International: Irish Heritage
GREENFINGERS — AOL UK: Green Fingers Gardening Tips
GREENHOUSE — AOL Studios [Web site]
GREENHOUSE NETWORKS — AOL Studios [Web site]
GREENSBORO — Digital City Greensboro
GREENSBORO LOCAL NEWS — Digital City Greensboro: Local News
GREENSBORO NEWS — Digital City Greensboro: Local News
GREENVILLE LOCAL NEWS — Digital City Greenville: Local News
GREENVILLE NEWS — Digital City Greenville: Local News
GREENWICH FESTIVAL — AOL UK: Greenwich & Docklands
    International Festival [Web site]
GREET ST — Greet Street
GREET STREET — Greet Street
GREETINGS — American Greetings Online Greetings
GRENADA — AOL International: Grenada
GRENADINES — AOL International: Grenadines
GRIEF SUPPORT — AOL Health: Grief Support Community
GRILLING — AOL Interests: Grilling
GRITTYNEWS — GrittySoft Newsletters
GRIZZLIES — Vancouver Grizzlies
GROCER — AOL WorkPlace: Grocers' Community
GROCERY STORE — AOL WorkPlace: Grocers' Community
GROLIER — The Grolier Multimedia Encyclopedia [Web site]
GROLIER'S — The Grolier Multimedia Encyclopedia [Web site]
GROLIERS — The Grolier Multimedia Encyclopedia [Web site]
GROOM — The Knot: Weddings for the Real World
GROUMET GOSSIP — Cindy Adams: Queen of Gourmet Gossip
GROUPWARE — AOL Computing: GroupWare SIG
GS — AOL Grandstand
GS ABL — AOL Grandstand: Simulation Basketball
GS ARTS — AOL Grandstand: Martial Arts Forum
GS AUTO — AOL Grandstand: Motor Sports Forum
GS BASEBALL — AOL Grandstand: Baseball Forum
GS BASKETBALL — AOL Grandstand: Basketball

GS BOWLING — AOL Grandstand: Bowling Forum
GS BOXING — AOL Grandstand: Boxing Forum
GS CENTRAL — AOL Games: Community
GS CHAT — Game Shows: Chat
GS COLLECTING — AOL Grandstand: Sports Cards Forum
GS COLLEGE BASKETBALL — AOL Grandstand: College Basketball
    Forum
GS COLLEGE BB — AOL Grandstand: College Basketball Forum
GS COLLEGE FOOTBALL — AOL Grandstand: Motor Sports Forum
GS COMM — AOL Games: Community
GS COMMUNITY — AOL Grandstand: Community Sports Forum
GS COMMUNITY SPORTS — AOL Grandstand: Community Sports Forum
GS DART — AOL Grandstand: Darts Forum
GS DARTS — AOL Grandstand: Darts Forum
GS DL — AOL Grandstand: Basketball
GS EXTREME — AOL Grandstand: Extreme Sports
GS EXTREME SPORTS — AOL Grandstand: Extreme Sports
GS FANTASY BASKETBALL — AOL Grandstand: Basketball
GS FANTASY HOCKEY — AOL Grandstand: Hockey
GS FANTASY HOOPS — AOL Grandstand: Basketball
GS FITNESS — AOL Grandstand: Fitness Forum
GS FOOTBALL — AOL Grandstand: Pro Football Forum
GS GOLF — AOL Grandstand: Golf Forum
GS HELP — Game Shows: Hints & Help
GS HINT — Game Shows: Hints & Help
GS HINTS — Game Shows: Hints & Help
GS HOCKEY — AOL Grandstand: Hockey Forum
GS HORSE — AOL Grandstand: Horse Forum
GS HUNTER — AOL Grandstand: Hunter/Jumper Forum
GS JUMPER — AOL Grandstand: Hunter/Jumper Forum
GS LACROSSE — AOL Grandstand: Lacrosse Forum
GS LEISURE — AOL Grandstand: Leisure Sports
GS LEISURE SPORTS — AOL Grandstand: Leisure Sports
GS MARTIAL ARTS — AOL Grandstand: Martial Arts Forum
GS MORE — AOL Grandstand: More Sports
GS MORE SPORTS — AOL Grandstand: More Sports
GS OUTDOOR — AOL Grandstand: Outdoor Sports Forum
GS OUTDOOR SPORTS — AOL Grandstand: Outdoor Sports Forum
GS OUTDOORS — AOL Grandstand: Outdoor Sports Forum
GS PAINTBALL — AOL Grandstand: Paintball Forum
GS PRO BASKETBALL — AOL Grandstand: NBA Forum
GS PRO FOOTBALL — AOL Grandstand: NFL Forum
GS QOTD — AOL Grandstand: Sports Trivia Question of the Day
GS SCUBA — AOL Grandstand: Scuba Forum
GS SIDELINE — AOL Grandstand: Sideline
GS SKATING — AOL Grandstand: Skating Forum

GS SOCCER — AOL Grandstand: Soccer Forum
GS SOFTBALL — AOL Grandstand: Softball Forum
GS SOFTWARE — AOL Grandstand: Sports Software HQ
GS SPORTS CARDS — AOL Grandstand: Sports Cards Forum
GS SPORTS TRIVIA — AOL Grandstand: Trivia
GS SPORTSMART — AOL Grandstand: SportsMart
GS SWIMMING — AOL Grandstand: Swimming/Water Sports Forum
GS TENNIS — AOL Grandstand: Tennis Forum
GS TRACK — AOL Grandstand: Track Forum
GS TRIVIA — AOL Grandstand: Trivia
GS TWIRL — AOL Grandstand: Twirling Forum
GS WESTERN — AOL Grandstand: Western Forum
GS WINTER — AOL Grandstand: Winter Sports Forum
GS WRESTLING — AOL Grandstand: Wrestling Forum
GSFL — AOL Grandstand: Simulation Football
GSHL — AOL Grandstand: Hockey
GSHOW CHAT — Game Shows: Chat
GSNBA — AOL Grandstand: NBA Forum
GSNC — AOL Grandstand: Simulation Auto
GSNFL — AOL Grandstand: NFL Forum
GTR — GTRworld for Guitars
GUAM — AOL International: Guam
GUATEMALA — AOL International: Guatemala
GUCCI — Gucci Parfums Counter
GUCCI COUNTER — Gucci Parfums Counter
<u>GUERILLA</u> — The Guerrilla Marketing Forum
<u>GUERILLA FORUM</u> — The Guerrilla Marketing Forum
GUERRILLA — The Guerrilla Marketing Forum
GUERRILLA FORUM — The Guerrilla Marketing Forum
<u>GUERRLLA CHAT</u> — The Guerrilla Marketing Forum: Chat
<u>GUERRLLA LIVE</u> — The Guerrilla Marketing Forum: Chat
GUESS — Guess [Web site]
GUFL — AOL Grandstand: Simulation Football
GUIDE PAGE — Notify AOL
GUIDE PAGER — Notify AOL
GUITAR — GTRworld for Guitars
GUITAR SIG — GTRworld for Guitars
GURU — The Gadget Guru Online
GUT INSTINCT — AboutWork: Gut Instinct
GUY IN THE HOOD — Digital City Boston: Neighborhood Guy
GUYANA — AOL International: Guyana
GW FEST — AOL UK: Greenwich & Docklands International Festival
    [Web site]
GWA — AOL Grandstand: Simulation Wrestling
GWF — AOL Grandstand: Simulation Wrestling
GYM ONQ — onQ: Men

GYMNASTIC — AOL Sports: Gymnastics Forum
GYMNASTICS — AOL Sports: Gymnastics Forum
H MILK — Digital City San Francisco: Harvey Milk Institute [Web site]
H2H — onQ: Relationships
H2H ONQ — onQ: Relationships
HACHETTE — Hachette Filipacchi New Media
HAIR LOSS — AOL Health: Baldness & Hair Loss
HAITI — AOL International: Haiti
HAL 9000 — Happy Birthday HAL 9000
HALITOSIS — AOL Health: Halitosis
HALLMARK — Hallmark Connections [Web site]
HALLMARK CONNECTIONS — Hallmark Connections [Web site]
HALLOWEEN — Haunted @AOL [seasonal]
HALLOWEEN HAPPENINGS — Halloween Travel [seasonal]
HALLOWEEN TRAVEL — Halloween Travel [seasonal]
HALLOWEEN TRIPS — Halloween Travel [seasonal]
HALLOWEEN@AOL — Haunted @AOL [seasonal]
HAM — The Ham Radio Forum
HAM RADIO — The Ham Radio Forum
HAM RADIO CLUB — The Ham Radio Forum
HAMPTON — Hampton Inn [Web site]
HAMPTON INN — Hampton Inn [Web site]
HAMPTON INNS — Hampton Inn [Web site]
HAMPTON LOCAL NEWS — Digital City Hampton Roads: Local News
HAMPTON ROADS DINING — Digital City Hampton Roads: Dining
HAMPTON ROADS EVENTS — Digital City Hampton Roads: Events
HAMPTON ROADS KIDS — Digital City Hampton Roads: KidSafe
HAMPTON ROADS LOCAL NEWS — Digital City Hampton Roads: Local News
HAMPTON ROADS MOVIES — Digital City Hampton Roads: Movies
HAMPTON ROADS NEWS — Digital City Hampton Roads: News
HAMPTON ROADS SINGLES — Digital City Hampton Roads: Singles Magazine
HANDBALL — AOL Sports: Handball
HANDLE — Create/Delete Screen Names
HANES — One Hanes Place
HANSON — Hanson [Web site]
HANUKKAH — Jewish Community: Chanukah [seasonal]
HAPPY NEW YEAR — New Year's @ AOL [seasonal]
HAPPY NEW YEARS DAY — New Year's @ AOL [seasonal]
HAPPYLAND — Happyland Comic Strip [Web site]
HARDWARE — AOL Computing: Hardware Forum
HARDWARE CENTER — AOL Store: Hardware Shop
HARDWARE COMPANIES — AOL Computing: Companies
HARDWARE FORUM — AOL Computing: Hardware Forum
HARDWARE SHOP — AOL Store: Hardware Shop

HARDWARE STORE — AOL Store: Hardware Shop
HARING — Image Exchange: Keith Haring
HARLEY — Big Twin Magazine
HARLEY DAVIDSON — Big Twin Magazine
HARRISBURG LOCAL NEWS — Digital City Harrisburg: Local News
HARRISBURG NEWS — Digital City Harrisburg: Local News
HARRY & DAVID — Harry and David [Web site]
HARRY DAVID — Harry and David [Web site]
HARTFORD — Digital City Hartford
HARTFORD LOCAL NEWS — Digital City Hartford: Local News
HARTFORD NEWS — Digital City Hartford: Local News
HARTFORD WHALERS — Carolina Hurricanes
HARVEY MILK — Digital City San Francisco: Harvey Milk Institute
    [Web site]
HARVEY MILK INSTITUTE — Digital City San Francisco: Harvey Milk
    Institute [Web site]
HAUNTED — Haunted @AOL [seasonal]
HAUNTED@AOL — Haunted @AOL [seasonal]
HAUTE STUFF — AOL Canada: Fashion
HAWKS — Atlanta Hawks
HAWTHORNE AND HAMILTON — Collectibles Today [Web site]
HAY FEVER — AOL Health: Hay Fever & Other Airborne Allergies
HBN — Hunting Broadcast Network
HBO — HBO Online [Web site]
HBO.COM — HBO Online [Web site]
HBS PUB — Harvard Business School Publishing
HDSL — xDSL Field Trial
HEADACHE — AOL Health: Headaches
HEADACHES — AOL Health: Headaches
HEADHUNTER — Motley Fool: Ask the Headhunter
HEADLINE NEWS — Today's News
HEADLINES — Today's News
HEALTH — AOL Health channel
HEALTH AND VITAMIN — Health & Vitamin Express
HEALTH CARE INDUSTRY — AOL WorkPlace: Health & Nutrition
    Professional Forum
HEALTH CLUB — AOL WorkPlace: Sports & Recreation Industry
    Community
HEALTH EXP — Health & Vitamin Express
HEALTH EXPERTS — AOL Health: Ask the Medical Experts
HEALTH EXPRESS — Health & Vitamin Express
HEALTH FAIR — AOL Health: Assesses Your Health Area
HEALTH FOCUS — Better Health & Medical: Health Focus
HEALTH FRONT 1 — Thrive@Healthy Living: Healthfront
HEALTH INTERACTIVE — AOL Health: Health Interactive
HEALTH MAGAZINE — Health Magazine Online

HEALTH MAGAZINES — Health Magazine Online
HEALTH MANAGER — Health Manager [Web site]
HEALTH NEWS — AOL Health: News
HEALTH PENN — Digital City Philadelphia: University of Pennsylvania Health System
HEALTH PROS — AOL WorkPlace: Health & Nutrition Professional Forum
HEALTH REFERENCE — AOL Health: Medical Reference
HEALTH SHOP — Health & Fitness Shops
HEALTH STORE — Health & Fitness Shops
HEALTH SUPER STORE — AOL Shoppers Advantage: Health & Beauty
HEALTH SUPPORT — AOL Health: Support Groups & Experts
HEALTHY BABIES — AOL Health: Raising Healthy Babies
HEALTHY EATING — AOL Health: Healthy Eating
HEALTHY GIVING — AOL Health: Healthy Giving
HEALTHY HOLIDAY — AOL Health: Healthy Holiday Forum
HEALTHY HOLIDAYS — AOL Health: Healthy Holidays
HEALTHY LIVING — AOL Health: Healthy Living
HEALTHY SUMMER — AOL Health: Healthy Summer
HEARING DISORDERS — AOL Health: Deafness & Hearing Disorders
HEART — AOL Health: Heart & Blood Disorders
HEART ATTACK — AOL Health: Heart Disease/Heart Attack
HEART ATTTACK — AOL Health: Heart Disease/Heart Attack
HEART DISEASE — AOL Health: Heart Disease/Heart Attack
HEART TO HEART — onQ: Relationships
HEARTBURN — AOL Health: Heartburn
HEARTLAND — AOL WorkPlace: Working From The Heartland
HEARTS — WorldPlay: Hearts
HEATING CONTRACTOR — AOL WorkPlace: Contractor's Community
HEAVEN — Heaven
HEBREW — AOL Lifestyles: Judaism
HECKLER — Hecklers Online
HECKLERS — Hecklers Online
HECKLERS CLUBS — Hecklers Online: Clubs
HECKLER'S ONLINE — Hecklers Online
HECKLERS ONLINE — Hecklers Online
HECKLERS TOP TEN — Hecklers Online: Interactive Top Ten
HECKLING CLUBS — Hecklers Online: Clubs
HEISMAN — Real Fans: Heisman Watch
HELIX — DC Comics: Helix Science Fiction Comics
HELP — AOL Member Services
HELP DESK — AOL Computing: Help Desk
HELP FORUM — Help Selections
HEM — Home Education Magazine
HEMORRHOIDS — AOL Health: Hemorrhoids
HEPATITIS — AOL Health: Hepatitis

HERALD — Digital City Boston: Boston Herald
HERBAL REMEDIES — AOL Health: Herbal Remedies
HERBFARM — Food & Drink Network: An HerbFarm Diary
<u>HERCEGOVINA</u> — AOL International: Bosnia Herzegovina
HERITAGE FOUNDATION — Heritage Foundation
HERPES — AOL Health: Herpes
HERZEGOVINA — AOL International: Bosnia Herzegovina
HEY BUDDY — Buddy List: View Buddies
HFC — Highlights Magazine
HFC NEWS — Highlights Magazine: Online Newsletter
HFM MAGNETWORK — Hachette Fillipachi New Media
HH ADULT — AOL Research & Learn: Ask-A-Teacher
HI ONQ — onQ: HIV
HICKORY — Hickory Farms
HICKORY FARM — Hickory Farms
HICKORY FARMS — Hickory Farms
HIGH BLOOD PRESSURE — AOL Health: Hypertension/High Blood
    Pressure
HIGH POINT — Digital City High Point
HIGH SPEED — High Speed Access
HIGHER ED — AOL Research & Learn: College Preparation
HIGHLAND — Digital City Philadelphia: Highland
HIGHLIGHTS — Highlights Magazine
<u>HIGHLITES</u> — Highlights Magazine
HIGHMARK — Highmark Mutual Funds
HIGHSMITH — Digital City Philadelphia: Highland
HIKER — Backpacker Magazine
HIKING — Backpacker Magazine
HINDI — AOL International: India
HINDU — AOL Lifestyles: Hinduism
HINDUISM — AOL Lifestyles: Hinduism
HIP HOP — AOL Entertainment: R&B/Rap
HISPANIC — AOL Lifestyles: Ethnicity
HISPANIC MAGAZINE — Hispanic Online
HISPANIC ONLINE — Hispanic Online
HISTORIC PHILLY — Digital City Philadelphia: Independence Hall
    Association Virtual Walking Tour
HISTORY — AOL Research & Learn: History
HISTORY CHANNEL — The History channel
HI-TECH INVESTING — AOL Personal Finance: Investing In Technology
HIV — AOL Health: AIDS & HIV
HIV BOARDS — onQ: HIV/AIDS Boards
HIV BOARDS ONQ — onQ: HIV/AIDS Boards
HIV CHAT — onQ: HIV/AIDS Chat
HIV CHAT ONQ — onQ: HIV/AIDS Chat
HIV LIBRARIES — onQ: HIV/AIDS Libraries

HIV LIBRARIES ONQ — onQ: HIV/AIDS Libraries
HIV ONQ — onQ: HIV/AIDS
HIV RESOURCES — onQ: HIV/AIDS Resources
HIV RESOURCES ONQ — onQ: HIV/AIDS Resources
HIV/AIDS ONQ — onQ: HIV/AIDS
HK — AOL International: Hong Kong
HK 97 — AOL International: Hong Kong
HK BIZ — AOL Personal Finance: Hong Kong Business
HM CURRENT — Health Magazine Online: Current
HM FITNESS — Health Magazine Online: Fitness
HM FOOD — Health Magazine Online: Food
HM RELATIONSHIPS — Health Magazine Online: Relationships
HM REMEDIES — Health Magazine Online: Remedies
HO — Hecklers Online
HO CLUBS — Hecklers Online: Clubs
HO PRIZES — Hecklers Online: The Prize Cellar
HOBBIES — AOL Interests: Hobbies
HOBBY — AOL Interests: Hobbies
HOBBY CENTRAL — AOL Interests: Hobbies
HOBBY CHAT — Hobby Shop Chat Room
HOBBY SHOP — AOL WorkPlace: Hobby Shops' Community
HOC — Home Office Computing Magazine
HOCKEY SCOREBOARD — AOL Sports: Hockey Scores
HOCKEY SCORES — AOL Sports: Hockey Scores
HOCKEY STARS — AOL Sports: Hockey Stars
HOCKEY TRIVIA — NTN Hockey Trivia
HOFFMAN ESTATES — Digital City Hoffman Estates [Web site]
HOH — AOL Health: Deaf Community
HOL PRO — AOL Entertainment: The Biz
HOLIDAY — Holidays @AOL [seasonal]
HOLIDAY CENTRAL ONQ — onQ: Holidays
HOLIDAY ONQ — onQ: Holiday
HOLIDAYS — Holidays @AOL [seasonal]
HOLIDAYS ONQ — onQ: Holiday
HOLLAND — AOL International: Netherlands
HOLLYWOOD — Hollywood Online
HOLLYWOOD HILLS HOMES — Digital City Los Angeles: Kirk Frieden
    Real Estate
HOLLYWOOD ONLINE — Hollywood Online
HOLLYWOOD PRO — AOL Entertainment: The Biz
HOLLYWOOD WIRE — Entertainment Asylum: Hollywood Wire
HOLOCAUST — Jewish Community: The Holocaust
HOLYFIELD — Athlete Direct: Evander Holyfield
HOME & KITCHEN SHOP — AOL Shopping: Home, Kitchen & Garden
HOME — AOL Interests: Home & Garden
HOME AND FAMILY ONQ — onQ: Home & Family

HOME AUDIO — AOL Computing: Products 2000
HOME BANKING — Bank of America: HomeBanking
HOME BUSINESS — AOL WorkPlace: Your Business
HOME DESIGN — AOL Interests: Home & Garden
HOME FURNISHINGS — AOL Shopping: Home, Kitchen & Garden
HOME GUIDE — Digital City Hampton Roads: Home Guide
HOME IMPROVEMENT — AOL Interests: Home & Garden
HOME IMPROVEMENT SUPERSTORE — AOL Shoppers Advantage:
     Home Improvement
HOME MAG — Home Magazine Online
HOME MAGAZINE — Home Magazine Online
HOME OFFICE — Home Office Computing Magazine
HOME OFFICE COMPUTING — Home Office Computing Magazine
HOME ONQ — onQ: Home & Family
HOME PAGE — AOL Personal Publisher
HOME PAGE CONTEST — Member Home Page Contest
HOME PLANS — Home Magazine Online: Build Your Own Home
HOME REFERENCE — AOL Research & Learn: Home & Family
HOME SCHOOL — AOL Families: Home Schooling Forum
HOME SCHOOLING — AOL Families: Home Schooling Forum
HOME SPOT — Digital City South Florida: Market
HOME SUPERSTORE — AOL Shoppers Advantage: Home & Luggage
HOME TEAM SPORTS — Home Team Sports Online
HOME THEATER — Stereo Review Online
HOME VIDEO — Home Video Forum
HOMEARTS — HomeArts Network [Web site]
HOMEARTS.COM — HomeArts Network [Web site]
HOMEBASE — AOL Families: Family Fun
HOMEOPATHY — AOL Health: Homeopathy
HOMEPC — HomePC Magazine Online
HOMES — AOL Interests: Home & Garden
HOMEWORK — AOL Research & Learn: Ask-A-Teacher
HOMEWORK HELP — AOL Research & Learn: Ask-A-Teacher
HOMOSEXUAL — AOL Lifestyles: Gay & Lesbian
HONDURAS — AOL International: Honduras
HONEYMOON — The Knot: Weddings for the Real World
HONEYMOON MAGAZINE — The Knot: Honeymoon Magazine
HONG KONG — AOL International: Hong Kong
HONG KONG 97 — AOL International: Hong Kong
HONG KONG BIZ — AOL Personal Finance: Hong Kong Business
HONG KONG TRAVEL — AOL Travel: Hong Kong
HOOD GUY — Digital City Boston: Neighborhood Guy
HOOKED ON SOAP — Digital City Atlanta: Hooked On Soap
HOOKED ON SOAPS — Digital City Atlanta: Hooked On Soap
HOOP TRIVIA — NTN Trivia: Basketball Trivia
HOOPS SCOREBOARD — STATS Hoops Scoreboard

HOOPS TRIVIA — NTN Trivia: Basketball Trivia
HOOVER — Hoover's Business Resources
HOOVER PROFILE — Hoover's Business Resources
HOOVER'S — Hoover's Business Resources
HOOVERS — Hoover's Business Resources
HOOVER'S PROFILE — Hoover's Business Resources
HOPKINS — InteliHealth [Web site]
HORNETS — Charlotte Hornets
HOROSCOPE — Horoscope Selections
HOROSCOPES — Horoscope Selections
HORSE — Horse Selections
HORSE FORUM — Horse Selections
HORSE ONQ — onQ: Pets
HORSE RACING — Horse Selections
HORSE SPORTS — AOL Grandstand: Horse Forum
HORSES — Horse Selections
HOSPITALITY — AOL WorkPlace: Hospitality Services
HOT — What's New on AOL
HOT 5 — What's New on AOL
HOT BED — Love@AOL: Hot Bed Chat
HOT CARS — AOL Interests: Auto Center Wheels
HOT DEALS — AOL Shopping: Bargain Basement
HOT FILES — AOL Computing: Daily Download
HOT FIVE — What's New on AOL
HOT GAMES — AOL Games: Top Games Picks
HOT GIFTS — AOL Shopping: Holiday Hot Gifts
HOT NEWS — AOL News: What's Hot in News
HOT NEWZ — AOL News: What's Hot in News
HOT SAVINGS — AOL Shopping: Deal of the Day
HOT SITES — Internet Connection: Hot Web Sites
HOT SOFTWARE — AOL Computing: Daily Download
HOT SPORTS — AOL Sports: From The Cheap Seats
HOT SPOT — MTV Online: Hot Spot
HOT TIP — AOL Insider Tips
HOT TIPS — AOL Insider Tips
HOT TODAY — What's New on AOL
HOT TOPICS — AOL Research & Learn: Hot Topics
HOT TRAVEL — AOL Travel: What's Hot
HOT WEB — Internet Connection: Hot Web Sites
HOT WEB SITES — Internet Connection: Hot Web Sites
HOTEL — AOL Travel: Hotel Reservation Center
HOTEL CENTER — AOL Travel: Hotel Reservation Center
HOTEL DC — Digital City Washington: Destination Digital City Hotels
HOTEL PRO — AOL WorkPlace: Hotels & Motels Professional Forum
HOTELS — AOL Travel: Hotel Reservation Center
HOTLANTA — Digital City Atlanta

HOTWIRED — HotWired [Web site]
HOTWIRED.COM — HotWired [Web site]
HOUSE AND HOME — AOL Interests: Home & Garden
HOUSENET — HouseNet
HOUSES — Real Estate Corner
HOUSEWARES — AOL Shopping: Home, Kitchen & Garden
HOUSTON — Digital City Houston
HOUSTON ASTROS — Houston Astros
HOUSTON DIGITAL CITY — Digital City Houston
HOUSTON LOCAL NEWS — Digital City Houston: Local News
HOUSTON NEWS — Digital City Houston: Local News
HOW TO — AOL Member Services
HOW TO CONNECT — AOL Member Services: Connecting to AOL
HOW TO DOWNLOAD — AOL Member Services: Downloading Files &
    Attachments
HOW TO GET AROUND — AOL Member Services: Getting Around &
    Using AOL
HOW TO MEET PEOPLE — AOL Member Services: People Connection
HOW TO SEARCH — AOL Member Services: Using Search & Find
HOW TO USE AOL — AOL Member Services: Getting Around & Using
    AOL
HOWARD — Digital City Philadelphia: Howard Stern
HOWARD STERN — Digital City Philadelphia: Howard Stern
HOWDY — American Greetings: Daily Delights Postcards
HP — Hewlett Packard Forum
HP HOME — Hewlett Packard Forum
HP PRN — Hewlett Packard Forum
HP SCAN — Hewlett Packard Forum
HP STOR — Hewlett Packard Forum
HP SUPPORT — Hewlett Packard Forum
HPC — HomePC Magazine Online
HPN — Better Health & Medical: Health Professionals Network
HQ — Historical Quotes
HQ WEATH — AOL Headquarters Weather
HQ WEATHER — AOL Headquarters Weather
HR CHAT — Digital City Hampton Roads: Chat
HR DINING — Digital City Hampton Roads: Dining
HR EVENTS — Digital City Hampton Roads: Events
HR GARDEN — Digital City Hampton Roads: Gardening
HR GARDENING — Digital City Hampton Roads: Gardening
HR LOCAL NEWS — Digital City Hampton Roads: Local Weather
HR MOVIES — Digital City Hampton Roads: Movies
HR SINGLES — Digital City Hampton Roads: Singles Magazine
HR SINGLES MAGAZINE — Digital City Hampton Roads: Singles
    Magazine
HR TALK — Digital City Hampton Roads: Chat

HRC — Human Rights Campaign for Gay & Lesbian Rights
HRS — Better Health & Medical Network
HRVATSKA — AOL International: Croatia
HTML — AOL Computing: On the Net
HTS — Home Team Sports Online
HTTP — What is HTTP?: Help with URLs
HTTP: — What is HTTP?: Help with URLs
HTTP:/ — What is HTTP?: Help with URLs
HUBIE — Serendipity Software
HULL — AOL UK: Local Life
HULL EOL — AOL UK: North East Events Online
HUMAN RIGHTS CAMPAIGN — Human Rights Campaign for Gay &
    Lesbian Rights
**HUMANISM — Religion & Beliefs: The Humanism-
    Unitarianism Forum**
HUMOR THERAPY — AOL Health: Humor Therapy
HUMOR WRITE — Digital City Denver: Humorwrite Online
HUNGARY — AOL International: Hungary
HUNGRY MOUSE — Digital City Dallas-Fort Worth: Food
HUNTING — Hunting Broadcast Network
HUP — Digital City Philadelphia: University of Pennsylvania Health
    System [Web site]
HURLEY — Amazing Instant Novelist
HURRICANE — Today's Weather
HURRICANES — Carolina Hurricanes
HURRICANES HOCKEY — Carolina Hurricanes
HW — Entertainment Asylum: Hollywood Wire
HW SHOP — AOL Shopping: Computer Hardware
HYMNE — AOL International: National Anthems of the World
HYMNOS — AOL International: National Anthems of the World
HYPE — Hype! You be the Movie Critic [Web site]
HYPERCARD — AOL Computing: HyperCard Forum
HYPERLINK — AOL Member Services: Using Hyperlinks
HYPERLINKS — AOL Member Services: Using Hyperlinks
HYPERTENSION — AOL Health: Hypertension/High Blood Pressure
HYPOGLYCEMIA — AOL Health: Hypoglycemia
I CHING — Horoscope Selections
I HOUSE — Digital City Philadelphia: International House Presents
    Philadelphia Festival of World Cinema
I KNOW WHAT YOU DID LAST SUMMER — I Know What You Did Last
    Summer Movie
I NEED HELP — AOL Member Services: Notify AOL
IA — WB Online: Insomniacs Asylum
IA CAFE — WB Online: Insomniacs Asylum
IA DEMENTIA — WB Online: Insomniacs Asylum
IA GONZO — WB Online: Insomniacs Asylum

IA LOUNGE — WB Online: Insomniacs Asylum
IA NEWSROOM — WB Online: Insomniacs Asylum
<u>IA REDEZVOUS</u> — WB Online: Insomniacs Asylum
IBD — Investor's Business Daily
IBIKE — iBike
IBM — IBM on AOL
IBM MSR — IBM Direct Connection
IBM OS2 — AOL Computing: OS/2 Forum
IBN — AOL News: International Business News
IBS — AOL Health: Irritable Bowel Syndrome
IC — AOL Internet Connection
IC HILITES — Internet Connection: IC-Hilites Weekly Newsletter
IC NEWS — AOL International: News
IC SPORT — AOL International: Sports
IC SPORTS — AOL International: Sports
IC STORE — AOL Computing: Superstore
ICE — AOL Canada: Arctic Journal
ICE RICK — AOL Canada: Arctic Journal
ICE SKATING — United States Figure Skating Association
ICELAND — AOL International: Iceland
IC-HILITES — Internet Connection: IC-Hilites Weekly Newsletter
I-CHING — Digital City Denver: Mo's Mystical Metaphysical Tour
ICTLEP — onQ: Transgender Organizations
IDEAS FOR BETTER LIVING — Woman's Day: Ideas for Better Living
IE BROWSER — Microsoft Internet Explorer Browser
IE FIX — Internet Security Update [for Windows 95 AOL 3.0 members only]
IE PREVIEW — Microsoft Internet Explorer Browser
IF CONTESTS — InsideFlyer Online
IF PROGRAMS — InsideFlyer Online
IF WHAT'S HOT — InsideFlyer Online
IGOLF — iGolf
IGOLF CHAT — iGolf: Chat Lobby
IGS — Internet Graphic Sites
IGUIDE — TV Guide Entertainment Network [Web site]
IHA — Digital City Philadelphia: Independence Hall Association Virtual Walking Tour
ILENE DATES — Digital City Washington: Singles-Minded
ILENE DIAMOND — Digital City Washington: Singles-Minded
ILLNESS — AOL Health: Illness and Treatments
ILLNESSES — AOL Health: Illness and Treatments
ILLUMINATION — The Knot: Illumination Album
ILLUSTRATOR — AOL Computing: Vector Artists SIG
ILLUSTRATOR SIG — AOL Computing: Vector Artists SIG
IMAGE DESIGN — AOL WorkPlace: Designers' Community
IMAGE DISK — AOL Member Services: Share Your Image Photos

IMAGE EX — Image Exchange: Marketplace
IMAGE EXCHANGE — Image Exchange
IMAGE ONQ — onQ: Image
IMAGE SCAN — Love@AOL: Photo Scanning
IMAGE SCANNING — AOL Computing: Image Scanning
IMAGES — AOL Interests: Pictures
IMAGINATION BACKGAMMON — WorldPlay: Backgammon
IMAGINATION BRIDGE — WorldPlay: Bridge
IMAGINATION CRIBBAGE — WorldPlay: Cribbage
IMAGINATION GIN — WorldPlay: Gin
IMAGINATION HEARTS — WorldPlay: Hearts
IMAGINATION SPADES — WorldPlay: Spades
IMAGING — AOL Interests: Pictures
IMAGINGATION GAMES — WorldPlay Games
IMH — Issues in Mental Health
IMMIGRATION — Tell Us Your Story: Immigration Stories
IMPOTENCE — AOL Health: Impotence
IMTN BIKE — iBike
IMUS — Digital City New York: WFAN
IMUS AND CHARLES MCCORD — Digital City New York: Imus in the
    Morning
IMUS IN THE MORNING — Digital City New York: Imus in the Morning
IN — Investors' Network: Stock Talk
IN THE FAST LANE — Digital City San Francisco: In The Fast Lane
IN TOON — InToon with the News
INC — Inc. Online
INC MAGAZINE — Inc. Online
INC NOW — The Company Corporation: Incorporate In Four Steps
INC ONLINE — Inc. Online
INC. — Inc. Online
INC. MAGAZINE — Inc. Online
INC. ONLINE — Inc. Online
INCOME STATEMENT — Disclosure: Financial Statements
INCONTINENCE@THRIVE — Thrive@Healthy Living: Incontinence
INCORPORATE — The Company Corporation: Incorporate In Four Steps
INCORPORATE NOW — The Company Corporation: Incorporate In Four
    Steps
IND INV — Digital City New York: Individual Investor
INDEPENDENCE DAY — Independence Day@AOL [seasonal]
INDEPENDENCE HALL — Digital City Philadelphia: Independence Hall
    Association Virtual Walking Tour
INDIA — AOL International: India
**INDIAN RIVER — Global Gourmet: Indian River Gift
    Fruit Co.**
INDIANA UNIVERSITY — Indiana University [Web site]
INDIANAPOLIS — Digital City Indianapolis

INDIANAPOLIS LOCAL NEWS — Digital City Indianapolis: Local News
INDIANAPOLIS NEWS — Digital City Indianapolis: Local News
INDIANS — Cleveland Indians
INDIVIDUAL INVESTOR — Digital City New York: Individual Investor
INDONESIA — AOL International: Indonesia
INDUSTRIAL BIZ — AOL News: Industry News
INDUSTRIAL EQUIPMENT — AOL WorkPlace: Industrial Equipment &
    Supplies
INDUSTRIAL NEWS — AOL News: Industry News
INDUSTRIAL SUPPLIES — AOL WorkPlace: Industrial Equipment &
    Supplies
INDUSTRIES & NICHES — AOL WorkPlace: Professional Forums
INDUSTRY AP — AOL News: Industry News
INDUSTRY PROFILES — Industry Profiles
INDUSTRY REUTERS — AOL News: Industry News
INDUSTRY WIRES — AOL News: Industry News
INDY CAR — AOL Sports: Auto Racing
INET EXCHANGE — Internet Connection: Exchange
INET ORGS — Internet Connection: Organizations
INFANT — AOL Families: Babies
INFECTION — AOL Health: Infectious & Contagious Diseases
INFECTIOUS — AOL Health: Infectious & Contagious Diseases
INFERTILITY — AOL Health: Infertility
INFINITI — Infiniti Online [Web site]
INFINITI ONLINE — Infiniti Online [Web site]
INFLUENCE — AOL Influence channel
INFLUENCE SEARCH — AOL Influence: Search & Explore
INFLUENZA — AOL Health: Influenza
INFO SOURCE — Digital City Boston: Family Info Source [Web site]
INFONAUTICS — AOL Research & Learn: Electric Library@AOL
INFORMATION — AOL Member Services
INFORMATION PROVIDERS — Information Provider Resource Center
INFOSHOP — AOL Member Services
INLINE HOCKEY — AOL Sports: Roller Hockey MiniForum
INLINE SKATING — AOL Sports: Inline/Aggressive/Roller Skating
INN — WorldPlay Games
INN BACKGAMMON — WorldPlay: Backgammon
INN BRIDGE — WorldPlay: Bridge
INN CRIBBAGE — WorldPlay: Cribbage
INN GAMES — WorldPlay: Games
INN GIN — WorldPlay: Gin
INN HEARTS — WorldPlay: Hearts
INN SPADES — WorldPlay: Spades
INOVA — Digital City Washington: Inova Health Systems
INOVA HEALTH — Digital City Washington: Inova Health Systems
INQUEST — Inquest Gaming Magazine

INQUEST MAG — Inquest Gaming Magazine
INQUEST MAGAZINE — Inquest Gaming Magazine
INSIDE FLYER — InsideFlyer Online
INSIDE MEDIA — Cowles Business Media [Web site]
INSIDE OUT — AOL Canada: Inside Out [Web site]
INSIDE PHILLY HOME — Digital City Philadelphia: Home Realtors
INSIDE PITCH — Andy Strasberg's Baseball-Itis
INSIDE SOAP — Inside Soap Magazine
INSIDE THRIVE — Thrive@Healthy Living: Inside Thrive Newsletter
INSIDER — AOL Insider Tips
INSIDER TIPS — AOL Insider Tips
INSIGHT COM BOWL — Real Fans: Insight.com Bowl
INSOMNIACS — WB Online: Insomniacs Asylum
INSOMNIACS ASYLUM — WB Online: Insomniacs Asylum
INSTA-GIFT — Love@AOL: Insta-Gift
INSTAGIFT — Love@AOL: Insta-Gift
INSTAKISS — Love@AOL: Insta-Kiss
INSTANT ARTIST — AOL Computing: Print Artist
INSTANT ARTIST 1 — AOL Computing: Print Artist
INSTANT KISS — Love@AOL: Insta-Kiss
INSTANT MESSANGER — AOL Instant Messenger
INSTANT MESSENGER — AOL Instant Messenger
INSTANT NOVELIST — Amazing Instant Novelist
INSTAPOLL SAN DIEGO — Digital City San Diego: California Lottery
INSTAPOLL SD — Digital City San Diego: California Lottery
INSURANCE — AOL Insurance Center
INSURANCE CENTER — AOL Insurance Center
INT CULTURE — AOL International: Cultures
INT NEWSSTAND — AOL Interests: Newsstand
INTEL — Intel: PC Dads
INTEL INSIDE — Intel: PC Dads
INTELIHEALTH — InteliHealth [Web site]
INTELLECTUAL — AOL Influence channel
INTELLICAST — Intellicast [Web site]
INTELLIHEALTH — InteliHealth [Web site]
INTENSITY — EXTRA Online: Intensity
INTERACTIVE JERSEY — Digital City South Jersey
INTERACTIVE MONDAY — Rosie O'Donnell Online: Interactive Mondays
INTERACTIVE MONDAYS — Rosie O'Donnell Online: Interactive
    Mondays
INTERACTIVE SJ — Digital City South Jersey
INTERACTIVE TOP TEN — Hecklers Online: Interactive Top Ten
INTERCON — InterCon Systems Corporation
INTEREST — AOL Interests channel
INTEREST CHANNEL — AOL Interests channel
INTEREST PROFILES — AOL Member Services: Interest Profiles

INTERESTS — AOL Interests channel
INTERESTS NEWSSTAND — AOL Interests: Newsstand
INTERESTS SEARCH — AOL Interests: Search & Explore
INTERIOR DECORATOR — AOL WorkPlace: Interior Decorators
    Community
INTERIOR DESIGN — AOL Interests: House & Garden
INTERN — AOL News: Bill Clinton News Special
INTERNATIONAL — AOL International channel
INTERNATIONAL ACCESS — International Access
INTERNATIONAL ANTHEMS — AOL International: National Anthems of
    the World
INTERNATIONAL BUSINESS NEWS — AOL News: International Business
    News
INTERNATIONAL CAFE — AOL International: Cafe
INTERNATIONAL CULTURE — AOL International: Cultures
INTERNATIONAL FINANCE — AOL International: Business
INTERNATIONAL LOVE — AOL International: Passport To Love
INTERNATIONAL LOVE — Passport To Love
INTERNATIONAL MRKT — AOL International: Marketplace
INTERNATIONAL NETWORKS — International Access
INTERNATIONAL NEWS — AOL News: U.S. & World News
INTERNATIONAL SHOP — AOL International: Marketplace
INTERNATIONAL SPORTS — AOL International: Sports
INTERNATIONAL STORE — AOL International: Marketplace
INTERNATIONAL TAXES — AOL International: Tax Information
INTERNATIONAL TRADE — AOL WorkPlace: International
    Trade
INTERNATIONAL TRAV — AOL International: Travel
INTERNATIONAL US — AOL International channel
INTERNATIONAL WEATHER — AOL International: Weather Reports
INTERNET — Internet Connection
INTERNET AMERICA — Internet America [Web site]
INTERNET CENTER — Internet Connection
INTERNET CONNECTION — Internet Connection
INTERNET EXCHANGE — Internet Connection: Exchange
INTERNET FIND — AOL NetFind
INTERNET GRAPHICS — Internet Graphic Sites
INTERNET HELP — AOL Member Services: Internet & World Wide Web
INTERNET NEWS — Internet Connection: Newsstand
INTERNET ONE CLICK — AOL Member Services: The Internet is One
    Click Away
INTERNET ORGS — Internet Connection: Organizations
INTERNET STORE — AOL Computing: Superstore
INTERNET TIME SAVERS — AOL NetFind [Web site]
INTERNET WHITE PAGES — AOL NetFind: White Pages [Web site]

INTERNET WORLD — AOL Member Services: The Internet is One Click Away
INTERSEXED — onQ: Transgender Community Forum
INTL — AOL International channel
INTL ACCESS — International Access
INTL BIZ NEWS — AOL News: International Business News
INTL BUSINESS — AOL International: Business
INTL BUY — AOL International: Classifieds
INTL CDN — AOL Canada: International channel
INTL CLASSIFIEDS — AOL International: Classifieds
INTL COUNTRY — AOL International: Country Information Search
INTL CULTURE — AOL International: Cultures
INTL CULTURES — AOL International: Cultures
INTL EXPLORE — AOL International: Search and Explore
INTL FINANCE — AOL International: Business
INTL FIND — AOL International: Search and Explore
INTL FUN — AOL International: Fun and Games
INTL HONG KONG — AOL International: Hong Kong
INTL INDIA — AOL International: India
INTL LOVE — AOL International: Passport To Love
INTL MEETING — Global Meeting Place
INTL NEWS — AOL International: News
INTL NEWSTAND — AOL International: Newsstand
INTL PHONE NUMBERS — International Access
INTL PREMIUM GAMES — AOL Games: Games Guide
INTL SELL — AOL International: Classifieds
INTL SOCIETIES — AOL International: Cultures
INTL SOCIETY — AOL International: Cultures
INTL SPORT — AOL International: Sports
INTL SPORTS — AOL International: Sports
INTL SWEDEN — AOL International: Sweden
INTL TAX — AOL International: Taxes Information
INTL TAXES — AOL International: Taxes Information
INTL TELEPHONE NUMBERS — International Access
INTL TRAVEL — AOL International: Travel
INTL WEATHER — AOL International: Weather Reports
INTL WEATHER REPORTS — AOL International: Weather Reports
INTL WIRES — AOL News: International Business News
INTL WORD GAME — AOL International: Language Games
INTL WORD GAMES — AOL International: Language Games
INTREPID NEW YORKER — Digital City New York: Intrepid New Yorker
INTREPID NY — Digital City New York: Intrepid New Yorker
INTREPID NYER — Digital City New York: Intrepid New Yorker
INTUIT — Intuit
INVERNESS — AOL UK: Local Life
INVEST — AOL Personal Finance: Investing Forums

INVESTING — AOL Personal Finance: Investing Forums
INVESTING BASICS — AOL Personal Finance: Investing Basics
INVESTING FORUMS — AOL Personal Finance: Investing Forums
INVESTMENT — AOL Personal Finance: Investing Forums
INVESTMENT BASICS — AOL Personal Finance: Investing Basics
INVESTMENT LINGO — AOL Personal Finance: Lingo
INVESTMENTS — AOL Personal Finance: Investing Forums
INVESTMENTS WATCH — AOL Member Services: Keep an Eye on
    Investments
INVESTOR — AOL Personal Finance: Investing Forums
INVESTOR RELATIONS — AOL Full Disclosure
INVESTORS — AOL Personal Finance: Investing Forums
INVESTOR'S BUSINESS — AOL Personal Finance: Investors Business
    Daily
INVESTORS BUSINESS — AOL Personal Finance: Investors Business
    Daily
INVESTOR'S DAILY — AOL Personal Finance: Investors Business Daily
INVESTORS DAILY — AOL Personal Finance: Investors Business Daily
IOMEGA — Iomega Corporation
ION SAN DIEGO — Digital City San Diego: Tom Blair
IONA — Forefront Records: Iona
IPG — BPS Software
IPO — Hoover's Business Resources: IPO Central
IPO CENTRAL — Hoover's Business Resources: IPO Central
IQVC — iQVC Shopping [Web site]
IR — AOL Full Disclosure
IRACE — iRace
IRAN — AOL International: Iran
IRAQ — AOL International: Iraq
IRC — Winsock Information Area
IRELAND — AOL International: Ireland
ISDN — Future Connectivity Options
ISIKOFF — AOL News: Bill Clinton News Special
ISKI — iSki
ISKI GEAR — iSki
ISKI HOT — iSki
ISKI SHOP — iSki
ISKI TRAVEL — iSki
ISLAM — AOL Lifestyles: Islam
ISLAMIC — AOL Lifestyles:
ISLAMIC RESOURCES — AOL Lifestyles: Islam
ISLANDERS — New York Islanders
ISLANDS — AOL International: Jamaica
ISRAEL — AOL International: Israel
ISRC — AOL Computing: Image Scanning
ISREAL — AOL International: Israel

ISSUES PHILLY — Digital City Philadelphia: Hot-Button Issues
ITALIA — AOL International: Italy
ITALIAN WORDS — AOL International: Language Games
ITALY — AOL International: Italy
IVANHOE — Medical Breakthroughs reported by Ivanhoe Broadcast News [Web site]
IVILLAGE — iVillage: The Women's Network
IWP — AOL NetFind: White Pages [Web site]
J CREW — J. Crew [Web site]
J.CREW — J. Crew [Web site]
JAASPIN INTERACTIVE — Jaspin Interactive [Web site]
JACKSON & PERKINS — Jackson & Perkins [Web site]
JACKSON PERKINS — Jackson & Perkins [Web site]
JACKSONVILLE — Digital City Jacksonville
JACKSONVILLE LOCAL NEWS — Digital City Jacksonville: Local News
JACKSONVILLE NEWS — Digital City Jacksonville: Local News
JAGUAR VEHICLES — Destination Jaguar [Web site]
JAID — Love@AOL: Jaid Barrymore Uncensored
JAID BARRYMORE — Love@AOL: Jaid Barrymore Uncensored
JAID LIVE — Love@AOL: Jaid Barrymore Uncensored
JAM MAGAZINE — Digital City Orlando: Jam Magazine [Web site]
JAM MAGAZINE — Digital City Orlando: Jam Magazine [Web site]
JAMAICA — AOL International: Jamaica
JAMES BOND MOVIES — Tomorrow Never Dies: The Movie
JAMES CRAMER — TheStreet.com on AOL
JAPAN — AOL International: Japan
JAPAN SOFTWARE — Download the AOL Japan Software
JAPANESE — AOL International: Japan
JAPANIMATION — Japanimation Station!
JARRY PARK — Real Fans: Montreal Expos Team Club
JASPIN — Jaspin Interactive [Web site]
JAVA — AOL Computing: On The Net
JAVA FORUM — AOL Computing: On The Net
JAY CALDERIN — Digital City Boston: Style Eye
JAYS — Toronto Blue Jays
JAZZ — AOL Entertainment: Jazz
JBJ — Jon Bon Jovi Collection
JC PENNEY — JCPenney
JC PLUS & TALL — JCPenney: Plus & Tall store
JCLIENT — Download the AOL Japan Software
JCO KOSHER — Jewish Community: Kosher
JCOL — Jewish Community Online
JCP — JCPenney
JCS — Music Boulevard: Jazz Central Station [Web site]
JD — AOL Research & Learn: Graduate and Professional Schools
JEANS — Eddie Bauer

JEEP EAGLE — Eagle [Web site]
JEFF CO NEWS — Digital City Denver: Jefferson Sentinel Online
JEFFERSON COUNTY — Digital City Denver: Jefferson Sentinel Online
JEFFERSON SENTINEL — Digital City Denver: Jefferson Sentinel Online
JENNY JONES — Jenny Jones [Web site]
JENX — Digital City San Francisco: JenX Twentysomething Rants and Raves
JERRYS FORD — Digital City Washington: Jerry's Ford
JERSEY — Digital City South Jersey
JERSEY CHAT — Digital City South Jersey: Chat Schedule
JERSEY INTERACTIVE — Digital City South Jersey
JERSEY SHORE — Digital City South Jersey: Down the Shore
JERSEY SOCCER — Digital City South Jersey: Soccer Moms
JERUSALEM — Israel Selections
JESUS FREAK — Christianity Online: Jesus Freaks
JESUS FREAKS — Christianity Online: Jesus Freaks
JET — AOL Interests: Aviation & Aeronautics
JETSONS — The Jetsons and AOL?
JEWELER — AOL WorkPlace: Jewelers' Community
JEWELRY — AOL Shopping: Beauty & Jewelry
JEWELRY SHOP — AOL Shopping: Beauty & Jewelry
JEWISH — Jewish Community Online
JEWISH ART — Jewish Community: Arts
JEWISH ARTS — Jewish Community: Arts
JEWISH BOARDS — Jewish Community: Message Boards
JEWISH BOOKS — Jewish Community: Books
JEWISH CA — Jewish Community: California Chat
JEWISH CANADA — Jewish Community: Canada
JEWISH CHAT — Jewish Community: Chat
JEWISH CHICAGO — Jewish Community: Greater Chicago Area
JEWISH CLASSIFIEDS — Jewish Classifieds
JEWISH COM — Jewish Community Online
JEWISH COMM — Jewish Community Online
JEWISH COMMUNITY — Jewish Community Online
JEWISH DALLAS — Jewish Community: Dallas-Fort Worth
JEWISH DFW — Jewish Community: Dallas-Fort Worth
JEWISH DOWNLOADS — Jewish Community: Downloads
JEWISH EDUCATION — Jewish Community: Education
JEWISH FAMILIES — Jewish Community: Family & Personal Matters
JEWISH FAMILY — Jewish Community: Family & Personal Matters
JEWISH FOOD — Jewish Community: Food
JEWISH HOLIDAY — Jewish Community: Holiday
JEWISH HOLIDAYS — Jewish Holidays & Spirituality
JEWISH KOSHER — Jewish Community: Kosher
JEWISH MATCHMAKER — Jewish Community: Matchmaker
JEWISH NEW YORK — Jewish Community: New York

JEWISH NEWS — Jewish Community: News
JEWISH NY — Jewish Community: New York
JEWISH NYC — Jewish Community: New York
JEWISH SINGLES — Jewish Community: Matchmaker
JEWISH STORE — Jewish Community: Store
JEWISH SURVEY — Jewish Community: Survey
JEWISH TRAVEL — Jewish Community: Travel
JEWISH WEB — Jewish Community: Web Sites and Other Jewish
    Internet Resources
JEWISH YOUTH — Jewish Community: Youth
JFAX — JFAX.com [Web site]
JFK JR — George Magazine
JI — Jaspin Interactive [Web site]
JIM EDMONDS — Athlete Direct: Jim Edmonds
JIM HARBAUGH — Athlete Direct: Jim Harbaugh
JIM WHITE — Digital City Dallas-Fort Worth: Jim White's Food & Wine
    Online
JIM WHITES FOOD & WINE — Digital City Dallas-Fort Worth: Jim
    White's Food & Wine Online
JOB — AOL WorkPlace: Finding a Job
JOB CHANGE — AOL WorkPlace: Changing Direction
JOB FIND — AOL WorkPlace: Finding a Job
JOB STUDY — AOL WorkPlace: Career Research
JOBS — AOL WorkPlace: Finding a Job
JOCKO — ABC Sports: Jocko's Daily Column
JOE TORRE — The Book Report: Joe Torre
JOHN KENNEDY — George Magazine
JOHN KENNEDY JR. — George Magazine
JOHN LAING — Digital City Los Angeles: John Laing Homes
JOHN LAING HOMES — Digital City Los Angeles: John Laing Homes
JOIN 1ST SITE — Join Love@1st Site [Web site]
JOIN DC — Digital City: Become A Digital Citizen
JOIN DIGITAL CITY — Digital City: Become A Digital Citizen
JOINTS — AOL Health: Bones, Joints & Muscles
JOKES — Joke Selections
JOKES BOSTON — Digital City Boston: Joke of the Day
JON BON JOVI — Jon Bon Jovi Collection
JONATHAN — AOL Member Services: Jonathan's Letter
JONATHAN LIPNICKI — WB Online: Meego
JONATHAN'S LETTER — AOL Member Services: Jonathan's Letter
JORDAN — AOL International: Jordan
JOSH & JOLENA — Thrive@Healthy Living: Josh and Jolena
JOYZEE — Digital City South Jersey
JPEG — AOL Computing: PC Graphic Arts
JPG — AOL Computing: PC Graphic Arts
JT BRICK — SportsFan: Brickhouse

JUDAISM — AOL Lifestyles: Judaism
JUDAISM TODAY — Jewish Community: Judaism Today
JUJU CROSSROADS — Digital City Twin Cities: Crossroads Insider
JULY 4 — Independence Day@AOL [seasonal]
JULY 4TH — Independence Day@AOL [seasonal]
**JUMBO — Jumbo! The Shareware Download Network
    [Web site]**
JUMP MAGAZINE — Jump [Web site]
JUNE RICH — Digital City Philadelphia: June Rich [Web site]
JUST JOKING — Digital City Dallas-Fort Worth: Just Joking
JUST JOKING DFW — Digital City Dallas-Fort Worth: Just Joking
KAAL TV — ABC Online: KAAL TV in Rochester, MN
KABC TV — ABC Online: KABC TV in Los Angeles, CA
KAIT TV — ABC Online: KAIT TV in Joneston, AR
KAKE TV — ABC Online: KAKE TV in Wichita, KS
KANSAS CITY — Digital City Kansas City
KANSAS CITY LOCAL NEWS — Digital City Kansas City: Local News
KANSAS CITY NEWS — Digital City Kansas City: Local News
KANSAS CITY ROYALS — Kansas City Royals
KAPLAN — Kaplan Online: Virtual Campus
KAPLAN SUPPORT — Kaplan Interactive Software Support
KARAOKE — AOL International: Japan
KARATE — Hobby Central: Martial Arts
KAREN VOIGHT — Thrive@Healthy Living: Shape
KARL MARX — Net Yield [Web site]
KARROS — Athlete Direct: Eric Karros
KATE — Love@AOL: Dr. Kate
KATE DELANEY — Digital City Dallas-Fort Worth: Sports Princess
KAUFMAN — The Kaufmann Fund
KAUFMANN — The Kaufmann Fund
KAUFMANN FUND — The Kaufmann Fund
KAYAKING — AOL Sports: Fitness
KAZAKHSTAN — AOL International: Kazakstan
KAZASTAN — AOL International: Kazakstan
KCRW — Digital City Los Angeles: KCRW 89.9 FM
KD — Microsoft Knowledge Base [Web site]
KEEFE — InToon with the News
KEITH HARING — Image Exchange: Keith Haring
KENNELS — AOL WorkPlace: Pet Stores, Supplies & Kennels
KENNY S — Digital City San Francisco: NASCAR Racing Online
KENNY SHEPHERD — Kenny Shepherd Nascar Area
KENYA — AOL International: Kenya
KERRY BYRNE — Digital City Boston: Beer Guy
KESMAI — GameStorm
KESMAI LEGENDS — GameStorm: Legends of Kesmai
KESQ TV — ABC Online: KESQ TV in Palm Springs, FL

KEWL GRAFFITI — People Connection: Graffiti
KEYWORD — AOL Member Services: Keyword List
KEYWORD INFO — AOL Member Services: Using Keywords
KEYWORD LIST — AOL Member Services: Keyword List
KEYWORDS — AOL Member Services: Keyword List
KEZI TV — ABC Online: KEZI TV in Eugene, OR
KFSN TV — ABC Online: KFSN TV in Fresno, CA
KGO TV — ABC Online: KGO TV in San Francisco, CA
KGTV — Digital City San Diego: KGTV Channel 10
KGTV 10 — Digital City San Diego: KGTV Channel 10
KGTV NEWS — Digital City San Diego: KGTV Channel 10
KGTV TV — Digital City San Diego: KGTV Channel 10
KGUN TV — ABC Online: KGUN TV in Tucson, AZ
KHBS TV — ABC Online: KHBS TV in Fort Smith, AR
KICK BUTT — Better Health & Medical: Smoking Cessation Classes
KID — AOL Kids Only channel
KID BUSINESS — KidsBiz Invention Connection [Web pointer]
KID DESK — IBM on AOL
KID HELP — AOL Kids Only: I Need Help!
KID INVENT — KidsBiz Invention Connection [Web pointer]
KID MOVIES — Hollywood Online: Kids Corner
KID PATROL — AOL Families: The National Center for Missing &
    Exploited Children
KID SAFE ATLANTA — Digital City Atlanta: KidSafe
KID SAFETY — AOL Neighborhood Watch
KID SEARCH — Kids Only: The Web [Web site]
KID STUFF — AOL Shopping: Toys & Collectibles
KID TRAVEL — Family Travel Network
KIDNEY — AOL Health: Kidney & Urinary Tract Disorders
KIDNEY FAILURE — AOL Health: Kidney Failure
KIDNEY STONES — AOL Health: Kidney Stones
KIDS & INVESTING — AOL Personal Finance: Kids & Investing
KIDS — AOL Kids Only channel
KIDS AND INVESTING — AOL Personal Finance: **Kids & Investing**
KIDS AND TEENS — AOL Families: Kids & Teens
KIDS BIZ — KidsBiz Invention Connection [Web pointer]
KID'S DICTIONARY — Merriam-Webster's Kids Dictionary
KIDS DICTIONARY — Merriam-Webster's Kids Dictionary
KIDS FIND — Kids Only: The Web [Web site]
KIDS GUIDE PAGER — Kids Only: I Need Help!
KIDS KICKS — Digital City Washington: Kids Kicks
KIDS ONLY — AOL Kids Only channel
KIDS ONLY SEARCH — Kids Only: The Web [Web site]
KIDS PAGE — Kids Only: I Need Help!
KIDS PAGER — Kids Only: I Need Help!
KIDS READS — The Book Report: Kids Reads

KIDS SEARCH — Kids Only: The Web [Web site]
KIDS' WB — WB Online: Kids
KIDS WB — WB Online: Kids
KIDS WEB — Kids Only: The Web [Web site]
KIDS YAP — AOL UK: Kids Yap
KIDZBIZ — Kidsbiz
KIDZINE — ABC Online: Kidzine
KIFI TV — ABC Online: KIFI TV in Idaho Falls, ID
KI-JANA CARTER — Athlete Direct
KIM BALL — Digital City Denver: Humorwrite Online
KIM BONNELL — Electra: Your Fashion Style
**KIM KOMANDO — Kim Komando's Komputer Klinic
   [Web site]**
KING — NetNoir: Martin Luther King, Jr.
KIRIBATI — AOL International: Kiribati
KIRK FRIEDEN — Digital City Los Angeles: Kirk Frieden Real Estate
KIRK FRIEDEN REAL ESTATE — Digital City Los Angeles: Kirk Frieden
   Real Estate
KIRSTIE ALLEY — WB Online: Veronica's Closet
KISS-O-GRAM — Love@AOL: Insta-Kiss
KITCHEN SUPERSTORE — AOL Shoppers Advantage: Kitchen Store
KIVI TV — ABC Online: KIVI TV in Boise, ID
KIXX — Digital City Philadelphia: Kixx Online
KIXX ONLINE — Digital City Philadelphia: Kixx Online
KIXX SOCCER — Digital City Philadelphia: Kixx Online
KLKN — ABC Online: KLKN TV in Lincoln, NE
KLKN TV — ABC Online: KLKN TV in Lincoln, NE
KMBC TV — ABC Online: KMBC TV in Kansas City, MO
KMGH TV — ABC Online: KMGH TV in Denver, CO
KMIZ TV — ABC Online: KMIZ TV in Columbia, MO
KNICKS — New York Knicks
KNOCK KNOCK — AOL Member Services: About Internet Knock-Knock
KNOCKERS — AOL Australia: Knockers Online
KNOT — The Knot: Weddings for the Real World
KNOW DB — Microsoft Knowledge Base [Web site]
KNOWLEDGE BASE — Microsoft Knowledge Base [Web site]
KNOWLEDGE DATABASE — Microsoft Knowledge Base [Web site]
KNTV TV — ABC Online: KNTV TV in San Jose, CA
KNXV TV — ABC Online: KNXV TV in Phoenix, AZ
KO — AOL Kids Only channel
KO CENTRAL — Kids Only: Central
KO CHAT — Kids Only: Chat
KO CLUBS — Kids Only: Clubs
KO CREATE — Kids Only: Create
KO FAME — Kids Only: Hall of Fame
KO FIND — Kids Only: Find It

KO FIND IT — Kids Only: Find It
KO GAMES — Kids Only: Games
KO GET INVOLVED — Kids Only: Get Involved
KO HELP — Kids Only: I Need Help!
KO HOT — Kids Only: What's Hot
KO NEWS — Kids Only: News
KO PARENT — Kids Only: Parent Feedback
KO SEARCH — Kids Only: The Web [Web site]
KO SERVICE — Kids Only: Member Services
KO SERVICES — Kids Only: Member Services
KO SPEAK — Kids Only: Speak Out
KO SPORTS — Kids Only: Sports
KO SS — Kids Only: Shows + Stars
KOAT TV — ABC Online: KOAT TV in Albuquerque, NM
KOCO TV — ABC Online: KOCO TV in Oklahoma City, OK
KODAK WEB — Kodak [Web site]
KODE TV — ABC Online: KODE TV in Joplin, MO
KOMANDO — Kim Komando's Komputer Klinic [Web site]
**KOMANDO CLINIC — Kim Komando's Komputer Klinic
    [Web site]**
**KOMPUTER KLINIC — Kim Komando's Komputer Klinic
    [Web site]**
KOOL GRAFFITI — People Connection: Graffiti
KORAN — AOL International: Middle East
KOREA — AOL International: Korea
KORMAN — Digital City Philadelphia: Korman Suites and Apartments
KORMAN SUITE — Digital City Philadelphia: Korman Suites and
    Apartments
KORMAN SUITES — Digital City Philadelphia: Korman Suites and
    Apartments
KOSHER — Jewish Community: Kosher
KOTLER — Digital City Los Angeles: Robert Kotler, M.D. FACS
KQTV TV — ABC Online: KQTV TV in St. Joseph, MO
KRANK — MTV Online: Krank
KS 107.5 — Digital City Denver: KS 107.5
KS 1075 — Digital City Denver: KS 107.5
KS-107.5 — Digital City Denver: KS 107.5
KTBS TV — ABC Online: KTBS TV in Shreveport, LA
KTCK — Digital City Dallas-Fort Worth: KTCK 1310 AM Sports Radio
KTKA TV — ABC Online: KTKA TV in Topeka, KS
KTLA — KTLA Channel 5: Los Angeles
KTRK TV — ABC Online: KTRK TV in Houston, TX
KTVX TV — ABC Online: KTVX TV in Salt Lake City, UT
KTXL — Digital City San Francisco: Unabomber Trial
KTXS TV — ABC Online: KTXS TV in Abilene, TX
KUWAIT — AOL International: Kuwait

KVIA TV — ABC Online: KVIA TV in El Paso, TX
KVUE TV — ABC Online: KVUE TV in Austin, TX
KWANZAA — NetNoir: The Story of Kwanzaa [seasonal]
KWB CYBER CARD — WB Online: Cyber-Club Membership Card
KWB MEMBERS — WB Online: Cyber-Club Membership Card
KWGN — Digital City Denver: WB2 News, Weather and Sports
KYNG — Digital City Dallas-Fort Worth: Young Country 105.3
    [Web site]
KYNG RADIO — Digital City Dallas-Fort Worth: Young Country 105.3
    [Web site]
KYRGYZSTAN — AOL International: Kyrgyzstan
L & C — AOL Research & Learn channel
L.A. — Digital City Los Angeles
L.A. AUTOGUIDE — Digital City Los Angeles: AutoGuide
L.A. BEAUTY — Digital City Los Angeles: Beauty & Style
L.A. CONCERTS — Southern California's Concert Connection
L.A. CREDIT — Digital City Los Angeles: Personal Finance
L.A. LOANS — Digital City Los Angeles: Personal Finance
L.A. LOVE — Digital City Los Angeles: Love@1st Site
L.A. MONEY — Digital City Los Angeles: Personal Finance
L.A. PERSONAL FINANCE — Digital City Los Angeles: Personal Finance
L.A. POSTCARDS — Digital City Los Angeles: Virtual Postcards
L.A. STYLE — Digital City Los Angeles: Beauty & Style
L.L. BEAN — L.L. Bean [Web site]
LA — Digital City Los Angeles
LA ADVICE — Digital City Los Angeles: Advice Expert!
LA ALICE — Digital City Los Angeles: Advice Expert!
LA ANIMATION — Digital City Los Angeles: Animation Fest
LA ANIMATION FEST — Digital City Los Angeles: Animation Fest
LA ANNEX — Digital City Los Angeles: The Learning Annex
LA APARTMENTS — Digital City Los Angeles: Rental Connection
LA AUTOGUIDE — Digital City Los Angeles: AutoGuide
LA AUTOS — Digital City Los Angeles: AutoGuide
LA BANDS — Digital City Los Angeles: Music Guide
LA BEAUTY & STYLE — Digital City Los Angeles: Beauty & Style
LA BEAUTY — Digital City Los Angeles: Beauty & Style
LA BEC FIN — Digital City Philadelphia: Dining Guide
LA BUSINESS DIRECTORY — Digital City Los Angeles: Business
    Directory [Web site]
LA CAREERS — Digital City Los Angeles: Employment Classifieds
LA CHAT — Digital City Los Angeles: Chat
LA CLASSROOM — Digital City Los Angeles: The Learning Annex
LA CLIP — Los Angeles Clippers
LA CLIPPERS — Los Angeles Clippers
LA COMM — Digital City Los Angeles: Community

LA COMPUTE MP — Digital City Los Angeles: Technical Employment Resource

LA COMPUTER CURRENTS — Digital City Los Angeles: Computer Currents

LA COMPUTER GUIDE — Digital City Los Angeles: Computer Mart

LA COMPUTER MART — Digital City Los Angeles: Computer Mart

LA COMPUTERS — Digital City Los Angeles: Computer Mart

LA CONDOS — Digital City Los Angeles: Homes For Sale

LA CONFIDENTIAL — LA Confidential: The Movie

LA DESTINATIONS — Digital City Los Angeles: Sights

LA DINING — Digital City Los Angeles: Dining

LA DOLCE VITA — Image Exchange: La Dolce Vita

LA EMPLOYMENT — Digital City Los Angeles: Employment Classifieds

LA EVENTS — Digital City Los Angeles: Events

LA FEMME NIKITA — La Femme Nikita: The Movie

LA FINANCE — Digital City Los Angeles: Personal Finance

LA GALAXY — Digital City Los Angeles: Galaxy

LA HOMES — Digital City Los Angeles: Homes For Sale

LA HOUSES — Digital City Los Angeles: Homes For Sale

LA JOBS — DC Los Angeles: Employment Classifieds

LA LAKE — Los Angeles Lakers

LA LAKERS — Los Angeles Lakers

LA LEARNING — Digital City Los Angeles: The Learning Annex

LA LEARNING ANNEX — Digital City Los Angeles: The Learning Annex

LA LOCAL NEWS — Digital City Los Angeles: Local News

LA M4M — PlanetOut: FantasyMan Island in Los Angeles

LA MORTGAGE — Digital City Los Angeles: Homes For Sale

LA MOVIES — Digital City Los Angeles: Movies

LA MUSIC — Digital City Los Angeles: Music Guide

LA NEWCARS — Digital City Los Angeles: AutoGuide

LA NEWS — Digital City Los Angeles: News

LA NIGHTLIFE — Digital City Los Angeles: Music Guide

LA PEOPLE — Digital City Los Angeles: People

LA PERSONALS — Digital City Los Angeles: Personals

LA PHONE — Digital City Los Angeles: Business Directory [Web site]

LA PHONE DIRECTORY — Digital City Los Angeles: Business Directory [Web site]

LA PHONES — Digital City Los Angeles: Business Directory [Web site]

LA PHOTO LIBRARIES — Digital City Los Angeles: Photo Libraries!

LA PHOTOS — Digital City Los Angeles: Photo Libraries!

LA PICTURES — Digital City Los Angeles: Photo Libraries!

LA POSTCARDS — Digital City Los Angeles: Virtual Postcards

LA REAL ESTATE — Digital City Los Angeles: Homes For Sale

LA RENTALS — Digital City Los Angeles: Rental Connection

LA RESIDENTIAL REAL ESTATE — Digital City Los Angeles: Homes For Sale

LA SIGHTS — Digital City Los Angeles: Sights
LA SINGLE — Digital City Los Angeles: Personals
LA SOCCER — Digital City Los Angeles: Galaxy
LA SOUND FILES — Digital City Los Angeles: Sound Libraries
LA SOUND LIBRARIES — Digital City Los Angeles: Sound Libraries
LA SOUNDS — Digital City Los Angeles: Sound Libraries
LA STYLE — Digital City Los Angeles: Beauty & Style
LA TEENS — Digital City Los Angeles: Teens
LA TEN BEST — Digital City Los Angeles: Ten Best
LA TEST — What's New on AOL
LA TOUR — Digital City Los Angeles: Tour
LA TOURIST SPOTS — Digital City Los Angeles: Sights
LA TRAVEL AGENT — Digital City Los Angeles: Travel Agents
LA TV — Digital City Los Angeles: TV Navigator
LA USED CARS — Digital City Los Angeles: AutoGuide
LA WAV LIBRARIES — Digital City Los Angeles: Sound Libraries
LA WAVS — Digital City Los Angeles: Sound Libraries
LA WEATHER — Digital City Los Angeles: News
LA WEB — Digital City Los Angeles: WebGuide [Web site]
LA WEBGUIDE — Digital City Los Angeles: WebGuide [Web site]
LA WEEKLY — Digital City Los Angeles: L.A. Weekly
LA WHITE PAGES — Digital City Los Angeles: Business Directory
   [Web site]
LA YELLOW PAGES — Digital City Los Angeles: Business Directory
   [Web site]
LACROSSE — AOL Sports: Lacrosse Forum
LADY DI — AOL International: Royalty Forum
LAING HOMES — Digital City Los Angeles: John Laing Homes
LAKERS — Los Angeles Lakers
LAKEWOOD NEWS — Digital City Denver: News and Information
LAMBDA — Lambda Rising Bookstore Online
LAMBDA RISING — Lambda Rising Bookstore Online
LANCASTER EOL — AOL UK: North West Events Online
LAND END — Lands' End Store [Web site]
LAND ENDS — Lands' End Store [Web site]
LAND'S END — Lands' End Store [Web site]
LANDS' END — Lands' End Store [Web site]
LANDS END — Lands' End Store [Web site]
LANDSCAPE — AOL Interests: Gardening
LANDSCAPER — AOL WorkPlace: Landscaping & Gardening
   Community
LANDSCAPING — AOL Interests: Gardening
LANGUAGE — AOL International: The Bistro
LANGUAGE CHALLENGE — AOL International: Language Games
LANGUAGE GAME — AOL International: Language Games
LANGUAGE GAMES — AOL International: Language Games

LANIER — Pamela Lanier's Bed and Breakfast Guide
LAOS — AOL International: Laos
LAPTOP — AOL Computing: Superstore
LAPUB — People Connection: LaPub
LARRY MAGID — The Larry Magid Show
LAS VEGAS — Digital City Las Vegas
LAS VEGAS DC — Digital City Las Vegas
LAS VEGAS DCITY — Digital City Las Vegas
LAS VEGAS HOMES — Digital City Las Vegas: Homes for Sale
LAS VEGAS LOCAL NEWS — Digital City Las Vegas: Local News
LAS VEGAS NEWS — Digital City Las Vegas: Local News
LAS VEGAS NV — Digital City Las Vegas
LAS VEGAS REAL ESTATE — Digital City Las Vegas: Homes for Sale
LAST MINUTE — AOL Travel: Planing a Last Minute Vacation
LAST MINUTE TRAVEL — AOL Travel: Planing a Last Minute Vacation
LAST SHOT — Real Fans: The Last Shot
LATE SHOW — Late Show Online
LATINA — Hispanic Online
LATINA TAG TEAM — Digital City San Diego: Latina Tag Team
LATINA TT — Digital City San Diego: Latina Tag Team
LATINO — Hispanic Online
LATINONET — LatinoNet
LATINOPLEX — Digital City Dallas-Fort Worth: Hispanic
LATVIA — AOL International: Latvia
<u>LATVIJA</u> — AOL International: Latvia
LATZ TA — Online Psych: Latz Talk
LATZ TALK — Online Psych: Latz Talk
LAURA RAPOSA — Boston Herald: Gossip Gals
LAW — AOL Research & Learn: Law & Government
LAW CENTER — Court TV Law Center
LAW RESOURCES — AOL Research & Learn: Legal Resources
LAW SCHOOL — KAPLAN Online -or- The Princeton Review
LAX — AOL Sports: Lacrosse Forum
LBL — Allstate: Lincoln Benefit Life
LCI CLUBS — AOL UK: London Calling Clubs
LCI GIGS — AOL UK: London Calling Gigs
LCI LIFE — AOL UK: London Calling Life
LCS — LCS Guide to Hockey
LCS HOCKEY — LCS Guide to Hockey
LCS HOCKEY GUIDE — LCS Guide to Hockey
LD — AOL Long Distance Savings Plan
LD BILL — AOL Long Distance: Members Area
LD HELP — AOL Long Distance: Members Area
LD MEMBER — Long Distance: Members Area
LE BEC FIN — Digital City Philadelphia: DiningGuide
LE BEC-FIN — Digital City Philadelphia: DiningGuide

LEADER — AOL Influence: Media and Money
LEADERS — AOL Community Leader Program
LEADERS NETWORK — Christianity Online: Church Leaders Network
LEADERSHIP — Christianity Online: Leadership Journal
LEADERSHIP JOURNAL — Christianity Online: Leadership Journal
LEARN ABOUT SECURITY — AOL Member Services: Online Safety
LEARN ACCESS — AOL Member Services: Connecting to AOL
LEARN AOL — AOL Member Services: QuickStart
LEARN CHAT — AOL Member Services: Chatting Online
LEARN CONNECTING — AOL Member Services: Connecting to AOL
LEARN DOWNLOAD — AOL Member Services: How To Download
LEARN DOWNLOADING — AOL Member Services: How To Download
LEARN E-MAIL — AOL Member Services: Your E-mail Address
LEARN EMAIL — AOL Member Services: Your E-mail Address
LEARN FIND — AOL Member Services: Finding Places on AOL
LEARN FINDING — AOL Member Services: Finding Things Online
LEARN FINDING PEOPLE — AOL Member Services: Find Family and
    Friends Online
LEARN FINDING THINGS — AOL Member Services: Using Search &
    Find
LEARN GAMES — AOL Member Services: Play Games Online
LEARN IM — AOL Member Services: Instant Messages
LEARN IM'S — AOL Member Services: Instant Messages
LEARN IMS — AOL Member Services: Using Instant Messages
LEARN INSTANT MESSAGES — AOL Member Services: Instant Messages
LEARN INTERNET — AOL Member Services: About the Internet & Web
LEARN KEYWORDS — AOL Member Services: Using Keywords
LEARN KID SAFETY — AOL Member Services: Using Parental Controls
LEARN MEETING PEOPLE — AOL Member Services: Find Family &
    Friends Online
LEARN MESSAGE BOARDS — AOL Member Services: Using Message
    Boards
LEARN NAVIGATION — AOL Member Services: Getting Around
LEARN NEWS PROFILES — AOL Member Services: Get Only the News
    You Want
LEARN ONLINE SAFETY — AOL Member Services: Using Parental
    Controls
LEARN PARENT — AOL Member Services: Using Parental Controls
LEARN PARENT CONTROL — AOL Member Services: Using Parental
    Controls
LEARN PARENTS CONTROL — AOL Member Services: Using Parental
    Controls
LEARN PEOPLE — AOL Member Services: People Connection
LEARN PEOPLE CONNECTION — AOL Member Services: People
    Connection

LEARN PERSONAL PUBLISHER — AOL Member Services: Personal Publisher

LEARN PP — AOL Member Services: Personal Publisher

LEARN PUBLISHER — AOL Member Services: Create a Web Site in Minutes

LEARN QUOTES — AOL Member Services: Keep an Eye on Investments

LEARN RICH TEXT — AOL Member Services: Spice Up Your E-mail

LEARN SECURITY — AOL Member Services: Online Safety

LEARN TO USE AOL — AOL Member Services: Getting Around and Using AOL

LEARNING & CULTURE — AOL Research & Learn channel

LEARNING — AOL Research & Learn channel

LEARNING AND CULTURE — AOL Research & Learn channel

LEARNING ANNEX — Digital City Los Angeles: The Learning Annex

LEARNING DISABILITIES — Development and Learning Disorders

LEARNING DISORDERS — AOL Health: Learning Disorders

LEATHER SOULS — PlanetOut: Leather Community

LEBANON — AOL International: Lebanon

LECOQSPROTIF — AOL Canada: LCS Guide to Hockey

LEEDS — AOL UK: Local Life

LEEDS EOL — AOL UK: North East Events Online

LEGAL — AOL Research & Learn: Legal Resources

LEGAL INFORMATION NET — Legal Information Network

LEGAL NOTICE — Special Notice Regarding the Class Action Suit

LEGAL SIG — Legal Information Network

LEGENDS — Legends of Kesmai

LEGENDS OF KESMAI — Legends of Kesmai

L'EGGS — One Hanes Place

LEICESTER — AOL UK: Local Life

LEISURE — AOL Influence: Arts and Leisure

LEISURE SPORTS — AOL Sports: Leisure Sports

LENTEK — Digital City Orlando: Lentek Pest Control [Web site]

LENTEK PEST CONTROL — Digital City Orlando: Lentek Pest Control [Web site]

LEO — Horoscope Selections

LEPRECHAUN — AOL International: Irish Heritage

LESBIAN & GAY RIGHTS — Human Rights Campaign for Gay & Lesbian Rights

LESBIAN — AOL Lifestyles: Gay & Lesbian

LESBIAN BOARDS — onQ: Message Boards

LESBIAN BUSINESS — onQ: Business

LESBIAN CHAT — onQ: Chat and Conferences

LESBIAN ENTERTAINMENT — onQ: Arts

LESBIAN HOMES — onQ: Home & Garden

LESBIAN LIBRARY — onQ: Libraries

LESBIAN MARRIAGE — onQ: Marriage

LESBIAN MESSAGE — onQ: Message Boards
LESBIAN NEWS — onQ: News
LESBIAN ORG — onQ: Organizations
LESBIAN ORGS — onQ: Organizations
LESBIAN SF — Digital City San Francisco: Gay Community
LESBIAN SOFTWARE — onQ: Libraries
LESBIAN TEEN — onQ: Youth
LESBIAN TRIVIA — onQ: Gaymeland
LESBIAN UK — AOL UK: Utopia Gay & Lesbian Forum
LESBIAN YOUTH — onQ: Youth
LESOTHO — AOL International: Lesotho
LETTER — A Letter From Steve Case
LETTER 3 — A Letter From Steve Case
LETTERMAN — Late Show Online
LEUKEMIA — AOL Health: Leukemia
LEWINSKY — Bill Clinton News Special
LEWISVILLE — Digital City Dallas-Fort Worth: Lewisville Leader
    Newspaper
LEWISVILLE LEADER — Digital City Dallas-Fort Worth: Lewisville Leader
    Newspaper
LFF — AOL UK: London Film Festival
LHASA — AOL International: Tibet
LIBERIA — AOL International: Liberia
LIBERTARIAN — Libertarian Party
LIBERTARIAN PARTY — Libertarian Party
LIBERTARIANS — Libertarian Party
LIBERTY BELL — Digital City Philadelphia: Independence Hall
    Association Virtual Walking Tour
LIBERTY BELLE — Digital City Philadelphia: Liberty Belle Cruises
LIBERTYVILLE — Digital City Libertyville [Web site]
LIBRA — Horoscope Selections
LIBRARIES ONQ — onQ: Libraries
LIBYA — AOL International: Libya
LIECHTENSTEIN — AOL International: Liechtenstein
LIFE BASICS — Digital City New York: LoveCoach
LIFE COVER — AOL News: Life News
LIFE FRONT — AOL News: Life News
LIFE NEWS — AOL News: Life News
LIFE STORIES — AOL News: Life News
LIFESTAGES — AOL LifeStages: Advice & Planning
LIFESTAGES DIAPERS — AOL LifeStages: Diapers & Dollars
LIFESTAGES ESTATE — AOL LifeStages: Can't Take it With You
LIFESTAGES HEALTH — AOL LifeStages: Health Care Issues
LIFESTAGES KIDS — AOL LifeStages: Kids & Cash
LIFESTAGES MARRIAGE — AOL LifeStages: Marriage & Money
LIFESTAGES RETIRE — AOL LifeStages: Retire in Style

LIFESTAGES SCHOOL — AOL LifeStages: Saving for School
LIFESTAGES SINGLE — AOL LifeStages: On Your Own
LIFESTYLE — AOL Lifestyles channel
LIFESTYLE SEARCH — Lifestyles: Search & Explore
LIFESTYLES — AOL Lifestyles channel
LIFESTYLES CHANNEL — AOL Lifestyles channel
LIFESTYLES SEARCH — Lifestyles: Search & Explore
LIFETIME —· Lifetime Television For Women [Web site]
LIFETIME TELEVISION — Lifetime Television For Women [Web site]
LIFETIME TV — Lifetime Television For Women [Web site]
LILLIAN — Lillian Vernon Store
LILLIAN VERNON — Lillian Vernon Store
LIN — Legal Information Network
LINCOLN — AOL UK: Local Life
LINCOLN BENEFIT LIFE — Allstate: Lincoln Benefit Life
LINCOLN EOL — AOL UK: Midlands Events Online
LINGO — AOL Personal Finance: Investment Lingo
LIQUOR STORE — AOL WorkPlace: Liquor Stores & Suppliers
    Community
LIRR MAP — Digital City New York: Long Island Rail Road [Web site]
LIRR MAPS — Digital City New York: Long Island Rail Road [Web site]
LIS — Entertainment Asylum: Lost in Space
LIST GUY — NetGuide on AOL: The List Guy
LISTEN UP — Digital City Denver: ListenUp Audio and Video
LISTSERV — Internet Connection: Mailing List Directory
LISTSERVS — Internet Connection: Mailing List Directory
LITERARY CRITICISM — Barron's Booknotes
LITERARY CRITICISMS — Barron's Booknotes
LITERATURE — AOL Research & Learn: Reading & Writing
LITHUANIA — AOL International: Lithuania
LIVE — AOL Live
LIVE — Entertainment Online
LIVE EVENTS — AOL Live
LIVE GUIDE — AOL Live: Coming Attractions
LIVE SPORTS — AOL Sports: Live
LIVE TONIGHT — AOL Live
LIVE! — AOL Live
LIVERPOOL — AOL UK: Local Life
LIVERPOOL EOL — AOL UK: North West Events Online
LIVING BOOKS — Broderbund
LIVING HISTORY — The History Channel: Living History Forum
LJ — Christianity Online: Leadership Journal
LL BEAN — L.L. Bean
LOA ANGELES CURRENTS — Digital City Los Angeles: Computer
    Currents
LOBBY — People Connection

LOCAL — Digital City Online
LOCAL EMPLOYMENT — Digital City: Employment Classifieds
LOCAL MOVIE GUIDE — Digital City: Movie Information [Web site]
LOCAL MOVIES — Digital City: Local Movies
LOCAL NEWS — Digital City: Local News
LOCAL SKIING — Digital City: Skiing
LOCAL WEATHER STATION — Digital City Hampton Roads: Local Weather Station
LOCKS — AOL WorkPlace: Locks & Locksmiths Community
LOGO SHOP — AOL Store: Logo Shop
LOIS & CLARK — Lois & Clark
LOIS AND CLARK — Lois & Clark
LONDON — AOL UK: Local Life in London
LONDONDERRY — AOL UK: Local Life
LONELY PLANET SEARCH — Lonely Planet: Search
LONG DISTANCE — AOL Long Distance Savings Plan
LONG ISLAND RAIL ROAD — Digital City New York: Long Island Rail Road [Web site]
LONGO — Digital City Los Angeles: Longo Toyota
LONGO TOYOTA — Digital City Los Angeles: Longo Toyota
LONGTON CROWN — Collectibles Today [Web site]
LOS ANGELAS DODGERS — Los Angeles Dodgers
LOS ANGELES — Digital City Los Angeles
LOS ANGELES CHAT — Digital City Los Angeles: Chat
LOS ANGELES CLIPPERS — Los Angeles Clippers
LOS ANGELES DINING — Digital City Los Angeles: Dining
LOS ANGELES DODGERS — Los Angeles Dodgers
LOS ANGELES EVENTS — Digital City Los Angeles: Events
LOS ANGELES GALAXY — Digital City Los Angeles: Galaxy
LOS ANGELES JOKES — Digital City Los Angeles: The Joke Box
LOS ANGELES KIDS — Digital City Los Angeles: KidSafe
LOS ANGELES KIDS SAFE — Digital City Los Angeles: KidSafe
LOS ANGELES LAKERS — Los Angeles Lakers
LOS ANGELES MIXSTAR — Digital City Los Angeles: Home Mortgage Facilitator
LOS ANGELES MOVIE — Digital City Los Angeles: Movies
LOS ANGELES MOVIES — Digital City Los Angeles: Movies
LOS ANGELES MOVING — Digital City Los Angeles: Relocation Guide
LOS ANGELES NEWS — Digital City Los Angeles: News
LOS ANGELES PEOPLE — Digital City Los Angeles: People
LOS ANGELES PHOTOS — Digital City Los Angeles: Photo Libraries!
LOS ANGELES RELO — Digital City Los Angeles: Relocation Guide
LOS ANGELES RELOCATE — Digital City Los Angeles: Relocation Guide
LOS ANGELES RELOCATION — Digital City Los Angeles: Relocation Guide
LOS ANGELES SINGLES — Digital City Los Angeles: Personals

LOS ANGELES SOCCER — Digital City Los Angeles: Galaxy
LOS ANGELES TEN BEST — Digital City Los Angeles: Ten Best
LOS ANGELES TRANSFER — Digital City Los Angeles: Relocation Guide
LOS ANGELES TV — Digital City Los Angeles: TV Navigator
LOST IN SPACE — Entertainment Asylum: Lost in Space
LOTTERY — AOL News: Lottery Results by State
LOTTERY DRAWING — AOL News: Lottery Results by State
LOTTO — AOL News: Lottery Results by State
LOTTO TEXAS — Lotto Texas [Web site]
LOTUS 123 — AOL Computing: Spreadsheet Applications
LOVE — Romance channel
LOVE AT 1ST — Digital City Los Angeles: Love @ 1st Site
LOVE AT AOL — Love@AOL
LOVE AT AOL DIRTY LAUNDRY — Love@AOL: Dirty Laundry
LOVE AT AOL INSTAGIFT — Love@AOL: Insta-Gift
LOVE AT AOL LOVER OF THE YEAR — Love@AOL: Lover of the Year
    Contest
LOVE AT AOL MYSTERY LOVER — Love@AOL: Mystery Lover Game
LOVE AT AOL PERSONAL — Love@AOL: Love Personals
LOVE AT AOL PERSONAL UPDATE — Love@AOL: Personals
LOVE AT AOL PERSONALS — Love@AOL: Love Personals
LOVE AT AOL PERSONALS UPDATE — Love@AOL: Personals
LOVE AT AOL SUCCESS STORIES — Love@AOL: Online Romance
    Success Stories
LOVE AT AOL'S INSTANT ROSE — Love@AOL: InstaRose
LOVE AT AOL'S INSTAROSE — Love@AOL: InstaRose
LOVE AT AOLS MYSTERY LOVER — Love@AOL: Mystery Lover Game
LOVE AT FIRST — Love @ 1st Site
LOVE FILES — Digital City Philadelphia: The Love Files
LOVE HOLLY — Digital City New York: Love Advisors: Holly
LOVE LINK — Love@AOL: Love~Links
LOVE LINKS — Love@AOL: Love~Links
LOVE ONQ — onQ: Relationships
LOVE PROFILE — Love@AOL: Profile Form
LOVE SHACK — AOL UK: The Love Shack
LOVE SHOP — Love@AOL: The Love Shop
LOVE SHOPPING — Love@AOL: The Love Shop
LOVE STEPHEN — Digital City New York: Love Coach
LOVE SUCCESS STORIES — Digital City Los Angeles: Love @ 1st Site
LOVE@1ST SITE — Digital City Los Angeles: Love @ 1st Site
LOVE@1STSIGHT — Digital City Los Angeles: Love @ 1st Site
LOVE@1ST-SITE — Digital City Los Angeles: Love @ 1st Site
LOVE@AOL — Love@AOL
LOVE@AOL DIRTY LAUNDRY — Love@AOL: Dirty Laundry
LOVE@AOL INSTA-GIFT — Love@AOL: Insta-Gift

LOVE@AOL LOVER OF THE YEAR — Love@AOL: Lover of the Year Contest

LOVE@AOL MYSTERY LOVER — Love@AOL: Mystery Lover Game

LOVE@AOL PERSONAL — Love@AOL: Love Personals

LOVE@AOL PERSONAL UPDATE — Love@AOL: Personals

LOVE@AOL PERSONALS — Love@AOL: Love Personals

LOVE@AOL PERSONALS UPDATE — Love@AOL: Personals

LOVE@AOL SUCCESS STORIES — Love@AOL: Online Romance Success Stories

LOVE@AOLS DIRTY LAUNDRY — Love@AOL: Dirty Laundry

LOVE@AOL'S INSTANT ROSE — Love@AOL: InstaRose

LOVE@AOL'S INSTAROSE — Love@AOL: InstaRose

LOVE@AOLS MYSTERY LOVER — Love@AOL: Mystery Lover Game

LOVER OF THE YEAR — Love@AOL: Lover of the Year Contest

LOVER OF THE YEAR CONTEST — Love@AOL: Lover of the Year Contest

LOVES TORE — Love@AOL: The Love Shop

LOW FARE — Preview Travel: Travel Newswire

LOW FARES — Preview Travel: Travel Newswire

LOWE — Backpacker Magazine: Marketplace

LPS — Lonely Planet: Search

LS — AOL Lifestyles channel

LS DIAPERS — AOL LifeStages: Diapers & Dollars

LS ESTATE — AOL LifeStages: Can't Take it With You

LS HEALTH — AOL LifeStages: Health Care Issues

LS KIDS — AOL LifeStages: Kids & Cash

LS MARRIAGE — AOL LifeStages: Marriage & Money

LS RETIRE — AOL LifeStages: Retire in Style

LS SCHOOL — AOL LifeStages: Saving for School

LS SINGLE — AOL LifeStages: On Your Own

LSAT — KAPLAN Online -or- The Princeton Review

LTT — Digital City San Diego: Latina Tag Team

LUCKY 7 — AOL News: Lottery Results by State

LUNAR SCOPES — Digital City Philadelphia: DjunaVerse

LUNCHBYTES — Digital City Denver: Lunchbytes

LUNG DISORDERS — AOL Health: Lung and Respiratory Screen

LUPUS — AOL Health: Lupus

LURVE — AOL UK: The Love Shack

LUTHERAN BROTHERHOOD — Christianity Online: Lutheran Brotherhood [Web site]

LUXEMBOURG — AOL International: Luxembourg

LV — Lillian Vernon Store

LV HOMES — Digital City Las Vegas: Homes for Sale

LV JOBS — Lasvegasjobs.com [Web site]

LV REAL ESTATE — Digital City Las Vegas: Homes for Sale

LYME DISEASE — AOL Health: Lyme Disease

LYMPHOMA — AOL Health: Lymphoma
LYNCHBURG — Digital City Roanoke [Web site]
LYNN FISCHER — Electra: Low-Fat Life with Lynn Fischer
<u>LYNN FISHER</u> — Electra: Low-Fat Life with Lynn Fischer
LYNN VARGAS — Digital City Washington: Vargas' Interiors by Design
M4M — PlanetOut: Boystown
M4M BOSTON — PlanetOut: FantasyMan Island for Boston
M4M CHICAGO — PlanetOut: FantasyMan Island for Chicago
M4M DC — PlanetOut: FantasyMan Island for Washington DC
M4M FLORIDA — PlanetOut: FantasyMan Island for Florida
MA CHAT — AOL Computing: Events
MA CHATS — AOL Computing: Events
MAC — AOL Computing channel
MAC OS8 — Apple on AOL
MAC ALPT — AOL Grandstand: Simulation Golf
MAC APPLICATIONS — AOL Computing: Mac Applications
MAC APPS — AOL Computing: Mac Applications
MAC ART — AOL Computing: Mac Graphics Arts
MAC AVSC — AOL Computing: Mac Animation & Video Software Center
MAC BEGINNER — AOL Computing: Mac Help Desk
MAC BEGINNERS — AOL Computing: Mac Help Desk
MAC BFSC — AOL Computing: Mac Business and Finance Software
    Center
MAC BUSINESS — AOL Computing: Mac Applications
MAC CAD — AOL Computing: Mac Graphics Arts
MAC CHATS — AOL Computing: Chat!
MAC COMMUNICATION — AOL Computing: Mac Communications &
    Networking
MAC COMMUNICATIONS — AOL Computing: Mac Communications &
    Networking
MAC COMPUTING — AOL Computing channel
MAC CONFERENCE — AOL Computing: Chat!
MAC CONFERENCES — AOL Computing: Chat!
MAC DESKTOP — AOL Computing: Mac Desktop & Web Publishing
MAC DESKTOP VIDEO — AOL Computing: Mac Animation & Video
MAC DEVELOPMENT — AOL Computing: Mac Development
MAC DOWNLOAD — AOL Computing: Daily Download
MAC DOWNLOADING — AOL Computing: Download Software
MAC DPSC — AOL Computing: Mac Desktop & Web Publishing
    Software Center
MAC DTP — AOL Computing: Mac Desktop & Web Publishing
MAC DVSC — AOL Computing: Mac Development Software Center
MAC EARLY ED — AOL Computing: Preschool/Early Childhood SIG
MAC EARLY EDUCATION — AOL Computing: Preschool/Early
    Childhood SIG

MAC EDSC — AOL Computing: Mac Education & Reference Software Center

MAC EDUCATION — AOL Computing: Mac Education/Technology

MAC FORMAT — AOL UK: MacFormat Magazine

MAC FUSC — AOL Computing: Fun and Games Software Center

MAC GAME — AOL Games: Mac Games

MAC GAMES — Mac Games & Entertainment Forum

MAC GRAPHICS — AOL Computing: Mac Graphics Arts

MAC GRAPHICS FORUM — AOL Computing: Mac Graphics Arts

MAC GRSC — AOL Computing: Mac Graphic Arts Software Center

MAC HARDWARE — AOL Computing: Mac Hardware/OS

MAC HELP — AOL Computing: Help Desk

MAC HELP DESK — AOL Computing: Help Desk

MAC HOSC — AOL Computing: Mac Home & Hobby Software Center

MAC HYPERCARD — AOL Computing: Mac HyperCard Forum

MAC INSC — AOL Computing: Mac Internet Software Center

MAC LIBRARIES — AOL Computing: Download Software

MAC MSSC — AOL Computing: Mac Music and Sound

MAC MULTIMEDIA — AOL Computing: Mac Animation & Video

MAC MUSIC — AOL Computing: Mac Music and Sound

MAC NEWS — AOL News: Apple News & Corporate Releases

MAC NTSC — AOL Computing: Mac Networking and Telecom Software Center

MAC O/S — AOL Computing: MacOS Resource

MAC OFFICE — AOL Computing: Mac Applications

MAC OPERATING SYSTEMS — AOL Computing: MacOS Resource

MAC OS — AOL Computing: MacOS Resource

MAC OS 8 — Apple on AOL

MAC PRESCHOOL — AOL Computing: Preschool/Early Childhood SIG

MAC PRESS — AOL News: Apple News & Corporate Releases

MAC PROGRAMMING — AOL Computing: Mac Development

MAC SOFTWARE — AOL Computing: Download Software

MAC SOFTWARE CENTER — AOL Computing: Download Software

MAC SOUND — AOL Computing: Mac Music & Sound

MAC SOUND TOOL — AOL Computing: Sound & Midi Resource Center

MAC SOUND TOOLS — AOL Computing: Sound & Midi Resource Center

MAC SUPPORT — AOL Computing: Mac Help Desk

MAC TELECOM — AOL Computing: Mac Communications & Networking

MAC TELECOMM — AOL Computing: Mac Communications & Networking

MAC TIPS — AOL Computing: Tips

MAC TODAY — Mac Today Magazine

MAC UPDATE — AOL Computing: Update Your Mac Software

MAC UTILITIES — AOL Computing: Mac Utilities Forum

MAC UTSC — AOL Computing: Mac Utilities and Tools Software Center

MAC VID — AOL Computing: Mac Animation and Video

MAC VIDEO — AOL Computing: Mac Animation and Video
MAC VIRUS — AOL Computing: Mac Virus Information Center
MAC WORD PROCESSING — AOL Computing: Mac Word Processing
  Forum
MACEDONIA — AOL International: Macedonia
MACH IT — Global Gourmet: Match It Game
MACHESTER EOL — AOL UK: North West Events Online
MACHINE SHOP — AOL WorkPlace: Machine Shops Community
MACH-IT — Global Gourmet: Match It Game
MACINTAX — Parsons Technology
MACINTOSH — AOL Computing channel
MACINTOSH NEWS — AOL News: Apple News & Corporate Releases
MACKEREL — Mackerel Interactive Media
MACSCITECH — MacScitech Forum
MACWORLD — Macworld Magazine Online
MAD — AOL News: Mad, Mad World
MAD ABOUT — Mad About You Fan Forum
MAD ABOUT YOU — Mad About You Fan Forum
MAD MAGAZINE — Mad Magazine
MAD WORLD — AOL News: Mad, Mad World!
MADAGASCAR — AOL International: Madagascar
MADAME ADAMS — Cindy Adams: Queen of Gossip Gourmet
MAG OUTLET — AOL Magazine Outlet Store
MAGAZINE — AOL News: Newsstand
MAGAZINE OUTLET — AOL Magazine Outlet Store
MAGAZINE RACK — AOL Computing: Newsstand
MAGAZINES — AOL News: Newsstand
MAGE — Engage: Magestorm
MAGE STORM — Engage: Magestorm
MAGIC KINGDOM — Walt Disney World Resorts
MAGIC ONLINE — Digital City Denver: Magic Online
MAGIC TRICK — Digital City Denver: Magic Online
MAGICK — Religion & Beliefs: Pagan Religions & Occult Sciences
MAGICKAL — Religion & Beliefs: Pagan Religions & Occult Sciences
MAGID — The Larry Magid Show
MAGNETIC SOUTH — onQ: Sabrina Matthews
MAGS — AOL Magazine Outlet Store
MAGYARORSZAG — AOL International: Hungary
MAIL — AOL Mail Center
MAIL CENTER — AOL Mail Center
MAIL CONTROL — AOL Mail Center: Mail Controls
MAIL CONTROLS — AOL Mail Center: Mail Controls
MAIL EXTRA — AOL Mail Center: Mail Extras
MAIL EXTRAS — AOL Mail Center: Mail Extras
MAIL GATEWAY — AOL Mail Center

MAIL ORDER BUSINESS — AOL WorkPlace: Mail Order Business
   Community
MAIL SERVICE — AOL WorkPlace: Mail Services Community
<u>MAIL XTRA</u> — AOL Mail Center: Mail Extras
<u>MAIL XTRAS</u> — AOL Mail Center: Mail Extras
MAILING LIST — Internet Mailing List Directory
MAILING LIST HELP — AOL Member Services: Internet & World
   Wide Web
MAILING LISTS — Internet Mailing List Directory
MAJORDOMO — Internet Mailing List Directory
MAKE FRIENDS — AOL Member Services: Find Family and Friends
   Online
MALAWI — AOL International: Malawi
MALAYSIA — AOL International: Malaysia
MALDIVES — AOL International: Maldives
MALE ONQ — onQ: Men
MALI — AOL International: Mali
MALL — AOL Shopping channel
MALTA — AOL International: Malta
MAMA'S CUCINA — Food & Drink Network: Ragu
MAN OF THE WEEK — PlanetOut: FantasyMan Island
MANCHESTER — AOL UK: Local Life
MANGA — Wizard World -or- Japanimation Station
MANHATTAN USER'S GUIDE — Digital City New York: Manhattan
   User's Guide
MANHATTAN USERS GUIDE — Digital City New York: Manhattan User's
   Guide
MANIC — AOL Health: Bipolar Disorder/Manic Depression
MANIC DEPRESSION — AOL Health: Bipolar Disorder/Manic
   Depression
MAN'S HEALTH — AOL Health: Men's Health
MANS HEALTH — AOL Health: Men's Health
MANUFACTURE — AOL WorkPlace: Manufacturing Community
MANUFACTURING — AOL WorkPlace: Manufacturing Community
MAPLE — AOL Canada: Maple Square Internet Directory
MAPLE SQUARE — AOL Canada: Maple Square Internet Directory
MARCH MADNESS SHOPPING — AOL Shopping: March Madness
   [seasonal]
MARCH MADNESS STORE — AOL Shopping: March Madness [seasonal]
MARFA LIGHTS — Digital City Dallas-Fort Worth: The TEX Files
MARIANA — AOL International: North Mariana Islands
MARIANA ISLANDS — AOL International: North Mariana Islands
MARINE — Military City Online
MARINERS — Seattle Mariners
MARINES — Military City Online
MARITIME — AOL Canada: Virtual Atlantic Canada

MARITIMES — AOL Canada: Virtual Atlantic Canada
MARK SPORT — Fishing and Hunting Broadcast Networks
MARKET — AOL MarketDay
MARKET NEWS — AOL Personal Finance: Market News Center
MARKET NEWS CENTER — AOL Personal Finance: Market News Center
MARKET RESEARCH — AOL Rewards: Opinion Place
MARKET SCOPE — Business Week Online: S&P MarketScope
MARKETDAY — AOL MarketDay
MARKETING PREFERENCES — AOL Marketing Preferences
MARKETING PREFS — AOL Marketing Preferences
MARKETING YOUR BUSINESS — AOL WorkPlace: Sales & Marketing
MARKETPLACE — AOL Shopping channel
MARKETPLACE GOODS — AOL Shopping: The Weekly Goods Newsletter
MARKETPLACE SEARCH — AOL Shopping: Search
MARKETS — AOL Personal Finance: Market News Center
MARLINS — Florida Marlins
MARRIAGE PARTNERSHIP — Christianity Online: Marriage Partnership
MARS ATTACK — Mars Attacks
MARS ATTACKS — Mars Attacks
MARS EXPLORATION — Mars Pathfinder Information
MARS PATHFINDER — Mars Pathfinder Information
MARS TOKYO — Digital City San Francisco: Mars Tokyo Visual Diary
MARSHALL AUTO — Digital City Denver: Chesrown Autos
MARSHALL ISLANDS — AOL International: Marshall Islands
MARTAL ART — AOL Sports: Martial Arts
MARTAL ARTS — AOL Sports: Martial Arts
MARTELL GRAND NATIONAL — AOL UK: The Martell British Grand
    National
MARTIAL ART — AOL Sports: Martial Arts
MARTIAL ARTS — AOL Sports: Martial Arts
MARTIN — NetNoir: Martin Luther King, Jr.
MARTIN LUTHER — NetNoir: Martin Luther King, Jr.
MARTIN LUTHER KING — NetNoir: Martin Luther King, Jr.
MARTINI — Louis M Martini Winery Message Boards
MARTINIQUE — AOL International: Martinique
MARVEL — Marvel Comics
MARVEL STORE — Marvel Online Store
MARVEL ZONE — Marvel Comics
MARY PCB — AOL UK: Mary Branscombe
MASQUE POKER — Online Casino
MASSACHUSETTS — Massachusetts Forum
MASSACHUSETTS EMPLOYERS — Digital City Boston: Boston & New
    England Employers
MASSACHUSETTS EMPLOYMENT — Digital City Boston: Employment
    Classifieds

<u>MASSACHUSSETTS SPIRITS</u> — Digital City Boston: Spirits and Fancy Drinks

MASTERLIST — Hoover's Business Resources

MATCH — AOL Interest Profiles

MATCH IT — Global Gourmet: Match It Game

MATCH OF THE DAY — AOL UK: Match of the Day

MATCH-IT — Global Gourmet: Match It Game

MATCHMAKER — The Romance channel

MATE — AOL International: Australia and Oceania

MATERNITY — AOL Families: Babies

MATH — AOL Research & Learn: Math

MATH HELP — AOL Research & Learn: Math

MATH REFERENCE — AOL Research & Learn: Math

MATT — Athlete Direct: Matt Williams Corner

MATT WILLIAMS — Athlete Direct: Matt Williams Corner

MATTINGLY — Christianity Online: News Commentaries

MAURITANIA — AOL International: Mauritania

MAURITUS — AOL International: Mauritius

MAVEN — Business Week: Maven Computer Buying Guide [Web site]

MAVERICKS — Dallas Mavericks

MAVICA — Sony Digital Mavica

MAVS — Dallas Mavericks

MAWN CHAT — Martial Arts Worldwide Network: Chat Room

MAY — Mad About You Fan Forum

MB — Music Boulevard

MB CD — Music Boulevard

MB GIFT — Music Boulevard: Gifts [Web site]

MB STONES — Music Boulevard: Rolling Stones

MBA — AOL Research & Learn: Graduate & Professional Schools

MBANX — AOL Canada: Bank of Montreal

MBS — AOL Computing: Mac Applications

MC CHAT — AOL Computing: Chat!

MCAFEE — McAfee Associates

MCAT — KAPLAN Online -or- The Princeton Review

MCINTIRE — University of Virginia Alumni: McIntire School of Commerce

MCINTIRE ALUMNI — University of Virginia Alumni: McIntire School of Commerce

MCKINNEY — Digital City Dallas-Fort Worth: The McKinney Messenger

MCKINNEY MESSENGER — Digital City Dallas Fort Worth: The McKinney Messenger

MCM — AOL Computing: Mac Communications & Networking

MCO — Military City Online

MCO BASES — Military City Online: Bases

MCO CHAT — Military City Online: Live

MCO GATE — Military City Online

MCO HQ — Military City Online: Headquarters
MCO LIVE — Military City Online: Live
MCO MAIN — Military City Online: Headquarters
MCO MC — Military City Online: Message Center
MCO NEWS — Military City Online: Newsroom
MCO ONLINE — Military City Online
MCO PORT — Military City Online: Internet Port
MCO SHOP — Military City Online: Shop
MCO TOUR — Military City Online: Tour
MCVEIGH — Digital City Denver: McVeigh Trial
MCVEIGH TRIAL — Digital City Denver: McVeigh Trial
MD HOTEL — Digital City Washington: Destination Hotels
MD LOTTERY — Digital City Washington: Lottery Numbers
MDTP — AOL Computing: Mac Desktop & Web Publishing
MDV — AOL Computing: Mac Development
MEALS ONLINE — Meals.com [Web site]
MEALS.COM — Meals.com [Web site]
MEAT — AOL Shopping: Gourmet Gifts
MECCA — AOL International: Middle East
MED — AOL Computing: Education/Technology Forum
MEDALLION — Christianity Online: Gold Medallion Winners
MEDFORD — Digital City Philadelphia: South Jersey Interactive
MEDIA AND MONEY — AOL Influence: Media and Money
MEDIA CABLE — Digital City Philadelphia: Greater Media Cable
    Company
MEDIA CENTER — AOL Computing: Library Media Center SIG
MEDIA INFORMATION — Cowles Business Media [Web site]
MEDIA ONQ — onQ: Media
MEDIA SPACE WEB — AOL Mediaspace [Web site]
MEDIA WEB — AOL Mediaspace [Web site]
MEDICAL — AOL WorkPlace: Medical Services Community
MEDICAL BILLING — AOL WorkPlace: Medical Billing & Claims
    Processing
MEDICAL CLAIMS — AOL WorkPlace: Medical Billing & Claims
    Processing
MEDICAL DICTIONARY — Merriam-Webster Medical Dictionary
MEDICAL EXPERTS — AOL Health: Ask the Medical Experts
MEDICAL REFERENCE — AOL Health: Medical Reference
MEDICAL SCHOOL — KAPLAN Online -or- The Princeton Review
MEDICAL SERVICES — AOL WorkPlace: Medical Services Community
MEDICAL TRANSCRIPTION — AOL WorkPlace: Medical Transcription
    Forum
MEDICINE — AOL Health channel
MEDIZINE — Better Health & Medical: Pharmacists Network
MEDLINE — Better Health & Medical: Medline
MEEGO — WB Online: Meego

MEG — AOL Insider Tips
MEGA STORIES — AOL Canada: Out There News [Web site]
MEISSNER — Digital City Philadelphia: Meissner Chevrolet/Geo/Oldsmobile
MEL TOXIC — Digital City Philadelphia: Entertainment
MELROSE — Melrose Place Fan Forum
MELROSE MONDAY — Melrose Place Fan Forum
MELROSE MONDAYS — Melrose Place Fan Forum
MELTING POT — Tell Us Your Story: Immigration Stories
MEMBER BENEFITS — AOL Member Perks
MEMBER DIRECTORY — AOL Member Directory
MEMBER EXCLUSIVES — AOL Member Perks
MEMBER PERKS — AOL Member Perks
MEMBER POINT — AOL Rewards
MEMBER POINTS — AOL Rewards
MEMBER PROFILE — AOL Member Directory
MEMBER REWARDS — AOL Rewards
MEMBER SERVICES — AOL Member Services
MEMBER SUPPORT — AOL Member Services
MEMBERS — AOL Member Directory
MEMBER'S CHOICE — AOL Members' Choice
MEMBERS' CHOICE — AOL Members' Choice
MEMBERS CHOICE — AOL Members' Choice
MEMBERS HELPING MEMBERS — AOL Members Helping Members
MEMBERS' RIDES — Wheels Exchange
MEMBERS RIDES — Wheels Exchange
MEMPHIS — Digital City Memphis
MEMPHIS LOCAL NEWS — Digital City Memphis: Local News
MEMPHIS NEWS — Digital City Memphis: Local News
MEN ON VACATION — onQ: Travel
MEN ONQ — onQ: Men
MENOPAUSE — AOL Health: Menopause
MENOPAUSE@THRIVE — Thrive@Healthy Living: Menopause
MEN'S HEALTH — AOL Health: Men's Health
MENS HEALTH — AOL Health: Men's Health
MENSCH — Digital City New York: How to Meet a Mensch in New York
MENSCH FIND — Digital City New York: How to Meet a Mensch in New York
MENSCH FINDER — Digital City New York: How to Meet a Mensch in New York
MENSCH FINDERS — Digital City New York: How to Meet a Mensch in New York
MENTAL HEALTH — AOL Health: Mental Health
MENTAL HEALTH AWARENESS — AOL Health: Mental Health Awareness Month
MENTAL HEALTH WEB — AOL Health: Mental Health Internet Sites

MERCHANDISE — AOL Shopping channel
MERRIAM — Merriam-Webster
MERRIAM WEBSTER — Merriam-Webster
MERRIAM-WEBSTER — Merriam-Webster
MESQUITE — Digital City Dallas-Fort Worth: The Mesquite News
MESQUITE NEWS — Digital City Dallas-Fort Worth: The Mesquite News
MESQUITE TEXAS — Digital City Dallas-Fort Worth: The Mesquite News
MESSIAH COLLEGE — Christianity Online: Messiah College Online
MET HOME — Metropolitan Home
METRO AUTO — Digital City Philadelphia: Metro Dealerships
METRO BANDS — Digital City Dallas-Fort Worth: Metro Music
METRO CLUBS — Digital City Dallas-Fort Worth: Metro Music
METRO DEALERS — Digital City Philadelphia: Metro Dealerships
METRO GAY — Digital City Dallas-Fort Worth: Gay & Lesbian
METRO MUSIC — Digital City Dallas-Fort Worth: Music
METRO SPORTS — Digital City New York: Metro Sports
METRO TEENS — Digital City Dallas-Fort Worth: Teens
METRO TOURISTER — Digital City Twin Cities: Metro Tourist Insider
METRO UNDERGROUND — Digital City Dallas-Fort Worth: Teens
METROPLEX RELIGION — Digital City Dallas-Fort Worth: Religion
METROPOLITAN HOME — Metropolitan Home
METS — New York Mets
MEXICO — AOL International: Mexico
MF — Motley Fool
MF CANADA — AOL Canada: Mutual Fund Centre
MF CENTER — AOL Personal Finance: Mutual Fund Center
MF CENTRE — AOL Canada: Mutual Fund Centre
MFC — AOL Personal Finance: Mutual Fund Center
MFC LIVE — Mutual Fund Center: Live
MFC VAULT — Mutual Fund Center: Vault
MG MAP STORE — Magellan Geographix Maps
MG MAPS — AOL Games: Mac Games
MGM — Mac Games & Entertainment Forum
MGR — AOL Computing: Mac Graphics Arts
MHC — AOL Computing: Mac Hypercard Forum
MHM — AOL Members Helping Members
MHS — AOL Computing: Mac Hypercard Forum
MHW — AOL Computing: Mac Hardware
MIAMI BLACK VOICES — Black Voices: South Florida
MIAMI BUSINESS — Digital City South Florida: Business news from
    dbusiness.com
MIAMI HEAT — Miami Heat
MIAMI LOCAL NEWS — Digital City Miami: Local News
MIAMI NEWS — Digital City Miami: Local News
MIB — ParaScope: Men In Black
MICHIGAN J FROG — WB Online

MICRON — Micron Electronics [Web site]
MICRONESIA — AOL International: Micronesia
MICROSOFT — AOL Computing: PC Windows Forum
MICROSOFT ACCESS — AOL Computing: MS Access Resource Center
MICROWAREHOUSE — Microwarehouse Web Pointer
MIDDLE EAST — AOL International: Middle East
MIDI — AOL Computing: Music & Sound Forum
MIGHTY MITES — Mackerel Interactive Media
MIKE & DOG — Digital City New York: Mike & the Mad Dog
MIKE & MAD DOG — Digital City New York: Mike & the Mad Dog
MIKE AND THE MAD DOG — Digital City New York: Mike & the
    Mad Dog
MIKE FRANCESA — Digital City New York: Mike & the Mad Dog
MIKE KEEFE — InToon with the News
MIKE MISSANELLI — Digital City Philadelphia: Mike Missanelli
MIL 2000 — Millennium Countdown
MIL FAM — Military City Online: Family Center
MILESTONE — DC Comics
MILITARY — Military City Online
MILITARY BRATS — Military City Online: Locator
MILITARY CITY — Military City Online
MILITARY CITY ONLINE — Military City Online
MILITARY FAMILY — Military City Online: Family Center
MILITARY HISTORY — AOL Research & Learn: Military History Forum
MILITARY ONQ — onQ: Military
MILK CARTON — National Center for Missing & Exploited Children
MILLENIUM TICKER — Millennium Countdown
MILWAUKEE — Digital City Milwaukee
MILWAUKEE BREWERS — Milwaukee Brewers
MILWAUKEE LOCAL NEWS — Digital City Milwaukee: Local News
MILWAUKEE NEWS — Digital City Milwaukee: Local News
MIME — AOL Member Services: About MIME
MIND GAMES — Online Psych: Mind Games
MINN FUN — Digital City Twin Cities: Entertainment
MINN MARKET — Digital City Twin Cities: Marketplace
MINN PEOPLE — Digital City Twin Cities: People
MINN SPORTS — Digital City Twin Cities: Sports
MINN TWINS — Minnesota Twins
MINNEAPOLIS — Digital City Minneapolis
MINNEAPOLIS CHAT — Digital City Twin Cities: Chat Screen
MINNEAPOLIS FUN — Digital City Twin Cities: Entertainment
MINNEAPOLIS LOCAL NEWS — Digital City Twin Cities: Local News
MINNEAPOLIS MARKET — Digital City Twin Cities: Marketplace
MINNEAPOLIS PEOPLE — Digital City Twin Cities: People
MINNEAPOLIS SPORTS — Digital City Twin Cities: Sports
MINNEAPOLIS TOUR — Digital City Twin Cities: Minnesota Living

MINNESOTA BUSINESS — Digital City Twin Cities: Business
MINNESOTA EMPLOYMENT — Digital City Twin Cities: Employment Classifieds
MINNESOTA MONTHLY — Digital City Twin Cities: Minnesota Monthly
MINNESOTA TWINS — Minnesota Twins
MIRABELLA — Mirabella
MIRABELLA ONLINE — Mirabella
MISSANELLI — Digital City Philadelphia: Mike Missanelli
MISSING CHILDREN — National Center for Missing & Exploited Children
MISSING KIDS — National Center for Missing & Exploited Children
MITES — Mackerel Interactive Media
MIX CITICORP — MixStar Mortgage Information Exchange
MIX CMBA — MixStar Mortgage Information Exchange
MIX COMMENTARY — MixStar Market Commentary
MIX DATA TRACK — Data Track Systems, Inc.
MIX TRAINING — MixStar Mortgage Information Exchange
MLB — AOL Sports: Baseball
MLK — NetNoir: Martin Luther King, Jr.
MLS — AOL Real Estate Center
MLS LIVE — Major League Soccer Live
MM — AOL Computing: Animation & Video Forums
MM BROWSER 40 — Enhanced Web Browser 40 bit
MM SHOW — AOL Multimedia Showcase [Web site]
MM SHOWCASE — AOL Multimedia Showcase [Web site]
MM STORE — AOL Shopping: March Madness [seasonal]
MMA — Image Exchange: Metropolitan Museum of Art
MMC — Music Messaging Center
MMM — AOL Computing: Mac Animation & Video
MMS — AOL Computing: Mac Music & Sound
MMS TOOL — AOL Computing: Mac Sound Resource Center
MMS TOOLS — AOL Computing: Mac Sound Resource Center
MN — Digital City Twin Cities: Minnesota Online
MN BIZ — Digital City Twin Cities: Business
MN BUSINESS — Digital City Twin Cities: Business
MN CONNECTION — Digital City Twin Cities: Minnesota Online
MN EDGE — The Edge Online Newspaper
MN ENTERTAINMENT — Digital City Twin Cities: Entertainment
MN FILM BOARD — Digital City Twin Cities: Film Board
MN MONTHLY — Digital City Minneapolis: Minnesota Monthly
MN ONLINE — Digital City Twin Cities: Minnesota Online
MN PEOPLE — Digital City Twin Cities: People
MN SPORTS — Digital City Twin Cities: Sports
MNC — Market News Center
MNC BONDS — Market News Center: Bonds & Money
MNC CURRENCIES — Market News Center: Currencies

MNC ECONOMY — Market News Center: U.S. Economy
MNC FUTURES — Market News Center: Futures
MNC INTERNATIONAL — Market News Center: International
MNC STOCKS — Market News Center: Stocks & Mutuals
MNC-XRAY — MNC X-ray
MO — Moms Online
MODEL PLANE — AOL Interests: Scale Models
MODEL PLANES — AOL Interests: Scale Models
MODEL TRAIN — AOL Interests: Scale Models
MODEL TRAINS — AOL Interests: Scale Models
MODEM — High Speed Access
MODEM HELP — High Speed Access
MODEM SHOP — AOL Store: Modem Shop
MODIFY ADDRESS — Change Your Billing Information
MOGUL — AOL Influence: Media and Money
MOLDOVA — AOL International: Moldova
MOLSON — Molson's [Web site]
MOLSON'S — Molson's [Web site]
MOLSONS — Molson's [Web site]
MOM — AOL Families
MOM ONLINE — Moms Online
MOM TRAVEL — AOL Travel: Mother's Day Travel [seasonal]
MOMS — AOL Families
MOMS ONLINE — Moms Online
MONACO — AOL International: Monaco
MONDAY MELROSE — Melrose Place Fan Forum
MONEY — AOL Personal Finance channel
MONEY MATTERS — Digital City Washington: Money Matters
MONEYWHIZ — MoneyWhiz
MONEYWISE — AOL UK: Moneywise Magazine [Web site]
MONEYWIZ — MoneyWhiz
MONGOLIA — AOL International: Mongolia
MONSTER ISLAND — AOL Games: Adventures By Mail
MONTREAL EXPOS — Montreal Expos
MOORESTOWN — Digital City Philadelphia: South Jersey Interactive
MORE GAMES — AOL Games: More Games
MORE REFERENCES — AOL Research & Learn: More References
MORNINGSTAR — Morningstar Mutual Funds
MORNINGSTAR FUNDS — Morningstar Mutual Fund Area
MORNINGSTAR MF — Morningstar Mutual Fund Area
MOROCCO — AOL International: Morocco
MOS — AOL Computing: MacOS Resource
MOS UPDATE — AOL Computing: Update Your Mac Software
MOSLIM — AOL Lifestyles: Islam
MOTD — AOL UK: Match of the Day
MOTD LIVE — AOL UK: Match of the Day

MOTD LIVE EVENT — AOL UK: Match of the Day
MOTEL — AOL Travel: Hotel Center
MOTEL PRO — AOL WorkPlace: Hotels & Motels Professional Forum
MOTELS — AOL Travel: Hotel Center
MOTHER — AOL Families
MOTHERHOOD — Moms Online
MOTHERS — AOL Families
MOTHER'S DAY — Mother's Day @ AOL [seasonal]
MOTHERS DAY — Mother's Day @ AOL [seasonal]
MOTIVATIONAL — Image Exchange: Motivational Gallery
MOTLEY — Motley Fool
MOTLEY FOOL — Motley Fool
MOTLEY FOOL.COM — Motley Fool.com [Web site]
MOTORCYCLE — Wheels
MOTORCYCLES — Wheels
MOTORCYCLING — Wheels
MOTORSPORT — Motorsport '98 Online
MOTORSPORTS — Motorsport '98 Online
MOUNT PROSPECT — Digital City Chicago: Mount Prospect
MOUNT ST HELENS — Volcano Resources
MOUNTAIN BIKING — AOL Sports: Mountain Biking
MOVERS & SHAKERS — AOL Influence channel
MOVERS — AOL WorkPlace: Movers & Moving Services
MOVIE CRITIC — Hype! You be the Movie Critic
MOVIE DEN — Entertainment Asylum: Drama Den
MOVIE FORUM — AOL Entertainment: Movie Forums
MOVIE FORUMS — AOL Entertainment: Movie Forums
MOVIE GUY — Digital City Boston: Movie Guy
MOVIE MAVEN — Digital City San Francisco: Movie Reviews
MOVIE REVIEW DATABASE — EXTRA: Film Reviews
MOVIE SHOW TIMES — MovieLink [Web site]
MOVIE STAR — AOL Entertainment channel
MOVIE TIMES — MovieLink [Web site]
MOVIELINK — MovieLink [Web site]
MOVIES LA — Digital City Los Angeles: Movies
MOVIES SD — Digital City San Diego: MovieGuide
MOVING SERVICES — AOL WorkPlace: Movers & Moving Services
    Community
MOZAMBIQUE — AOL International: Mozambique
MP — Christianity Online: Marriage Partnership
MP DEAL — AOL Shopping: Real Deals Newsletter
MP DEALS — AOL Shopping: Real Deals Newsletter
MPM — Christianity Online: Marriage Partnership
MRC FAMILY — Novartis MRC Family Practice
MRC FAMILY PRACTICE — Novartis Medical Resource Center: Family
    Practice

MRC NEURO — Novartis Medical Resource Center: Neurology
MRC NEUROLOGY — Novartis Medical Resource Center: Neurology
MRC SALES — Novartis Medical Resource Center: Sales
MS — AOL Health: Multiple Sclerosis
M'S — Seattle Mariners
MS ACCESS — AOL Computing: MS Access Resource Center
MS DOS 6 — AOL Computing: MS-DOS 6.0 Resource Center
MS DOS 60 — AOL Computing: MS-DOS 6.0 Resource Center
MS EXCEL — AOL Computing: Spreadsheet Applications
MS KB — Microsoft Knowledge Base [Web site]
MS WINDOWS — AOL Computing: PC Windows Forum
MS WORD — AOL Computing: Word Processing Applications
MSCOPE — Business Week Online: S&P MarketScope
MSQUARE — AOL Canada: Maple Square Internet Directory
MSTAR — Morningstar Mutual Fund Area
MT PRODUCTIONS — Digital City San Francisco: Lesbian Bars [Web site]
MTC — AOL Computing: Mac Communications & Networking
MTN BIKE — AOL Sports: Mountain Biking
MTV — MTV Online
MTV ARENA — MTV Online
MTV HOUSE OF STYLE — MTV Online
MTV IDIOT SAVANTS — MTV Online
MTV LOVELINE — MTV Online
MTV MESSAGE BOARDS — MTV Online: Message Boards
MTV NEWS — MTV Online
MTV ONLINE — MTV Online
MTV TUBESCAN — MTV Online
MTV XCLUSIVE — MTV Xclusive
MTV.COM — MTV Online
MTVD — Digital City San Francisco: Mars Tokyo Visual Diary
MTVO — MTV Online
MU GUIDE — Digital City New York: Manhattan User's Guide
MUCH — MuchMusic
MUCHM — MuchMusic
MUCHMUSIC — MuchMusic
MUCHMUSIC ONLINE — MuchMusic
MUG — AOL Shopping: Gifts & Gadgets
MULTIMEDIA — AOL Computing: Animation & Video Forums
MULTIMEDIA FORUM — AOL Computing: Animation & Video Forums
MULTIMEDIA SHOW — AOL Multimedia Showcase [Web site]
MULTIMEDIA SHOWCASE — AOL Multimedia Showcase [Web site]
MULTIPLE SCLEROSIS — AOL Health: Multiple Sclerosis
MUM — Mother's Day @ AOL [seasonal]
MURPHY BROWN — Murphy Brown
MUSCLES — AOL Health: Bones, Joints & Muscles

MUSCULAR DYSTROPHY — AOL Health: Muscular Dystrophy
MUSEUM NY — Digital City New York: Museums
MUSEUMS NY — Digital City New York: Museums
MUSIC & SOUND — AOL Computing: Music & Sound Forum
MUSIC — AOL Entertainment: Music
MUSIC AND SOUND FORUM — AOL Computing: Music & Sound Forum
MUSIC AWARDS — SPIN Online: Online Music Awards
MUSIC AXIS — Entertainment Asylum: Music Axis
MUSIC BIZ — AOL WorkPlace: Musical Instrument Dealers' Community
MUSIC BLVD — Music Boulevard
MUSIC BOULEVARD — Music Boulevard
MUSIC BUSINESS — AOL WorkPlace: Musical Instrument Dealers'
    Community
MUSIC CITY — Digital City Nashville
MUSIC FORUM — AOL Computing: Music & Sound Forum
MUSIC MEDIA — AOL Entertainment: Music Media
MUSIC MESSAGE — AOL Entertainment: Music Community
MUSIC MESSAGE BOARDS — AOL Entertainment: Music Community
MUSIC MESSAGING — AOL Entertainment: Music Community
MUSIC STORE — AOL Shopping: Books & Music
MUSIC WEB — AOL Entertainment: Music Web Sites
MUSICSPACE — AOL Entertainment: Music
MUSICSPACE WEB — AOL Entertainment: Music Web Sites
MUSLIM — AOL Lifestyles: Islam
MUT — AOL Computing: Mac Utilities Forum
MUTUAL FUND — AOL Personal Finance: Mutual Fund Center
MUTUAL FUND CENTER — AOL Personal Finance: Mutual Fund Center
MUTUAL FUND CENTER VAULT — Mutual Fund Center: Vault
MUTUAL FUND LIVE — Mutual Fund Center: Live
MUTUAL FUND PORTFOLIO — Mutual Fund Center: Portfolio
MUTUAL FUND TAX GUIDE — Mutual Fund Center: Fund Investor's Tax
    Guide
MUTUAL FUNDS — AOL Personal Finance: Mutual Fund Center
MUTUAL FUNDS 202 — Mutual Funds 202
MUTUAL FUNDS LIVE — Mutual Fund Center: Live
<u>MUTUTAL FUNDS CENTER</u> — AOL Personal Finance: Mutual Fund
    Center
MVC — Military & Vets Club
MVD — AOL Computing: Mac Animation and Video
MW — Merriam-Webster
MW DICT — Merriam-Webster Collegiate Dictionary
M-W DICTIONARY — Merriam-Webster Collegiate Dictionary
MW DICTIONARY — Merriam-Webster Collegiate Dictionary
MW NEWS — Macworld Magazine Online: News
MW SOFTWARE — Macworld Magazine Online: Software
MW THESAURUS — Merriam-Webster Thesaurus

MWISE — AOL UK: Moneywise Magazine [Web site]
MWP — AOL Computing: Mac Desktop & Web Publishing
MY ACCOUNT — AOL Rewards
MY AOL — My AOL
MY BALANCE — AOL Rewards
MY BOARDS — Message Boards for Offline Reading
MY HOME PAGE — AOL Personal Publisher
MY PLACE — My Place (for FTP Space)
MY PLACE HELP — Web Publishing Help Central
MY PROFILE — AOL Member Directory
MY WEB PAGE — Personal Publisher 4.0
MYANMAR — AOL International: Myanmar
MYNDTALK — Online Psych: MyNDTALK
MYRTLE — Genealogy Forum: DearMYRTLE Daily Column
MYST — Myst Forum
MYST US — Myst Forum
MYSTERIOUS PLACES — Mystical Places of the World
MYSTERY LOVER GAME — Love@AOL: Mystery Lover Game
MYSTICAL PLACES — Mystical Places of the World
N 64 — Antagonist, Inc.
N AND B — Numerology & Beyond
N ENGLAND — AOL UK: Northern England
N IRELAND — AOL UK: Northern Ireland
N MARIANA ISLANDS — AOL International: Northern Mariana Islands
N&B — Numerology & Beyond
N&V — USA Weekend [Web pointer]
N@N — Nick at Nite
NAEA — NAEA Tax channel
NAEA TAX CHANNEL — NAEA Tax channel
NAGF — Non-Affiliated Gaming Forum
NAME — Create/Delete Screen Names
NAMES — Create/Delete Screen Names
NAMI — National Association of Mentally Ill
NAMIBIA — AOL International: Namibia
NAN — Nick at Nite
NANCY FRIDAY — Online Psych: Nancy Friday
NANDO — The Sports Server [Web site]
NANDO.NET — The Nando Times [Web site]
NAPC — National Association of Personnel Consultants
NAPERVILLE — Digital City Naperville [Web site]
NAREE — AOL Real Estate Desk
NASA — Space Exploration Online
NASA.GOV — NASA [Web site]
NASCAR — AOL Sports: Auto Racing
NASCAR CHAT — Athlete Direct: NASCAR Family Chat Room
NASH VEGAS — Digital City Nashville

NASHVILLE — Digital City Nashville
NASHVILLE LOCAL NEWS — Digital City Nashville: Local News
NASHVILLE NEWS — Digital City Nashville: Local News
NATIONAL ANTHEMS — AOL International: National Anthems of the World
NATIONAL GUARD — Military City Online
NATIONAL PARKS — AOL Grandstand: America's Parks Forum
NATIONAL URBAN LEAGU — National Urban League
NATIONWIDE — Nationwide Insurance
NATIONWIDE INSURANCE — Nationwide Insurance
NATIVE — AOL Interests: Ethnicity
NATL ARTHRITIS MONTH — AOL Health: National Arthritis Month
NATURE — AOL Research & Learn: Environment & Nature
NATUROPATHIC — AOL Health: Naturopathic Medicine
NAURU — AOL International: Nauru
NAVIGATE — Find Central
NAVIGATOR — Download Netscape Navigator for AOL
NAVIPRESS — AOL PrimeHost
NAVY — Military City Online
NBA — AOL Sports: Pro Basketball
NBA DRAFT — AOL Sports: NBA Draft Fan Central
NBA DRAFT FAN CENTRAL — AOL Sports: NBA Draft Fan Central
NBA SCOREBOARD — AOL Sports: NBA Scoreboard
NBA SCORES — AOL Sports: NBA Scoreboard
NBR — Nightly Business Report
NCAA BASKETBALL — AOL Sports: AOL College Basketball
NCAA BASKETBALL SCORES — AOL Sports: NCAA Basketball Scores
NCAA BB SCORES — AOL Sports: NCAA Basketball Scores
NCAA HOOPS — AOL Sports: AOL College Basketball
NCAA SCORES — AOL Sports: NCAA Basketball Scores
NCMEC — National Center for Missing and Exploited Children
NE EOL — AOL UK: North East Events Online
NEA PUBLIC — National Education Association
NEARSIGHTED — AOL Health: Nearsightedness
NEARSIGHTEDNESS — AOL Health: Nearsightedness
NEC — NEC Online
NEC TECH — NEC Online
NECN — New England Cable News
NEDERLANDS — AOL International: Netherlands
NEEDLECRAFT — AOL Interests: Sewing
NEEDLEPOINT — AOL Interests: Sewing
NEIGHBORHOOD GUY — Digital City Boston: Neighborhood Guy
NEIGHBORHOOD WATCH — AOL Neighborhood Watch
NEIGHBORS SD — Digital City San Diego: Community
NEMOURS — KidsHealth.Org
NEOW NEOW — Nikolai@AOL

NEOW-NEOW — Nikolai@AOL
NEPAL — AOL International: Nepal
NER EVOLUTION — New England Revolution Soccer
NERVOUS SYSTEM — AOL Health: Brain & Nervous System Disorders
NESN — NESN SportsCircuit
NESN BASEBALL — NESN: Baseball
NESN FOOTBALL — NESN: Football
NESN HOCKEY — NESN: Hockey
NESN OUTDOORS — NESN: Outdoors
NESN SPORTCIRCUIT — NESN SportsCircuit
NESN SPORTS — NESN SportsCircuit
NET — Internet Connection
NET EXCHANGE — Internet Connection: Exchange
NET HELP — AOL Member Services: Internet & World Wide Web
NET HIGHLIGHTS — Internet Connection
NET HLEP — AOL Member Services: Internet & World Wide Web
NET KNOW-HOW — NetGuide: Net Know-How
NET KNOWHOW — NetGuide: Net Know-How
NET MAGAZINE — AOL UK: Internet Magazine
NET NEWS — Internet Connection: News
NET ORGS — Internet Connection: Organizations
NET SURF — Youth Tech: Net Surf
NET TODAY — NetGuide: The Net Today
NET.HELP — AOL Member Services: Internet & World Wide Web
NET_NOIR — NetNoir
NET_NOIRE — NetNoir
NETCOACH — NetGuide: NetCoach
NETFIND — AOL NetFind [Web site]
NETFIND ADS — AOL NetFind: Advertising Link [Web site]
NETFIND ADVERTISE — AOL NetFind: Advertising Link [Web site]
NETFIND ADVERTISING — AOL NetFind: Advertising Link [Web site]
NETFIND FOR KIDS — AOL NetFind: Kids [Web site]
NETFIND KIDS — AOL NetFind: Kids [Web site]
NETFIND REVIEWS — AOL NetFind: Search Newsgroups [Web site]
NETFIND TIMESAVER — AOL Netfind [Web site]
NETFIND TIMESAVERS — AOL Netfind [Web site]
NETFIND TIPS — AOL Netfind: NetFind Tips [Web site]
NETFINDER — AOL NetFind [Web site]
NETGAME — AOL Grandstand: Tennis Forum
NETGIRL — Love@AOL: NetGirl
NETGUIDE — NetGuide [Web site]
NETGUIDE BTS — NetGuide: Behind the Scenes
NETGUIDE COACH — NetGuide: NetCoach
NETGUIDE ON AOL — NetGuide [Web site]
NETHERLANDS — AOL International: Netherlands
NETHERLANDS ANTILLES — AOL International: Netherlands Antilles

NETIQUETTE — Netiquette: Life in Cyberspace [Web site]
NETMAIL — AOL NetMail
NETMAIL INFO — AOL NetMail
NETNOIR — NetNoir
NETNOIRE — NetNoir
NETS — New Jersey Nets
NETSCAPE — Download Netscape Navigator for AOL
NETSCAPE COMMUNICATOR — Download Netscape Navigator for AOL
NETSCAPE NAVIGATOR — Download Netscape Navigator for AOL
NETWORKING — AOL Computing: Telecom & Networking Forums
NETWORKING FORUM — AOL Computing: Telecom & Networking
    Forums
NETYEILD — NetYield [Web site]
NETYIELD — NetYield [Web site]
NEUROLOGICAL — AOL Health: Brain & Nervous System Disorders
NEVERWINTER — AD&D Online: Neverwinter Nights
NEVIS — AOL International: St. Kitts and Nevis
NEW — What's New on AOL
NEW AGE — AOL Lifestyles: New Age
NEW AOL — Upgrade to Latest AOL Software Version
NEW AOL 3.0 — Upgrade to the Latest AOL Software Version
NEW AOL 30 — Upgrade to the Latest AOL Software Version
NEW AOL 95 — Upgrade to the Latest AOL Software Version
NEW AUTO — AOL Auto Center
NEW BREED — Digital City Twin Cities: Music Insider
NEW BROWSER — Microsoft Internet Explorer Browser
NEW CAR — AOL Auto Center
NEW CASTLE — AOL UK: Local Life
NEW CASTLE EOL — AOL UK: Far North Events Online
NEW CHANNEL LINE-UP — AOL Click and Go
NEW CHANNEL LINEUP — AOL Click and Go
NEW CHANNELS — AOL Click and Go New
NEW COMPUTER — AOL Computing: New Computer User's Guide
NEW ENGLAND BASEBALL — NESN: Baseball
NEW ENGLAND BOATING — Digital City Boston: Boating
NEW ENGLAND CABLE — Digital City Boston: New England Cable News
NEW ENGLAND CABLE NEWS — Digital City Boston: New England
    Cable News
NEW ENGLAND CLASSIFIEDS — Digital City Boston: Classifieds
NEW ENGLAND CRUISING — Digital City Boston: Sailing
NEW ENGLAND EMPLOYERS — Digital City Boston: Boston & New
    England Employers
NEW ENGLAND FISHING — Digital City Boston: Boating
NEW ENGLAND FOOTBALL — NESN: Football
NEW ENGLAND GOLF — Digital City Boston: Golf
NEW ENGLAND HOCKEY — NESN: Hockey

NEW ENGLAND NEWS — Digital City Boston: New England Cable News
NEW ENGLAND OUTDOORS — NESN: Outdoors
NEW ENGLAND REVOLUTION — New England Revolution Soccer
NEW ENGLAND SAILING — Digital City Boston: Sailing
NEW ENGLAND SKIING — Digital City Boston: Skiing
NEW ENGLAND SOCCER — New England Revolution Soccer
NEW ENGLAND SPORTS — NESN SportsCircuit
NEW FILES — AOL Computing: PC Weekly New Files
NEW GAMES — Antagonist, Inc.: The Daily Dose
NEW GUINEA — AOL International: Papua New Guinea
NEW HAMPSHIRE CHILD CARE — Digital City Boston: Family Info
    Source
NEW HAVEN — Digital City New Haven
NEW HAVEN NEWS — Digital City Hartford: Local News
NEW HOME NETWORK — New Home Network [Web site]
NEW INTERESTS — AOL Research & Learn: New Interests
NEW JERSEY CHAT — Digital City Philadelphia: South Jersey
    Interactive Chat
NEW JERSEY HOMES — Digital City Philadelphia: Real Estate
NEW JERSEY SHORE — Digital City Philadelphia: Down The Shore
NEW LIFE CLINIC — New Life Clinics
NEW LOVE AT AOL PERSONAL — Love@AOL: Update Your Personal
NEW LOVE AT AOL PERSONALS — Love@AOL: Update Your Personal
NEW LOVE@AOL PERSONAL — Love@AOL: Updated Your Personal
NEW LOVE@AOL PERSONALS — Love@AOL: Update Your Personal
NEW MAC — AOL Computing: Mac Help Desk
NEW MAIL — AOL Mail Center
NEW MEMBER — AOL Member Services: QuickStart
NEW MUSIC — AOL Entertainment: Music
NEW ONQ — onQ: New
NEW ORLEANS LOCAL NEWS — Digital City New Orleans: Local News
NEW ORLEANS NEWS — Digital City New Orleans: Local News
NEW PC — AOL Computing: PC Help Desk
NEW PRICE — AOL Member Services: Accounts & Billing
NEW PRICING — AOL Member Services: Accounts & Billing
NEW PRODUCT NEWS — AOL Computing: Buyer's Guide
NEW SOFTWARE — AOL Computing: New Releases
NEW TV — AOL Entertainment: Television
NEW USER — AOL Computing: New Computer User's Guide
NEW USER'S GUIDE — AOL Computing: New Computer User's Guide
NEW USERS GUIDE — AOL Computing: New Computer User's Guide
NEW YEAR — New Year's @ AOL [seasonal]
NEW YEAR ONQ — onQ: New Year [seasonal]
NEW YEARS @AOL — New Year's @ AOL [seasonal]
NEW YEARS — New Year's @ AOL [seasonal]
NEW YEARS DAY — New Year's @ AOL [seasonal]

NEW YORK — Digital City New York
NEW YORK 1 — Digital City New York: NY1 News
NEW YORK AROUND THE WORLD — Digital City New York: Around the World
NEW YORK AROUND WORLD — Digital City New York: Around the World
NEW YORK CITY — Digital City New York
NEW YORK CITY LOCAL NEWS — Digital City New York: Local News
NEW YORK CITY NEWS — Digital City New York: Local News
NEW YORK CITYGUIDE — Digital City New York: CityGuide
NEW YORK COMPLAINTS — Digital City New York: Complaints
NEW YORK DINING — Digital City New York: Dining
NEW YORK EAT — Digital City New York: Dining
NEW YORK EATS — Digital City New York: Dining
NEW YORK EMPLOYMENT — Digital City New York: Employment Classifieds
NEW YORK GIANTS — New York Giants: Pro Football
NEW YORK LINKS — Digital City New York: Links
NEW YORK LOCAL NEWS — Digital City New York: Local News
NEW YORK METS — New York Mets
NEW YORK MOVIES — Digital City New York: Movies
NEW YORK NEWS — Digital City New York: News
NEW YORK OBSERVER — New York Observer
NEW YORK ONE — Digital City New York: NY1 News
NEW YORK PERSONALS — Digital City New York: Personals
NEW YORK RANGERS — Digital City New York: Rangers
NEW YORK SEARCH — Digital City New York: Search
NEW YORK SPORTS — Digital City New York: News
NEW YORK SUBWAY — Digital City New York: Subway Maps
NEW YORK TIMES — New York Times Online
NEW YORK TIMES CHAT — New York Times: Live Events
NEW YORK WB11 — Digital City New York: WB11
NEW YORK WEBGUIDE — Digital City New York: WebGuide
NEW YORK WHITE PAGES — Digital City New York: White Pages
NEW YORK YANKEES — New York Yankees
NEW YORK YELLOW PAGES — Digital City New York: Yellow Pages
NEW ZEALAND — AOL International: New Zealand
NEWBIE — AOL Member Services: QuickStart
<u>NEWGROUP FINDER</u> — AOL NetFind: Search Newsgroups [Web site]
NEWS & VIEWS — USA Weekend [Web pointer]
NEWS — AOL News channel
NEWS BEST — AOL News: What's Hot in News
NEWS BOARD — AOL News: NewsTalk Live
NEWS BOARDS — AOL News: NewsTalk Live
NEWS GOSSIP — AOL News: The Back Page

NEWS IN YOUR BOX — AOL Member Services: Get Only the News You Want

NEWS INTL — AOL International: News

NEWS MESSAGE BOARD — AOL News: NewsTalk Live

NEWS MESSAGE BOARDS — AOL News: NewsTalk Live

NEWS ONQ — onQ: News

NEWS QUIZ — Tribune News Quiz

NEWS RADIO WGST — Digital City Atlanta: News & Weather

NEWS SAN DIEGO — Digital City San Diego: News

NEWS SEARCH — AOL News: Search

NEWS TEXT — AOL News channel

NEWS TICKER — AOL News channel

NEWS YOU WANT — AOL Member Services: Get Only the News You Want

NEWS.COM — ABC NEWS.com [Web site]

NEWSGROUP — Internet USENET Newsgroups

NEWSGROUP FINDER — AOL NetFind: Newsgroup Finder

NEWSGROUP HELP — AOL Member Services: Internet & World Wide Web

NEWSGROUP REVIEWS — AOL NetFind: Search Newsgroups [Web site]

NEWSGROUP SCOOP — AOL NetFind: Search Newsgroups [Web site]

NEWSGROUP SEARCH — AOL NetFind [Web site]

NEWSGROUPS — Internet USENET Newsgroups

NEWSLETTER — Online Newsletters

NEWSLETTERS — Online Newsletters

NEWSMAKERS — AOL News: The Back Page Newsmakers

NEWSPAPER — AOL News: Newsstand

NEWSPAPERS — AOL News: Newsstand

NEWSROOM — AOL News channel

NEWSSTAND — AOL News: Newsstand

NEWSSTAND SEARCH — AOL News: Newsstand Search

NEWSTALK — AOL News: NewsTalk Live

NEWSTAND — AOL News: Newsstand

NEWSTAND SEARCH — AOL News: Newsstand Search [Web site]

NEWSWEEK — Newsweek Interactive

NEWT — AOL News: Eye on Newt

NEWT GINGRICH — AOL News: Eye on Newt

NEWTER — AOL News: Eye on Newt

NEWTON — AOL Computing: Newton Resource Center

NEWTON BOOK — AOL Computing: PDA & Palmtop Forum

NF APT — AOL NetFind: Find an Apartment or Home [Web site]

NF CAR — AOL NetFind: Car Corner [Web site]

NF COMPUTER — AOL NetFind: Buy a Computer [Web site]

NF FAMILY — AOL NetFind: Home & Family [Web site]

NF GOVT — AOL NetFind: Your Government [Web site]

NF HEALTH — AOL NetFind: Your Health [Web site]

NF JOB — AOL NetFind: Find a Job [Web site]
NF MONEY — AOL NetFind: Find an Apartment or Home [Web site]
NF NIGHT IN — AOL NetFind: Plan a Night In [Web site]
NF NIGHT OUT — AOL NetFind: Plan a Night Out [Web site]
NF REFERENCE — AOL NetFind: Reference Source [Web site]
NF TRAVEL — AOL NetFind: Find an Airline/Hotel [Web site]
NFL CATALOG — AOL Sports: Official NFL Catalog
NFL DRAFT 97 — AOL Sports: NFL Draft
NFL FOOTBALL — AOL Sports: Pro Football
NFL NEWS — AOL Sports: TeamNFL Newsletter
NFL NEWSLETTER — AOL Sports: TeamNFL Newsletter
NFL PHOTO — AOL Sports: NFL Photo
NFL PHOTOS — NFL Photo
NFL SCORES — AOL Sports: NFL Scores
NFL SIGN UP — AOL Sports: TeamNFL Newsletter
NG BTS — NetGuide: Behind the Scenes
NG COACH — NetGuide: NetCoach
NG LBA — onQ: Business Center
NG LIST GUY — NetGuide: Listguy
NG SPOTLIGHT — NetGuide: Product Spotlight
NGLTF — National Gay and Lesbian Task Force
NHL ALL STAR — AOL Sports: 1998 NHL All Star Area
NHL ALL STAR GAME — AOL Sports: 1998 NHL All Star Area
NHL ALL STARS — AOL Sports: 1998 NHL All Star Area
NHL SCOREBOARD — AOL Sports: NHL Scores
NHL SCORES — AOL Sports: NHL Scores
NICARAGUA — AOL International: Nicaragua
NICHES — AOL WorkPlace: Professional Forums
NICK — Nickelodeon
NICK AT NITE — Nick at Nite
NICK HALLOWEEN — Nickelodeon: Halloween [seasonal]
NICK PROFILES — Nickelodeon: All About the Ops!
NICK@NITE — Nick at Nite
NICKELODEON — Nickelodeon
NICOTINE — AOL Health: Nicotine/Tobacco Addiction
NIGER — AOL International: Niger
NIGERIA — AOL International: Nigeria
NIGHTLINE — ABC News.com [Web site]
NIKITA — La Femme Nikita
NIKOLAI — Nikolai@AOL
NINE PATCH — Quilting Forum: Nine Patch Newsletter
NINE PATCH NEWS — Quilting Forum: Nine Patch Newsletter
NINETY ONE X — Digital City San Diego: 91x
NINTENDO — AOL Games: Video Games Forum
NISSAN — Nissan Online [Web site]

NISSAN PAVILION — Digital City Washington: Cellar Door Entertainment

NJ CHAT — Digital City Philadelphia: South Jersey Interactive Chat

NJ FIGHTING — Digital City Philadelphia: Boxing

NJ HOMES — Digital City Philadelphia: Real Estate

NJ REAL ESTATE — Digital City Philadelphia: Real Estate

NJ SHORE — Digital City Philadelphia: Down The Shore

NL — AOL Sports: Baseball

NMSS — National Multiple Sclerosis Society [Web pointer]

NN BLACK BOOKS — NetNoir: Books

NN BLACK BUSINESS — NetNoir: Black Business

NN BLACK LITERATURE — NetNoir: Literature

NN BLACK MUSIC — NetNoir: Music

NN BLACK PRODUCTS — NetNoir: Products

NN BLACK TEENS — NetNoir: Teens

NN BOOKS — NetNoir: Books

NN EBONY — NetNoir: Ebony

NN LITERATURE — NetNoir: Literature

NN MLK — NetNoir: Martin Luther King, Jr.

NN MUSIC — NetNoir: Music

NN SHOP — NetNoir: Products

NN SHOPPING — NetNoir: Products

NN TEENS — NetNoir: Teens

NO CHASER — Digital City Denver: Music Scene

NO CHASER — Digital City Denver: Straight No Chaser

NOCKERS — AOL Australia: Knockers Online

NOIRNET — NetNoir

NOLO — Nolo Press Self-Help Law Center

NOLOPRESS — Nolo Press Self-Help Law Center

NOMADIC — Nomadic Computing

NOR AMERICA — AOL International: North America

NORFOLK LOCAL NEWS — Digital City Hampton Roads: Local News

NORGE — AOL International: Norway

NORTH AFRICA — AOL International: Middle East

NORTH AMERICA — AOL International: North America

NORTH COUNTY HOMES — Digital City San Diego: Real Estate

NORTH EAST SKIING — Digital City Boston: Skiing

NORTH KOREA — AOL International: North Korea

NORTH MARIANA — AOL International: North Mariana Islands

NORTH MARIANA ISLE — AOL International: North Mariana Islands

NORTH TEXAS AUTOGUIDE — Digital City Dallas-Fort Worth: AutoGuide

NORTHERN IRELAND — AOL UK: Northern Ireland

NORTON — Symantec Corporation

NORWAY — AOL International: Norway

NORWICH — AOL UK: Local Life

NOSE — AOL Health: Ear, Nose & Throat
NOT POLITICS AS USUAL — George Magazine
NOTEBOOK — AOL Computing: Superstore
NOTIFY AOL — Notify AOL
NOTTINGHAM — AOL UK: Local Life
NOTTINGHAM EOL — AOL UK: Midlands Events Online
NOVA HEALTH — Digital City Washington: Inova Health System
NOVEL — Amazing Instant Novelist
NOVELL — Novell World Wide [Web site]
NOVICE — AOL Member Services: QuickStart
NOW PLAYING — Entertainment Asylum: Now Playing [Web site]
NPR — National Public Radio Outreach
NS HOT — AOL News: Newsstand What's Hot
NS HOT — Newsstand: What's Hot on the Web
NSBA — AOL Grandstand: Simulation Basketball
NSS — Space Exploration Online
NTN — NTN Trivia
NTN BASEBALL — NTN Trivia: Online Drive
NTN BASKETBALL TRIVIA — NTN Trivia: Basketball Trivia
NTN CANADA — AOL Canada: NTN Trivia
NTN DIAMONDBALL — NTN Trivia: Sports
NTN FOOTBALL — NTN Trivia: Playbook
NTN HOCKEY — NTN Trivia: Hockey Trivia
NTN HOCKEY TRIVIA — NTN Trivia: Hockey Trivia
NTN HOOP TRIVIA — NTN Trivia: Basketball Trivia
NTN HOOPS TRIVIA — NTN Trivia: Pro Basketball Trivia
NTN PLAYBOOK — NTN Trivia: Playbook
NTN QB1 — NTN Trivia: QB1
NTN TRIVIA — NTN Trivia
NUG — AOL Computing: New Computer User's Guide
NUGGETS — Denver Nuggets
NUL — National Urban League
NUMBERS — Accessing America Online
NUMEROLOGY — Numerology & Beyond
NURSERIES — AOL WorkPlace: Landscaping & Gardening Community
NUTRITION — AOL Health: Eating Well
NUTRITION PHYSICIAN — iVillage: Nutrition Physician
NUTRITION PROS — AOL WorkPlace: Health & Nutrition Professional
    Forum
NUTRITIONIST — AOL WorkPlace: Health & Nutrition Professional
    Forum
NUTRITIONISTS — AOL WorkPlace: Health & Nutrition Professional
    Forum
NUTS MAG — AOL Canada: Nuts Magazine
NUTS MAGAZINE — AOL Canada: Nuts Magazine
NW — Newsweek Interactive

NW EOL — AOL UK: North West Events Online
NWFL — AOL Grandstand: Simulation Football
NWN — AD&D Online: Neverwinter Nights
NY — Digital City New York
NY ADVICE — Digital City New York: Love Advisors
NY AROUND THE WORLD — Digital City New York: Around the World
NY AUTO — Digital City New York: AutoGuide
NY CAREERS — Digital City New York: Employment Classifieds
NY CARS — Digital City New York: AutoGuide
NY CHAT — Digital City New York: Chat
NY CHATS — Digital City New York: Chat
NY CITY — Digital City New York: Citywise
NY CITYGUIDE — Digital City New York: CityGuide
NY CITYGUIDES — Digital City New York: CityGuide
NY CITYWISE — Digital City New York: Citywise
NY CLASSIFIEDS — Digital City New York: Employment Classifieds
NY CLUB — Digital City New York: Dining
NY CLUB LEADERS — Digital City New York: Club Leaders [Web site]
NY COMPLAINTS — Digital City New York: Complaints
NY CONSUMER — Digital City New York: Complaints
NY CONSUMER COMPLAINTS — Digital City New York: Complaints
NY CULTURE — Digital City New York: CultureFinder
NY CULTUREFINDER — Digital City New York: CultureFinder
NY DINING — Digital City New York: Dining
NY DININGS — Digital City New York: Dining
NY EAT — Digital City New York: Dining
NY EATS — Digital City New York: Dining
NY EMPLOYMENT — Digital City New York: Employment Classifieds
NY ENTERTAINMENT — Digital City New York: Entertainment
NY EVENT GUIDE — Digital City New York: Event Guide
NY EVENT GUIDES — Digital City New York: Event Guide
NY EVENTS — Digital City New York: Event Guide
NY FIND — Digital City New York: CultureFinder
NY FINDER — Digital City New York: CultureFinder
NY GALLERIES — Digital City New York: Museums
NY GALLERY — Digital City New York: Museums
NY GIANTS — New York Giants: Pro Football
NY HOROSCOPE — Digital City New York: Horoscopes
NY HOROSCOPES — Digital City New York: Horoscopes
NY HOST — Digital City New York: Meet Your Hosts
NY HOSTS — Digital City New York: Meet Your Hosts
NY INVEST — Digital City New York: Investing
NY INVESTING — Digital City New York: Investing
NY JOBS — Digital City New York: Employment Classifieds
NY JOIN — Digital City New York: Join the Virtual Neighborhood
    [Web site]

NY JOIN A CLUB — Digital City New York: Dining
NY LINK — Digital City New York: Links
NY LINKS — Digital City New York: Links
NY LOCAL NEWS — Digital City New York: Local News
NY LOVE — Digital City New York: Love Advisors
NY LOVE ADVICE — Digital City New York: Love Advisors
NY LOVE ADVISORS — Digital City New York: Love Advisors
NY MAP — Digital City New York: Subway Maps
NY MAPS — Digital City New York: Subway Maps
NY MENSCH — Digital City New York: How to Meet a Mensch in
     New York
NY MOVIE — Digital City New York: Movies
NY MOVIE GUIDE — Digital City New York: Movies
NY MOVIE GUIDES — Digital City New York: Movies
NY MOVIES — Digital City New York: Movies
NY MUSEUM — Digital City New York: Museums
NY MUSEUMS — Digital City New York: Museums
NY MUSIC — Digital City New York: Music
NY NEIGHBORHOOD EAT — Digital City New York: Dining
NY NEIGHBORHOOD EATS — Digital City New York: Dining
NY NEW — Digital City New York: News
NY NEWS — Digital City New York: News
NY NIGHT — Digital City New York: Nightlife
NY NIGHTLIFE — Digital City New York: Nightlife
NY NIGHTS — Digital City New York: Nightlife
NY OBSERVER — New York Observer
NY ONE — Digital City New York: NY1 News
NY PASSPORT — Digital City New York: Dining
NY PEOPLE — Digital City New York: Investing
NY PERSONAL — Digital City New York: Personals
NY PERSONALS — Digital City New York: Personals
NY PUBLISHER — Digital City New York: Virtual Neighborhood
     Publisher Page [Web site]
NY RANGERS — New York Rangers
NY REAL FAN — Digital City New York: Real Fans
NY REAL FANS — Digital City New York: Real Fans
NY REGISTER — Digital City New York: Join the Virtual Neighborhood
     [Web site]
NY SALE — Digital City New York: Sales and Bargains
NY SALES & BARGAINS — Digital City New York: Sales and Bargains
NY SALES — Digital City New York: Sales and Bargains
NY SALES AND BARGAINS — Digital City New York: Sales and Bargains
NY SB — Digital City New York: New York School Board
NY SCHOOL BD — Digital City New York: New York School Board
NY SEARCH — Digital City New York: Search
NY SITE HOSTS — Digital City New York: Meet Your Hosts

NY SPORT — Digital City New York: News
NY SPORTS — Digital City New York: News
NY SSBA — Digital City New York: New York School Board
NY SUBWAY — Digital City New York: Subway Maps
NY SUBWAY MAPS — Digital City New York: Subway Maps
NY SUBWAYS — Digital City New York: Subway Maps
NY THEATER — Digital City New York: Theater Page
NY THEATRE — Digital City New York: Theater Page
NY TIMES — New York Times Online
NY TOOLBOX — Digital City New York: VN Toolbox
NY WABC — Digital City New York: WABC-TV 7 News
NY WABC TV — Digital City New York: WABC-TV 7 News
NY WEBGUIDE — Digital City New York: WebGuide
NY WHITE PAGES — Digital City New York: White Pages
NY YELLOW PAGES — Digital City New York: Yellow Pages
NY1 — Digital City New York: NY1 News
NY1 NEWS — Digital City New York: NY1 News
NYC — Digital City New York
NYC CARS — Digital City New York: Auto
NYC LOCAL NEWS — Digital City New York: Local News
NYC M4M — PlanetOut: FantasyMan Island for New York
NYC NEWS — Digital City New York: Local News
NYC PICKS — Digital City New York: Events Picks
NYG — New York Giants: Pro Football
NYT — New York Times Online
NYT ARCHIVE — New York Times: Archives
NYT ARTS — New York Times: Arts News
NYT ARTS GUIDE — New York Times: Arts Guide
NYT AUTOS — New York Times: Autos
NYT BESTSELLERS — New York Times: Books
NYT BIZ — New York Times: Business News
NYT BOARDS — New York Times: Message Boards
NYT BOOK REVIEW — New York Times: Books
NYT BOOKS — New York Times: Books
NYT BR — New York Times: Books
NYT BRIDGE — New York Times: Bridge
NYT BULLETIN — New York Times: Subscription
NYT BUSINESS — New York Times: Business News
NYT BUSINESS DAY — New York Times: Business News
NYT C&T — New York Times: Computers & Technology
NYT CD — New York Times: CDs
NYT CD REVIEWS — New York Times: CDs
NYT CDS — New York Times: CDs
NYT CHAT — New York Times: Live Events
NYT CHESS — New York Times: Chess
NYT COMPUTERS — New York Times: Computers & Technology

NYT CONTENTS — New York Times: Contents
NYT CROSSWORD — New York Times: Crossword Puzzles
NYT CROSSWORDS — New York Times: Crossword Puzzles
NYT DANCE — New York Times: Music & Dance
NYT DINING — New York Times: Dining
NYT DINING GUIDE — New York Times: Dining
NYT DIVERSIONS — New York Times: Diversions
NYT EDITORIAL — New York Times: Op-Ed & Editorials
NYT EDUCATION — New York Times: Education
NYT FASHION — New York Times: Fashion
NYT FEEDBACK — New York Times: Feedback
NYT FILM — New York Times: Film
NYT FILM REVIEWS — New York Times: Film
NYT FINANCE — New York Times: Personal Finance
NYT FIND — New York Times: Search
NYT FITNESS — New York Times: Health & Fitness
NYT FOOD — New York Times: Food
NYT FRONT PAGE — New York Times: Page One
NYT GALLERIES — New York Times: Museums & Galleries
NYT GAMES — New York Times: Diversions
NYT GARDEN — New York Times: Gardening
NYT GARDENING — New York Times: Gardening
NYT H&F — New York Times: Health & Fitness
NYT H&L — New York Times: Home & Living
NYT H&L GUIDE — New York Times: Home & Living Guide
NYT HEADLINES — New York Times: News Preview
NYT HEALTH & FITNESS — New York Times: Health & Fitness
NYT HEALTH — New York Times: Health & Fitness
NYT HEALTH AND FITNESS — New York Times: Health & Fitness
NYT HELP — New York Times: Help
NYT HOME & LIVING — New York Times: Home & Living
NYT HOME & LIVING GUIDE — New York Times: Home & Living Guide
NYT HOME — New York Times: Home
NYT HOME AND LIVING — New York Times: Home & Living
NYT HOME AND LIVING GUIDE — New York Times: Home & Living
    Guide
NYT HOME GUIDE — New York Times: Home & Living Guide
NYT INDEX — New York Times: Contents
NYT INT — New York Times: International News
NYT INTERNATIONAL — New York Times: International News
NYT LETTERS — New York Times: Feedback
NYT LIVE — New York Times: Live Events
NYT LIVING — New York Times: Home & Living
NYT LIVING GUIDE — New York Times: Home & Living Guide
NYT M&G — New York Times: Museums & Galleries
NYT MAG — New York Times: Magazine

NYT MAGAZINE — New York Times: Magazine
NYT MESSAGE BOARDS — New York Times: Message Boards
NYT METRO — New York Times: National/Metro News
NYT MOVIES — New York Times: Film
NYT MUSEUMS & GALLERIES — New York Times: Museums & Galleries
NYT MUSEUMS — New York Times: Museums & Galleries
NYT MUSIC — New York Times: CDs
NYT NATIONAL — New York Times: National/Metro News
NYT NATIONAL/METRO — New York Times: National/Metro News
NYT NEWS CHAT — New York Times: News Chat
NYT NEWS UPDATE — New York Times: News Update
NYT NWR — New York Times: Week in Review
NYT OBIT — New York Times: Obituaries
NYT OBITUARIES — New York Times: Obituaries
NYT OP ED — New York Times: Op-Ed & Editorials
NYT OP ED/EDITORIAL — New York Times: Op-Ed & Editorials
NYT PAGE ONE — New York Times: Page One
NYT PEOPLE — New York Times: People
NYT PEOPLE IN THE NEWS — New York Times: People
NYT PERSONAL FINANCE — New York Times: Personal Finance
NYT PF — New York Times: Personal Finance
NYT PREVIEW — New York Times: News Preview
NYT PUZZLES & GAMES — New York Times: Diversions
NYT QUIZ — New York Times: Weekly News Quiz
NYT RELIGION — New York Times: Religion
NYT SCI — New York Times: Science News
NYT SCIENCE — New York Times: Science News
NYT SCIENCE Q&A — New York Times: Science Q & A
NYT SEARCH — New York Times: Search
NYT SPORTS — New York Times: Sports News
NYT STYLE — New York Times: Fashion
NYT TALK — New York Times: Live Events
NYT TECH — New York Times: Computers & Technology
NYT TECHNOLOGY — New York Times: Computers & Technology
NYT THEATER — New York Times: Theater
NYT TRAVEL — New York Times: Travel
NYT UPDATE — New York Times: News Update
NYT VIDEO — New York Times: Film
NYT WEEK — New York Times: Week in Review
NYT WEEK IN REVIEW — New York Times: Week in Review
NYT WINE — New York Times: Wine
NYT WORLD — New York Times: International News
OAKLAND A'S — Oakland Athletics
OAKLAND ATHLETICS — Oakland Athletics
OAO — Outdoor Adventure Online
OASIS WINE — Food & Drink Network: Oasis Wine

OBJECTS DESIRE — Objects of Desire
OBJECTS OF DESIRE — Objects of Desire
OC — Digital City Orange County
OC CARS — Digital City Orange County: New and Used Auto Source
OC COMMUNITY — Digital City Orange County: Community!
OC ENTERTAINMENT — Digital City Orange County: Entertainment!
OC NEWS — Digital City Orange County: News, Weather & Traffic!
OC PEOPLE — Digital City Orange County: People!
OC RECREATION — Digital City Orange County: Interactive Sports
    Central!
OC SPORTS — Digital City Orange County: Interactive Sports Central!
OC TRAFFIC — Digital City Orange County: News, Weather & Traffic!
OC WEATHER — Digital City Orange County: News, Weather & Traffic!
OCCULT — Religion & Beliefs: Pagan Religions & Occult Sciences
OCEANIA — AOL International: Australia and Oceania
OCI COMMUNITY — Digital City Orange County: Community!
OCI ENTERTAINMENT — Digital City Orange County: Entertainment!
OCI NEWS — Digital City Orange County: News, Weather & Traffic!
OCI PEOPLE — Digital City Orange County: People!
OCI SPORTS — Digital City Orange County: Interactive Sports Central!
ODEON — AOL Live
O'DONNELL — Rosie O'Donnell Online
ODONNELL — Rosie O'Donnell Online
OESTERREICH — AOL International: Austria
OFFBEAT BOSTON — Digital City Boston: Offbeat Boston
OFFICE RELATIONSHIPS — AOL WorkPlace: Office Romance
OFFICE ROMANCE — AOL WorkPlace: Office Romance
OFFICE SERVICES — AOL WorkPlace: Office Services
OFFICE SHOP — AOL Shopping: Home Office
OFFICE SUPERSTORE — AOL Shoppers Advantage: Office Store
OFFICE SUPPLIER — AOL WorkPlace: Office Supply Store Community
OFFICE SUPPLIERS — AOL WorkPlace: Office Supply Store Community
OFFICE SUPPLIES — OfficeMax
OFFICE SUPPLY — OfficeMax
OFFICE SUPPLY STORE — AOL WorkPlace: Office Supply Store
    Community
OFFICE SUPPLY STORES — AOL WorkPlace: Office Supply Store
    Community
OFFICEMAX — OfficeMax
OFFICIAL HOME PAGES — AOL Games: Official Games Sites [Web site]
OFS — AOL Personal Finance: Banking Center
OGF — AOL Games: Online Gaming Forums
OGTS — AOL Games: Online Games Technical Support
OI — The Online Investor
OKC BOMB — Digital City Denver: McVeigh Trial
OKC BOMB TRIAL — Digital City Denver: McVeigh Trial

OKLAHOMA CITY — Digital City Oklahoma City: Local News
OKLAHOMA CITY BOMBING — Digital City Denver: McVeigh Trial
OKLAHOMA CITY LOCAL NEWS — Digital City Oklahoma City: Local News
OKLAHOMA CITY NEWS — Digital City Oklahoma City: Local News
OL' BLUE EYES — Entertainment Asylum: Club Sinatra
OLD WEST — Digital City Denver: OutWest Online
OLI — The Online Investor
OLP — Online Psych
OLP ASK AREA — Online Psych: Experts
OLP ASK EXPERTS — Online Psych: Experts
OLP ASK GAYE — Online Psych: Ask Gaye
OLP ASK MICHELE — Online Psych: Ask Michele
OLP ASK PEGGY — Online Psych: Ask Peggy
OLP CHAT — Online Psych: Chat
OLP COVER STORY — Online Psych: Cover Story
OLP CS — Online Psych: Cover Story
OLP DOCS — Online Psych: Ask the Psychiatrists
OLP DR. ADD — Online Psych: Ask Dr. ADD
OLP EXPERTS — Online Psych: Experts
OLP FAQ FILES — Online Psych: FAQ Files
OLP FRIDAY — Online Psych: Nancy Friday
OLP GAMES — Online Psych: Mind Games
OLP LIVE — Online Psych: Chat
OLP LIVE SEMINAR — Online Psych: Seminar
OLP LOCATOR — Online Psych: Locator
OLP MB — Online Psych: Message Boards
OLP MESSAGE BOARD — Online Psych: Message Boards
OLP MIND GAMES — Online Psych: Mind Games
OLP MPD — Online Psych: Ask MPD
OLP MYND — Online Psych: MyNDTALK
OLP SEM — Online Psych: Seminar
OLP SEMINAR — Online Psych: Seminar
OLP STORIES — Online Psych: Cover Story
OLP STRESS DOC — Online Psych: Stress Doc
OLP TALK — Online Psych: Chat
OLP TEEN — Online Psych Teens
OLP TESTS — Online Psych: Mind Games
OLP THE DOCS — Online Psych: Ask the Psychiatrists
OLSON — Digital City Los Angeles: The Olson Company
OLSON CO — Digital City Los Angeles: The Olson Company
OLSON COMPANY — Digital City Los Angeles: The Olson Company
OMA — SPIN Online: Online Music Awards
OMAHA — Omaha Steaks International
OMAHA STEAKS — Omaha Steaks International
OMAHA WEB — Omaha Steaks: Special Offer [Web site]

OMAN — AOL International: Oman

OMAS — SPIN Online: Online Music Awards

O'MEARA — Digital City Denver: O'Meara Ford Center

OMEARA — Digital City Denver: O'Meara Ford Center

OMNI — OMNI Magazine Online [Web site]

OMNI MAGAZINE — OMNI Magazine Online [Web site]

OMNI ONLINE — OMNI Magazine Online [Web site]

ON HOOPS — On Hoops [Web site]

ON THE NET — AOL Computing: On the Net

ONE CLICK AWAY — AOL Member Services: The Internet is One Click Away

ONE LAP — Car and Driver Online

ONE LIFE TO LIVE — ABC Online: Daytime

ONE SCARY NIGHT — Halloween@AOL [seasonal]

ONE SPORT — Backpacker Magazine: Marketplace

ONLINE ALICE — Digital City Los Angeles: Advice Expert

ONLINE BANKING — AOL Personal Finance: Banking Center

ONLINE BUSINESS — AOL WorkPlace: Doing Business Online

ONLINE CAMPUS — AOL Research & Learn: Online Campus

ONLINE CASINO — GameStorm: Online Casino

ONLINE CLASSES — AOL Computing: Online Classroom

ONLINE CLASSROOM — AOL Computing: Online Classroom

ONLINE CLOCK — Online Clock

ONLINE COURSES — AOL Research & Learn: Courses Online

ONLINE DRIVE — NTN Trivia: Online Drive

ONLINE GAMING — AOL Games: Online Gaming Forums

ONLINE GARAGE — Digital City Twin Cities: The Online Garage

ONLINE GREETINGS — American Greetings Online Greetings

ONLINE INVESTOR — The Online Investor

ONLINE MUSIC AWARDS — SPIN Online: Online Music Awards

ONLINE POSTCARDS — America Greetings Online Greetings

ONLINE PSYCH — Online Psych

ONLINE SUPPORT — AOL Member Services

ONLINE TIPS — AOL Insider Tips

ONLINE TRANSACTIONS — AOL Personal Finance: Banking Center

ONLINE WEDDING — Love@AOL: CyberVows

ONLY — What's New on AOL

ONLY AOL — What's New on AOL

ONLY ON AOL — What's New on AOL

ONQ — onQ Gay & Lesbian Community

ONQ CARDS — onQ: Tzabaco

ONQ GREETINGS — onQ: Tzabaco

ONQ HIV BOARDS — onQ: HIV Boards

ONQ HIV CHAT — onQ: HIV Chat

ONQ HIV LIBRARIES — onQ: HIV Libraries

ONQ HIV RESOURCES — onQ: HIV Resources

ONQ HIV TREATMENT — onQ: HIV Treatment
ONQ LIBRARIES — onQ: Libraries
ONQ MILITARY — onQ: Military
ONQ NEWS — onQ: News
ONQ SAN FRANCISCO — onQ: San Francisco
ONQ SEARCH — onQ: Channel Search
ONQ SF — onQ: San Francisco
ONQ SOLDIER — onQ: Military
ONQ TRAVEL — onQ: Travel
ONSALE — Onsale Online Auction [Web site]
ONSALE AUCTION — Onsale Online Auction [Web site]
ONSALE AUCTIONS — Onsale Online Auction [Web site]
OP — AOL Rewards: Opinion Place
OPERATION CONDOR — EXTRA: Operation Condor
OPINION — AOL Rewards: Opinion Place
OPINION PLACE — AOL Rewards: Opinion Place
OPINIONS — AOL Rewards: Opinion Place
OPP — Paramount: Other People's Problems [Web site]
OPRAH — Oprah Online
OPRAH ONLINE — Oprah Online
OPRAH WINFREY — Oprah Online
ORAL HEALTH — AOL Health: Dental & Oral Health
ORANGE BOWL — AOL Sports: Orange Bowl
ORANGE COMMUNITY — Digital City Orange County: Community!
ORANGE COUNTY — Digital City Orange County
ORANGE COUNTY SPORTS — Digital City Orange County: Interactive
   Sports Central!
ORANGE CURTAIN — Digital City Orange County
ORANGE ENTERTAINMENT — Digital City Orange County:
   Entertainment!
ORANGE PEOPLE — Digital City Orange County: People!
ORANGE SPORTS — Digital City Orange County: Interactive Sports
   Central!
ORGANIZATION — AOL Lifestyles: Communities
ORIENT — AOL International: Asia
ORIENTAL — AOL International: Asia
ORIENTATION — AOL Member Services: QuickStart
ORIOLES — Baltimore Orioles
ORL CHAT — Digital City Orlando: Chat Room
ORL COMMUNITY — Digital City Orlando: Community
ORL ENTERTAIN — Digital City Orlando: Entertainment
ORL HEALTH — Digital City Orlando: Healthy U.
ORL MAGIC — Digital City Orlando: Orlando Magic
ORL MARKET — Digital City Orlando: Market
ORL MOVIES — Digital City Orlando: Movies
ORL NEWS — Orlando Sentinel News

ORL RECRUITING — Digital City Orlando: College Sports Recruiting
[Web site]
ORLAND PARK — Digital City Orland Park [Web site]
ORLANDO — Digital City Orlando
ORLANDO CHAT — Digital City Orlando: Chat Room
ORLANDO COMMUNITY — Digital City Orlando: Community
ORLANDO ENTERTAINMENT — Digital City Orlando: Entertainment
ORLANDO HEALTH — Digital City Orlando: Healthy U.
ORLANDO KIDS — Digital City Orlando: KidSafe
ORLANDO KIDS SAFE — Digital City Orlando: KidSafe
ORLANDO LOCAL NEWS — Digital City Orlando: Local News
ORLANDO MAGIC — Orlando Magic
ORLANDO MARKETPLACE — Digital City Orlando: Market
ORLANDO NEWS — Orlando Sentinel News
ORLANDO SENTINEL — Orlando Sentinel Online
ORLANDO THEME PARKS — Digital City Orlando: Go2Orlando Travel
Service
ORLANDO TRAVEL — Digital City Orlando: Go2Orlando Travel Service
ORLANDO TURKEY — Digital City Orlando: Let's Talk Turkey!
[Web site]
O'S — Baltimore Orioles
OS SPECIAL — Omaha Steaks International
OS TWO — AOL Computing: The OS/2 Forum
OS/2 — AOL Computing: The OS/2 Forum
OS2 — AOL Computing: The OS/2 Forum
OS8 — Apple on AOL
OSO — Orlando Sentinel Online
OSO ARCHIVE — Orlando Sentinel Online: Archives
OSO ARCHIVES — Orlando Sentinel Online: Archives
OSO BLACK — Orlando Sentinel Online: Black Voices
OSO BUSINESS — Orlando Sentinel Online: Business
OSO CHAT — Orlando Sentinel Online: Chat
OSO CLASSIFIED — Orlando Sentinel Online: Classified
OSO CLASSIFIEDS — Orlando Sentinel Online: Classified
OSO DOWNLOAD — Orlando Sentinel Online: Download
OSO FEATURES — Orlando Sentinel Online: Features
OSO GOVERNMENT — Orlando Sentinel Online: Politics
OSO HOMES — Orlando Sentinel Online: Homes
OSO LIVING — Orlando Sentinel Online: Features
OSO MAGIC — Orlando Sentinel Online: Magic
OSO MERCHANDISE — Orlando Sentinel Online: Merchandise
OSO MOVIES — Orlando Sentinel Online: Movies
OSO NET — Orlando Sentinel Online: Net
OSO PHOTO — Orlando Sentinel Online Photos
OSO PHOTOS — Orlando Sentinel Online Photos
OSO POLITICS — Orlando Sentinel Online: Politics

OSO RECRUITING — Digital City Orlando: College Sports Recruiting [Web site]

OSO SOUND OFF — Orlando Sentinel Online: Sound Off

OSO SPORTS — Orlando Sentinel Online: Sports

OSO STORM — Orlando Sentinel Online: Hurricane Survival Guide

OSO TOP — Orlando Sentinel Online: Top Stories

OSO TOP STORIES — Orlando Sentinel Online: Top Stories

OSO WEATHER — Orlando Sentinel Online: Weather

OSTEOPATHY — AOL Health: Osteopathy

OSTEOPOROSIS — AOL Health: Osteoporosis

OSTEOPOROSIS@THRIVE — Thrive@Healthy Living: Osteoporosis

OSTRICH — AOL Interests: Pets

OTHER PEOPLES PROBLEMS — Paramount: Other People's Problems [Web site]

OTITIS MEDIA — AOL Health: Otitis Media

OTN — AOL Computing: On the Net

OUR BROKER — AOL Personal Finance: Real Estate Desk

OUR OWN — Digital City Hampton Roads: Gay & Lesbian Community

OUR WEDDING PAGE — The Wedding Shopper [Web site]

OUT AND AT HOME — NetNoir: Gay & Lesbian

OUT ONQ — onQ: Coming Out

OUT THERE — Out There News [Web site]

OUT THERE NEWS — Out There News [Web site]

OUTBACK — AOL International: Australia and Oceania

OUTDOOR ADVENTURE — Outdoor Adventure Online

OUTDOOR FUN — AOL Interests: Outdoor Fun

OUTDOOR TRAVEL — AOL Travel: Adventure and Outdoor Travel

OUTDOORS SF — Digital City San Francisco: Outdoor Recreation

OUTPOST — Cyberian Outpost [Web site]

OUTPOST.COM — Cyberian Outpost [Web site]

OUTWEST — Digital City Denver: OutWest Online

OUTWEST ONLINE — Digital City Denver: OutWest Online

OVARIAN CANCER — AOL Health: Ovarian Cancer

OVER 40 CDN — AOL Canada: Over 40 Chat

OWL MAGAZINE — Owl Magazine

OXFORD — Better Health & Medical: Oxford Health Plans

OXFORD AVEDA SALON — Digital City Denver: Oxford/Aveda Spa at Oxford Hotel

OXFORD CLUB — Digital City Denver: Oxford/Aveda Spa at Oxford Hotel

OXFORD HP — Better Health & Medical: Oxford Health Plans

OXFORD SALON — Digital City Denver: Oxford/Aveda Spa at Oxford Hotel

OXFORD SPA — Digital City Denver: Oxford/Aveda Spa at Oxford Hotel

OZ.COMMUNITY — AOL Australia: AOL Today

PACERS — Indiana Pacers
PACIFIC STOCK EXCHANGE — Pacific Stock Exchange [Web site]
PADREISMS — Digital City San Diego: Andy Strasberg's Baseball-Itis
PADRES — San Diego Padres
PAGAN — Religion & Beliefs: Pagan Religions & Occult Sciences
PAGE — MobileComm: Send a Page
PAGEBOOK — MobileComm: Paging Address Book
PAGER — AOL Computing: Products 2000
PAIN — AOL Health: Pain Relief
PAIN RELIEF — AOL Health: Pain Relief
PAINTBALL — AOL Grandstand: Paintball Forum
PAINTBALL FORUM — AOL Grandstand: Paintball Forum
PAINTWAR — Engage: Splatterball
PAKISTAN — AOL International: Pakistan
PALATINE — Digital City Chicago: Palatine [Web site]
PALAU — AOL International: Palau
PALESTINE — AOL International: Palestine
PALLADIUM — Book Central: Community
PALMISTRY — Digital City Denver: Mo's Mystical Metaphysical Tour
PALMPILOT — 3Com: Palm Computing
PALMTOP — AOL Computing: PDA & Palmtop Forum
PANAMA — AOL International: Panama
PANIC — AOL Health: Anxiety & Panic Disorders
PAP — AOL Computing: PC Application Forums
PAPUA — AOL International: Papua New Guinea
PAPUA NEW GUINEA — AOL International: Papua New Guinea
PARADOX — DC Comics: Paradox Press
PARAGON — Paragon Online [Web site]
PARAGON ONLINE — Paragon Online [Web site]
PARAGUAY — AOL International: Paraguay
PARASCOPE — ParaScope
PARENT — AOL Families
PARENT CLUB — Parent Soup: Triaminic Parents Club
PARENT SOUP — Parent Soup
PARENT SOUP CHAT — Parent Soup: Chat
PARENTAL CONTROL — AOL Parental Controls
PARENTAL CONTROLS — AOL Parental Controls
PARENTING — AOL Families: Parenting
PARENTS — AOL Families
PARENTS CLUB — Parent Soup: Triaminic Parents Club
PARENTS SOUP — Parent Soup
PARGH — The Gadget Guru Online
PARIS — AOL International channel
PARK RIDGE — Digital City Chicago: Park Ridge [Web site]
PARKINSON'S — AOL Health: Parkinson's Disease
PARKINSONS — AOL Health: Parkinson's Disease

PARKINSON'S DISEASE — AOL Health: Parkinson's Disease
PARKINSONS DISEASE — AOL Health: Parkinson's Disease
PARLOR — AOL Games: Parlor Games
PARROT — Parrot Key: Tropical Rock Forum
PARSONS — Parsons Technology
PARSONS TECHNOLOGY — Parsons Technology
PARTNER ABUSE — Massachusetts Coalition of Battered Women
　　Service Groups
PARTNER VIOLENCE — Massachusetts Coalition of Battered Women
　　Service Groups
PARTY GAMES — Love@AOL: Party Games
PASADENA HOMES — Digital City Los Angeles: Susan & Brad Mohr
　　Realtors
PASSIONS — AOL Interests channel
PASSOVER — Passover [seasonal]
PASSPORT — AOL International: Passport to Love
PASSPORT LOVE — AOL International: Passport to Love
PASSPORT TO LOVE — AOL International: Passport to Love
PASSPORT TO NY — Digital City New York: Dining
PASSWORD — Change Your Password
PASSWORD TIPS — Password Protection Tips
PASSWORDS — Change Your Password
PATERNO — Paterno Imports
PAVING CONTRACTOR — AOL WorkPlace: Contractor's Community
PAWN BROKER — AOL WorkPlace: Pawnbrokers' Community
PBK — AOL Sports: Pro Basketball
PBM — AOL Games: Play-by-Mail Forum
PBM CLUBS — AOL Games: Play-by-Mail Forum
PC — People Connection
PC APPLICATIONS — AOL Computing: PC Applications Forums
PC APPLICATIONS FORUM — AOL Computing: PC Applications Forums
PC APPS — AOL Computing: PC Applications Forums
PC APS — AOL Computing: PC Applications Forums
PC AVSC — AOL Computing: Animation & Video Software Center
PC BEGINNER — AOL Computing: PC Help Desk
PC BFSC — AOL Computing: Business & Finance Software Center
PC BIZ — AOL Computing: Business Applications
PC BUS — AOL Computing: Business Applications
PC BUSINESS — AOL Computing: Business Applications
PC CHAT — AOL Computing: Events
PC CHATS — AOL Computing: Events
PC CONFERENCE — AOL Computing: Events
PC CONFERENCES — AOL Computing: Events
PC CRAFTS — AOL Computing: Home & Hobby Applications
PC DADS — Intel: PC Dads
PC DATA — PC Data

PC DB — AOL Computing: Database Applications
PC DEV — AOL Computing: PC Development
PC DEVELOPMENT — AOL Computing: PC Development
PC DEVELOPMENT FORUM — AOL Computing: PC Development
PC DOWNLOAD — AOL Computing: Daily Download
PC DPSC — AOL Computing: Desktop Publishing Software Center
PC DTP — AOL Computing: Desktop & Web Publishing Forum
PC DVSC — AOL Computing: Development and Programming Software Center
PC ED — AOL Computing: Education & Reference Applications
PC EDSC — AOL Computing: Education & Reference Software Center
PC EDU — AOL Computing: Education & Reference Applications
PC EDUCATION — AOL Computing: Education & Reference Applications
PC FIN — AOL Computing: Finance Computing Forum
PC FINANCE — AOL Computing: Finance Applications
PC FINANCIAL — DLJ Direct Brokers
PC FINANCIAL NETWORK — DLJ Direct Brokers
PC FORT — Antagonist, Inc.: PC Games
PC FORTRESS — Antagonist, Inc.: PC Games
PC FORUMS — AOL Computing: Help Desk
PC FUSC — AOL Computing: Fun and Games Software Center
PC GAMES — AOL Games: PC Games Forum
PC GRAPHICS — AOL Computing: PC Graphic Arts Forum
PC GRSC — AOL Computing: Graphics Software Center
PC HARDWARE — AOL Computing: PC Hardware Forum
PC HARDWARE FORUM — AOL Computing: PC Hardware Forum
PC HELP — AOL Computing: PC Help Desk
PC HH — AOL Computing: Home & Hobby Applications
PC HOBBY — AOL Computing: Home & Hobby Applications
PC HOME — AOL Computing: Home & Hobby Applications
PC HOSC — AOL Computing: Home and Hobby Software Center
PC INSC — AOL Computing: Internet Software Center
PC INVEST — AOL Computing: Finance Applications
PC INVESTMENT — AOL Computing: Finance Applications
PC LEARN — AOL Computing: Education & Reference Applications
PC MALL — PCMall [Web site]
PC MM — AOL Computing: PC Animation & Video
PC MONEY — AOL Computing: Finance Applications
PC MSSC — AOL Computing: Music & Sound Software Center
PC MU — AOL Computing: PC Music & Sound Forum
PC MULTIMEDIA — AOL Computing: PC Animation & Video
PC MULTIMEDIA FORUM — AOL Computing: PC Animation & Video
PC MUSIC & SOUND FORUM — AOL Computing: PC Music & Sound Forum
PC MUSIC — AOL Computing: PC Music & Sound Forum
PC MUSIC FORUM — AOL Computing: PC Music & Sound Forum

PC NEW FILES — AOL Computing: PC Weekly New Files
PC NTSC — AOL Computing: Telecom & Networking
PC PLAZA — People Connection: Plaza
PC PRODUCTIVITY — AOL Computing: Productivity Applications
PC REF — AOL Computing: Education & Reference Applications
PC REFERENCE — AOL Computing: Education & Reference Applications
PC SEARCH — People Connection: Search Featured Chats
PC SECURITY — AOL Computing: Virus Information
PC SOFTWARE — AOL Computing: Download Software
PC SOUND — AOL Computing: PC Music & Sound Forum
PC SOUND FORUM — AOL Computing: PC Music & Sound Forum
PC SPORTS — AOL Computing: Home & Hobby Applications
PC STUDIO — People Connection: Studio
PC SUPPORT — AOL Computing: PC Help Desk
PC TEACH — AOL Computing: Education & Reference Applications
PC TELECOM — AOL Computing: Telecom & Networking
PC TELECOM FORUM — AOL Computing: Telecom & Networking
PC TIPS — AOL Computing: Tips
PC TOOL — AOL Computing: PC Essential Utilities
PC TOOLBOX — AOL Computing: PC Essential Utilities
PC TOOLS — AOL Computing: PC Essential Utilities
PC TOYS — Objects of Desire
PC UTSC — AOL Computing: Utilities & Tools Software Center
PC WEBOPAEDIA — AOL Computing: Webopædia [Web site]
PC WEBOPEDIA — AOL Computing: Webopædia [Web site]
PC WORD — AOL Computing: Word Processing Applications
PC WORLD — PC World Online
PC WORLD ONLINE — PC World Online
PC ZONE — PC Games Zone [Web site]
P-C-D — Global Gourmet: Professional Cutlery Direct
PCD — Global Gourmet: Professional Cutlery Direct
PCF — DLJ Direct Brokers
PCF APPLY — Pet Care Forum: Apply
PCF AS — Pet Care Forum: Animals & Society
PCF BIRDS — Pet Care Forum: Birds
PCF BOARDS — Pet Care Forum: Message Boards
PCF CATS — Pet Care Forum: Cats
PCF CHAT — Pet Care Forum: Chat
PCF DOGS — Pet Care Forum: Dogs
PCF FML — Pet Care Forum: Fish & Marine Life
PCF HORSES — Pet Care Forum: Horses
PCF LIBRARIES — Pet Care Forum: Libraries
PCF PET — Pet Care Forum: Gina Spadafori's Pet Connection
PCF POLL — Pet Care Forum: Poll
PCF RA — Pet Care Forum: Reptiles and Amphibians
PCF SME — Pet Care Forum: Small Mammals and Exotics Forum

PCF TODAY — Pet Care Forum: Today in Pet Care
PCF VET — Pet Care Forum: The Veterinary Hospital
PCFN — DLJ Direct Brokers
PCFN ACCT — DLJ Direct Brokers
PCFN LINGO — AOL Personal Finance: Lingo
PCH — Entertainment Asylum: Pulp Cult Horror Highway
PCH HIGHWAY — Entertainment Asylum: Pulp Cult Horror Highway
PCM — AOL Computing: Telecom & Networking
PCW ONLINE — PC World Online
PDA — AOL Computing: PDA & Palmtop Forum
PDA DEV — AOL Computing: PDA Development
PDA DEV SIG — AOL Computing: PDA Development
PDA FORUM — AOL Computing: PDA & Palmtop Forum
PDA GUIDE — AOL Computing: The PDA Buyers' Guide
PDA SEARCH — AOL Computing: The PDA Buyers' Guide
PDA SELECT — AOL Computing: The PDA Buyers' Guide
PDA SHOP — AOL Computing: The PDA Buyers' Guide
PDA STORE — AOL Computing: The PDA Buyers' Guide
PDC — Portfolio Direct
PDV — AOL Computing: PC Development
PEACEMAKER — EXTRA: The Peacemaker
PEAPOD — Digital City Chicago: Peapod [Web site]
PEEPS — Peeps Republic [Web site]
PEEPS REPUBLIC — Peeps Republic [Web site]
PEN — Better Health & Medical: Personal Empowerment Network
PEN DEAF — Better Health & Hearing: Deaf & Hard of Hearing
    Community
PEN HOH — Better Health & Hearing: Deaf & Hard of Hearing
    Community
PEN PAL — Digital City or International Pen Pals
PEN PALS — Digital City or International Pen Pals
PENN HEALTH — Digital City Philadelphia: University of Pennsylvania
PENNEY'S — JCPenney
PEOPLE — People Connection
PEOPLE CONNECTION — People Connection
PEOPLE CONNECTION HELP — AOL Member Services: People
    Connection
PEOPLE CONNECTION SEARCH — People Connection: Search Featured
    Chats
PEOPLE DCSD — Digital City San Diego: People
PEOPLE FINDER — AOL NetFind: Find a Person [Web site]
PEOPLE SD — Digital City San Diego: People
PEOPLE SEARCH — People Connection: Search Featured Chats
PEOPLES GRAFFITI — People Connection: Graffiti
PERFUME — The Fragrance Counter
PERIODONTAL — AOL Health: Periodontal Disease

PERISCOPE — ParaScope
PERKIN — Perkin Elmer Customer Service [Web site]
PERKIN ELMER — Perkin Elmer Customer Service [Web site]
PERKS — AOL Member Perks
PERON — AOL International: Evita
PERRIER — Digital City Philadelphia: Dining Guide
PERS CLASSIFIEDS — AOL Classifieds: Personals
PERSHING — DLJ Direct Brokers
PERSIAN GULF — AOL International: Middle East
PERSON FIND — AOL NetFind: Find a Person [Web site]
PERSON FINDER — AOL NetFind: Find a Person [Web site]
PERSON OF INFLUENCE — AOL Influence: Person of Influence
PERSONAL EMPOWERMENT — Better Health & Medical: Personal
    Empowerment Network
PERSONAL FILING CABINET — AOL Member Services: Personal Filing
    Cabinet
PERSONAL FINANCE — AOL Personal Finance channel
PERSONAL FINANCE AUTO GUIDE — AOL Personal Finance: Auto Guide
PERSONAL FINANCE HOME — AOL Personal Finance: Real Estate
PERSONAL FINANCE STORE — AOL Personal Finance: Store
**PERSONAL PERIPHERALS — Personal Computer Peripherals
    Corp**
PERSONAL PUBLISHER — AOL Personal Publisher
PERSONAL PUBLISHER 2 — AOL Personal Publisher
PERSONAL SAN DIEGO — Digital City San Diego: Personals
PERSONAL SHOPPER — Electra: Personal Shopper
PERSONAL WEALTH — S&P Personal Wealth
PERSONALS — Romance channel
PERSONALS CLASSIFIEDS — AOL Classifieds: Personals
PERSONALS DCSD — Digital City San Diego: Personals
PERSONALS SD — Digital City San Diego: Personals
PERU — AOL International: Peru
PESACH — Passover [seasonal]
PEST CONTROL — AOL WorkPlace: Pest Control Services' Community
PET — AOL Interests: Pets
PET CARE — Pet Care Forum
PET CARE FORUM — Pet Care Forum
PET STUFF — AOL Interests: Pets
PET SUPPLIER — AOL WorkPlace: Pet Shops, Supplies & Kennels
    Community
PET SUPPLIERS — AOL WorkPlace: Pet Shops, Supplies & Kennels
    Community
PET SUPPLIES — AOL WorkPlace: Pet Shops, Supplies & Kennels
    Community
PETE HAMILL — Digital City New York: Pete Hamill's NY Chronicle
PETER MCNAMARA — Digital City Boston: Cigar Guy

PETER MELTZER — Digital City New York: Dining
PETER NORTON — Symantec Corporation
PETRO — Sports Fan: The Soren Petro Experience
PETS — AOL Interests: Pets
PETS ONQ — onQ: Pets
PF — AOL Personal Finance channel
PF ADVICE — AOL Personal Finance: LifeStages Advice & Planning
PF AUTO GUIDE — AOL Personal Finance: Auto Guide
PF BANKS — AOL Personal Finance: Banking Center
PF BASICS — AOL Personal Finance: Investing Basics
PF CLOSED-END FUND — Closed-End Funds
PF EXPLORE — AOL Personal Finance: Search & Explore
PF FORUMS — AOL Personal Finance: Investing Forums
PF GAME DAY — Pro Football Game Day
PF GD — Pro Football Game Day
PF HOME & AUTO — AOL Personal Finance: Home & Auto
PF LIVE — AOL Personal Finance: Live
PF LOOKING — Real Estate Center: Looking
PF NEWSLETTER — AOL Personal Finance: Newsletters
PF PLANNING — AOL Personal Finance: LifeStages Advice & Planning
PF REC FINANCING — Real Estate Center: Financing
PF REC LOOKING — Real Estate Center: Looking
PF REC MOVING — Real Estate Center: Moving
PF REC RENTING — Real Estate Center: Renting
PF REC SELLING — Real Estate Center: Selling
PF SEARCH — AOL Personal Finance: Search & Explore
PF SEARCH EXPLORE — AOL Personal Finance: Search & Explore
PF STORE — AOL Personal Finance: Store
PFB — AOL Sports: Pro Football
PFB GAME DAY — Pro Football Game Day
PFB SCOREBOARD — STATS Football Scoreboard
PFC — AOL Member Services: Personal Filing Cabinet
PFCN — DLJ Direct Brokers
PFIZER — Pfizer: Exploring Your Health
PGA — iGolf
PH — Simon & Schuster College Online
PH COMM — AOL PrimeHost
PH COMMERCIAL — AOL PrimeHost
PH HELP — AOL PrimeHost: Online Support
PH MEMBER SERVICES — AOL PrimeHost: Online Support
PH SERVICE — AOL PrimeHost: Online Support
PHIL END — Digital City Philadelphia: Philadelphia Weekend
PHIL HEALTH — Digital City Philadelphia: Health
PHIL MARKET — Digital City Philadelphia: Market
PHILA ZOO — Digital City Philadelphia: Philadelphia Zoo
PHILADELPHIA — Digital City Philadelphia

PHILADELPHIA AUTO DIGEST — Digital City Philadelphia: Auto Digest
PHILADELPHIA AUTO UPDATE — Digital City Philadelphia: Auto Digest
PHILADELPHIA BUSINESS — Digital City Philadelphia: Market
PHILADELPHIA CHAT — Digital City Philadelphia: Chat
PHILADELPHIA EAGLES — Digital City Philadelphia: The Eagles
PHILADELPHIA KIDS — Digital City Philadelphia: KidSafe
PHILADELPHIA KIDS SAFE — Digital City Philadelphia: KidSafe
PHILADELPHIA LOCAL NEWS — Digital City Philadelphia: Local News
PHILADELPHIA MUSIC — Digital City Philadelphia: Music
PHILADELPHIA SOUND — Digital City Philadelphia: Music
PHILADELPHIA STORES — Digital City Philadelphia: Shopping
PHILADELPHIA TRAVEL — Digital City Philadelphia: Travel
PHILEDELPHIA PHILLIES — Philadelphia Phillies
PHILIPPINES — AOL International: Philippines
PHILLIES — Philadelphia Phillies
PHILLY — Digital City Philadelphia
PHILLY 4TH — Digital City Philadelphia: Welcome America
PHILLY AA — Digital City Philadelphia: Alcoholics Anonymous
PHILLY ARCA — Digital City Philadelphia: Andy Belmont Racing
PHILLY AUCTION — Digital City Philadelphia: DiningGuide Charity
    Auction
PHILLY AUTO — Digital City Philadelphia: Automart
PHILLY AUTO DIGEST — Digital City Philadelphia: Auto Digest
PHILLY AUTO UPDATE — Digital City Philadelphia: Auto Digest
PHILLY AUTOGUIDE — Digital City Philadelphia: Automart
PHILLY AUTOMART — Digital City Philadelphia: Automart
PHILLY BASEBALL — Digital City Philadelphia: Baseball
PHILLY BASKETBALL — Digital City Philadelphia: Basketball
PHILLY BIZ — Digital City Philadelphia: Business
PHILLY BOX — Digital City Philadelphia: Boxing
PHILLY BOXING — Digital City Philadelphia: Boxing
PHILLY BUSINESS — Digital City Philadelphia: Market
PHILLY CABLE — Digital City Philadelphia: Greater Media Cable
    Company
PHILLY CAREERS — Digital City Philadelphia: Employment Classifieds
PHILLY CARS — Digital City Philadelphia: Automart
PHILLY CHAT — Digital City Philadelphia: Chat
PHILLY DEALERS ONLY — Digital City Philadelphia: Auto Dealers
PHILLY DIGITAL CITY — Digital City Philadelphia
PHILLY DINING — Digital City Philadelphia: Dining
PHILLY EMPLOYMENT — Digital City Philadelphia: Employment
    Classifieds
PHILLY FANTASY BASEBALL — Digital City Philadelphia: Fantasy
    Baseball
PHILLY FIGHTING — Digital City Philadelphia: Boxing
PHILLY FILM — Digital City Philadelphia: International House

PHILLY FILMFEST — Digital City Philadelphia: International House
PHILLY FIT — Digital City Philadelphia: Health
PHILLY FLORIST — Digital City Philadelphia: Polites Florist
PHILLY FOOD — Digital City Philadelphia: Dining
PHILLY FOOTBALL — Digital City Philadelphia: Pro Football
PHILLY FOURTH — Digital City Philadelphia: Welcome America
PHILLY GAY — Digital City Philadelphia: Gay / Lesbian Links
PHILLY GOING OUT — Digital City Philadelphia: Nightlife Listings
PHILLY GRANDSTAND — Digital City Philadelphia: Fantasy Baseball
PHILLY HEALTH — Digital City Philadelphia: Health
PHILLY HOCKEY — Digital City Philadelphia: Hockey
PHILLY HOCKY — Digital City Philadelphia: Hockey
PHILLY HOOPS — Digital City Philadelphia: Basketball
PHILLY HOT DEALS — Digital City Philadelphia: Auto Hot Deals
PHILLY HOT ZONE — Digital City Philadelphia: Teens
PHILLY ISSUES — Digital City Philadelphia: Hot-Button Issues
PHILLY JOBS — Digital City Philadelphia: Employment Classifieds
PHILLY KIXX — Digital City Philadelphia: Kixx
PHILLY LOCAL NEWS — Digital City Philadelphia: Local News
PHILLY LOVE — Digital City Philadelphia: Star Sites
PHILLY MARKET — Digital City Philadelphia: Market
PHILLY MOVE — Digital City Philadelphia: Relocation
PHILLY MOVIES — Digital City Philadelphia: Movies
PHILLY MOVING — Digital City Philadelphia: Relocation
PHILLY MUSIC — Digital City Philadelphia: Music
PHILLY NASCAR — Digital City Philadelphia: Andy Belmont Racing
PHILLY NIGHTLIFE — Digital City Philadelphia: Nightlife Listings
PHILLY OLYMPICS — Digital City Philadelphia: Olympics
PHILLY PERSONALS — Digital City Philadelphia: Personals
PHILLY PHOTOS — Digital City Philadelphia: Photo Galleries
PHILLY PICS — Digital City Philadelphia: Photo Galleries
PHILLY PIG SKIN — Digital City Philadelphia: Pro Football
PHILLY PIX — Digital City Philadelphia: Photo Galleries
PHILLY POETRY — Digital City Philadelphia: Poetry & Stories
PHILLY POLL — Digital City Philadelphia: Poll
PHILLY POLLING — Digital City Philadelphia: Poll
PHILLY RACING — Digital City Philadelphia: Andy Belmont Racing
PHILLY RAGE — Digital City Philadelphia: Basketball
PHILLY RELOCATION — Digital City Philadelphia: Relocation
PHILLY REVIEWER — Digital City Philadelphia: Member Music Reviews
PHILLY SEX — Digital City Philadelphia: Star Sites
PHILLY SHORT STORIES — Digital City Philadelphia: Poetry & Stories
PHILLY SIXERS — Digital City Philadelphia: Basketball
PHILLY SOCCER — Digital City Philadelphia: Kixx
PHILLY SOUND — Digital City Philadelphia: Music

PHILLY SPRING BASEBALL — Digital City Philadelphia: Phillies Spring Training
PHILLY STERN — Digital City Philadelphia: Howard Stern
PHILLY STORE — Digital City Philadelphia: Shopping
PHILLY STORES — Digital City Philadelphia: Shopping
PHILLY STORIES — Digital City Philadelphia: Poetry & Stories
PHILLY SUMMIT — Digital City Philadelphia: Presidential Summit
PHILLY SUNBALL — Digital City Philadelphia: Phillies Spring Training
PHILLY TALK — Digital City Philadelphia: Chat
PHILLY TEEN — Digital City Philadelphia: Teens
PHILLY TEENS — Digital City Philadelphia: Teens
PHILLY THRIVE — Digital City Philadelphia: Health
PHILLY TOURISM — Digital City Philadelphia: Travel
PHILLY TRAVEL — Digital City Philadelphia: Travel
PHILLY TRUCKS — Digital City Philadelphia: Automart
PHILLY WEEKEND — Digital City Philadelphia: Weekend
PHILLY YOUTH — Digital City Philadelphia: Teens
PHILLY ZOO — Digital City Philadelphia: Philadelphia Zoo
PHILLY@THE MOVIES — Digital City Philadelphia: Movies
PHISH — The Grateful Dead Forum: The Phorum
PHISH FORUM — The Grateful Dead Forum: The Phorum
PHISH PHORUM — The Grateful Dead Forum: The Phorum
PHL — Digital City Philadelphia: WPHL-TV
PHL 17 — Digital City Philadelphia: WPHL-TV
PHMS — PrimeHost: Online Support
PHOBIA — AOL Health: Phobias
PHOBIAS — AOL Health: Phobias
PHOENIX — Arizona Central
PHOENIX LOCAL NEWS — Phoenix Local News
PHOENIX NEWS — Phoenix Local News
PHONE HELP — Accessing America Online
PHONE NUMBER — Accessing America Online
PHONE NUMBERS — Accessing America Online
PHONEBOOK — AOL Research & Learn: Phone & Addresses
PHOTO — AOL Interests: Pictures
PHOTO OF THE MONTH — Daily Press: Photo of the Month
PHOTO PERSONALS — Love@AOL: Photo Personals
PHOTO PHILLY — Digital City Philadelphia: Photo Galleries
PHOTOGRAPH — AOL Interests: Pictures
PHOTOGRAPHER — AOL WorkPlace: Photography
PHOTOGRAPHS — AOL Interests: Pictures
PHOTOGRAPHY — AOL Interests: Pictures
PHOTOGRAPHY FORUM — Photography Forum
PHOTOSCAN — Love@AOL: Photo Scanning
PHOTOSHOP — AOL Computing: Photoshop SIG
PHOTSHOP SIG — AOL Computing: Photoshop SIG

PHRASE CHALLENGE — AOL International: Language Games
PHRASE GAME — AOL International: Language Games
PHRASE GAMES — AOL International: Language Games
PHRASES GAMES — AOL International: Language Games
PHS — AOL Families: Practical Homeschooling
PHW — AOL Computing: PC Hardware Forum
PHYSICALLY DISABLED — DisABILITIES Community Forum
PICTURE — AOL Interests: Pictures
PICTURE DISK — Using your Image Disk in e-mail
PICTURE PERFECT — Picture Perfect: The Movie
PICTURES — AOL Interests: Pictures
PICTURES OF THE WEEK — AOL News: Pictures of the Week
PIERIAN — Pierian Spring Software
PIERIAN SP — Pierian Spring Software
PIG — AOL Interests: Pets
PILOTS — AOL Interests: Aviation & Aeronautics
PIM — AOL Computing: Productivity Forum
PIMS — AOL Computing: Productivity Forum
PIRATES — Pittsburgh Pirates
PISCES — Horoscope Selections
PISTONS — Detroit Pistons
PITTSBURGH LOCAL NEWS — Digital City Pittsburgh: Local News
PITTSBURGH NEWS — Digital City Pittsburgh: Local News
PITTSBURGH PIRATES — Pittsburgh Pirates
PITUITARY — AOL Health: Pituitary Disorders
PIX O WEEK — AOL News: Pictures of the Week
PIZZA — AOL WorkPlace: Pizza Parlors, Restaurants & Delivery
PIZZA DELIVERY — AOL WorkPlace: Pizza Parlors, Restaurants &
    Delivery
PIZZA PARLOR — AOL WorkPlace: Pizza Parlors, Restaurants &
    Delivery
PLACES TO EXPLORE — Places To Explore
PLAIN TALK — Electra: Plain Talk with Jane
PLANEBIZ — PlaneBusiness Online
PLANET EALING — AOL UK: Planet Ealing Film
PLANET EALING KIDS — AOL UK: Planet Ealing for Kids
PLANET MARS — Mars Pathfinder Information
PLANETOUT — PlanetOut
PLANETOUT LIVE — PlanetOut: Live
PLANETRADIO — Digital City Atlanta: News
PLANNER — AOL WorkPlace: Planning & Specifications Community
PLANNERS — AOL WorkPlace: Planning & Specifications Community
PLANO — Digital City Dallas-Forth Worth: Plano Star Courier
PLANO BALLOON — Digital City Dallas-Forth Worth: Annual Balloon
    Festival

PLANO BALLOON FEST — Digital City Dallas-Forth Worth: Annual Balloon Festival

PLANO STAR COURIER — Digital City Dallas-Forth Worth: Plano Star Courier

PLAY GAMES — AOL Member Services: Play Games Online

PLAYBILL — Playbill On-Line [Web site]

PLAY-BY-MAIL — Play-by-Mail Forum

PLAYSTATION — Antagonist, Inc.: Sony Playstation

PLAYTEX — One Hanes Place

PLEASURE DOME ONQ — onQ: Backroom

PLUBMING CONTRACTOR — AOL WorkPlace: Contractor's Community

PLUG IN — Plug In

PLUG INS — AOL Multimedia Showcase [Web site]

PLUGGED — Plug In

PLUGGED IN — Plug In

PLUS & TALL — JCPenney: Plus & Tall store

PLUS & TALLS — JCPenney: Plus & Tall store

PLUS — PLUS ATM Network

PLUS AND TALL — JCPenney: Plus & Tall store

PLUS AND TALLS — JCPenney: Plus & Tall store

PLUS SIZE CONCEPTS — Electra: Plus Size Concepts

PLUS SYSTEMS — PLUS ATM Network

PLYMOUTH — Digital City Plymouth [Web site]

PMM — AOL Computing: PC Animation & Video

PMU — AOL Computing: PC Music & Sound Forum

PNEUMONIA — AOL Health: Pneumonia

PNO — PlanetOut

PNO AIDS — PlanetOut: HIV & AIDS Resource Area

PNO ARTS — PlanetOut

PNO BI — PlanetOut: Bisexual Community

PNO BISEXUAL — PlanetOut: Bisexual Community

PNO BOYSTOWN — PlanetOut: Men's Community

PNO COMMUNITIES — PlanetOut: Community

PNO COMMUNITY — PlanetOut: Community

PNO FANTASYMAN — PlanetOut: FantasyMan Island

PNO FETISH — PlanetOut: Leather Community

PNO FMI LOCAL — PlanetOut: FantasyMan Island

PNO GAY MEN — PlanetOut: Men's Community

PNO HEALTH — PlanetOut

PNO HIV — PlanetOut: HIV & AIDS Resource Area

PNO LEATHER — PlanetOut: Leather Community

PNO LESBIAN — PlanetOut: Women's Community

PNO LIVE — PlanetOut

PNO MAN OF THE WEEK — PlanetOut: FantasyMan Island

PNO MEN — PlanetOut: Men's Community

PNO MILITARY M4M — PlanetOut: Military M4M

PNO TRANS — PlanetOut: Transland
PNO TRANSEXUAL — PlanetOut: Transland
PNO TRAVEL — PlanetOut: Travel
PNO US — PlanetOut
PNO WOMEN — PlanetOut: Women's Community
PNO YOUNG AND RESTLESS — PlanetOut: Youth Community
PNO YOUTH — PlanetOut: Youth Community
POA — AOL Member Services: AOL Update
POET — Writers Club: Poetry Place
POETRY PLACE — Writers Club: Poetry Place
POI — AOL Influence: Person of Influence
POINT — AOL Rewards
POINTS — AOL Rewards
POINTS BALANCE — AOL Rewards
POINTS PROGRAM — AOL Rewards
POKER — Online Casino
POKER WORLD — Online Casino
POL HOURLY — AOL News: Politics News Summary
POL NEWS — AOL News: Politics
POL TALK — AOL News: Politics
POL UPDATE — AOL News: Politics News Summary
POLAND — AOL International: Poland
POLARFREE — AOL Canada: Arctic Journal
POLARIS — Polaris Grant Center/Mac Education Forum
POLAROID — Parent Soup: Polaroid and Parenting
POLI AP — AOL News: More Politics News
POLI REUTERS — AOL News: More Politics News
POLICE — Public Safety Center
POLICY REVIEW — Heritage Foundation
POLITES FLORIST — Digital City Philadelphia: Polites Florist
POLITICAL — AOL News: Politics News
POLITICAL COMIC — AOL News: The Back Page Cartoon
POLITICAL INSITE — Digital City San Francisco: Politics and Power
POLITICS — AOL News: Politics News
POLITICS FEED — AOL News: More Politics News
POLITICS HOURLY — AOL News: Politics News Summary
POLITICS ONQ — onQ: News
POLITICS SUMMARY — AOL News: Politics News Summary
POLITICS UPDATE — AOL News: Politics News Summary
POLITICS WIRE — AOL News: More Politics News
POLL ONQ — onQ: Poll
POLL PHILLY — Digital City Philadelphia: Poll
POLO SPORT — Ralph Lauren Fragrance
POLSKA — AOL International: Poland
PONDEROSA — Digital City Denver: Ponderosa Realty & Property

PONDEROSA REALTY — Digital City Denver: Ponderosa Realty & Property

POOL — Engage: Virtual Pool

POP — AOL Entertainment: Rock/Pop

POP MUSIC — AOL Entertainment: Rock/Pop

POP PHOTO — Popular Photography

POP ROCK — AOL Entertainment: Rock/Pop

POP SCI — Popular Science [Web site]

POP SCI AUTO — Popular Science: Auto [Web site]

POP SCI HOME — Popular Science: Home Tech [Web site]

POP SCI HOME TECH — Popular Science: Home Tech [Web site]

POP SCI SCIENCE — Popular Science: Science [Web site]

POPE — Catholic Community

POPULAR PHOTOGRAPHY — Popular Photography

POPULAR SCIENCE — Popular Science [Web site]

POPULAR SHAREWARE — AOL Computing: Most Popular Software Titles

POPULAR SOFTWARE — AOL Computing: Most Popular Software Titles

PORK — Pork Online

PORT DIR — Portfolio Direct

PORT GUIDE — AOL Personal Finance: Guide to Portfolios

PORT HELP — AOL Personal Finance: Guide to Portfolios

PORT TRAK — Motley Fool: PortTrak

PORTFOLIO — Stock Portfolio Summary

PORTFOLIO DIRECT — Portfolio Direct

PORTFOLIO GUIDE — AOL Personal Finance: Guide to Portfolios

PORTFOLIO ONQ — onQ: Business

PORTLAND — Digital City Portland: WebGuide [Web site]

PORTLAND LOCAL NEWS — Digital City Portland: Local News

PORTLAND NEWS — Digital City Portland: Local News

PORTUGAL — AOL International: Portugal

POS GEN — AOL UK: Positive Generation

POSITIVE GENERATION — AOL UK: Positive Generation

POSITIVE LIVING — onQ: HIV

POSITIVE ONQ — onQ: Positive Living

POST OFFICE — AOL Mail Center

POSTCARD — American Greetings Online Greetings

POSTCARDS — American Greetings Online Greetings

POSTMASTER — Postmaster Online

POV — AOL Computing: 3D Rendering

POV-TRACE — AOL Computing: 3D Rendering

POWDER BURN — Digital City Washington: Powder Burn Skiing

POWER BALL — AOL News: Lottery Results by State

POWER BROKERS — AOL Influence: Media and Money

POWER EQUIPMENT — American Woodworker: Tool Reviews

POWER STATION — Paragon Online [Web site]

POWER SURGE@THRIVE — Thrive@Healthy Living: Power Surge
    Menopause Support Group
POWER TOOLS — American Woodworker: Tool Reviews
POWERBOATS — AOL Interests: Boating & Sailing
POWERBOOK — AOL Computing: Mac Hardware/OS
POWERMAC — AOL Computing: Mac Hardware/OS
POWERSUITE — AOL Store: PowerSuite
PP AD — AOL Personal Publisher: Athlete Direct
PP AVIATION — AOL Personal Publisher: Aviation Sites
PP COLLECTING — AOL Personal Publisher: Collecting Sites
PP FAMILY — AOL Personal Publisher: Family Sites
PP GRAPHICS — AOL Personal Publisher: Graphic Resource Sites
PP HELP — Web Publishing Help Central
PP MELROSE — AOL Personal Publisher: Melrose Sites
PP MUSIC ALT — AOL Personal Publisher: Music/Alternative Sites
PP SKI — AOL Personal Publisher: Ski Zone Sites
PP WHEELS — AOL Personal Publisher: Wheels Sites
PP WWF — AOL Personal Publisher: WWF Sites
PP X FILES — AOL Personal Publisher: X-Files Sites
PP2 — AOL Personal Publisher
PP2 HELP — Web Publishing Help Central
PPL — AOL International: Passport To Love
PPV — Digital City Washington: Media General Cable Pay Per View
PPYB — AOL Personal Publisher
PR — Princeton Review [Web site]
PR CHRONIC — Pain Relief Center: Chronic Pain
PR CHRONIC FATIGUE — Pain Relief Center: Fibromyalgia/CFIDS
PR FIBROMYALGIA — Pain Relief Center: Fibromyalgia/CFIDS
PR HEADACHES — Pain Relief Center: Headaches
PRAGUE — Time Out's Guide to Prague [Web site]
PRAIRIE — The Prairie Group [Web site]
PRAYER NET — Christianity Online: The Prayer Network
PRC — Pain Relief Center
PREAKNESS — ABC Sports: Triple Crown
PREFERED MAIL — AOL Mail Center: Junk Mail
PREFERRED MAIL — AOL Mail Center: Junk Mail
PREGNANCY — AOL Health: Pregnancy
PREGNANT — AOL Health: Pregnancy
PREMIERE — Premiere Magazine Online
PREMIERE MAGAZINE — Premiere Magazine Online
PREMIUM — AOL Games: Games Guide
PREMIUM AREA — AOL Games: Games Guide
PREMIUM CHARGES — AOL Games: Games Guide
PREMIUM GAMES — AOL Games: Games Guide
PREMIUM PRICING — AOL Games: Games Guide
PREMIUM SERVICES — AOL Games: Games Guide

PRENTICE HALL — Simon & Schuster College Online
PRESENTING — Presenting New AOL Channels
PRESIDENT — AOL News: Bill Clinton News Special
PRESIDENT CLINTON — AOL News: Bill Clinton News Special
PRESIDENTIAL SUMMIT — Digital City Philadelphia: Presidential Summit [Web site]
PRESIDENTS SUMMIT — Digital City Philadelphia: Presidential Summit [Web site]
PRESLEY HOMES — Digital City Los Angeles: Presley Home Developments
PRESS — America Online Press Releases
PRESS ONQ — onQ: Media
PRESS RELEASE — America Online Press Releases
PRESTIGE — AOL Influence channel
PREVIEW — AOL Software Preview
PREVIEW 4.0 — AOL Software Preview
PREVIEW TRAVEL — Preview Travel
PREVIEW TRAVEL NEWS — Preview Travel: News
PREVIEW VACATIONS — Preview Travel: Vacations
PRICELINE — Priceline.com
PRICING — AOL Member Services: Account & Billing
PRIDE ONQ — onQ: Pride Press
PRIDE PRESS — onQ: Pride Press
PRIDE RUN — AOL Canada: Pride and Remembrance Run
PRILOSEC — Prilosec: Frequent Heartburn Sufferers Community
PRIME HELP — AOL PrimeHost: Online Support
PRIME WEB — AOL PrimeHost
PRIMEHOST — AOL PrimeHost
PRIMETIME LIVE — ABC News.com [Web site]
PRINCE — AOL International: Royalty Forum
PRINCESS — AOL International: Royalty Forum
PRINCESS DI — AOL International: Royalty Forum
PRINCESS DIANA — AOL International: Royalty Forum
PRINCETON — Princeton Review [Web site]
PRINCETON REVIEW — Princeton Review [Web site]
PRINT ARTIST — AOL Computing: Print Artist
PRINT SHOP — AOL WorkPlace: Printers & Print Shops
PRINT SHOP CONNECTION — Broderbund: The Print Shop Connection
PRINTER — AOL Computing: Printer Knowledge Base
PRINTER RESOURCE — AOL Computing: Printer Knowledge Base
PRINTERS — AOL Computing: Printer Knowledge Base
PRINTWEASELS — AOL Canada: PrintWeasels
PRISM ELITE — Prism Elite Software
PRO BASKETBALL — AOL Sports: Pro Basketball
PRO BASKETBALL SCOREBOARD — AOL Sports: NBA Scores
PRO BASKETBALL SCORES — AOL Sports: NBA Scores

PRO BASKETBALL STARS — AOL Sports: Pro Basketball Stars
PRO FOOTBALL — AOL Sports: Pro Football
PRO FOOTBALL GD — Pro Football Game Day
PRO FOOTBALL SCOREBOARD — AOL Sports: NFL Scores
PRO FOOTBALL SCORES — AOL Sports: NFL Scores
PRO FOOTBALL STARS — AOL Sports: Pro Football Stars
PRO HOOPS — AOL Sports: Pro Basketball
PRODUCTIVITY — AOL Computing: Productivity Applications
PRODUCTIVITY FORUM — AOL Computing: Productivity Applications
PROF DOSH — AOL UK: Prof Dosh
PROFESSION — AOL WorkPlace: Professional Forums
PROFESSIONAL FORUMS — AOL WorkPlace: Professional Forums
PROFESSIONS — AOL WorkPlace: Professional Forums
PROFILE — AOL Member Directory
PROFILES — AOL Member Directory
PROGRAMMER U — AOL Computing: Programmer University
PROGRAMMING — AOL Computing: PC Development
PROMISE C — Christianity Online: Promise Checks
PROMISE CHECKS — Christianity Online: Promise Checks
PROPERTY MANAGE — AOL WorkPlace: Property Management
    Community
PROPERTY MGMT — AOL WorkPlace: Property Management
    Community
PROSTATE CANCER — AOL Health: Prostate Cancer
PROSTATE DISORDERS — AOL Health: Prostate Disorders Forum
PROTFOLIO WATCH — AOL Member Services: Keep an Eye on
    Investments
PROVIDENCE — Digital City Providence
PROVIDENCE LOCAL NEWS — Digital City Providence: Local News
PROVIDENCE NEWS — Digital City Providence: Local News
PRTMD — Pain Relief Center: Temporomandibular Disorder
PRTMJ — Pain Relief Center: Temporomandibular Disorder
PRUDENTIAL — Prudential Insurance Center
PS — Parent Soup
PS AL GORE — Parent Soup: Al Gore
PS AMERICAN BABY — Parent Soup: American Baby
PS BABIES — Parent Soup: Babies
PS BABY & TODDLER — Parent Soup: Baby & Toddler
PS CHILL — Parent Soup: Chill Out
PS DRUG FREE — Parent Soup: Drug Free
PS ED CENTRAL — Parent Soup: Education Central
PS EDUCATION — Parent Soup: Education Central
PS EXPECTING — Parent Soup Expecting Parents
PS EXPERTS — Parent Soup: Experts
PS FAMILY COUNSELOR — Parent Soup: Ask the Eliums
PS FAMILY COUNSELORS — Parent Soup: Ask the Eliums

PS FATHER — Parent Soup: Father's Day [seasonal]
PS FATHERS — Parent Soup: Father's Day [seasonal]
PS FUN — Parent Soup: Chill Out
PS FUN AND GAMES — Parent Soup: Chill Out
PS GAMES — Parent Soup: Chill Out
PS GI — Parent Soup: Gut Instinct Quiz
PS GRADE — Parent Soup: Making the Grade
PS JOIN — Parent Soup: Family Profiles
PS LA LECHE LEAGUE — Parent Soup: La Leche League
PS MESSAGES — Parent Soup: Message Boards
PS NEWSFLASH — Parent Soup: News Flash
PS PARENTS CONNECT — Parent Soup: Connection
PS QUIZ — Parent Soup: Gut Instinct Quiz
PS SCHOOL — Parent Soup: Parents of School-Age Children
PS SCHOOL SPIRIT — Parent Soup: School Spirit
PS SCHOOL YEARS — Parent Soup: School Years
PS SOFTWARE — Parent Soup: Software Library
PS SPOOKY — Parent Soup: Spooky Soup [seasonal]
PS SUMMER — Parent Soup: Summer Solstice [seasonal]
PS TEEN YEARS — Parent Soup: Teen Years
PS TEENS — Parent Soup: Teens
PS TODDLERS — Parent Soup: Toddlers
PSA — Public Safety Center
PSC — Public Safety Center
PSC CLUB — Public Safety Center: Registration
PSC HQ — Public Safety Center: Registration
PSCP — ParaScope
PSE — Pacific Stock Exchange [Web site]
PSORIASIS — AOL Health: Psoriasis
PSUITE — AOL Store: PowerSuite
PSX — Pro Sports Xchange -or- PlayStation Fortress
PSYCH — AOL Health: Mental Health
PSYCH LOCATOR — Online Psych: Locator
PSYCH ONLINE — Online Psych
PSYCHOLOGY — AOL Health: Mental Health
PT — Parsons Technology
PTC — AOL Computing: Telecom & Networking
PTWJ — Electra: Plain Talk with Jane
PU — AOL Computing: Programmer University
PUBLIC RADIO — National Public Radio Outreach
PUBLICATIONS — AOL News: Newsstand
PUBLISH YOUR WEB SITE — AOL Member Services: Create a Web Site
    in a Minute
PUBLISHER — AOL WorkPlace: Publishing
PUBLISHERS — AOL WorkPlace: Publishing
PUERTO RICO — AOL International: Puerto Rico

PULP — Reebok
PULSE — Pulse Online
PULSE MAGAZINE — Pulse Online
PULSE OF AOL — AOL Member Services: AOL Update
PULSE ONLINE — Pulse Online
PULSE! — Pulse Online
PURCHASE SURVEY — AOL Rewards: Survey
PURIM — Jewish Community: Purim
PYRAMID — WorldPlay: Schwa Pyramid
Q101 — Digital City Chicago: WKQX-FM Q101 Radio Online
QATAR — AOL International: Qatar
QB — Real Fans: Armchair Quarterback
QB1 — NTN Trivia: QB1
QFN — Intuit
QMILITARY — onQ: Military
QOTD — Sports Trivia Question of the Day
QRG — AOL Quick Reference Guide
QT — AOL Computing: Mac Animation & Video
QUAKE CLANS — Gibbed.Com Gamesite Hosting [Web site]
QUAKE NEWS — Gibbed.Com Gamesite Hosting [Web site]
QUANTUM GROUP — the.quantum.group [Web site]
QUARK — Quark
QUARTERLY REVIEW — Sage: Mutual Fund Quarterly Review
QUATTRO — AOL Computing: Spreadsheet Forum
QUE — People Connection: Quantum Que
QUEEN — AOL International: Royalty Forum
QUEEN'S PARK GRAND PRIX — AOL Canada: Queen's Park Grand Prix
QUEER MARRIAGE — onQ: Marriage
QUEST FOR THE CUP — Digital City Philadelphia: Flyers Cup Coverage
QUEST TENTS — Backpacker Magazine: Marketplace
QUEST TEST — AOL Kids Only: Quest Test
QUESTION OF THE DAY — Sports Trivia Question of the Day
QUESTIONS — AOL Member Services
QUICK CAM HQ — Connectix Corporation
QUICK FIXES — Internet Connection: QuickFixes
QUICK GIFT — AOL Shopping: Quick Gifts
QUICK GIFTS — AOL Shopping: Quick Gifts
QUICK MENU — Quick Menu for New Members
QUICK REFERENCE — AOL Quick Reference Guide
QUICK REFERENCE GUIDE — AOL Quick Reference Guide
QUICK START — AOL Member Services: QuickStart
QUICKCAM — Connectix Corporation
QUICKEN — Intuit
QUICKEN FINANCIAL NETWORK — Intuit
QUICKTIME — AOL Computing: Mac Animation & Video
QUICKVERSE — Parsons Technology

QUIK MENU — Quick Menu for New Members
QUILT — AOL Interests: Quilters Online Forum
QUILTERS — AOL Interests: Quilters Online Forum
QUILTING — AOL Interests: Quilters Online Forum
QUIOSCODE PERIODICOS — AOL International: Newsstand
QUOTE — AOL Personal Finance: Quotes & Portfolios
QUOTES — AOL Personal Finance: Quotes & Portfolios
QUOTES BETA — AOL Personal Finance: Quotes & Portfolios
QURL — onQ: The Queer Resource Locator [Web site]
QVC — iQVC Shopping [Web site]
R & L MATH — AOL Research & Learn: Math
R AND B — AOL Entertainment: R&B/Rap
R HUNTER — The Grateful Dead Forum: Robert Hunter Focus
R SLAM — Redskins Slam
R&B — AOL Entertainment: R&B/Rap
R&B MUSIC — AOL Entertainment: R&B/Rap
R&E — Religion & Ethics Forum
R&L ENVIRONMENT — AOL Research & Learn: Environmental &
    Nature
R&T — Road & Track Online
RABBITJACKS — RabbitJack's Casino
RABBITJACKS CASINO — RabbitJack's Casino
RABIES — AOL Health: Rabies
RACE CARS — AOL Sports: Auto Racing
RACE RELATION — Race Relations
RACE RELATIONS — Race Relations
RACING — AOL Sports: Auto Racing
RACING STARS — AOL Sports: Auto Racing Stars
RADIO 91X — Digital City San Diego: 91x
RADIO COMMUNICATION — The Ham Radio Forum
RADIO COMMUNICATIONS — The Ham Radio Forum
RADSL — xDSL Field Trial
RAGU — Food & Drink Network: Ragu
RAILROADING — AOL Interests: Scale Models
RAISING HEALTHY BABIES — AOL Health: Raising Health Babies
RALEIGH — Digital City Raleigh-Durham
RALEIGH LOCAL NEWS — Digital City Raleigh-Durham: Local News
RALEIGH NEWS — Digital City Raleigh-Durham: Local News
RALPH LAUREN — Ralph Lauren Fragrance
RALPH LAUREN FRAGRANCES — Ralph Lauren Fragrance
RAMADAN — AOL Lifestyles: Islam
RAMADHAN — AOL Lifestyles: Islam
RAMDOUBLER — Connectix Corporation
RANDOM — Random Keyword Roulette
RANGERS — Texas Rangers
RAP — AOL Entertainment: R&B/Rap

RAPTORS — Toronto Raptors
RATHER BE BOATING — Rather Be Boating
RATITE — AOL Interests: Pets
RAW — World Wrestling Federation Online
RAYTRACE — AOL Computing: 3D Rendering
RBB — Rather Be Boating
RDI — AOL Games: Free-Form Gaming Forum
RE CLASSIFIEDS — AOL Classifieds: Real Estate
RE/MAX — Digital City Philadelphia: RE/MAX
REACH THE BEACH — Digital City Washington: Guide to The Eastern
    Shore
REACHOUT — AOL Neighborhood Watch
REACHOUT ZONE — AOL Neighborhood Watch
READ MY BOARDS — Message Boards for Offline Reading
READING — AOL Research & Learn: Reading & Writing
READINGS — Horoscope Selections
REAL DEAL — AOL Shopping: Bargain Basement
REAL ESTATE — AOL Personal Finance: Real Estate Center
REAL ESTATE CLASSIFIEDS — Real Estate Classifieds
REAL ESTATE DESK — AOL Personal Finance: Real Estate Desk
REAL FANS — Real Fans Sports Network
REAL HITS — AOL UK: Charts
REAL LIFE — MoneyWhiz
REBA WHAT IF — Reba What If at Thanksgiving [seasonal]
REBECCA ST JAMES — Forefront Records: Rebecca St. James
REBECCA ST. JAMES — Forefront Records: Rebecca St. James
REC FINANCING — AOL Personal Finance: Real Estate Center
REC LOOKING — AOL Personal Finance: Real Estate Center
REC MOVING — AOL Personal Finance: Real Estate Center
REC RENTING — AOL Personal Finance: Real Estate Center
REC SELLING — AOL Personal Finance: Real Estate Center
REC SKATE — AOL Grandstand: Roller/Inline Skating Forum
REC SKATING — AOL Grandstand: Roller/Inline Skating Forum
RECIPE — AOL Interests: Food
RECIPES — AOL Interests: Food
RECIPIES — AOL Interests: Food
RECORD CHRONICLE — Digital City Dallas-Fort Worth: Denton Record-
    Chronicle [Web site]
RECORD-CHRONICLE — Digital City Dallas-Fort Worth: Denton Record-
    Chronicle [Web site]
RECOVERY ONQ — onQ: Support & Recovery
RECREATION — AOL Sports channel
RECREATION SF — Digital City San Francisco: Outdoor Recreation
RECREATIONAL SKATING — AOL Grandstand: Roller/Inline Skating
    Forum
RED CARPET BUDDY — AOL Canada: Red Carpet to Buddy Lists

RED CARPET CACHE — AOL Canada: Red Carpet to Web Cache
RED CARPET FIND — AOL Canada: Red Carpet to AOL Find
RED CARPET FP — AOL Canada: Red Carpet to Favourite Places
RED CARPET HELP — AOL Canada: Red Carpet to Finding Help
RED CARPET IM — AOL Canada: Red Carpet to Instant Messages
RED CARPET KEY — AOL Canada: Red Carpet to Keywords
RED CARPET KEYWORDS — AOL Canada: Red Carpet to Keywords
RED CARPET MAIL — AOL Canada: Red Carpet to E-mail
RED CARPET NAMES — AOL Canada: Red Carpet to Screen Names
RED ORB — Broderbund: Red Orb Entertainment
RED ROCKET — Red Rocket [Web site]
RED SKINS NETWORK — Digital City Washington: WJFK Redskins
    Network Online
RED SKINS SLAM — Digital City Washington: Redskins Slam
RED SOX — Boston Red Sox
RED SOX BASEBALL — Boston Red Sox
RED STAR STATION — Digital City San Francisco: Red Star Station
    Creative Artists Forum
REDIAL — AOL Autodialer
REDIALER — AOL Autodialer
REDS — Cincinnati Reds
REDZONE — NESN Football
REEBOK ANTHEM — Reebok
REEBOK DMX — Reebok: DMX Series 2000
REF 50 — AOL Research & Learn: The Fifty States
REF ART — AOL Research & Learn: The Arts
REF COMPUTER — AOL Research & Learn: Computing
REF COMPUTING — AOL Research & Learn: Computing
REF CONSUMER — AOL Research & Learn: Consumer & Money Matters
REF CURRENT EVENT — AOL Research & Learn: Current Events
REF CURRENT EVENTS — AOL Research & Learn: Current Events
REF DICTIONARIES — AOL Research & Learn: Dictionaries
REF ENTERTAINMENT — AOL Research & Learn: Entertainment
REF FAMILY — AOL Research & Learn: Home & Family
REF GENERAL — AOL Research & Learn: More References
REF GEOGRAPHY — AOL Research & Learn: Geography & Maps
REF GOVERNMENT — AOL Research & Learn: Law & Government
REF HEALTH — AOL Research & Learn: Health
REF HISTORY — AOL Research & Learn: History
REF HOME — AOL Research & Learn: Home & Family
REF LEGAL — AOL Research & Learn: Legal Resources
REF LEISURE — AOL Research & Learn: Entertainment
REF LITERATURE — AOL Research & Learn: Reading & Writing
REF MATH — AOL Research & Learn: Math
REF MUSIC — The Arts
REF SCIENCE — AOL Research & Learn: Science

REF SEARCH — AOL Research & Learn: Search & Explore
REF SPORTS — AOL Research & Learn: Sports & Leisure
REF STATES — AOL Research & Learn: The Fifty States
REF TECHNOLOGY — AOL Research & Learn: Computing
REF TRAVEL — AOL Research & Learn: Geography & Maps
REF USA — AOL Research & Learn: The Fifty States
REFERENCE — AOL Research & Learn channel
REFERENCE BOOKSHELF — AOL Research & Learn: Bookshelf
REFERENCE CANADA — AOL Research & Learn: Bookshelf
REFERENCE DICTIONARIES — AOL Research & Learn: Dictionaries
REFERENCE GUIDE — AOL Quick Reference Guide
REFERENCE SEARCH — AOL Research & Learn: Search & Explore
REFLEX SYMPATHETIC DYSTROPHY SYNDROME — AOL Health: Reflex
    Sympathetic Dystrophy Syndrome
REFRESH — Change Your Billing Information
REFUND — AOL Access Refund Policy
REGIONAL RESOURCES — AOL Research & Learn: Regional Resources
REGISTERED RETIREMENT SAVINGS PLAN — AOL Canada: Registered
    Retirement Savings Plan
RELATED WORDS — Merriam-Webster Thesaurus
RELATIONSHIPS — AOL Health: Relationships & Sexuality
RELATIONSHIPS ONQ — onQ: Relationships
RELATIVITY — ABC Online: Relativity
RELIEF — Pain Relief Center
RELIGION & ETHICS — Religion & Beliefs: Humanism-Unitarianism
    Area
RELIGION NEWS — Christianity Online: Religion News Update
RELIGION ONQ — onQ: Spirituality
RELIX — Relix Records
RELIX RECORDS — Relix Records
REMAX — Digital City Philadelphia: RE/MAX
REMINDER — AOL Reminder Service
REMODEL — AOL Interests: Home & Garden
REMODELING — AOL Interests: Home & Garden
RENDER — AOL Computing: 3D Rendering
RENDERING — AOL Computing: 3D Rendering
RENEWAL — Motley Fool: Subscription Renewals
RENOVATE — AOL Interests: Home & Garden
RENT A CAR — AOL Travel: Car Rental Reservation Center
RENT NET — Rent Net Comprehensive Rental Listings [Web site]
RENTAL CAR — AOL Travel: Car Rental Reservation Center
RENTAL CARS — AOL Travel: Car Rental Reservation Center
RENTAL SOLUTIONS — Digital City San Francisco: Rental Solutions
REPRODUCTION — AOL Health: Reproduction & Sexual Health
REPUBLIC OF BURUNDI — AOL International: Burundi
REPUBLICA Y'U BURUNDI — AOL International: Burundi

REPUBLICAN — Republican National Committee [Web site]

REPUBLICANS — Republican National Committee [Web site]

RESEARCH & LEARN — AOL Research & Learn channel

RESEARCH — AOL Research & Learn channel

RESEARCH ZONE — Electric Library@AOL

RESERVATION — AOL Travel: Reservation Center

RESERVATIONS — AOL Travel: Reservation Center

RESOURCE BY LOCATION — AOL Research & Learn: Regional Resources

RESOURCES BY REGION — AOL Research & Learn: Regional Resources

RESTAURANTS SD — Digital City San Diego: Dining Guide

RESUMAIL — Digital City Dallas-Fort Worth: Resumail

RETAIL TOYS — AOL WorkPlace: Toy Shops' Community

RETAIL WORLD — Retail World Cartoons

RETARDATION — AOL Health: Mental Retardation

RETIREMENT — AOL Personal Finance: Advice & Planning Retire

RETURN OF THE JEDI — Digital City Philadelphia: Star Wars

REVIEW NEWSGROUPS — AOL NetFind: Search Newsgroups [Web site]

REVOLUTION SOCCER — New England Revolution Soccer

REWARD — AOL Rewards

REWARD POINTS — AOL Rewards

REWARD PROGRAM — AOL Rewards

REWARD TOWN — AOL Rewards

REWARDS — AOL Rewards

REWARDS PROGRAM — AOL Rewards

REWARDS PROGRAMS — AOL Rewards

RF — Real Fans Sports Network

RF AUDIO — Real Fans: Insight.com Bowl

RF BASEBALL — Real Fans: Baseball

RF BOARDS — Real Fans: Chat Rooms

RF BOBBY O — Real Fans: Boston Bruins Team Club

RF BOSSY — Real Fans: New York Islanders Team Club

RF BOWLS — Real Fans: Bowls

RF BRODEUR — Real Fans: New Jersey Devils Team Club

RF C HOOPS — Real Fans: College Basketball

RF CHAT — Real Fans: Chat Rooms

RF CHOMP — Real Fans: San Jose Sharks Team Club

RF CLUBS — Real Fans: Join Your Team Club

RF CONTENT — Real Fans: Index

RF CONTENTS — Real Fans: Index

RF CRISP — Real Fans: Tampa Bay Lightning Team Club

RF DIONNE — Real Fans: LA Kings Team Club

RF DRILL — Real Fans: One Minute Drill

RF ERIC — Real Fans: Philadelphia Flyers Team Club

RF EVENT — Real Fans: Insight.com Bowl

RF FANTASY — Real Fans: Fantasy Land

RF FUHR — Real Fans: St. Louis Blues Team Club
RF GAMEROOM — Real Fans: Gameroom
RF GAMES — Real Fans: Gameroom
RF GIACOMIN — Real Fans: New York Rangers Team Club
RF GILMOUR — Real Fans: Toronto Maple Leafs Team Club
RF GORDIE — Real Fans: Detroit Red Wings Team Club
RF GREAT ONE — Real Fans: Florida Team Club
RF HOCKEY — Real Fans: NHL Today
RF HULL — Real Fans: Phoenix Coyotes Team Club
RF INDEX — Real Fans: Index
RF JAGR — Real Fans: Pittsburgh Penguins Team Club
RF KEY — Real Fans: Keywords
RF KEYS — Real Fans: Keywords
RF KEYWORDS — Real Fans: Keywords
RF LABRE — Real Fans: Washington Capitals Team Club
RF LAFLEUR — Real Fans: Montreal Team Club
RF LANNY — Real Fans: Calgary Flames Team Club
RF LIVE — Real Fans: Insight.com Bowl
RF MIKITA — Real Fans: Chicago Blackhawks Team Club
RF MODANO — Real Fans: Dallas Stars Team Club
RF NBA — Real Fans: Pro Basketball
RF NHL — Real Fans: NHL Today
RF NIEDERMAYER — Real Fans: Florida Panthers Team Club
RF P HOOPS — Real Fans: Pro Basketball
RF PERREAULT — Real Fans: Buffalo Sabres Team Club
RF POLL — Real Fans: Polls
RF POLLS — Real Fans: Polls
RF POND — Real Fans: Mighty Ducks Team Club
RF QUINTON — Real Fans: Tampa Bay Devil Rays Team Club
RF RADIO — Real Fans: Insight.com Bowl
RF ROY — Real Fans: Colorado Avalanche Team Club
RF SCORE — Real Fans: Score Ticker
RF SCORE... — Real Fans: Score Ticker
RF SCORES — Real Fans: Score Ticker
RF SMYL — Real Fans: Vancouver Canucks Team Club
RF SPORTS — Real Fans Sports Network
RF SPORTSBAR — Real Fans: Sportsbar
RF STORE — Real Fans: Store
RF STORM — Real Fans: Carolina Hurricanes Team Club
RF SUPER BOWL — Real Fans: Playoffs and Super Bowl Area
RF TOP TEN — Real Fans: Gameroom
RF TRACKER — Real Fans: Score Ticker
RF TRAVIS — Real Fans: Arizona Diamondbacks Team Club
RF YASHIN — Real Fans: Ottawa Senators Team Club
RHEUMATIC FEVER — AOL Health: Rheumatic Fever
RIC EDELMAN — Ric Edelman: Your Financial Planner

RICHMOND LOCAL NEWS — Digital City Richmond: Local News
RICHMOND NEWS — Digital City Richmond: Local News
RICK EDELMAN — Ric Edelman: Your Financial Planner
RICKI LAKE — The Ricki Lake Show
RINCON LATINO — Digital City Dallas-Fort Worth: Hispanic
RISING RIVERS — AOL News: Flood Information Zone
RIVEN — Broderbund: Riven Sequel to MYST
RJ CASINO — RabbitJack's Casino
RJ DONOVAN — Digital City Boston: Theater Guy
RL ART — AOL Research & Learn: The Arts
RL ARTS — AOL Research & Learn: The Arts
RL BUSINESS — AOL Research & Learn: Business Forum
RL CONSUMER — AOL Research & Learn: Consumer & Money Matters
RL HEALTH — AOL Research & Learn: Health
RL LAW — AOL Research & Learn: Law & Government
RL LEGAL — AOL Research & Learn: Legal Resources
RL MUSIC — AOL Research & Learn: The Arts
RL SEARCH — AOL Research & Learn: Search & Explore
RL SPORTS — AOL Research & Learn: Sports & Leisure
RMB — Message Boards for Offline Reading
RNC — Republican National Committee [Web site]
RNN FAIRFIELD — Digital City New York: RNN Fairfield
RNN HUDSON VALLEY — Digital City New York: RNN Hudson Valley
RNN NORTH NJ — Digital City New York: New Jersey
RNN WESTCHESTER — Digital City New York: RNN Westchester
RNU — Religion News Update
ROAD & TRACK — Road & Track Online
ROAD — Road & Track Online
ROAD AND TRACK — Road & Track Online
ROAD TO COLLEGE — AOL Research & Learn: College Preparation
ROAD TRIP — AOL Road Trips
ROAD TRIPS — AOL Road Trips
ROANOKE — Digital City Roanoke
ROANOKE LOCAL NEWS — Digital City Roanoke: Local News
ROANOKE NEWS — Digital City Roanoke: Local News
ROAR — EXTRA: Roar
ROBERT HUNTER — The Grateful Dead Forum: Robert Hunter Focus
ROCHESTER — Digital City Rochester
ROCHESTER CITY NEWS — Digital City Rochester: Local News
ROCHESTER LOCAL NEWS — Digital City Rochester: News
ROCHESTER NEWS — Digital City Rochester: News
ROCK & ROLL — AOL Entertainment: Rock and Roll
ROCK — AOL Entertainment: Rock
ROCK AND ROLL — AOL Entertainment: Rock and Roll
ROCK CLIMBING — AOL Sports: Fitness
ROCK N ROLL — Hail Hail Rock and Roll

ROCKETS — Houston Rockets
ROCKIES — Colorado Rockies
ROCKTROPOLIS — Music Boulevard: Rocktropolis [Web site]
RODEO — AOL Grandstand: Rodeo MiniForum
RODMAN — Athlete Direct: Dennis Rodman
ROLEMASTER — Engage: Rolemaster Magestorm
ROLEPLAYING — AOL Games: Role Playing Games Forum
ROLLER BLADING — AOL Sports: Fitness
ROLLER DERBY — AOL Grandstand: Roller Derby Miniforum
ROLLER GAMES — AOL Grandstand: Roller Derby Miniforum
ROLLER HOCKEY — AOL Grandstand: Roller Hockey Miniforum
ROLLER SKATING — AOL Sports: Inline/Aggressive/Roller Skating
    Forum
ROLLING MEADOWS — Digital City Chicago: Rolling Meadows
    [Web site]
ROLLING STONE — Rolling Stone Online
ROMANCE — Romance channel
ROMANCE GROUP — Writers Club: Romance Group
ROMANCE NOVELS — Writers Club: Romance Group
ROMANCE TIMES — Writers Club: Romance Group
ROMANIA — AOL International: Romania
RON WYNN — Digital City Los Angeles: Ron Wynn's West Real Estate
RON'S TRAILS — Digital City Denver: Trail Guide
ROOFING CONTRACTOR — AOL WorkPlace: Contractor's Community
ROOTS — Genealogy Forum
ROSE BOWL — AOL Sports: Rose Bowl
ROSES — 1-800-FLOWERS
ROSH HASHANA — Rosh Hashanah [seasonal]
ROSH HASHANAH — Rosh Hashanah [seasonal]
ROSIE — Rosie O'Donnell Online
ROSIE ODONNELL — Rosie O'Donnell Online
ROSS SIMMONS — Ross-Simons [Web site]
ROSS SIMONS — Ross-Simons [Web site]
ROSS-SIMONS — Ross-Simons [Web site]
ROSS-SIMONS GIFTWORKS — 911 Gifts Online Store
ROSS-SIMONS HARRY AND DAVID — Harry and David [Web site]
ROSS-SIMONS JACKSON & PERKINS — Jackson & Perkins [Web site]
ROSS-SIMONS MICROWARHOUSE — MicroWarehouse [Web site]
ROSWELL — ParaScope: Anniversary of Roswell Crash
ROTO ZONE — Real Fans: Roto Zone
ROTUNDA — AOL Computing: Events
ROYALS — Kansas City Royals
ROZ — AOL Neighborhood Watch
RPG — AOL Games: Role Playing Games Forum
RPGA — RPGA Selections
RPGA NETWORK — AOL Games: Fellowship of Online Gamers

RPMC — AOL Travel: RPMC Event Travel
RRSP — AOL Canada: Registered Retirement Savings Plan
RRSP CHAT — AOL Canada: RRSP Chat
RS JAMES — Forefront Records: Rebecca St. James
RSDS — AOL Health: Reflex Sympathetic Dystrophy Syndrome
RSFL — AOL Grandstand: Simulation Football
RSJ — Forefront Records: Rebecca St. James
RSO — Rolling Stone Online
RSP — RSP Funding Focus
RSS — Digital City San Francisco: Red Star Station Creative Artists
　　Forum
RTB — Digital City Washington: Guide to The Eastern Shore
RUGBY — AOL Sports: More Sports
RUGBY CLUB — AOL UK: The Rugby Club
RUGBY UNION — AOL UK: The Rugby Club
RUN — AOL Sports: Running
RUNNER — AOL Sports: Running
RUNNER'S WORLD — Runner's World
RUNNERS WORLD — Runner's World
RUNNING — AOL Sports: Running
RUSS & STEVE — Digital City New York: The Sweater & the
　　Schmoozer
RUSSELL — Russell Grant's Stars
RUSSELL GRANT — Russell Grant's Stars
RUSSELLS STARS — Russell Grant's Stars
RUSSIA — AOL International: Russian Federation
RUSSIAN FEDERATION — AOL International: Russian
　　Federation
RW — Runner's World
RWANDA — AOL International: Rwanda
RX — Health & Vitamin Express
RYDER CUP — AOL Sports: Ryder Cup Coverage
RYOBI — Ryobi Tools
S & S — Simon & Schuster College Online
S ENGLAND — AOL UK: Southern England
S FAN BASEBALL — SportsFan: Baseball
S FAN COLLEGE B — SportsFan: College Basketball
S FAN COLLEGE F — Sports Fan: College Football
S FAN HOCKEY — SportsFan: Hockey
S FAN NBA — SportsFan: Basketball
S FAN NFL — SportsFan: Pro Football
S FAN OPINION — SportsFan: Opinion
S FAN PREGAME — SportsFan: Pre-Game Plus
S FAN WOMEN — SportsFan: Women's Sports
S JERSEY CHAT — Digital City Philadelphia: Chat Schedule
S TRIB — Minneapolis Star Tribune

S TRIB VOICES — Minneapolis Star Tribune Online: Voices
S&P PERSONAL WEALTH — S&P Personal Wealth [Web site]
S&P PW — S&P Personal Wealth [Web site]
S&P WEALTH — S&P Personal Wealth [Web site]
S&R ONQ — onQ: Support & Recovery
S&S BIOLOGY — Simon & Schuster College Online: Biology
S&S CRIMINAL JUSTICE — Simon & Schuster College Online: Criminal Justice
S&S ENGLISH — Simon & Schuster College Online: English
S&S MATH — Simon & Schuster College Online: Mathematics
S&S PHYS ED — Simon & Schuster College Online: Health, Phys Ed and Rec
S&S POLI SCI — Simon & Schuster College Online: Political Science
S&S SOCIAL WORK — Simon & Schuster College Online: Social Work
S&S SOCIOLOGY — Simon & Schuster College Online: Sociology & Anthropology
S.B.A. — U.S. Small Business Administration
S.D. POSTCARDS — Digital City San Diego: Postcards
SA — AOL Shoppers Advantage
SA BEST BUYS — AOL Shoppers Advantage: Best Buys
SA COMPUTER SUPERSTORE — AOL Shoppers Advantage: Computer Hardware
SA MED — Scientific American: Medical Publications
SA SPORTS SUPERSTORE — AOL Shoppers Advantage: Sports Superstore
SA SWEEPS — AOL Shoppers Advantage: Sweepstakes
SABRINA MATTHEWS — onQ: Sabrina Matthews
SAC KINGS — Sacramento Kings
SACRAMENTO — Digital City Sacramento
SACRAMENTO LOCAL NEWS — Digital City Sacramento: Local News
SACRAMENTO NEWS — Digital City Sacramento: Local News
SAF — Scientific American: Frontiers
SAFE IN THE SUN — AOL Health: Safe in the Sun
SAFEST KID — Digital City Atlanta: KidSafe
SAFEST KID ATLANTA — Digital City Atlanta: KidSafe
SAFEST KIDS — Digital City Atlanta: KidSafe
SAFETY — AOL Neighborhood Watch
SAFETY HELP — AOL Member Services: Online Safety & Security
SAFETY ONLINE — Safety Online with Dr Solomon
SAFEWARE — Safeware Online: Computer Insurance
SAGE — Sage: Making Sense of Mutual Funds
SAGE CHAT — Sage: Chat
SAGE SCHOOL — Sage: School
SAGE TALK — Sage: Chat
SAGITTARIUS — Horoscope Selections
SAIL — AOL Grandstand: Sailing Forum

SAILING — AOL Interests: Boating & Sailing
SAILING FORUM — AOL Grandstand: Sailing Forum
SALE — AOL Shopping: Bargain Basement
SALES & MARKETING — AOL WorkPlace: Sales & Marketing
SALON — Salon Magazine [Web site]
SALON MAGAZINE — Salon Magazine [Web site]
SALT LAKE CITY — Digital City Salt Lake City
SALT LAKE CITY LOCAL NEWS — Digital City Salt Lake City: Local News
SALT LAKE CITY NEWS — Digital City Salt Lake City: Local News
SALT WATER FISHING — Fishing Broadcast Network
SAM — Boxer*Jam's Strike-A-Match
SAM 2 — Boxer*Jam's Strike-A-Match
SAMOA — AOL International: Samoa
SAN ANTONIO — Digital City San Antonio: Local News
SAN ANTONIO LOCAL NEWS — Digital City San Antonio: Local News
SAN ANTONIO NEWS — Digital City San Antonio: Local News
SAN DEIGO NEWS — Digital City San Diego: KGTV Channel 10
SAN DIEGO — Digital City San Diego
SAN DIEGO ADVICE — Digital City San Diego: Dear Lisa
SAN DIEGO AUTOGUIDE — Digital City San Diego: AutoGuide
SAN DIEGO AUTOS — Digital City San Diego: AutoGuide
SAN DIEGO BASEBALL — Digital City San Diego: Andy Strasberg's
    Baseball-Itis
SAN DIEGO BIZ — Digital City San Diego: Business Matters
SAN DIEGO BUSINESS — Digital City San Diego: Business Matters
SAN DIEGO CAREERS — Digital City San Diego: Employment Classifieds
SAN DIEGO CARS — Digital City San Diego: AutoGuide
SAN DIEGO CHAT — Digital City San Diego: Chat
SAN DIEGO CLASSIFIEDS — Digital City San Diego: Employment
    Classifieds
SAN DIEGO COMICS — Digital City San Diego: Comics
SAN DIEGO DINING — Digital City San Diego: Dining Guide
SAN DIEGO ED — Digital City San Diego: Education Site
SAN DIEGO EMPLOYMENT — Digital City San Diego: Employment
    Classifieds
SAN DIEGO EVENTS — Digital City San Diego: Zoom Events
SAN DIEGO FUNNIES — Comics: Digital City San Diego
SAN DIEGO GARDEN — Digital City San Diego: Online Gardener
SAN DIEGO HACKSAW — Digital City San Diego: Hacksaw's Headlines
SAN DIEGO HOMES — Digital City San Diego: Real Estate
SAN DIEGO HOSTS — Digital City San Diego: Hosts
SAN DIEGO HOUSES — Digital City San Diego: Real Estate
SAN DIEGO INDEX — Digital City San Diego: Index
SAN DIEGO INSTAPOLL — Digital City San Diego: California Lottery
SAN DIEGO JOBS — Digital City San Diego: Employment Classifieds
SAN DIEGO KIDS — Digital City San Diego: KidSafe

SAN DIEGO LISA — Digital City San Diego: Dear Lisa
SAN DIEGO LOCAL NEWS — Digital City San Diego: Local News
SAN DIEGO LOTTO — Digital City San Diego: California Lottery
SAN DIEGO MAG — Digital City San Diego: Magazine
SAN DIEGO MAGAZINE — Digital City San Diego: Magazine
SAN DIEGO MOVIES — Digital City San Diego: MovieGuide
SAN DIEGO NEWS — Digital City San Diego: News
SAN DIEGO PADRES — San Diego Padres
SAN DIEGO PEOPLE — Digital City San Diego: People
SAN DIEGO PERSONAL — Digital City San Diego: Personals
SAN DIEGO POLL — Digital City San Diego: California Lottery
SAN DIEGO RELO — Digital City San Diego: Relocation Guide
SAN DIEGO RELOCATION — Digital City San Diego: Relocation Guide
SAN DIEGO RESTAURANTS — Digital City San Diego: Dining Guide
SAN DIEGO SCHOOLS — Digital City San Diego: Education Site
SAN DIEGO SHOPPING — Digital City San Diego: Marketplace
SAN DIEGO SKIING — Digital City San Diego: Ski Guide
SAN DIEGO SPORTS — Digital City San Diego: Sports
SAN DIEGO TELE — Digital City San Diego: TV Navigator
SAN DIEGO TOUR — Digital City San Diego: Tour
SAN DIEGO TOURISM — Digital City San Diego: Tour
SAN DIEGO TRAIL GUY — Digital City San Diego: Trail Guy
SAN DIEGO TRAILS — Digital City San Diego: Trail Guy
SAN DIEGO TRANSFER — Digital City San Diego: Relocation Guide
SAN DIEGO TRAVEL — Digital City San Diego: Tour
SAN DIEGO TV — Digital City San Diego: TV Navigator
SAN DIEGO YOUTH SPORTS — Digital City San Diego: Youth Sports
    Directory
SAN DIEGO'S 10 — Digital City San Diego: KGTV Channel 10
SAN FRAN GIANTS — San Francisco Giants: Pro Baseball
SAN FRANCISCO AUTOS — Digital City San Francisco: AutoGuide
SAN FRANCISCO CARS — Digital City San Francisco: AutoGuide
SAN FRANCISCO EL NINO — Digital City San Francisco: El Nino Guide
SAN FRANCISCO EMPLOYMENT — Digital City San Francisco:
    Employment
SAN FRANCISCO EVENTS — Digital City San Francisco: Entertainment
SAN FRANCISCO GAY PRIDE — Digital City San Francisco: Gay Pride
SAN FRANCISCO GIANTS — San Francisco Giants: Pro Baseball
SAN FRANCISCO KIDS — Digital City San Francisco: KidSafe
SAN FRANCISCO KIDS SAFE — Digital City San Francisco: KidSafe
SAN FRANCISCO LESBIAN BARS — Digital City San Francisco: Lesbian
    Bars
SAN FRANCISCO LOCAL NEWS — Digital City San Francisco: Local News
SAN FRANCISCO M4M — PlanetOut: FantasyMan Island for San
    Francisco
SAN FRANCISCO MIXSTAR — Digital City San Francisco: MixStar

SAN FRANCISCO NEWS — Digital City San Francisco: News

SAN FRANCISCO ONQ — onQ: San Francisco

SAN FRANCISCO RELO — Digital City San Francisco: Relocation Guide

SAN FRANCISCO RELOCATION — Digital City San Francisco: Relocation Guide

SAN FRANCISCO TRANSFER — Digital City San Francisco: Relocation Guide

SAN JOSE AUTO GUIDE — Digital City San Diego: AutoGuide

SAN JOSE CARS — Digital City San Diego: AutoGuide

SAN JOSE JAZZ — Digital City San Jose: Jazz Festival

SAN JOSE JAZZ FESTIVAL — Digital City San Jose: Jazz Festival

SAN JOSE PERSONALS — Digital City San Diego: Personals

SAN MARINO — AOL International: San Marino

SANDY BLOCK — Digital City Boston: Wine Guy

SANTA — Holidays@AOL [seasonal]

SANTA FE — Digital City Santa Fe

SANWA — Sanwa Bank

SANWA BANK — Sanwa Bank

SANWA BANK CALIFORNIA — Sanwa Bank

SANWA PC — Sanwa Bank

SANWHA — Sanwa Bank

SARAH MCLACHLAN — Sarah McLachlan Surfacing Contest

SARAH MCLACHLAN CONTEST — Sarah McLachlan Surfacing Contest

SARCOIDOSIS — AOL Health: Sarcoidosis

SAT — KAPLAN Online -or- The Princeton Review

SATELLITE SOUL — Forefront Records: Satellite Soul

SATURDAY NIGHT — ABC Online: Saturday Night [Web site]

SATURN — Saturn Corporation [Web site]

SATURN OF SANTA CLARITA — Digital City Los Angeles: Saturn of Santa Clarita!

SATURN OF THE VALLEY — Digital City Los Angeles: Saturn of Santa Clarita!

SAUDI ARABIA — AOL International: Saudi Arabia

SAVINGS — AOL Shopping: Deal of the Day

SAVINGS CLUB — AOL Savings Clubs

SB PERSONALS — Digital City San Diego: Personals

SBA — U.S. Small Business Administration

SCA — The History Channel's Living History Forum

SCALE MODELS — AOL Interests: Scale Models

SCAN IMAGE — Love@AOL: Photo Scanning

SCAN PHOTO — Love@AOL: Photo Scanning

SCANNERS — AOL Computing: Superstore

SCANNING — AOL Computing: Image Scanning

SCARE ME — ABC Online: Kidzine Halloween [seasonal]

SCHAUMBURG — Digital City Chicago: Schaumburg [Web site]

SCHOLARS — AOL Research & Learn: The Scholar's Hall

SCHOLAR'S HALL — AOL Research & Learn: The Scholar's Hall
SCHOLARS' HALL — AOL Research & Learn: The Scholar's Hall
SCHOLARS HALL — AOL Research & Learn: The Scholar's Hall
SCHOLARSHIPS — AOL Research & Learn: Financial Aid
SCHOLASTIC — Scholastic Network
SCHOOL DAYS — AOL Shopping: Back To School Sale [seasonal]
SCHOOLHOUSE — The Electronic Schoolhouse
SCHUT — The AOL Greenhouse
SCHWA — WorldPlay: SCHWA Pyramid
SCHWA PYRAMID — WorldPlay: SCHWA Pyramid
SCHWAB — Charles Schwab Online
SCHWAB ONLINE — Charles Schwab Online
SCHWARZ — FAO Schwarz
SCI AM — Scientific American
SCI FI CHANNEL — The SciFi Channel [Web site]
SCI FI ZONE — Entertainment Asylum: Sci Fi Zone
SCI FI ZONE CHAT — Entertainment Asylum: Sci-Fi Zone Chat
SCIENCE — AOL Research & Learn: Science
SCIENCE FAIR — AOL Research & Learn: Science Fair Central
SCIENCE FAIR CENTRAL — AOL Research & Learn: Science Fair Central
SCIENCE FAIRS — AOL Research & Learn: Science Fair Central
SCIENCE PLACE — Digital City Dallas-Fort Worth: Science Place
    Museum
SCIENCE PROJECT — AOL Research & Learn: Science Fair Central
SCIENCE REFERENCE — AOL Research & Learn: Science and Math
    Reference
SCIENTIFIC AMERICAN — Scientific American
SCI-FI ZONE — Entertainment Asylum: Sci-Fi Zone
SCOOP — AOL NetFind: Search Newsgroup [Web site]
SCOOP FIND — AOL NetFind: Search Newsgroup [Web site]
SCOOP FINDER — AOL NetFind: Search Newsgroup [Web site]
SCOPE — ParaScope
SCORE! — Love@AOL: Virtual Dating Game
SCOREBOARD — AOL Sports: Scoreboard
SCOREBOARDS — AOL Sports: Scoreboards
SCORPIO — Horoscope Selections
SCOTLAND — AOL International: Scotland
SCOUNDREL — Villains of Fact & Fiction
SCOUNDRELS — Villains of Fact & Fiction
SCOUTING — AOL Families: Scouting Forum
SCOUTS — AOL Families: Scouting Forum
SCP — Digital City San Francisco: Sports channel
SCPA-LA — Society for the Prevention of Cruelty to Animals
SCRAPBOOK — Creative Scrapbooking
SCREEN NAME — Create/Delete Screen Names
SCREEN NAMES — Create/Delete Screen Names

SCREEN TEAM — Entertainment Asylum: Screen Team
<u>SCREENAME</u> — Create/Delete Screen Names
<u>SCREENAMES</u> — Create/Delete Screen Names
SCUBA — AOL Scuba Forum
SCUBA FORUM — AOL Scuba Forum
SCUDDER — Scudder
<u>SCWIEZ</u> — AOL International: Switzerland
SD — Digital City San Diego
SD AUTO — Digital City San Diego: AutoGuide
SD AUTOGUIDE — Digital City San Diego: AutoGuide
SD BICYCLING — Digital City San Diego: Guy
SD BIZ — Digital City San Diego: Business Matters
SD BLAIR — Digital City San Diego: Tom Blair
SD BUSINESS — Digital City San Diego: Business Matters
SD BUSINESS MATTERS — Digital City San Diego: Business Matters
SD CARS — Digital City San Diego: AutoGuide
SD CARTOONS — Digital City San Diego: Comics
SD CHAT — Digital City San Diego: Chat
SD CHATS — Digital City San Diego: Chat
SD COMICS — Digital City San Diego: Comics
SD COMM — Digital City San Diego: People
SD COMMUNITY — Digital City San Diego: Community
SD DEAR LISA — Digital City San Diego: Dear Lisa
SD DIGITAL CITY — Digital City San Diego
SD DINING — Digital City San Diego: Dining Guide
SD ED — Digital City San Diego: Education Site
SD EDUCATION — Digital City San Diego: Education Site
SD EMPLOYMENT — Digital City San Diego: Jobs/Employment
SD ENTERTAINMENT — Digital City San Diego: Entertainment
SD EVENTS — Digital City San Diego: Zoom
SD FIND — Digital City San Diego: Index
SD FIND IT — Digital City San Diego: Index
SD FUN — Digital City San Diego: Entertainment
SD FUNNIES — Digital City San Diego: Comics
SD FUNNY — Digital City San Diego: Comics
SD GARDEN — Digital City San Diego: Online Gardener
SD HACKSAW — Digital City San Diego: Hacksaw's Headlines
SD HIKE — Digital City San Diego: Guy
SD HOMES — Digital City San Diego: Real Estate
SD HOSTS — Digital City San Diego: Hosts
SD HOUSES — Digital City San Diego: Real Estate
SD INDEX — Digital City San Diego: Index
SD INSTAPOLL — Digital City San Diego: California Lottery
SD JOBS — Digital City San Diego: Jobs/Employment
SD KID SPORTS — Digital City San Diego: Youth Sports Directory
SD KIDS SPORTS — Digital City San Diego: Youth Sports Directory

SD LISA — Digital City San Diego: Dear Lisa
SD LOCAL NEWS — Digital City San Diego: Local News
SD LOTTERY — Digital City San Diego: California Lottery
SD LOTTO — Digital City San Diego: California Lottery
SD MAG — Digital City San Diego: Magazine
SD MAGAZINE — Digital City San Diego: Magazine
SD MARKET — Digital City San Diego: Marketplace
SD MARKETPLACE — Digital City San Diego: Marketplace
SD MOVIES — Digital City San Diego: MovieGuide
SD NEIGHBORS — Digital City San Diego: Community
SD NEWS — Digital City San Diego: News
SD PEOPLE — Digital City San Diego: People
SD PERSONALS — Digital City San Diego: Personals
SD POLL — Digital City San Diego: California Lottery
SD POSTCARDS — Digital City San Diego: Postcards
SD REAL ESTATE — Digital City San Diego: Real Estate
SD RESTAURANTS — Digital City San Diego: Dining Guide
SD SHOPPING — Digital City San Diego: Marketplace
SD SKI — Digital City San Diego: Ski Guide
SD SKIING — Digital City San Diego: Ski Guide
SD SNOW — Digital City San Diego: Ski Guide
SD SPORTS — Digital City San Diego: Sports
SD TELE — Digital City San Diego: TV Navigator
SD TELEVISION — Digital City San Diego: TV Navigator
SD TOUR — Digital City San Diego: Tour
SD TOURISM — Digital City San Diego: Tour
SD TRAILS — Digital City San Diego: Guy
SD TRAVEL — Digital City San Diego: Tour
SD TRAVEL GROUP — Digital City San Diego: San Diego Travel
SD TV — Digital City San Diego: TV Navigator
SD TV GUIDE — Digital City San Diego: TV Navigator
SD WEATHER — Digital City San Diego: News
SD YOUTH SPORTS — Youth Sports Directory of San Diego
SD YS — Youth Sports Directory of San Diego
SDJ — Forefront Records: Seven Day Jesus
SDSL — xDSL Field Trial
SEA & SKI — AOL Classifieds: Sea & Ski Getaways
SEA AND SKI — AOL Classifieds: Sea & Ski Getaways
SEAFOOD MARKET — Hickory Farms: Seafood Market
SEARCH — AOL Find
SEARCH AOL LIVE — Search AOL Live
SEARCH COMPUTING — AOL Computing: Search and Explore
SEARCH EMAIL — AOL NetFind: Email Finder [Web site]
SEARCH ENTERTAINMENT — AOL Entertainment: Search & Explore
SEARCH EVENTS — Search AOL Live
SEARCH GAMES — AOL Games: Search & Explore

SEARCH GUESTS — Search AOL Live
SEARCH HELP — AOL Member Services: Using Search & Find
SEARCH INFLUENCE — AOL Influence: Search and Explore
SEARCH LIFESTYLES — AOL Lifestyles: Search & Explore
SEARCH MARKETPLACE — AOL Shopping: Search
SEARCH MS — AOL Entertainment: Music Search [Web site]
SEARCH MUSIC — AOL Entertainment: Music Search [Web site]
SEARCH MUSICSPACE — AOL Entertainment: Music Search [Web site]
SEARCH NEWS — AOL News: Search
SEARCH NEWSGROUPS — AOL NetFind: Search Newsgroups [Web site]
SEARCH ONQ — onQ: Channel Search
SEARCH PC — People Connection: Search Featured Chats
SEARCH PEOPLE CONNECTION — People Connection: Search Featured
   Chats
SEARCH PF — AOL Personal Finance: Search & Explore
SEARCH REF — AOL Research & Learn: Search & Explore
SEARCH REFERENCE — AOL Research & Learn: Search & Explore
SEARCH RL — AOL Research & Learn: Search & Explore
SEARCH SHAREWARE — AOL Computing: File Search
SEARCH SHOPPING — AOL Shopping: Search
SEARCH SPORTS — AOL Sports: Search & Explore
SEARCH TRAVEL — AOL Travel: Search & Explore
SEARS — STATS, Inc.
SEARS DIEHARD — STATS, Inc.
SEATTLE — Digital City Seattle
SEATTLE DIGITAL CITY — Digital City Seattle
SEATTLE LOCAL NEWS — Digital City Seattle: Local News
SEATTLE MARINERS — Seattle Mariners
SEATTLE NEWS — Digital City Seattle: Local News
SECOND CHANCE — Your Second Chance
SECOND CHANCES — Your Second Chance
SECRET — AOL Secrets
SECRETARYS DAY — AOL Shopping: Secretary's Day [seasonal]
SECRETARYS SHOP — AOL Shopping: Secretary's Day [seasonal]
SECRETARYS STORE — AOL Shopping: Secretary's Day [seasonal]
SECRETS — AOL Secrets
SECURITY — AOL Neighborhood Watch
SECURITY HELP — AOL Member Services: Online Safety & Security
SECURITY SERVICE — AOL WorkPlace: Security Services Community
SEGA — AOL Games: Video Games Forum
SELECT OFFERS — AOL Rewards: Select Offers
SELF EMPLOYED — AOL WorkPlace: Your Business
SELF HELP — AOL Lifestyles: Self Improvement
SELF IMPROVEMENT — AOL Lifestyles: Self Improvement
SELF-HELP — Self-Help Forum
SELL COMPUTER — AOL Computing: Classifieds

SEND A KISS — Love@AOL: Insta-Kiss
SENEGAL — AOL International: Senegal
SENIOR CONNECTION — Christianity Online: Senior Citizens
SENIOR HEALTH — AOL Health: Seniors' Health
SENIORNET — SeniorNet Online
SENIORS — AOL Lifestyles: Ages & Stages
SENIOR'S HEALTH — AOL Health: Seniors' Health
SENIORS HEALTH — AOL Health: Seniors' Health
SENTINEL — Sun Sentinel South Florida
SENTINEL FEATURES — Orlando Sentinel Online: Features
SERVENET — SERVEnet
SERVICE — AOL Member Services
SETON NOTES — Seton.noteS: News Commentary
SEVEN DAY JESUS — Forefront Records: Seven Day Jesus
SEVENTEEN — Seventeen Online
SEVENTEEN MAGAZINE — Seventeen Online
SEW — AOL Interests: Sewing
SEW NEWS — Sew News Magazine
SEWING — AOL Interests: Sewing
SEX — AOL Health: Relationships & Sexuality
SEX ADDICTION — AOL Health: Sex Addiction
SEX SF — Digital City San Francisco: The Couch
SEXUAL DYSFUNCTION — AOL Health: Sexual Dysfunction
SEXUAL HEALTH — AOL Health: Reproduction & Sexual Health
SEXUALITY — AOL Health: Relationships & Sexuality
SEYCHELLES — AOL International: Seychelles
SF APARTMENTS — Digital City San Francisco: Rent Tech
SF ASTROBYTES — Digital City San Francisco: Zodiac
SF ASTROLOGY — Digital City San Francisco: Astrobytes Daily
    Horoscopes
SF AUTOGUIDE — Digital City San Francisco: AutoGuide
SF AUTOS — Digital City San Francisco: AutoGuide
SF BAY AREA QUESTIONS — Digital City San Francisco: Questions
SF BAY KAHUNA — Digital City San Francisco: Questions
SF BRIDGES — Digital City San Francisco: WWWomen
SF CAR DEALS — Digital City San Francisco: Hot Deals
SF CAREERS — Digital City San Francisco: Employment Classifieds
SF CARS — Digital City San Francisco: AutoGuide
SF CLASSIFIEDS — Digital City San Francisco: Employment Classifieds
SF COMM — Digital City San Francisco: Community
SF COMMUNITY — Digital City San Francisco: Community
SF COMPUTER CURRENTS — Digital City San Francisco: Computer
    Currents
SF COMPUTERS — Digital City San Francisco: Computer Currents
SF CONTESTS — Digital City San Francisco: Fun & Games
SF COUCH — Digital City San Francisco: The Couch

SF CRITICAL MASS — Digital City San Francisco: Critical Mass
SF CURRENTS — Digital City San Francisco: Computer Currents
SF DATE — Digital City San Francisco: Dating Scene
SF DATING — Digital City San Francisco: Dating Scene
SF DINING — Digital City San Francisco: Dining Guide
SF DIVORCE — Digital City San Francisco: Divorce Chat
SF DIVORCE CHAT — Digital City San Francisco: Divorce Chat
SF EGG — Digital City San Francisco: Electronic Gourmet Guide
SF EL NINO — Digital City San Francisco: El Nino Guide
SF EMPLOYMENT — Digital City San Francisco: Employment Classifieds
SF ENTERTAINMENT — Digital City San Francisco: Entertainment
SF EVENTS — Digital City San Francisco: Entertainment
SF GAMES — Digital City San Francisco: Fun & Games
SF GAY — Digital City San Francisco: Gay Community
SF GAY CHAT — Digital City San Francisco: Gay & Lesbian Chat
SF GAY PRIDE — Digital City San Francisco: Gay Pride
SF GIANTS — Digital City San Francisco: Giants: Pro Baseball!
SF GOOF OFF — Digital City San Francisco: Fun & Games
SF GORP — Digital City San Francisco: Outdoor Recreation
SF HANG — Digital City San Francisco: Hangout
SF HANG OUT — Digital City San Francisco: Hangout
SF HARVEY MIL — Digital City San Francisco: Harvey Milk Institute
   [Web site]
SF HOMES — Digital City San Francisco: Real Estate
SF HOROSCOPES — Digital City San Francisco: Astrobytes Daily
   Horoscopes
SF HOT DEALS — Digital City San Francisco: Hot Deals
SF HOT JOBS — Digital City San Francisco: Hot Jobs of the Day
SF JOBS — Digital City San Francisco: Employment Classifieds
SF JOKE — Digital City San Francisco: Joke of the Day Page
SF JOKES — Digital City San Francisco: Joke of the Day Page
SF LEARNING ANNEX — Digital City San Francisco: Learning Annex
SF LESBIAN — Digital City San Francisco: Gay Community
SF LESBIAN CHAT — San Francisco Gay & Lesbian Chat
SF LOCAL NEWS — Digital City San Francisco: Local News
SF M4M — PlanetOut: FantasyMan Island for San Francisco
SF MAP — Digital City South Florida: Map
SF MOVIES — Digital City San Francisco: Movie Maven's Movie
   Reviews
SF NEWS — Digital City San Francisco: News
SF ONQ — onQ: San Francisco
SF OUTDOORS — Digital City San Francisco: Outdoor Recreation
SF PEOPLE — Digital City San Francisco: Community Area
SF PERSONALS — Digital City San Francisco: Personals
SF PRIDE — Digital City San Francisco: Gay Pride
SF QUESTIONS — Digital City San Francisco: Questions

SF REAL ESTATE — Digital City San Francisco: Real Estate Area
SF RECREATION — Digital City San Francisco: Outdoor Recreation
SF RENTALS — Digital City San Francisco: Rent Tech
SF RENTALS — Digital City San Francisco: Rent Tech
SF RESTAURANTS — Digital City San Francisco: Dining Guide
SF SEX — Digital City San Francisco: The Couch
SF SINGLES — Digital City San Francisco: Dating Scene
SF SITE MAP — Digital City South Florida: Map
SF SPORTS CONNECTION — Digital City San Francisco: Sports
    Connection
SF TEEN BUZZ — Digital City San Francisco: Teen Buzz
SF TRANSMEDIA — Digital City San Francisco: Transmedia
SF TRIVIA — Digital City San Francisco: Fun & Games
SF WEATHER — Digital City San Francisco: Weather
SF WOMEN — Digital City San Francisco: A Woman's Place
SF WOMEN — Digital City San Francisco: WWWomen
SF ZODIAC — Digital City San Francisco: Zodiac
SF ZONE — Entertainment Asylum: Sci Fi Zone
SF ZONE CHAT — Entertainment Asylum: Sci-Fi Zone Chat
SF-EGG — Digital City San Francisco: Electronic Gourmet Guide
SFJB — Digital City San Francisco: Junior Buzz
SFJR — Digital City San Francisco: Junior Buzz
SFOL — AOL Games: Space Fleet Online
SFRN — SportsFan Radio Network
SGMA — Sporting Goods Super Store
SGREEN — Athlete Direct: Shawn Green's Journal Online
SHADES.COM — Brands For Less [Web site]
SHADOW WARRIOR — AOL Games: Shadow Warrior
SHALOM — Jewish Community Online
SHAMROCK — AOL International: Irish Heritage
SHAQ — Los Angeles Lakers
SHAREWARE — AOL Computing: Download Software
SHAREWARE RELEASES — AOL Computing: New Releases
SHAREWARE SEARCH — AOL Computing: File Search
SHARK — Shark Attack Trading Forum
SHARK ATTACK — Shark Attack Trading Forum
SHARP — AOL Computing: PDA & Palmtop Forum
SHARPER IMAGE — Sharper Image Store
SHAWN — Athlete Direct: Shawn Green's Journal Online
SHAWN GREEN — Athlete Direct: Shawn Green's Journal Online
SHEENA SHOPPER — AOL Canada: It's Sheena
SHEEP — AOL Interests: Pets
SHEETS — AOL Shopping: Home, Kitchen & Garden
SHEFFIELD — AOL UK: Local Life
SHEFFIELD EOL — AOL UK: North East Events Online
SHH — AOL Secrets

SHHH — AOL Secrets
SHHHH — AOL Secrets
SHIFT — Shift [Web site]
SHIP CRITIC — Cruise Critic
SHIP CRITICS — Cruise Critic
SHNS — Digital City Boston: Politics Today
SHOP — AOL Shopping channel
SHOP A MATE — AOL UK: Sign On A Friend
SHOP BOOKSTORE — AOL Store: Book Shop
SHOP FITNESS — Sports Superstore: Fitness Store
SHOP GOLF — Sports Superstore: Golf Pro Store
SHOP MODEM — AOL Store: Modem Shop
SHOP SOFTWARE — AOL Store: Software Shop
SHOP TALK — AOL Shopping: Message Boards
SHOP@EATS — Thrive@Healthy Living: Eats Shop
SHOP@GIFT — Thrive@Healthy Living: Gift Shop
SHOP@HEALTH — Thrive@Healthy Living: Health Shop
SHOP@OUTDOORS — Thrive@Healthy Living: Outdoors Shop
SHOP@SEX — Thrive@Healthy Living: Sex Shop
SHOP@SHAPE — Thrive@Healthy Living: Shape Shop
SHOP@THRIVE — Thrive@Healthy Living: Shop
SHOPPERS ADVANTAGE — AOL Shoppers Advantage
SHOPPING — AOL Shopping channel
SHOPPING BOARDS — AOL Shopping: Message Boards
SHOPPING CHAT — AOL Shopping: Message Boards
SHOPPING SEARCH — AOL Shopping: Search
SHOPPING SERVICES — AOL Shopping: May We Help You?
SHOPPING SHOWCASE — AOL Shopping: Showcase
SHORTHAND — Online Shorthands
SHORTHANDS — Online Shorthands
SHORTWAVE — The Ham Radio Forum
SHOW BIZ — AOL Entertainment: The Industry
SHOW BIZ INFO — AOL Entertainment: Daily Fix
SHOW BIZ NEWS — AOL Entertainment: Daily Fix
SHOW ME — People Connection: Show Me How
SHOW ME HOW — People Connection: Show Me How
SHOW ME THE MONEY — AOL Personal Finance
SHOW TIMES — MovieLink [Web site]
SHOWCASE — AOL Shopping: Showcase
SICK — AOL Health: Illness and Treatments
SICKNESS — AOL Health: Illness and Treatments
SIDEKICK — Starfish Software
SIERRA LEONE — AOL International: Sierra Leone
SIGNET — Signet Bank
SIGNET BANK — Signet Bank
SIGNET ONLINE — Signet Bank

SIGNS — AOL WorkPlace: Signs Community
SILICON VALLEY — Digital City San Francisco: High Tech Jobs & News
SIM — AOL Games: Simming Forum
SIM RACING — iRace
SIMBA — Cowles Business Media [Web site]
SIMI — Simi Winery
SIMI WINERY — Simi Winery
SIMMING — AOL Games: Simming Forum
SIMON & SCHUSTER — Simon & Schuster College Online
SIMS — AOL Games: Simming Forum
SIMULATION — AOL Games: PC Games Forum
SIMULATION AUTO — AOL Grandstand: Simulation Auto
SIMULATION BASEBALL — AOL Grandstand: Simulation Baseball
SIMULATION BASKETBALL — AOL Grandstand: Simulation Basketball
SIMULATION FOOTBALL — AOL Grandstand: Simulation Football
SIMULATION GOLF — AOL Grandstand: Simulation Golf
SIMULATION HOCKEY — AOL Grandstand: Simulation Hockey
SIMULATION LEAGUE — Cyber Sports Simulation Leagues
SIMULATION LEAGUES — Cyber Sports Simulation Leagues
SIMULATION WRESTLING — AOL Grandstand: Simulation Wrestling
SINATRA — Entertainment Asylum: Club Sinatra
SINGAPORE — AOL International: Singapore
SINGLES MINDED — Digital City Washington: Singles-Minded
SINGLES SF — Digital City San Francisco: Dating Scene
SINUS — AOL Health: Sinusitis
SINUSITIS — AOL Health: Sinusitis
SIXERS — Philadelphia 76ers
SJ BALL TALK — Digital City Philadelphia: SportsLine
SJ CHAT — Digital City Philadelphia: Chat Schedule
SJ GAS — Digital City Philadelphia: South Jersey Gas Company
SJ INTERACTIVE — Digital City South Jersey
SJ JAZZ — Digital City San Jose: Jazz Festival
SJ MOVIES — Digital City Philadelphia: Movies
SJ PERSONALS — Digital City San Diego: Personals
SJ SPORTS LINE — Digital City Philadelphia: SportsLine
SKARE ME — ABC Online: Kidzine Halloween [seasonal]
SKATEBOARD — Surflink
SKATEBOARDING — Surflink
SKATING — AOL Grandstand: Skating Forum
SKATING RINK — AOL WorkPlace: Sports & Recreation Industry
    Community
SKEL STORE — The Grateful Dead Forum: Skeleton Collection
SKELETON STORE — The Grateful Dead Forum: Skeleton Collection
SKI — AOL Sports: Skiing
SKI AMERICA 98 — Travel America: Ski America
SKI BOSTON — AOL Sports: Skiing

SKI CONDITIONS — U.S. Ski Reports [seasonal]
SKI DC — Digital City Washington: Powder Burn Skiing
SKI DIRECT — Thomas Cook Ski Direct
SKI INSTRUCTOR — iSki
SKI NET — AOL Sports: Ski Net
SKI NEW ENGLAND — Digital City Boston: Snow Sports
SKI NORTHEAST — AOL Sports: Skiing
SKI REPORT — U.S. Ski Reports [seasonal]
SKI REPORTS — U.S. Ski Reports [seasonal]
SKI SCHOOL — iSki
SKI WEATHER — U.S. Ski Reports [seasonal]
SKI ZONE — AOL Travel: Ski Zone
SKIING — AOL Sports: Skiing
SKILLET — Christianity Online: Skillet
SKIN — AOL Health: Skin, Hair & Nails
SKIN CANCER — AOL Health: Skin Cancer/Melanoma
SKIN HAIR NAILS — AOL Health: Skin, Hair & Nails
SKINS SLAM — Redskins Slam
SKYDIVING — AOL Interests: Aviation & Aeronautics
SLDN — onQ: Military
SLDR — Digital City Philadelphia: SportsLine
SLEEP DISORDERS — AOL Health: Sleep Disorders
SLIDESHOW — AOL Slideshows
SLIDESHOWS — AOL Slideshows
SLOANE — Digital City Philadelphia: Sloane Toyota/Nissan
SLOVAKIA — AOL International: Slovakia
SLOVENIA — AOL International: Slovenia
SLOVENIJA — AOL International: Slovenia
SLOVENSKA — AOL International: Slovakia
SLOW ROOSEVELT — Digital City Dallas-Fort Worth: Slow Roosevelt
SMALL BIZ TIP — AOL WorkPlace: Today's Business Tip
SMALL BUSINESS — AOL WorkPlace: Your Business
SMALL BUSINESS ADMIN — U.S. Small Business Administration
SMALL BUSINESS STORE — AOL WorkPlace: Business Services
SMALL BUSINESS TIP — AOL WorkPlace: Today's Business Tip
SMALLTOWN POETS — Christianity Online: Smalltown Poets
SMART BOOKMARK — Smart Bookmarks [Web site]
SMART BOOKMARKS — Smart Bookmarks [Web site]
SMART KIDS — AOL Computing: Youth Tech
SMART MOUTHS — Smart Mouths [Web site]
SMART TEENS — AOL Computing: Youth Tech
SMILE 4 U — Don't Worry Be Happy!
SMILEY — AOL Canada: Smileys and Shorthand
SMILEYS — AOL Canada: Smileys and Shorthand
SMILEYS AND SHORTHAND — AOL Canada: Smileys and Shorthand
SMITHSONIAN — Smithsonian Online

SMITHSONIAN MAGAZINE — Smithsonian Online
SMOKE — AOL Health: Smoking Cessation
SMOKEOUT — Great American Smokeout Area
SMOKING — AOL Health: Smoking Cessation
SMOKING CESSATION — AOL Health: Smoking Cessation
SN LIBRARIES — Search Scholastic Libraries
SN LIT GAME — AOL Research & Learn: Literature Game
SN SPACE — Space and Astronomy
SNOWBIRD — AOL Canada: Canadian Snowbird Association
SNOWBIRDS — AOL Canada: Canadian Snowbird Association
SNOWBOARD — AOL Sports: Snowboarding
SNOWBOARDING — AOL Sports: Snowboarding
SO CAL APARTMENTS — Digital City Los Angeles: Rental Connection
SO CAL CHAT — Digital City Los Angeles: Chat
SO CAL COMPUTERS — Digital City Los Angeles: Source for Computer
   Shopping
SO CAL DINING — Digital City Los Angeles: Dining
SO CAL EVENTS — Digital City Los Angeles: Events
SO CAL MOVIES — Digital City Los Angeles: Movies
SO CAL MUSIC — Digital City South Florida: Music Guide
SO CAL NEWS — Digital City Los Angeles: News
SO CAL PEOPLE — Digital City Los Angeles: People
SO CAL PERSONALS — Digital City Los Angeles: Personals
SO CAL PUB — Digital City Los Angeles: Social Group
SO CAL RENTALS — Digital City Los Angeles: Rental Connection
SO CAL SINGLES — Digital City Los Angeles: Personals
SO FLA 50 PLUS — Digital City South Florida: 50 Plus
SO FLA 50+ — Digital City South Florida: 50 Plus
SO FLA ADULTS — Digital City South Florida: 50 Plus
SO FLA BUSINESS — Digital City South Florida: Local Business
SO FLA CALENDAR — Digital City South Florida: Events Calendar
SO FLA CHAT — Digital City South Florida: Chat
SO FLA COMMUNITY — Digital City South Florida: Community Section
SO FLA ENTERTAIN — Digital City South Florida: Entertainment
SO FLA FIFTY PLUS — Digital City South Florida: 50 Plus
SO FLA INTERACT — Digital City South Florida: Interact
SO FLA LOCAL NEWS — Digital City South Florida: Local News
SO FLA MARKET — Digital City South Florida: Market
SO FLA MONEY — Digital City South Florida: Local Business
SO FLA NEWS — Digital City South Florida: News
SO FLA PERSONALS — Digital City South Florida: Personals
SO FLA SENIORS — Digital City South Florida: 50 Plus
SO FLA SPORTS — Digital City South Florida: Sports
SO FLA STAGE — Digital City South Florida: Stage
SO FLA WEATHER — Digital City South Florida: News
SO FLA YOU — Digital City South Florida: You

SOAF — Sign on a Friend
SOAF UK — AOL UK: Sign On A Friend
SOAP DIGEST — Soap Opera Digest
SOAP OPERA DIGEST — Soap Opera Digest
SOAPLINE — ABC Online: Daytime
SOAPS — AOL Entertainment: Soap Operas
SOCIETY — AOL Influence channel
SOD — Soap Opera Digest
SOFT SHOP — AOL Store: Software Shop
SOFTWARE — AOL Computing: Download Software
SOFTWARE COMPANIES — AOL Computing: Companies
SOFTWARE HARDTALK — Software Hardtalk
SOFTWARE HELP — AOL Computing: Software Help
SOFTWARE NET — Software.net [Web site]
SOFTWARE RELEASES — AOL Computing: New Releases
SOFTWARE SEARCH — AOL Computing: File Search
SOFTWARE SHOP — Computer Shop Selections
SOFTWARE STORE — Computer Shop Selections
SOFTWARE SUPERSTORE — AOL Shoppers Advantage: Software &
    Video Games
SOHO — Home Office Computing Magazine
SOI — AOL Canada: Stars On Ice
SOL 3 — AOL Games: Sol III Sci-Fi Role Playing
SOL ASYLUM — Entertainment Asylum
SOL III — AOL Games: Sol III Sci-Fi Role Playing
SOLAR ECCLIPSE — Solar Eclipse
SOLAR ECLIPSE — Solar Eclipse
SOLOMON ISLANDS — AOL International: Solomon Islands
SOMALIA — AOL International: Somalia
SONICS — Seattle Supersonics
SONY — Sony Digital Mavica
SONY MUSIC — Sony Music [Web site]
SONY MUSIC D — Sony Music [Web site]
SORE THROAT — AOL Health: Sore Throat
SOUND ROOM — The Sound Room
SOUSAL ABUSE — Massachusetts Coalition of Battered Women Service
    Groups
SOUTH AFRICA — AOL International: South Africa
SOUTH AMERICA — AOL International: South America
SOUTH BAY — Digital City San Diego: South Bay Interactive
SOUTH BAY AUTO GUIDE — Digital City San Diego: AutoGuide
SOUTH BAY DEALS — Digital City San Diego: AutoGuide
SOUTH BAY HOMES — Digital City San Diego: Real Estate
SOUTH BAY HOT DEALS — Digital City San Diego: AutoGuide
SOUTH BAY INTERACTIVE — Digital City San Diego: Interactive
SOUTH BAY PERSONALS — Digital City San Diego: Personals

SOUTH FLORIDA BIZ — Digital City South Florida: Local Business
SOUTH FLORIDA BLACK VOICES — Black Voices: South Florida
SOUTH FLORIDA BUSINESS — Digital City South Florida: Local
   Business page
SOUTH FLORIDA HEADLINE CHAT — Digital City South Florida: News
SOUTH FLORIDA KIDS — Digital City South Florida: KidSafe
SOUTH FLORIDA KIDS SAFE — Digital City South Florida: KidSafe
SOUTH FLORIDA LOCAL NEWS — Digital City South Florida: Local News
SOUTH FLORIDA NEWS — Digital City South Florida: News
SOUTH FLORIDA PERSONALS — Digital City South Florida: Personals
SOUTH FLORIDA SITE MAP — Digital City South Florida: Map
SOUTH JERSEY — Digital City Philadelphia: South Jersey Interactive
SOUTH JERSEY BALL — Digital City Philadelphia: SportsLine
SOUTH JERSEY GAS — Digital City Philadelphia: South Jersey Gas
   Company
SOUTH JERSEY MOVIES — Digital City Philadelphia: Movies
SOUTH JERSEY ONLINE — Digital City South Jersey
SOUTH KOREA — AOL International: South Korea
SOUTH OF THE BORDER — AOL International: South America
SOUTHAMPTON — AOL UK: Local Life
SOUTHERN MANAGEMENT — Digital City Washington: Southern
   Management Corporation
SP PW — S&P Personal Wealth [Web site]
SPACE — National Space Society
SPACE FLEET — AOL Games: Space Fleet Online
SPACE WARS — AOL Games: Space Wars Sim Forum
SPADES — WorldPlay: Spades
SPAIN — AOL International: Spain
SPAM UPDATE — AOL Spam Update
SPANISH — AOL International: The Bistro
SPANISH DICTIONARY — AOL International: Language Dictionaries &
   Resources
SPANISH WORDS — AOL International: Language Word Games
SPARTANBURG — Digital City Greenville: Local News
SPARTANBURG LOCAL NEWS — Digital City Greenville: Local News
SPARTANBURG NEWS — Digital City Greenville: Local News
SPCA — Society for the Prevention of Cruelty to Animals
SPCALA — Society for the Prevention of Cruelty to Animals
SPEAKER GINGRICH — AOL News: Eye on the Newt
SPEAKER OF THE HOUSE — AOL News: Eye on the Newt
SPEC WRITER — AOL WorkPlace: Planning & Specifications Community
SPEC WRITERS — AOL WorkPlace: Planning & Specifications
   Community
SPECIAL D — AOL International: Special Delivery
SPECIAL DELIVERY — AOL International: Special Delivery
SPECIAL NOTICE — Special Notice Concerning Class Action Suit

SPECIFICATIONS — AOL WorkPlace: Planning & Specifications Community
SPEED BOATS — Boating Selections
SPEED SKATING — Speed Skating MiniForum
SPEEDNET — Arizona Central: SpeedNet
SPEIGEL — Spiegel [Web site]
SPEND POINTS — AOL Rewards
SPICE GIRLS — The SPICE Girls
SPICE UP EMAIL — AOL Member Services: Spice Up Your E-mail
SPIDER-MAN — Marvel Comics
SPIDERMAN — Marvel Comics
SPIEGEL — Spiegel [Web site]
SPIKE REPORT — Digital City Los Angeles: News
SPIN — SPIN Online
SPIN ONLINE — SPIN Online
SPIRITS OF MASSACHUSETTS — Digital City Boston: Spirits
SPIRITUALITY — AOL Lifestyles: Spirituality
SPIRITUALITY ONQ — onQ: Spirituality
SPLATTER — Engage: Splatterball
SPLATTER BALL — Engage: Splatterball
SPOOKY SOUP — Parent Soup: Halloween [seasonal]
SPOR — AOL International: Sports
SPORT & REC PRO — AOL WorkPlace: Sports & Recreation Industry Community
SPORT & REC PROFESSIONAL — AOL WorkPlace: Sports & Recreation Industry Community
SPORT & REC PROFESSIONALS — AOL WorkPlace: Sports & Recreation Industry Community
SPORT & REC PROS — AOL WorkPlace: Sports & Recreation Industry Community
SPORT — AOL Sports channel
SPORT COVER — AOL News: Sports News
SPORT FISHING — Fishing Broadcast Network
SPORT OS — AOL News: Sports News
SPORT SUPERSTORE — Sports Superstore Online
SPORTING CLAYS — Hunting Broadcast Network
SPORTING NEWS — The Sporting News
SPORTLINK — Digital City Philadelphia: Sportslink Live!
SPORTS & REC — AOL WorkPlace: Sports & Recreation Industry Community
SPORTS — AOL Sports channel
SPORTS AUDITORIUMS — AOL Grandstand: Sports Live
SPORTS BOARDS — AOL Grandstand: Message Boards
SPORTS CHAT — AOL Grandstand: Chat
SPORTS CHAT — AOL Grandstand: Chat
SPORTS CIRCUIT — NESN Sports Circuit

SPORTS CONNECTION — Digital City San Francisco: Sports Connection
SPORTS CONNECTION SF — Digital City San Francisco: Sports Connection
SPORTS DCSD — Digital City San Diego: Sports
SPORTS EVENTS — AOL Grandstand: Sports Live
SPORTS FAN — SportsFan Radio Network
SPORTS FRONT — AOL News: Sports News
SPORTS GUY — Digital City Boston: Sports Guy
SPORTS HOT — AOL Sports: From The Cheap Seats
SPORTS IC — AOL Sports: Internet Center
SPORTS INTL — AOL International: Sports
SPORTS LIBRARIES — AOL Sports: Libraries
SPORTS LIVE — AOL Grandstand: Sports Live
SPORTS NEWS — AOL News: Sports News
SPORTS NEWSSTAND — AOL Sports: Newsstand
SPORTS NOTEBOOK — Garry Cobb's Sports Notebook
SPORTS PICTURES OF THE WEEK — AOL News: Sports Pictures of the Week
SPORTS PIX — AOL News: Sports Pictures of the Week
SPORTS POTW — AOL News: Sports Pictures of the Week
SPORTS PRINCESS — Digital City Dallas-Fort Worth: Sports Princess
SPORTS ROOM — AOL Grandstand: Chat
SPORTS ROOMS — AOL Grandstand: Chat
SPORTS SAN DIEGO — Digital City San Diego: Sports
SPORTS SD — Digital City San Diego: Sports
SPORTS SEARCH — AOL Sports: Search & Explore
SPORTS SHOP — AOL Shopping: Sports & Fitness
SPORTS STARS — Athlete Direct
SPORTS SUPER — Sports Superstore Online
SPORTS SUPERSHOP — Sports Superstore Online
SPORTS SUPERSTORE — Sports Superstore Online
SPORTS SUPERSTORE ONLINE — Sports Superstore Online
SPORTS TALK — AOL Grandstand: Chat
SPORTSLINE SJ — Digital City Philadelphia: SportsLine
SPORTSLINK — Digital City Philadelphia: Sportslink Live!
SPORTSLINK LIVE — Digital City Philadelphia: Sportslink Live!
SPOTW — AOL News: Sports Pictures of the Week
SPRAIN — AOL Health: Sprain
SPREADSHEET — AOL Computing: Spreadsheet Applications
SPREADSHEETS — AOL Computing: Spreadsheet Applications
SPRING BREAK — Warm Weather Travel [seasonal]
SPRING INTO SUMMER — AOL Canada: Spring into Summer
SPRING SELECTIONS — AOL Shopping: Spring Catalog [seasonal]
SPRING SELECTIONS STORE — AOL Shopping: Spring Catalog [seasonal]
SPRING SHOP — AOL Shopping: Spring Catalog [seasonal]

SPRING SHOPPING — AOL Shopping: Spring Catalog [seasonal]
SPRING STORE — AOL Shopping: Spring Catalog [seasonal]
SPRING TRAINING — Digital City Philadelphia: Phillies Spring Training
SPRINT PCS — Sprint PCS Online Store
SPROT — AOL Sports channel
SPURS — San Antonio Spurs
SRI LANKA — AOL International: Sri Lanka
SRS — onQ: Organizations
SS BIOLOGY — Simon & Schuster College Online: Biology
SS CRIMINAL JUSTICE — Simon & Schuster College Online: Criminal
    Justice Forum
SS DE CHAT — Sun-Sentinel Digital Edition Chat Schedule
SS ENGLISH — Simon & Schuster College Online: English Forum
SS MATH — Simon & Schuster College Online: Mathematics Forum
SS PHYS ED — Simon & Schuster College Online: Health, Phys Ed
    and Rec
SS POLI SCI — Simon & Schuster College Online: Political Science
    Forum
SS SOCIAL WORK — Simon & Schuster College Online: Social Work
    Area
SS SOCIOLOGY — Simon & Schuster College Online:
    Anthropology/Sociology Forum
SSO — Sports Superstore Online
ST KITTS — AOL International: St. Kitts and Nevis
ST LOUIS — Digital City St. Louis
ST LOUIS LOCAL NEWS — Digital City St. Louis: Local News
ST LOUIS NEWS — Digital City St. Louis: Local News
ST PADDYS DAY — St. Patrick's Day [seasonal]
ST PATRICK — St. Patrick's Day [seasonal]
ST PATRICKS DAY — St. Patrick's Day [seasonal]
ST PATS — St. Patrick's Day [seasonal]
ST PAUL — Digital City Twin Cities
ST PAUL CHAT — Digital City Twin Cities: Chat
ST PAUL DIGITAL CITY — Digital City Twin Cities
ST PAUL FUN — Digital City Twin Cities: Entertainment
ST PAUL MARKET — Digital City Twin Cities: Marketplace
ST PAUL PEOPLE — Digital City Twin Cities: People
ST PAUL SPORTS — Digital City Twin Cities: Sports
ST PAUL TOUR — Digital City Twin Cities: Living
ST PETE COMM — Digital City Tampa Bay: Community
ST PETE NEWS — Digital City Tampa Bay: News
ST PETE PEOPLE — Digital City Tampa Bay: People
ST PETE WEATHER — Digital City Tampa Bay: News
ST PETERSBURG — Digital City Tampa Bay
ST VALENTINE'S DAY — Valentine's Day @AOL [seasonal]
ST. LOUIS — Digital City St. Louis

ST. LOUIS CARDINALS — St. Louis Cardinals
ST. LOUIS LOCAL NEWS — Digital City St. Louis: Local News
ST. LOUIS NEWS — Digital City St. Louis: Local News
ST. LUCIA — AOL International: St. Lucia
ST. PATRICK'S DAY — St. Patrick's Day [seasonal]
ST. PAUL LOCAL NEWS — Twin Cities Local News
ST. VINCENT — AOL International: St. Vincent and Grenadines
STADIUM SHOP — The Stadium Shop
STAFF DEVELOPMENT — AOL Computing: Staff Development SIG
STAFF ONQ — onQ: Apply to onQ
STAGE — Playbill Online [Web site]
STAMP BIZ — AOL WorkPlace: The Stamp Professionals Community
STAMP BUSINESS — AOL WorkPlace: The Stamp Professionals Community
STAMP PROFESSIONAL — AOL WorkPlace: The Stamp Professionals Community
STAMPRO — AOL WorkPlace: The Stamp Professionals Community
STANFORD UNIVERSITY — Stanford University [Web site]
STANLEY MARTIN — Stanley Martin Homes [Web site]
STAR COURIER — Plano Star Courier
STAR SEARCH — EXTRA: Star Search
STAR TRACKS — Teen People: Stars & Stuff
STAR TREK — Star Trek Club
STAR TREK CLUB — Star Trek Forum
STAR TRIB — Minneapolis Star Tribune
STAR TRIBUNE — Minneapolis Star Tribune
STAR TRIBUNE ONLINE — Minneapolis Star Tribune
STAR TRIBUNE VOICES — Minneapolis Star Tribune: Voices
STAR TRIBUNE.COM — Minneapolis Star Tribune Online
STAR WARS — Digital City Philadelphia: Star Wars
STARBUCKS — Starbucks Coffee
STARFISH — Starfish Software
STARKEY — Starkey Laboratories, Inc.
STARLOG — AOL Entertainment: Newsletter Subscription
STARS & SHOWS — ABC Online: Stars & Shows
STARS — EXTRA: Stars
STARS CLUB — Stars Club
STARS ON ICE — AOL Canada: Stars On Ice
STARTING YOUR BUSINESS — AOL WorkPlace: Getting Started
STARTUP — AOL WorkPlace: Getting Off The Ground
STARZ — EXTRA: Stars
STAT COLLEGE FOOTBALL — STATS: College Football
STATE — AOL Research & Learn: The Fifty States
STATE HOUSE NEWS SERVICE — Digital City Boston: Politics Today
STATES — AOL Research & Learn: The Fifty States

STATS — STATS: Sports
STATS ABL — STATS: ABL
STATS BASKETBALL — STATS: Professional and College Hoops
STATS BK — STATS: Pro Basketball
STATS CBK — STATS: College Basketball
STATS CFB — STATS: College Football
STATS COLLEGE — STATS: NCAA Football and Basketball
STATS COLLEGE BASKETBALL — STATS: College Basketball
STATS COLLEGE FOOTBALL — STATS College Football
STATS COLLEGE HOOPS — STATS: College Basketball
STATS FB SCOREBOARD — STATS: Football Scoreboard
STATS HOOPS — STATS: Professional and College Hoops
STATS INC — STATS: Sports
STATS INC. — STATS: Sports
STATS NBA — STATS: Pro Basketball
STATS NCAA — STATS: NCAA Football and Basketball
STATS NCAA FOOTBALL — STATS: College Football
STATS NCAA HOOPS — STATS: College Basketball
STATS PBK — STATS: Pro Basketball
STATS PFB SCOREBOARD — STATS: Football Scoreboard
STATS PRO BASKETBALL — STATS: Pro Basketball
STATS PRO HOOPS — STATS: Pro Basketball
STATS WBK — STATS: WNBA
STATS WNBA — STATS: WNBA
STATS, INC — STATS: Sports
STATS, INC. — STATS: Sports
STATUE — Tell Us Your Story: Immigration Stories
STATUE OF LIBERTY — Tell Us Your Story: Immigration Stories
STD — AOL Health: Sexually Transmitted Diseases
STDS — AOL Health: Sexually Transmitted Diseases
STEAKS — Omaha Steaks International
STEAMROOM ONQ — onQ: Backroom
STEEPLE CHASE — AOL UK: The Martell British Grand National
STEPHEN BRAY — AOL Canada: Stephen Bray Clay Pipes
STEREO — Stereo Review
STEREO EQUIPMENT — Stereo Review
STEREO REVIEW — Stereo Review
STERN — Digital City Philadelphia: Howard Stern
STEVE — A Letter From Steve Case
STEVE CASE — A Letter From Steve Case
STEVE CASE LETTER — A Letter From Steve Case
STEVE WB 17 — Digital City Philadelphia: Highland
STEVE YOUNG — Athlete Direct
STEVE'S LETTER — A Letter From Steve Case
STICKMAX — OfficeMax: Search for Stick Max Contest
STIMULANTS — AOL Health: Stimulant Addiction

STIRLING — AOL UK: Local Life
STIRLING EOL — AOL UK: Scotland Events Online
STN — AOL Canada: Skate The Nation
STO — Minneapolis Star Tribune
STO VOICES — Star Tribune Online: Voices
STOCK — AOL Personal Finance: Quotes & Portfolios
STOCK ONQ — onQ: Business
STOCK PORTFOLIO — AOL Personal Finance: Stock Portfolios
STOCK QUOTES — AOL Personal Finance: Quotes & Portfolios
STOCK REPORT — AOL Personal Finance: Market Guide [Web site]
STOCK REPORTS — AOL Personal Finance: Market Guide [Web site]
STOCK TALK — AOL Personal Finance: Stock Talk
STOCK TIMING — Decision Point Timing & Charts
STOCKBURGER — Digital City Philadelphia: Stockburger Dealers
STOCKLINK — AOL Personal Finance: Quotes & Portfolios
STOCKS — AOL Personal Finance: Quotes & Portfolios
STOKE — AOL UK: Local Life
STOKE EOL — AOL UK: Midlands Events Online
STONES — Virgin Records: Rolling Stones Tour
STOOD UP — PlanetOut: Stood Up
STOOD-UP — PlanetOut: Stood Up
STORE — AOL Shopping channel
STORE ONQ — onQ: Store
STORES — AOL Shopping channel
STORIES — AOL Stories
STRAIGHT DOPE — The Straight Dope
STRAIGHT DOPE SEARCH — The Straight Dope: Search
STRAIGHT NO CHASER — Digital City Denver: Music Scene
STRATEGIES — AOL WorkPlace: Business Know-How Forum
STRATEGY FORUM — Strategy Forum
STREP THROAT — AOL Health: Strep Throat
STRESS — AOL Health: Emotional Well-Being
STRESS DOC — Online Psych: Stress Doc
STRESS MANAGEMENT — AOL Health: Emotional Well-Being
STRIKE A MATCH — Boxer*Jam's Strike-A-Match
STRIKE-A-MATCH — Boxer*Jam's Strike-A-Match
STROKE — AOL Health: Stroke
STUDIO I — Entertainment Asylum: Chat
STUDIO L — Entertainment Asylum: Chat
STUDIO-I — Entertainment Asylum: Chat
STUDIO-L — Entertainment Asylum: Chat
STUDY SKILLS — Study Smart Service
STUDY SMART — Study Smart Service
STUDY SMART — Study Smart Service
STYLE HH — The AOL Greenhouse
STYLE — AOL Influence: The Good Life

STYLE EYE — Digital City Boston: Style Eye
SUCCESS STORIES — Love@AOL: Online Romance Success Stories
SUCK — Suck.com [Web site]
<u>SUD AMERICA</u> — AOL International: South America
SUDAN — AOL International: Sudan
SUDDENLY SUSAN — WB Online: Suddenly Susan
SUGAR BOWL — AOL Sports: Sugar Bowl
SUGGEST — Suggestion Boxes
SUGGESTION — Suggestion Boxes
SUGGESTIONS — Suggestion Boxes
<u>SUISSE</u> — AOL International: Switzerland
SUMMER CANADA — AOL Canada: Spring into Summer
SUMMER TRAVEL — AOL Travel: Summer Travel Planning
SUMMER TRAVEL PLANNING — AOL Travel: Summer Travel Planning
SUMO — AOL International: Sports
SUN BOWL — AOL Sports: Sun Bowl
<u>SUN SENTINAL CHAT</u> — Sun-Sentinel: Chat Room
SUN SENTINEL — Sun Sentinel South Florida
SUN SENTINEL CHAT — Sun-Sentinel: Chat Room
SUNDANCE SQUARE — Digital City Dallas-Fort Worth: Sundance
    Square
SUNDERLAND — AOL UK: Local Life
SUNDERLAND EOL — AOL UK: Far North Events Online
<u>SUNGLASS</u> — Brands for Less: Shades [Web site]
SUNS — Phoenix Suns
SUN-SENTINEL — Sun Sentinel South Florida
SUN-SENTINEL CHAT — Sun-Sentinel: Chat Room
SUNSET PARK HOMES — Digital City Los Angeles: Ron Wynn Real
    Estate
SUNSET PARK REAL ESTATE — Digital City Los Angeles: Ron Wynn Real
    Estate
<u>SUOMI</u> — AOL International: Finland
SUPER BOWL SHOP — Super Bowl Store
SUPER BOWL SHOPPING — Super Bowl Store
SUPER BOWL STORE — Super Bowl Store
SUPER PLUMBER — Warner Plumbing [Web site]
SUPER SPORTS STORE — Sports Superstore Online
SUPERCARD — AOL Computing: SuperCard Resource Center
SUPERMAN — DC Comics
SUPERSITE — Onsale Online Auction Supersite [Web site]
SUPERSONICS — Seattle Supersonics
SUPERSTORE — AOL Shoppers Advantage
SUPPORT — AOL Member Services
SUPPORT FORUMS — AOL Computing: Help Desk
SUPPORT ONQ — onQ: Support & Recovery
SURCHARGE — AOL Games: Guide

SURETRADE — Suretrade.com [Web site]

SURF — Surflink

SURFACING — Sarah McLachlan Surfacing Contest [Web site]

SURFACING CONTEST — Sarah McLachlan Surfacing Contest [Web site]

SURFER — Surflink

SURFING — Surflink

SURFLINK — Surflink

SURINAME — AOL International: Suriname

SURVEYS — AOL Rewards: Opinion Place

SURVIVE IN LONDON — AOL UK: Digital City London: Survival

SUSAN — WB Online: Suddenly Susan

SUSAN WEBER — Electra: Plus Size Concepts

SUSHI — AOL International: Japan

SUUNTO — Backpacker Magazine: Marketplace

SUZYN WALDMAN — Digital City New York: Suzyn Waldman's Yankees Beat

SVIZZERA — AOL International: Switzerland

SW NET — Software.net [Web site]

SW SHOP — AOL Shopping: Computer Software

SWAMI — AOL Australian: Swami Area

SWANSEA — AOL UK: Local Life

SWAZILAND — AOL International: Swaziland

SWEDEN INTL — AOL International: Sweden

SWEETWATER — Backpacker Magazine: Marketplace

SWIM — AOL Sports: Swimming

SWIMMING — AOL Sports: Swimming

SWISS ARMY — Brands for Less [Web site]

SWISS ARMY DEPOT — Brands for Less [Web site]

SWISS BANKS — AOL International: Swiss Banks and Nazi Plunder

SWITCHBOARD — AOL White Pages [Web site]

SWITCHBOARD.COM — AOL White Pages [Web site]

SWITZERLAND — AOL International: Switzerland

SWOON — Passport to Love: Swoon-O-Matic

SWSF — Space Wars Sim Forum

SYDNEY — AOL International: Australia and Oceania

SYMANTEC — Symantec Corporation

SYNAGOGUE — Jewish Community: Synagogue Life

SYNAGOGUES — Jewish Community: Synagogue Life

SYNONYMS — Merriam-Webster Thesaurus

SYRIA — AOL International: Syria

SYSOP — AOL Member Services

SYSTEM RESPONSE — System Response Report

T & L — American Express: Travel & Leisure Magazine Online

T NEWS — AOL Research & Learn: Teachers' Newsstand

T ROWE PERFORMANCE — T. Rowe Price: Funds Performance [Web site]

T ROWE PRICE — T. Rowe Price: Welcome
T ROWE PRICES — T. Rowe Price: Fund Prices [Web site]
T SHIRT — AOL Shopping: Apparel & Accessories
T SHIRTS — AOL Shopping: Apparel & Accessories
T SQUARE — Apple Computer: Town Square Chat Room
T TALK — Teacher's Forum
TA — AOL Travelers Advantage
TA SWEEPS — AOL Travelers Advantage: Las Vegas Sweepstakes
TAC — Top Advisors' Corner
TACOMA — Digital City Seattle: Web Guide [Web site]
TACOMA DIGITAL CITY — Digital City Seattle: Web Guide [Web site]
TAHOE — Digital City San Francisco: Lake Tahoe
TAILORS — AOL WorkPlace: Apparel Professionals Forum
TAIWAN — AOL International: Taiwan
TAJIKISTAN — AOL International: Tajikistan
TAJMAHAL — AOL International: India
TALK — People Connection
TALK BACK — Digital Cities Twin Cities: Talk Back
TALK ONQ — onQ: Chat
TALK WOMAN — TalkWomen
TALK WOMEN — TalkWomen
TAMC CHAT — Entertainment Asylum: Teen Asylum Chat
TAMPA — Digital City Tampa Bay: WebGuide [Web site]
TAMPA BAY — Digital City Tampa Bay: WebGuide [Web site]
TAMPA BAY DEVIL RAYS — Tampa Bay Devil Rays
TAMPA BAY LOCAL NEWS — Digital City Tampa Bay: NewsGuide
TAMPA COMM — Digital City Tampa Bay: Community
TAMPA DEVIL RAYS — Tampa Bay Devil Rays
TAMPA LOCAL NEWS — Digital City Tampa Bay: NewsGuide
TAMPA NEWS — Digital City Tampa Bay: News & Weather
TAMPA PEOPLE — Digital City Tampa Bay: People
TAMPA WEATHER — Digital City Tampa: News & Weather
TANKGIRL — Dead OnLine [Web site]
TANZANIA — AOL International: Tanzania
TAO — Travel America Online
TAPESTRY OF WOMEN — Online Psych: Tapestry of Women
TARA — Tara Lapinski
TARA LAPINSKI — Tara Lapinski
TARA LIPINSKI — Tara Lapinski
TAROT — Horoscope Selections
TAROT SCOPES — Digital City Philadelphia: DjunaVerse
TASTE UK FOOD — AOL UK: Good Taste
TAURUS — Horoscope Selections
TAVERN — AOL WorkPlace: Restaurants, Taverns & Bars
TAX — AOL Tax Planning
TAX CHANNEL — NAEA Tax channel

TAX EDGE — Parsons Technology
TAX FORUM — AOL Tax Planning
TAX PLANNING — AOL Tax Planning
TAX PREPARATION — AOL Tax Planning
TAXES — AOL Tax Planning
TAXES INTL — AOL International: Tax Information
TAXICAB — AOL WorkPlace: Taxicab Community
TAXLOGIC — TaxLogic
TAY — Taylor University
TAYLOR UNIVERSITY — Taylor University
TB — AOL Health: Tuberculosis
TB NEWS — Digital City Tampa Bay: Local News
TBB — The Book Bag for Teens
TBR — The Book Report
TBR TEEN READS — The Book Bag for Teens
TBR TEENS — The Book Bag for Teens
TBS — The Body Shop: Skin and Hair Care Products for Every Body
TBSF — Digital City San Francisco: Teen Buzz
TC AUTOS — Digital City Twin Cities: AutoGuide
TC BIZ — Digital City Twin Cities: Business
TC BOOK EM — Digital City Twin Cities: Book 'Em Book Reviews
TC BUSINESS — Digital City Twin Cities: Business
TC CENTER STAGE — Digital City Twin Cities: Center Stage with Chris
    Kliesen
TC CHAT — Digital City Twin Cities: Chat
TC CLICKED ON — Digital City Twin Cities: Newsletter
TC COMMUNITY — Digital City Twin Cities: Community Pages
TC DINING — Digital City Twin Cities: Dining
TC ENTERTAIN — Digital City Twin Cities: Entertainment
TC ENTERTAINMENT — Digital City Twin Cities: Entertainment
TC EVENTS — Digital City Twin Cities: Events
TC FAMILY — Digital City Twin Cities: Family
TC HEALTH — Digital City Twin Cities: Health & Wellness
TC HOME — Digital City Twin Cities: Home & Family
TC HOMES — Digital City Twin Cities: Real Estate
TC LIVING — Digital City Twin Cities: Minnesota Living
TC LOCAL NEWS — Digital City Twin Cities: Local News
TC MARKET — Digital City Twin Cities: Marketplace
TC MARKETPLACE — Digital City Twin Cities: Marketplace
TC MOVIE MAVEN — Digital City Twin Cities: Movie Reviews
TC MOVIES — Digital City Twin Cities: Movies
TC PEOPLE — Digital City Twin Cities: People
TC REAL ESTATE — Digital City Twin Cities: Cities Real Estate
TC SEASONAL — Digital City Twin Cities: Summer in the Cities
    [seasonal]
TC SEASONS — Digital City Twin Cities: Summer in the Cities [seasonal]

TC SLACKER — Digital City Twin Cities: Ask A Slacker
TC SPORTS — Digital City Twin Cities: Sports
TC SUMMER — Digital City Twin Cities: Summer in the Cities [seasonal]
TC TRAVEL — Digital City Twin Cities: Travel
TC VIRTUAL PARENT — Digital City Twin Cities: Virtual Parent
TC VISITOR — Digital City Twin Cities: Visitor's Guide
TCF — onQ: Transgender Community Forum
TCF CHAT — onQ: Transgender Community Chat and Conference
     Rooms
TCF CHATS — onQ: Transgender Community Chat and Conference
     Rooms
TCF ONQ — onQ: Transgender Community Forum
TD GREEN LINE — AOL Canada: Green Line Discount Broker
TDAY — Thanksgiving @AOL [seasonal]
TEACHER PAGER — AOL Research & Learn: Ask-A-Teacher
TEACHER'S INSURANCE — TIAA Teachers' Insurance [Web site]
TEACHERS' INSURANCE — TIAA Teachers' Insurance [Web site]
TEACHERS INSURANCE — TIAA Teachers' Insurance [Web site]
TEACHER'S LOUNGE — AOL Research & Learn: Teacher's Lounge
TEACHERS' LOUNGE — AOL Research & Learn: Teacher's Lounge
TEACHERS LOUNGE — AOL Research & Learn: Teacher's Lounge
TEAM CLUBS — Real Fans: Join Your Team Club
TEAM NFL DRAFT — TeamNFL Draft
TEAM NFL NEWSLETTER — TeamNFL Newsletter
TEAM NFL STORE — The Official NFL Catalog
TECH BIZ — AOL WorkPlace: Computers & Technology Professional
     Forum
TECH HELP — AOL Member Services
TECH HELP LIVE — AOL Member Services
TECH LIVE — AOL Member Services
TECH NEWS — AOL News: Technology
TECH SUPPORT — AOL Member Services
TECHIE PALS — AOL Computing: Youth Tech Techie Pals
TECHNICAL SUPPORT — AOL Member Services
TECHNOLOGY FRONT — AOL News: Technology News
TECHNOLOGY INVESTING — AOL Personal Finance: Investing In
     Technology
TECHNOLOGY NEWS — AOL News: Technology
TECHNOLOGY REFERENCE — AOL Research & Learn: Computing
TECNICA — Backpacker Magazine: Marketplace
TEEN — AOL Teens channel
TEEN ASYLUM — Entertainment Asylum: Teen Asylum
TEEN ASYLUM CHAT — Entertainment Asylum: Teen Asylum Chat
TEEN BUZZ SF — Digital City San Francisco: Teen Buzz
TEEN CHANNEL — AOL Teens channel
TEEN CHAT — Teen Scene

TEEN FASHION — AOL Teens: Style
TEEN FRIENDS — AOL Teens: Friends
TEEN FUN — AOL Teens: Fun
TEEN HANGOUT — Teen Scene
TEEN HELP — AOL Teens: I Need Help!
TEEN LIFE — AOL Teens: Life
TEEN MOVIES — AOL Teens: Fun
TEEN MUSIC — AOL Teens: Fun
TEEN PEOPLE — Teen People Magazine Online
TEEN PEOPLE DAILY DISH — Teen People: Daily Dish
TEEN PEOPLE HOROSCOPES — Teen People: Horoscopes
TEEN PEOPLE LIVE — Teen People: Live
TEEN PEOPLE MESSAGE BOARDS — Teen People: Message Boards
TEEN PEOPLE ONLINE — Teen People Magazine Online
TEEN PEOPLE SEARCH — Teen People: Search
TEEN PEOPLE STARS & STUFF — Teen People: Stars & Stuff
TEEN PEOPLE STYLE — Teen People: Looks & Love
TEEN PEOPLE STYLEGRRL — Teen People: Looks & Love
TEEN PEOPLE SUBSCRIPTION — Teen People Subscription
TEEN PEOPLE: STARS & STUFF — Teen People: Stars & Stuff
TEEN PHILLY — Digital City Philadelphia: Teens
TEEN SEARCH — AOL Teens: Search the Web [Web site]
TEEN STYLE — Teens: Style
TEEN TALK — AOL Teens: Friends
TEEN WRITER — Writers Club: Teens
TEEN WRITERS — Writers Club: Teens
TEEN WRITING — Writers Club: Teens
TEENAGERS — AOL Teens channel
TEENS — AOL Teens channel
TEENS CHANNEL — AOL Teens channel
TEENS FASHION — AOL Teens channel
TEENS FRIENDS — AOL Teens: Friends
TEENS FUN — AOL Teens: Fun
TEENS LIFE — AOL Teens: Life
TEENS STYLE — AOL Teens: Style
TEENS@PHILLY — Digital City Philadelphia: Teens
TEHNOLOGY FRONT — AOL News: Technology
TEL AVIV — AOL International: Israel Interactive
TELE MEDIA — AOL Canada: Canadian Living Magazine
TELECOM — AOL Computing: Telecom & Networking
TELECOM FORUM — AOL Computing: Telecom & Networking
TELECOMMUNICATIONS — AOL Computing: Telecom & Networking
TELEPHONE — Accessing America Online
TELEPHONE NUMBERS — Accessing America Online
TELEPHONE REPAIR — AOL WorkPlace: Telephone Equipment &
    Systems Industry

TELEPHONE SERVICE — AOL WorkPlace: Telephone Equipment & Systems Industry

TELEPHONE SYSTEMS — AOL WorkPlace: Telephone Equipment & Systems Industry

TELESCAN — AOL Personal Finance: Telescan Users Group

TELEVISION — AOL Entertainment: Television

TELL US — Tell Us Your Story: Immigration Stories

TELL US YOUR STORY — Tell Us Your Story: Immigration Stories

TELNET — Telnet Center

TELNET ACCESS — Telnet Center

TELNET CENTER — Telnet Center

TEL-SAVE — AOL Long Distance Savings Plan

TEMP SERVICES — AOL WorkPlace: Employment Agencies & Services

TEN BEST — Digital City Los Angeles: Ten Best

TEN BEST OF LA — Digital City Los Angeles: Ten Best

TENNIS — AOL Sports: Tennis

<u>TERAPIN STATION</u> — The Grateful Dead Forum: Terrapin Station

TERMS — AOL Terms of Service

TERMS OF SERVICE — AOL Terms of Service

TERRAPIN STATION — The Grateful Dead Forum: Terrapin Station

TERRIS — AOL UK: Terris

TERRIS HELP — AOL UK: Terris Help & Information

TERRIS MESSAGES — AOL UK: Terris: Message Boards

TEST YOUR HEALTH — AOL Health: Assesses Your Health Area

TEX FILES — Digital City Dallas-Fort Worth: The Tex Files

TEXAS EMPLOYMENT — Digital City Dallas-Fort Worth: Employment Classifieds

TEXAS GAY FORUM — Digital City Dallas-Fort Worth: Gay & Lesbian

TEXAS INSTRUMENTS — Texas Instruments

TEXAS LOTTERY — Digital City Dallas-Fort Worth: Lottery

TEXAS MOTOR SPEEDWAY — Digital City Dallas-Fort Worth: NASCAR Racing

TEXAS NASCAR — Digital City Dallas-Fort Worth: NASCAR Racing

TEXAS PARKS — Digital City Dallas-Fort Worth: Parks and Wildlife Department

TEXAS RANGERS — Texas Rangers Baseball

TEXAS TEENS — Digital City Dallas-Fort Worth: Teens

TEXAS WILDLIFE — Digital City Dallas-Fort Worth: Parks and Wildlife Department

TEXAS WINES — Digital City Dallas-Fort Worth: Food & Wine Online

THAILAND — AOL International: Thailand

THANKS BABS — onQ: Travel

THANKSGIVING — Thanksgiving @AOL [seasonal]

THANKSGIVING CANADA — AOL Canada: Thanksgiving [seasonal]

THANKSGIVING SHOPPING — AOL Shopping: Thanksgiving [seasonal]

THE ANT HILL — Antagonist, Inc.: ANT Hill

THE ASYLUM — Entertainment Asylum
THE BAC — Bay Area California Group
THE BALLROOM — Digital City Washington: Cellar Door Entertainment
THE BAYOU — Digital City Washington: Cellar Door Entertainment
THE BIZ — AOL Entertainment: The Biz
THE BODY SHOP — The Body Shop: Skin and Hair Care Products for
    Every Body
THE BOOK BAG — The Book Bag for Teens
THE BOOK REPORT — The Book Report
THE BOSTON HERALD — Boston Herald
THE CAPS — The Washington Capitals
THE CASTRO — Digital City San Francisco: Gay, **Lesbian & Bi**
    Community
THE CATFISH REPORT — Digital City Philadelphia: The Catfish Report
THE CHAMPIONS BUICK — Digital City Atlanta: Champions Buick
THE COUCH — Digital City San Francisco: The Couch
THE CRICKETER — AOL UK: The Cricketer Magazine
THE DAILY FIX — AOL Entertainment: Daily Fix
THE DATE DOCTOR — Digital City Los Angeles: The Date Doctor
THE DATING DIVA — Electra: Dating Diva
THE DEAD — The Grateful Dead Forum
THE DISNEY STORE — The Disney Store
THE FAN — Digital City New York: Sports Radio 66 AM WFAN
THE FIX — AOL Entertainment: Daily Fix
THE FOURTH OF JULY AREA — Independence Day@AOL [seasonal]
THE GADGET GURU — The Gadget Guru Online
THE GAP — The Gap [Web site]
THE GOOD LIFE — AOL Influence: The Good Life
THE GRANDSTAND — AOL Grandstand
THE GRID — Entertainment Asylum: What's On TV
THE HARTFORD — AARP Insurance Program from The Hartford
    [Web site]
THE HERALD — Boston Herald
THE HISTORY CHANNEL — The History channel
THE HOLE — Mighty Mites
THE I-MAN — Digital City New York: Imus in the Morning
THE INDUSTRY — AOL Entertainment: The Industry
THE INVESTOR — The Investor: Personal Finance Channel Newsletter
THE KENTUCKY DERBY — AOL Sports: Kentucky Derby
THE KNOT — The Knot: Weddings for the Real World
THE LAST SHOT — Real Fans: Last Shot
THE LATEST — What's New on AOL
THE LEARNING ANNEX — Digital City Los Angeles: The Learning Annex
THE LIST — AOL UK: The List for Glasgow and Edinburgh Events
THE LIST GUY — NetGuide: AOL Listguy
THE LOFT 5 — The AOL Greenhouse

THE LOVE FILES — Digital City Philadelphia: The Love Files
THE MALL — AOL Shopping channel
THE MESQUITE NEWS — Digital City Dallas-Fort Worth: Mesquite Newspaper
THE MOTLEY FOOL — Motley Fool
THE MUSERS — Digital City Dallas-Fort Worth: KTCK 1310 AM Sports Radio
THE NANDO TIMES — The Nando Times [Web site]
THE NATURE CONSERVANCY — The Nature Conservancy
THE NET TODAY — NetGuide: The Net Today
THE NEW YORK TIMES — New York Times Online
THE OLSON CO — Digital City Los Angeles: The Olson Company
THE OLSON COMPANY — Digital City Los Angeles: The Olson Company
THE OMNI — Digital City Atlanta: The Omni
THE PEACEMAKER — EXTRA: The Peacemaker
THE PHILADELPHIA SOUND — Digital City Philadelphia: Music
THE PHILLY SOUND — Digital City Philadelphia: Music
THE PRINT SHOP — Broderbund Software: The Print Shop Connection
THE PRODIGY — British Bands: The Prodigy
THE REVOLUTION — New England Revolution Soccer
THE RUGBY CLUB — AOL UK: The Rugby Club
THE SCIENCE PLACE — Digital City Dallas-Fort Worth: Science Place Museum
THE SCREEN TEAM — Entertainment Asylum: Screen Team
THE SHARPER IMAGE — The Sharper Image Store
THE SPORTING NEWS — The Sporting News
THE SPORTS PRINCESS — Digital City Dallas-Fort Worth: Sports Princess
THE STADIUM SHOP — The Stadium Shop
THE STONES — SPIN Online: Rolling Stones Tour
THE STREET — TheStreet.com
THE STRIP — Comic Strip, Manga and Graphic Novel Forum [Web site]
THE SWEATER & THE SCHMOOZER — Digital City New York: The Sweater & The Schmoozer
THE TEEN ZONE — Digital City Dallas-Fort Worth: Teens
THE TEX FILES — Digital City Dallas-Fort Worth: The TEX Files
THE TOKEN MALE — Electra: Token Male
THE UNDERGROUND — Digital City Washington: Teens
THE WALL — Vietnam Veterans Memorial Wall
THE WASHINGTON TIMES — The Washington Times
THE WB — WB Online
THE WB NETWORK — WB Online
THE WEDDING CHANNEL — Digital City Los Angeles: Wedding Guide
THE WEDDING SHOPPER — The Wedding Shopper [Web site]
THE WHALE — Hartford Whalers
THE WU TANG CLAN — The Wu Tang Clan Contest

THEATER GUY — Digital City Boston: Theater Guy
THEATER PRO — AOL WorkPlace: Theaters Community
THEATER PROFESSIONAL — AOL WorkPlace: Theaters Community
THEATER PROFESSIONALS — AOL WorkPlace: Theaters Community
THEATER PROS — AOL WorkPlace: Theaters Community
THERE I WAS — Digital City Twin Cities: There I Was
THESAURUS — Merriam-Webster Thesaurus
THESTREET — TheStreet.com on AOL
THIRD AGE — Third Age [Web site]
THIS DAY IN HISTORY — The History Channel: This Day In History
THIS IS LONDON — AOL UK: Local London Area [Web site]
THIS WEEK — ABC News.com [Web site]
THOMAS COOK SKI — Thomas Cook Ski Direct Area
THOMAS COOK SKI DIRECT — Thomas Cook Ski Direct [Web site]
THRIVE — Thrive@Healthy Living
THRIVE ASTHMA — Thrive@Healthy Living: Asthma
THRIVE EATS — Thrive@Healthy Living: Eats
THRIVE EXPERTS — Thrive@Healthy Living: Experts
THRIVE MARKETPLACE — Thrive@Healthy Living: Marketplace
THRIVE ONLINE — Thrive@Healthy Living
THRIVE OUTDOORS — Thrive@Healthy Living: Active Sports
THRIVE OUTSIDE — Thrive@Healthy Living: Active Sports
THRIVE SEX — Thrive@Healthy Living: Passion
THRIVE SHAPE — Thrive@Healthy Living: Shape
THRIVE TALK — Thrive@Healthy Living: Talk
THRIVE@ — Thrive@Healthy Living
THRIVE@ADVENTURE — Thrive@Healthy Living: Active Sports
THRIVE@EATS — Thrive@Healthy Living: Eats
THRIVE@EXPERTS — Thrive@Healthy Living: Experts
THRIVE@FOOD — Thrive@Healthy Living: Eats
THRIVE@MARKETPLACE — Thrive@Healthy Living: Marketplace
THRIVE@OSTEOPOROSIS — Thrive@Healthy Living: Osteoporosis
THRIVE@OUTDOORS — Thrive@Healthy Living: Outdoors
THRIVE@PASSION — Thrive@Healthy Living: Passion
THRIVE@SEX — Thrive@Healthy Living: Passion
THRIVE@SHAPE — Thrive@Healthy Living: Shape
THRIVE@TALK — Thrive@Healthy Living: Talk
THRIVE@WEIGHTLOSS — Thrive@Healthy Living: Weight Loss
THROAT — AOL Health: Ear, Nose & Throat
THRV BRITTA — Thrive@Healthy Living: Brita Water [Web site]
TI — Texas Instruments
TI FOUNDERS IMAX — Digital City Dallas-Fort Worth: The Science Place Museum
TIAA — TIAA Teachers' Insurance [Web site]
TIAA/CREF — TIAA Teachers' Insurance [Web site]
TIBET — AOL International: Tibet

TICKER — AOL News Ticker
TICKETMASTER — Ticketmaster
TICKETS — Tickets.com [Web site]
TICKETS.COM — Tickets.com [Web site]
TIGERS — Detroit Tigers
TIL — AOL UK: Local London Area [Web site]
TIMBERWOLVES — Minnesota Timberwolves
TIME OUT AMSTERDAM — Time Out's Guide to Amsterdam [Web site]
TIME OUT BUDAPEST — Time Out Travel Guide to Budapest [Web site]
TIME OUT SHOPPING — Time Out Shopping & Services Guide [Web site]
TIMES — New York Times Online
TIMES ART — New York Times: Arts News
TIMES ARTS — New York Times Arts
TIMES BOOKS — New York Times: Books
TIMES CHAT — New York Times: Live Events
TIMES CROSSWORD — New York Times: Crossword
TIMES CROSSWORDS — New York Times: Crossword
TIMES DINING — New York Times: Dining Out
TIMES FILM — New York Times: Movies
TIMES MOVIES — New York Times: Movies
TIMES MUSIC — New York Times: Music & Dance
TIMES NEWS — New York Times Online
TIMES SPORTS — New York Times: Sports News
TIMES STORIES — New York Times: Page One
TIMES THEATER — New York Times: Theater
TIMES TOP NEWS — New York Times: Page One
TIMES TOP STORIES — New York Times: Page One
TIP — AOL Insider Tips
TIP OF DAY — AOL Member Services: Tip of the Day
TIP OF THE DAY — AOL Member Services: Tip of the Day
TIP SHEET — AOL UK: Charts
TIPS — AOL Insider Tips
TIPS FOR AOL NETFIND — AOL NetFind: NetFind Tips [Web site]
TIPS FOR NETFIND — AOL NetFind: NetFind Tips [Web site]
TITF — AOL Computing: Events
TLS — Real Fans: The Last Shot
TMAKER — Broderbund Software Online
TMJ — AOL Health: TMJ/TMD
TMS — AOL Health: Temporomandibular Syndrome
TN SEARCH — AOL News: Search
TNC — The Nature Conservancy
TO AM — Time Out's Guide to Amsterdam [Web site]
TO BUD — Time Out Travel Guide to Budapest [Web site]
TO INT — Time Out International [Web site]
TO INTERNATIONAL — Time Out International [Web site]

TO MERCHANDISE — Time Out Merchandise & Subscriptions
TO PRAG — Time Out's Guide to Prague [Web site]
TO PRAGUE — Time Out's Guide to Prague [Web site]
TO YOUR HEALTH — AOL Health: To Your Health Newsletter
TOBAGO — AOL International: Trinidad and Tobago
TODAY — AOL Today
TODAY'S EVENTS — AOL Live
TODAYS EVENTS — AOL Live
TODAY'S NEWS — AOL News channel
TODAYS NEWS — AOL News channel
TODAY'S NEWS BOARD — AOL News: Message Center
TODAY'S NEWS SEARCH — AOL News: Search
TODD ART — Image Exchange: Ask Todd Art
TODDLER — AOL Families: Babies
TOGO — AOL International: Togo
TOH — AOL Games: Official Game Sites [Web site]
TOKEN MALE — Electra: Token Male
TOLL FREE — AOL Research & Learn: Switchboard Toll Free Directory
    [Web site]
TOM BASS — AOL Sports: Coach Tom Bass
TOM BLAIR — Digital City San Diego: Tom Blair
TOM KIMBALL — Digital City Denver: Humorwrite Online
TOMORROW NEVER DIES — EXTRA: Tomorrow Never Dies
TONGA — AOL International: Tonga
TONY AWARD — AOL Influence: Tony Awards
TONY AWARDS — AOL Influence: Tony Awards
TONY MASSAROTTI — Boston Herald: Tony Massarotti
TONYS — AOL Influence: Tony Awards
TOOL REVIEW — American Woodworker: Tool Reviews
TOOL REVIEWS — American Woodworker: Tool Reviews
TOOLS & REFERENCE — AOL WorkPlace: Tools & Reference
TOON — InToon with the News
TOONZ — InToon with the News
TOP 10 — Late Show Online: Top Ten List
TOP 25 — Antagonist, Inc.: Slaughter's Top 25 Games
TOP 40 FUNDS — AOL Personal Finance: Top 40 Mutual Funds
TOP ADVISOR — Top Advisors' Corner
TOP ADVISORS — Top Advisors' Corner
TOP COMPANY SITES — Internet Connection: Top Company Sites
TOP GAME PICKS — AOL Games: Top Games Picks
TOP M — TopModel
TOP NEWS — Today's News
TOP TIPS — AOL Insider Tips
TOPMODEL — TopModel Online
TOPS TIPS — AOL Insider Tips
TORO SPORT — Digital City Toronto: Sports

TORO SPORTS — Digital City Toronto: Sports
TORO TRAVEL — Digital City Toronto: Travel
TORONTO — Digital City Toronto
TORONTO BLUE JAYS — Toronto Blue Jays
TORONTO DIGITAL CITY — Digital City Toronto
TORONTO DINING — Digital City Toronto: Restaurants
TORONTO EVENTS — Digital City Toronto: Events
TORONTO MOVIES — Digital City Toronto: Movie Guide
TORONTO NEWS — Digital City Toronto: News and Weather
TORONTO PLACES — Digital City Toronto: Events
TORONTO RESTAURANTS — Digital City Toronto: Restaurants
TORONTO SPORT — Digital City Toronto: Sports
TORONTO SPORTS — Digital City Toronto: Sports
TORONTO TRAVEL — Digital City Toronto: Travel
TORRE — The Book Report: Joe Torre
TOS — AOL Terms of Service
TOS ADVISOR — AOL Terms of Service
TOTN — National Public Radio Outreach
TOUR CANADA — AOL Canada: Guided Tour
TOUR GUIDE — AOL Store
TOUR JERUSALEM — Tour Jerusalem
TOUR SAN DIEGO — Digital City San Diego: Tour
TOUR SD — Digital City San Diego: Tour
TOURISM PHILLY — Digital City Philadelphia: Travel
TOWER — Tower Records
TOWER RECORDS — Tower Records
TOY BIZ — Pangea Toy Network
TOY BUZZ — Pangea Toy Network
TOY SHOP — AOL Shopping: Toys & Collectibles
TOY STORE — AOL Shopping: Toys & Collectibles
TOYS SUPERSTORE — AOL Shoppers Advantage: Toys & Video Games
TP — Time: Warner's Teen People Magazine Online
TP BOARDS — Teen People: Message Boards
TP CHAT — Teen People: Live
TP CHAT HOSTS — Teen People: Chat Host Profiles
TP DAILY DISH — Teen People: Daily Dish
TP DD — Teen People: Daily Dish
TP HOST — Teen People: Chat Host Profiles
TP HOST PROFILES — Teen People: Chat Host Profiles
TP LIVE — Teen People: Live
TP LOOKS — Teen People: Looks & Love
TP LOVE — Teen People: Looks & Love
TP ONLINE — Teen People Magazine Online
TP RC — Teen People: Reality Check
TP REALITY CHECK — Teen People: Reality Check
TP SEARCH — Teen People: Search

TP SS — Teen People: Stars & Stuff
TP STARS — Teen People: Stars & Stuff
TP STUFF — Teen People: Stars & Stuff
TP STYLE — Teen People: Looks & Love
TP STYLEGRRL — Teen People Online: Looks & Love
TP SUBSCRIBE — Teen People Online: Subscription Form [Web site]
TP ZINE — Teen People Online: Zine & Heard
TPN — Christianity Online: The Prayer Network
TPO — Teen People Magazine Online
TPR — Princeton Review [Web site]
TRACK — Road & Track Online
TRADERS — Shark Attack Trading Forum
TRAFFIC — Digital City: Traffic Guide
TRAIL BLAZERS — Portland Trail Blazers
TRAIL GUY — Digital City San Diego: Trail of the Week [Web site]
TRAILS ILLUSTRATED — Backpacker Magazine: Marketplace
TRANS TEST — Click & Go 4.0
TRANSCRIPT — AOL Live: Transcripts
TRANSCRIPTION — AOL WorkPlace: Office Services
TRANSCRIPTS — AOL Live: Transcripts
TRANSGENDER — onQ: Transgender Community Forum
TRANSLAND — PlanetOut: Transland
TRANSMEDIA — Digital City San Francisco: Transmedia Network Inc.
TRANSSEXUAL — onQ: Transgender Community Forum
TRANSWORLD — TransWorld Snowboarding
TRANSWORLD SNOWBOARDING — TransWorld Snowboarding
TRANTEST — Click & Go 4.0
TRAVEL & LEISURE — Travel & Leisure Magazine Online
TRAVEL — AOL Travel
TRAVEL ADVISORIES — U.S. & State Department Travel Advisories
TRAVEL ALABAMA — Travel America: Alabama
TRAVEL ALBUQUERQUE — Travel America: Albuquerque
TRAVEL ARIZONA — Travel America: Arizona
TRAVEL ATLANTA — Digital City Atlanta: Traveler
TRAVEL AUSTIN — Travel America: Austin
TRAVEL BARGAIN — AOL Travel: Bargains
TRAVEL BARGAINS — AOL Travel: Bargains
TRAVEL BOSTON — Travel America: Boston
TRAVEL CALIFORNIA — Travel America: California
TRAVEL CC — Travel America: Corpus Christi
TRAVEL CHICAGO — Travel America: Chicago
TRAVEL CINCINNATI — Travel America: Cincinnati
TRAVEL CLASSIFIEDS — AOL Classifieds: Travel
TRAVEL COLORADO — Travel America: Colorado
TRAVEL CONNECTICUT — Travel America: Connecticut
TRAVEL CORNER — Travel Corner

TRAVEL CORPUS CHRISTI — Travel America: Corpus Christi
TRAVEL DALLAS — Travel America: Dallas
TRAVEL DAYTONA BEACH — Travel America: Daytona Beach
TRAVEL DC — Digital City Washington DC: Visitor's Guide
TRAVEL DENVER — Travel America: Denver
TRAVEL EL PASO — Travel America: El Paso
TRAVEL EUGENE — Travel America: Eugene
TRAVEL FEATURES — AOL Travel: Current Destinations
TRAVEL FLORIDA — Travel America: Florida
TRAVEL FORT WORTH — Travel America: Fort Worth
TRAVEL GRACELAND — Travel America: Memphis
TRAVEL GRAND JUNCTION — Travel America: Grand Junction
TRAVEL GUY — Digital City Boston: Travel Guy
TRAVEL HAWAII — Travel America: Hawaii
TRAVEL HONG KONG — AOL Travel: Hong Kong Hand-Over
TRAVEL HOUSTON — Travel America: Houston
TRAVEL HUNTSVILLE — Travel America: Huntsville
TRAVEL INTERESTS — AOL Travel: Where to Go and What to Do
TRAVEL KANSAS — Travel America: Kansas
TRAVEL KENTUCKY — Travel America: Kentucky
TRAVEL KEY WEST — Travel America: Key West
TRAVEL KNOXVILLE — Travel America: Knoxville
TRAVEL LAKE TAHOE — Travel America: Lake Tahoe
TRAVEL LAS VEGAS — Travel America: Las Vegas
TRAVEL LONG BEACH — Travel America: Long Beach
TRAVEL LOS ANGELES — Travel America: Los Angeles
TRAVEL LOUISVILLE — Travel America: Louisville
TRAVEL MA — Travel America: Massachusetts
TRAVEL MAINE — Travel America: Maine
TRAVEL MASSACHUSETTS — Travel America: Massachusetts
TRAVEL MEMPHIS — Travel America: Memphis
TRAVEL MESSAGES & CHAT — AOL Travel: Messages & Chat
TRAVEL MIAMI — Travel America: Miami
TRAVEL MINNEAPOLIS — Travel America: Minneapolis
TRAVEL MINNESOTA — Travel America: Minnesota
TRAVEL MONTGOMERY — Travel America: Montgomery
TRAVEL NASHVILLE — Travel America: Nashville
TRAVEL NEW HAMPSHIRE — Travel America: New Hampshire
TRAVEL NEW ORLEANS — Travel America: New Orleans
TRAVEL NEW YORK — Travel America: New York City
TRAVEL NEW YORK CITY — Travel America: New York City
TRAVEL NEWPORT NEW — Travel America: Newport News
TRAVEL NEWPORT NEWS — Travel America: Newport News
TRAVEL NEWS — Preview Travel News
TRAVEL NH — Travel America: New Hampshire
TRAVEL NORTH DAKOTA — Travel America: North Dakota

TRAVEL NYC — Travel America: New York City
TRAVEL OAHU — Travel America: Oahu
TRAVEL OAKLAND — Travel America: Oakland
TRAVEL OHIO — Travel America: Ohio
TRAVEL ONQ — onQ: Travel
TRAVEL OREGON — Travel America: Oregon
TRAVEL ORLANDO — Travel America: Orlando
TRAVEL PALM SPRINGS — Travel America: Palm Springs
TRAVEL PENNSYLVANIA — Travel America: Pennsylvania
TRAVEL PHILADELPHIA — Travel America: Philadelphia
TRAVEL PHILLY — Digital City Philadelphia: Travel and Tourism
TRAVEL PHOENIX — Travel America: Phoenix
TRAVEL PICKS — AOL Travel: What's Hot
TRAVEL PITTSBURGH — Travel America: Pittsburgh
TRAVEL PORT — PlanetOut: Travel
TRAVEL PORTLAND — Travel America: Portland
TRAVEL PORTLAND ME — Travel America: Portland
TRAVEL PORTLAND OR — Travel America: Portland
TRAVEL PORTLAND OREGON — Travel America: Portland
TRAVEL PORTSMOUTH — Travel America: Portsmouth
TRAVEL REFERENCE — AOL Research & Learn: Geography & Maps
TRAVEL RESERVATION — AOL Travel: Reservations Center
TRAVEL RESERVATIONS — AOL Travel: Reservations Center
TRAVEL RHODE ISLAND — Travel America: Rhode Island
TRAVEL RI — Travel America: Rhode Island
TRAVEL RICHMOND — Travel America: Richmond
TRAVEL SACRAMENTO — Travel America: Sacramento
TRAVEL SALT LAKE — Travel America: Salt Lake City
TRAVEL SALT LAKE CITY — Travel America: Salt Lake City
TRAVEL SAN ANTONIO — Travel America: San Antonio
TRAVEL SAN DIEGO — Travel America: San Diego
TRAVEL SAN FRANCISCO — Travel America: San Francisco
TRAVEL SANTA BARBARA — Travel America: Santa Barbara
TRAVEL SB — Travel America: Santa Barbara
TRAVEL SCOTTSDALE — Travel America: Scottsdale
TRAVEL SEARCH — AOL Travel: Search & Explore
TRAVEL SEATTLE — Travel America: Seattle
TRAVEL SF — Travel America: San Francisco
TRAVEL ST PETE — Travel St. Petersburg
TRAVEL ST PETERSBURG — Travel St. Petersburg
TRAVEL ST. PETE — Travel St. Petersburg
TRAVEL ST. PETERSBURG — Travel St. Petersburg
TRAVEL STORIES — AOL Travel: Current Destinations
TRAVEL SUPERSTORE — AOL Shopping: Luggage & Travel Gear
TRAVEL TAHOE — Travel America: Lake Tahoe
TRAVEL TAMPA — Travel America: Tampa

TRAVEL TENNESSEE — Travel America: Tennessee
TRAVEL TEXAS — Travel America: Texas
TRAVEL TUCSON — Travel America: Tucson
TRAVEL UTAH — Travel America: Utah
TRAVEL VERMONT — Travel America: Vermont
TRAVEL VIRGINIA — Travel America: Virginia
TRAVEL VISA — Traveling With Visa
TRAVEL WARNINGS — U.S. State Department Travel Advisories
TRAVEL WASHINGTON — Travel America: Washington
TRAVEL WASHINGTON DC — Travel America: Washington DC
TRAVEL WEATHER — Worldwide Weather Conditions & Forecasts
TRAVEL WISCONSIN — Travel America: Wisconsin
TRAVEL ZINE — Photo Rents Online: Vacation Rentals
TRAVELERS ADVANTAGE — AOL Travelers Advantage
TRAVELERS CORNER — Travel Corner
TREATMENTS — AOL Health: Illness and Treatments
TREE HUGGERS — EnviroLink Network
TREE SERVICE — AOL WorkPlace: Landscaping & Gardening
     Community
TREK — Star Trek Club
TREK CLUB — Star Trek Club
TREKKER — 800-Trekker Online Store
TREKKIES — Star Trek Club
TREND — AOL Influence channel
TRENDS — AOL Influence channel
TRENDY — AOL Influence channel
TRENTON — Digital City Philadelphia
TRIAD ONLINE — Digital City Greensboro, High Point, and Winston-
     Salem
TRIAMINIC — Triaminic Parents Club
TRIB — Chicago Tribune AOL Edition
TRIB ADS — Chicago Tribune: Classifieds
TRIB CLASSIFIED — Chicago Tribune: Classifieds
TRIB COLUMNISTS — Chicago Tribune: Columnists
TRIB COLUMNS — Chicago Tribune: Columnists
TRIB ENTERTAINMENT — Chicago Tribune: Entertainment Guide
TRIB LOTTERY — Chicago Tribune: Lottery
TRIB NEWS — Chicago Tribune AOL Edition
TRIB SPORTS — Chicago Tribune: Sports
TRIBE — Cleveland Indians
TRIBUNE — Chicago Tribune AOL Edition
TRIESS — onQ: Transgender Organizations
TRINIDAD — AOL International: Trinidad and Tobago
TRIP PLAN — AOL Travel: European Elites
TRIPLE A — American Automobile Association (AAA) Online
TRIPOD — Tripod.com [Web site]

TRIPP — AOL News: Bill Clinton News Special
TRIVIA — Trivia Selections
TRIVIA FORUM — AOL Trivia Forum
TRIVIANA — Digital City San Francisco: Trivian Games
TROPHY HOMES — Digital City Las Vegas: Trophy Homes
TROPICAL STORM — Today's Weather
TROPICAL WEATHER — Today's Weather
TROY AIKMAN — Athlete Direct
TRUE TALES — True Tales from the Internet
TRUFFLES — AOL Shopping: Gourmet Gifts
TRY MIXSTAR — MixStar: One-Month Free Trial
TSC — TheStreet.com [Web pointer]
T-SHIRTS — AOL Shopping: Apparel & Accessories
TSN — The Sporting News
TSN COLLEGE HOOPS — The Sporting News: College Hoops
TSP — Digital City Dallas/Ft. Worth: The Science Place Museum
TUBE — AOL Entertainment: TV Today
TUBERCULOSIS — AOL Health: Tuberculosis
TUNISIA — AOL International: Tunisia
TURKEY — AOL International: Turkey
TURKEY DAY — Thanksgiving @AOL [seasonal]
TURKISH — AOL International: Middle East
<u>TURKIYE</u> — AOL International: Turkey
TURKMENISTAN — AOL International: Turkmenistan
TURTLE ISLAND — AOL Lifestyles: Ethnicity
TUTORING — AOL Research & Learn: Ask-A-Teacher
TUVALU — AOL International: Tuvalu
TV — AOL Entertainment: TV Today
TV DEALER — AOL WorkPlace: TV & Radio Community
TV DEN — Entertainment Asylum: Drama Den
TV GAL — Digital City Boston: TV Gal Amy Amatangelo
TV GAL BOSTON — Digital City Boston: TV Gal Amy Amatangelo
TV GOSSIP — TV Shows Gossip
TV INDUSTRY — AOL Entertainment: Word of Mouth
TV LA — Digital City Los Angeles: TV Navigator
TV LAND — Nick at Nite: TV Land Online
TV LISTINGS — TV Quest
TV NAVIGATOR — Digital City: TV Navigator
TV NETWORKS — TV Networks
TV ONLINE — AOL Entertainment: TV Today
<u>TV PARAODIES</u> — TV Spoofs
TV PEOPLE — AOL Entertainment: TV Today
TV QUEST — TV Quest
TV REPAIR — AOL WorkPlace: TV & Radio Community
TV SATIRES — TV Spoofs
TV SHOWS — AOL Entertainment: TV Today

TV SOURCE — TV Quest
TV SPOOFS — TV Spoofs
TV TODAY — AOL Entertainment: TV Today
TV VIEWERS — TV Viewers Forum
TWANG — Twang This! [Web site]
TWANG THIS — Twang This! [Web site]
TWANG THIS! — Twang This! [Web site]
TWIL — Love@AOL: This Week In Love
TWIN CITIES — Digital City Minneapolis
TWIN CITIES BUSINESS — Digital City Twin Cities: Business
TWIN CITIES CAREERS — Digital City Twin Cities: Employment
    Classifieds
TWIN CITIES CHAT — Digital City Twin Cities: Chat
TWIN CITIES CLASSIFIEDS — Digital City Twin Cities: Employment
    Classifieds
TWIN CITIES EMPLOYMENT — Digital City Twin Cities: Employment
    Classifieds
TWIN CITIES FUN — Digital City Twin Cities: Entertainment
TWIN CITIES JOBS — Digital City Twin Cities: Employment Classifieds
TWIN CITIES KIDS — Digital City Twin Cities: Kids Safe
TWIN CITIES KIDS SAFE — Digital City Twin Cities: Kids Safe
TWIN CITIES LIVING — Digital City Twin Cities: Living
TWIN CITIES LOCAL NEWS — Digital City Twin Cities: Local News
TWIN CITIES MARKET — Digital City Twin Cities: Marketplace
TWIN CITIES PEOPLE — Digital City Twin Cities: People
TWIN CITIES SPORTS — Digital City Twin Cities: Sports
TWN CHAT — iVillage: Live Chats
TWOLVES — Minnesota Timberwolves
TX MOTOR SPEEDWAY — Digital City Dallas-Ft. Worth: Speed On The
    Fast Track
TYPESETTING — AOL WorkPlace: Office Services Forum
TYPHOON — Today's Weather
TZABACO — PlanetOut: Tzabaco Catalog
U IOWA — The University of Iowa [Web site]
U MICH — University of Michigan [Web site]
U OF P HEALTH — Digital City Philadelphia: University of Pennsylvania
U PENN — University of Pennsylvania [Web site]
U TEXAS — University of Texas as Austin [Web site]
U.S.S.B.A. — U.S. Small Business Administration
UA — Unlimited Adventures
UBOC — Union Bank of California
UCAL — University of California Extension Online
UCAOL — University of California Extension Online
UCF — Digital City Orlando: UCF Future [Web site]
UCF FUTURE — Digital City Orlando: UCF Future [Web site]
UCX — University of California Extension Online

UDSL — xDSL Information
UFC — The UFC: Ultimate Fighting Championships
UGANDA — AOL International: Uganda
UGF — The User Group Network [Web site]
UIUC — University of Illinois at Urbana-Champaign [Web site]
UK — AOL UK (United Kingdom)
UK BIKING — AOL UK: Back Street Heroes: Motorcycle Forum
UK CRICKET — AOL UK: Cricketer International Magazine
UK DC NEWS — AOL UK: Local Life Newsletters
UK ELECTION — AOL UK: Election '97
UK ELECTION 97 — AOL UK: Election '97
UK FOOL — AOL UK: The Motley Fool UK
UK FOOTBALL — AOL UK: Football (Soccer)
UK FOOTBALL — AOL UK: Football (Soccer)
UK FOOTBALL CAPTION COMPETITION — AOL UK: Football Caption Competition
UK FOOTBALL CHAT — AOL UK: Football Chat
UK FOOTBALL NEWS — AOL UK: Football News
UK FOOTY NEWS — AOL UK: Football News
UK GAME SPOT — AOL UK: GameSpot
UK GAY — AOL UK: Utopia - Gay & Lesbian Forum
UK GORILLAS — AOL UK: Saving Gorillas in the Mist
UK HOTELS — AOL UK: Online Hotels Guide [Web site]
UK HOTELS GUIDE — AOL UK: Online Hotels Guide [Web site]
UK LESBIAN — AOL UK: Utopia - Gay & Lesbian Forum
UK MAIN — AOL UK (United Kingdom)
UK MF — AOL UK: The Motley Fool UK
UK MOTORBIKES — AOL UK: Back Street Heroes: Motorcycle Forum
UK NEWS — AOL UK: News
UK NEWS STAND — AOL UK: News Stand
UK PUB — AOL UK: Pub
UK SCHOOL — AOL UK: Forum for Secondary Schools
UK SCHOOLS — AOL UK: Forum for Secondary Schools
UK SOAF — AOL UK: Sign On A Friend
UK SOCCER — AOL UK: Football (Soccer)
UK SOCCER — AOL UK: Football (Soccer)
UK SOCCER CHAT — AOL UK: Football Chat
UK SOCCER NEWS — AOL UK: Football News
UK SPECIAL REPORT — AOL UK: Special News Report [Web site]
UK VOTE — AOL UK: Election '97
UK VOTING — AOL UK: Election '97
UK WOMEN — AOL UK: Utopia for Women
UK WRITE — The Writers Club: UK Writers
UK WRITERS — The Writers Club: UK Writers
UK WRITING — The Writers Club: UK Writers

UKRAINE — AOL International: Ukraine
UKRAYINA — AOL International: Ukraine
ULCER — AOL Health: Ulcers
ULCERS — AOL Health: Ulcers
ULTIMATE — The UFC: Ultimate Fighting Championships
ULTRALIGHTS — Hobby Central: Aviation
UMD — Universal Multimedia & Design, Inc. [Web site]
UMD.COM — Universal Multimedia & Design, Inc.
 [Web site]
UNABOM — Digital City San Francisco: Unabomber Trial
UNABOMB — Digital City San Francisco: Unabomber Trial
UNABOMBER — Digital City San Francisco: Unabomber Trial
UNABOMBER TRIAL — Digital City San Francisco: Unabomber Trial
UNCENSORED — Love@AOL: Jaid Barrymore Uncensored
UNDERGROUND — Digital City Washington: Teens
UNION — Union Bank of California
UNION BANK — Union Bank of California
UNITARIAN — Religion & Beliefs: The Humanism-
 Unitarianism Forum
UNITARIANISM — Religion & Beliefs: The Humanism-
 Unitarianism Forum
UNITED ARAB EMIRATES — AOL International: United Arab
 Emirates
UNITED KINGDOM — AOL UK (United Kingdom)
UNITED MEDIA — The Comic Zone [Web site]
UNITED MEDIA.COM — The Comic Zone [Web site]
UNITED STATES — The Fifty States
UNIVERSAL — Universal Studios [Web site]
UNIVERSAL.COM — Universal Studios [Web site]
UNIVERSITY — AOL Research & Learn: College Preparation
UNLIMITED ADVENTURES — Unlimited Adventures
UNSUBSCRIBE — Subscribe to an Online Newsletter
UPDATE ACCOUNT — AOL Member Services: Change Your Billing
 Information
UPDATE BILLING INFO — AOL Member Services: Change Your Billing
 Information
UPGRADE — Upgrade to the Latest Version of AOL Software
UPGRADE ORDER — Order AOL Software Upgrade Kits
UPGRADE ORDERS — Order AOL Software Upgrade Kits
UPHS — Digital City Philadelphia: University of Pennsylvania
UPSET STOMACH — AOL Health: Heartburn/GERD
URBAN LEAGUE — The National Urban League
URINARY TRACT — AOL Health: Kidney & Urinary Tract Disorders
URL — What is HTTP?
URUGUAY — AOL International: Uruguay
US — AOL International: North America

US AP — AOL News: US & World News
US HEADLINES — AOL News: US & World Hourly News Summary
US NEWS — AOL News: US & World News Front Page
US OPEN GOLF — AOL Sports: Golf
US REUTERS — US World Wire
US ROBOTICS — U.S. Robotics Online
US SMALL BUSINESS — U.S. Small Business Administration
US SUMMARY — AOL News: US & World Hourly News Summary
US TAX FORMS — Tax Forms, Schedules, and Instructions
US WEATH — Today's Weather
US WEATHER — Today's Weather
US WIRE — AOL News: US & World News
US WORLD — AOL News: US & World News Front Page
USA — The Fifty States
USA TODAY — USA Today [Web site]
USA TODAY.COM — USA Today [Web site]
USENET — Internet Newsgroups/USENET
USER GROUP — The User Group Network [Web site]
USER GROUPS — The User Group Network [Web site]
USER NAME — Create, Delete, Restore and Update Screen Names
USFSA — United States Figure Skating Association
USPS — United States Postal Service
USPS WEB — United States Postal Service [Web site]
USR — U.S. Robotics Online
USS ENTERPRISE — Star Trek Club
USSBA — U.S. Small Business Administration
UTAH — Utah Forum
UTAH FORUM — Utah Forum
UTAH JAZZ — Utah Jazz
UTI — AOL Health: Urinary Tract Infections
UTILITIES — AOL Computing: Productivity Applications
UTILS — AOL Computing: Productivity Applications
UTOPIA — AOL UK: Utopia - Gay & Lesbian Forum
UTOPIA CHAT — AOL UK: Gay & Lesbian Chat
UTOPIA EMAIL — AOL UK: Utopia - Email List
UTOPIA EMAIL LIST — AOL UK: Utopia - Email List
UTOPIA LIST — AOL UK: Utopia - Email List
UTOPIA LISTSERV — AOL UK: Utopia - Email List
UTOPIA LOVE — AOL UK: Utopia - Personal Adverts
UTOPIA NEWS — AOL UK: Utopia - News Center
UTOPIA PERSONALS — AOL UK: Utopia - Personal Adverts
UTOPIA PHOTOS — AOL UK: Utopia - Users Picture Library
UTOPIA PICS — AOL UK: Utopia - Users Picture Library
UTOPIA PICTURES — AOL UK: Utopia - Users Picture Library
UTOPIA PIX — AOL UK: Utopia - Users Picture Library
UTOPIA VIRTUAL PLACES — Utopia Virtual Places

UTOPIA VP — Utopia Virtual Places
UTOPIA WOMEN — AOL UK: Utopia - Women
UTOPIA YOUTH — AOL UK: Utopia - Youth
UTOPIAN NEWS — AOL UK: Utopia - News Center
UTOPIAN WOMEN — AOL UK: Utopia - Women
UZBEKISTAN — AOL International: Uzbekistan
V ACCOUNT — The Vanguard Group: Access [Web site]
V COMMS — The Vanguard Group: Contact Information [Web site]
V DAY — Valentine's Day @ AOL [seasonal]
V FITZGERALD — Digital City Los Angeles: Valerie Fitzgerald Real
     Estate
V FUNDS — The Vanguard Group [Web site]
V NEWS — The Vanguard Group [Web site]
V POOL — Virtual Pool
V STATS — The Vanguard Group: Daily Prices and Yields [Web site]
V STRATEGY — The Vanguard Group [Web site]
V WEBB — Electra: Veronica Webb's Digital Eye
V103 — Digital City Chicago: V103 Online 106 JAMZ
VA BEACH LOCAL NEWS — Digital City Hampton Roads: News
VA HOTEL — Digital City Washington DC: Visitor's Guide to Hotels
VA LOTTERY — Digital City Washington: Lottery Numbers
VACATION — AOL Travel channel
VACATION PLAN — AOL Travel: European Elites
VACATION RENTAL — Vacation Rentals Express
VACATION RENTALS — Vacation Rentals Express
VACATION RENTALS EXPRESS — Vacation Rentals Express
VACATIONS — AOL Travel channel
VACATIONS.COM — Preview Travel [Web site]
VALENTINE — Valentine's Day @ AOL [seasonal]
VALENTINE VACATIONS — Preview Travel's Top 10 Romantic Getaways
VALENTINE'S — Valentine's Day @ AOL [seasonal]
VALENTINES — Valentine's Day @ AOL [seasonal]
VALENTINE'S DAY — Valentine's Day @ AOL [seasonal]
VALENTINES ONQ — onQ: Finding the One
VALENTINES VACATIONS — Preview Travel's Top 10 Romantic
     Getaways
VALERIE F — Digital City Los Angeles: Valerie Fitzgerald Real Estate
VALERIE FITZGERALD — Digital City Los Angeles: Valerie Fitzgerald
     Real Estate
VALUES — Religion & Beliefs: Ethics & Values
VALUTOOL — The Motley Fool: The Foolish Valuation Tool
VAN KAMPEN — Van Kampen American Capital
VANGUARD — The Vanguard Group [Web site]
VANGUARD ONLINE — The Vanguard Group [Web site]
VANUATU — AOL International: Vanutu
VARGAS — Interiors By Design with Lynn Vargas

VARGAS DESIGNS — Interiors By Design with Lynn Vargas
VARIABLE ANNUITIES — Retirement Planning & Variable Annuities
VATICAN CITY — AOL International: Vatican City
VAULT — Mutual Fund Center: fundsVault
VB — Visual Basic
VDE — Electra: Veronica Webb's Digital Eye
VECTOR — AOL Computing: Illustrator and Vector Art
VECTOR ART — AOL Computing: Illustrator and Vector Art
VECTOR SIG — AOL Computing: Illustrator and Vector Art
VEGAN — Vegetarians Online
VEGANS — Vegetarians Online
VEGAS — Digital City Las Vegas
VEGAS INSIDER — Vegas Insider [Web site]
<u>VEGATARIAN</u> — Vegetarians Online
<u>VEGATARIANS</u> — Vegetarians Online
VEGETARIAN — AOL Interests: Food
VEGETARIAN — AOL Interests: Vegetarian Living
VEHICLES CLASSIFIEDS — AOL Classifieds: Vehicles
**VENDING — AOL WorkPlace: Vending and Coin-Op
  Machines**
**VENDING MACHINE — AOL WorkPlace: Vending and Coin-
  Op Machines**
**VENDING MACHINES — AOL WorkPlace: Vending and Coin-
  Op Machines**
VENDORS — AOL Computing: Companies
VENEZUALA — AOL International: Venezuala
VERONICA — Gopher
VERONICA WEBB — Electra: Veronica Webb's Digital Eye
VERONICA'S CLOSET — WB Online: Veronica's Closet
VERONICAS CLOSET — WB Online: Veronica's Closet
VERONICAS DIGITAL EYE — Electra: Veronica Webb's Digital Eye
VERTIGO — DC Comics: Vertigo Comics
VET — AOL WorkPlace: Veterinarian Community
VETERANS — Military & Vets Club
VETERANS DAY — Veteran' Day Tribute [seasonal]
VETERINARIAN — AOL WorkPlace: Veterinarian Community
VETERINARIANS — AOL WorkPlace: Veterinarian Community
VETERINARY — AOL WorkPlace: Veterinarian Community
VG — The Vanguard Group [Web site]
VGA PLANETS — VGA Planets Gaming Forum
VGAP — VGA Planets Gaming Forum
VGF — Video Games Forum
VGS — Video Games Forum
VH1 — VH1 Online
VIC — AOL Computing: Virus Information
VID ZONE — The Video Zone

VIDEO EQUIPMENT — Video Magazine Online
VIDEO GAME — Video Games Forum
VIDEO GAMES — Video Game Selections
VIDEO MAG — Video Magazine Online
VIDEO MAGAZINE — Video Magazine Online
VIDEO OL — Video Magazine Online
VIDEO ONLINE — Video Magazine Online
VIDEO PRODUCTION — AOL WorkPlace: Video Production Community
VIDEO SIG — Video Special Interest Group
VIDEO ZONE — The Video Zone
VIETNAM — Vietnam Areas
VIETNAM MEMORIAL — Vietnam Veterans Memorial Wall
VIEW ACCOUNT ACTIVITY — AOL Rewards
VIEW ACCOUNT HISTORY — AOL Rewards
VIEWER — AOL Computing: Recommended Viewers
VIEWERS — AOL Computing: Recommended Viewers
VIEWERS TAKE CONTROL — TV Viewers Forum
VIEWZ — Viewz: The Online Magazine for Personal Computing
VILLAIN — Military City Online: Villains of Fact & Fiction
VILLAINS — Military City Online: Villains of Fact & Fiction
VIN — Veterinary Information Network
VIP — VIP for a Day Contest Winners
VIP FOR A DAY — VIP for a Day Contest Winners
VIRGIN — Virgin Records America
VIRGIN ISLANDS — AOL International: Virgin Islands
VIRGIN RECORDS — Virgin Records America
VIRGO — Horoscope Selections
VIRTUAL ATLANTIC — AOL Canada: Virtual Atlantic
VIRTUAL CAMPUS — Kaplan Online: Virtual Campus
VIRTUAL FRUITCAKE — Virtual Fruitcake
VIRTUAL FUN — Youth Tech: Virtual Fun
VIRTUAL HUMOR — Christianity Online: Contests and Fun Stuff
VIRTUAL JOB FAIR — Westech Virtual Job Fair
VIRTUAL PLANET — AOL Atlas: Virtual Planet
VIRTUAL POOL — Virtual Pool
VIRTUAL REALITY — AOL Computing: Virtual Reality
VIRTUAL TORCH — Virtual Torch Relay
VIRTUAL VINEYARDS — Virtual Vineyards [Web site]
VIRTUAL VOWS — Love@AOL: CyberVows
VIRTUAL WALES — Virtual Wales
VIRTUAL WEDDINGS — Love@AOL: CyberVows
VIRTUAL YARD SALE — AOL Classifieds
VIRTUE — iVillage: The Nutrition Physician
VIRTUES — iVillage: The Nutrition Physician
VIRUS — AOL Computing: Virus Information
VIRUS GUARD — Safety Online with Dr Alan Solomon

VIRUS UPDATE — Computer Protection Center
VIS HELP — Visual Help: AOL Graphic Representations of Hints
    and Tips
VISA INFO — AOL Visa Card Information
VISA INFORMATION — AOL Visa Card Information
VISION — AOL Health: Eyes and Vision
VISION VIDEO — Christianity Online: Gateway Films/Vision Video
VISIT SAN DIEGO — Digital City San Diego: Tour
VISTA — Chase Manhattan Bank on AOL
VISUAL BASIC — Visual Basic
VISUAL HELP — Visual Help: AOL Graphic Representations of Hints
    and Tips
VISUAL PROPERTIES — Apartments.com
VITAMIN — Health & Vitamin Express
VITAMIN EXP — Health & Vitamin Express
VITAMIN EXPRESS — Health & Vitamin Express
VITAMIN(S) — Health & Vitamin Express
VJF — Westech Virtual Job Fair
VKAC — Van Kampen American Capital
VOICE — Entertainment Asylum: Club Sinatra
VOIGHT — Thrive@Healthy Living: Shape
VOLATILITY — AOL Personal Finance: Market Correction
VOLCANO — Volcano Resources
VOLCANOS — Volcano Resources
VOLLEYBALL — Volleyball
VOTE 97 — AOL News: The Vote '97
VP — Virtual Pool
VP UTOPIA — Utopia - Virtual Places
VR — AOL Computing: Virtual Reality
VRE — Vacation Rentals Express
VROOM — Digital City South Florida: Marketplace
VSH — Virtual Summer House [seasonal]
VV — Christianity Online: Gateway Films/Vision Video
VZ — The Video Zone
VZONE — The Video Zone
W. LOS ANGELES HOMES — Digital City Los Angeles: Ron Wynn Homes
WABC TV — Digital City New York: WABC-TV
WABC-TV — Digital City New York: WABC-TV
WAIS — Gopher
WAKEBOARDING — AOL Sports: Sailing Forum
WALES — AOL UK: Wales
WALES EOL — AOL UK: Wales Events Online
WALKING — AOL Sports: Fitness
WALL — Vietnam Veterans Memorial Wall
WALL STREET WORDS — Wall Street Words
WALLPAPER — AOL Computing: Windows Wallpaper

WALT DISNEY WORLD — Walt Disney World Resorts
WALT WHITMAN — Digital City Philadelphia: Walt Whitman Bridge
WALT WHITMAN BRIDGE — Digital City Philadelphia: Walt Whitman
 Bridge
**WALTER ANDERSEN — Digital City San Diego: Walter
 Andersen Nursery**
**WALTER ANDERSEN NURSERY — Digital City San Diego:
 Walter Andersen Nursery**
WAND TV — ABC Online: WAND TV in Decatur, IL
WANGER — Jerry Wenger's Stock Picks
WANNABE — AOL Community Leader Program
WANTMAN — Digital City Philadelphia: The Love Files
WARCRAFT — Warcraft II: Tides of Darkness
WARCRAFT 2 — Warcraft II: Tides of Darkness
WARCRAFT II — Warcraft II: Tides of Darkness
WARNER — Warner Records
WARNER BROS SS — Warner Bros. Studio Store
WARNER MUSIC — Warner/Reprise Records Online
WARNER PLUMBING — Warner Plumbing [Web site]
WARNER PLUMBING — Warner Plumbing [Web site]
WARNER RECORDS — Warner/Reprise Records Online
WARNER STORE — Warner Bros. Studio Store
WARNER SUPER PLUMBING — Warner Plumbing [Web site]
WARRIORS — Golden State Warriors
WART — AOL Health: Warts
WARTS — AOL Health: Warts
WASH AGENTS — Digital City Washington: Real Estate Agents
WASH CAPS — Washington Capitals
WASH DC — Digital City Washington DC
WASH PERSONALS — Digital City Washington: Personals
WASH TIMES — Digital City Washington: The Washington Times
WASHING TOONS — Digital City Washington: Washing-Toons from Exit
 Poll
WASHINGTON — Digital City Washington DC
WASHINGTON AGENTS — Digital City Washington: Real Estate Agents
WASHINGTON CAPITALS — Washington Capitals
WASHINGTON DC — Digital City Washington DC
WASHINGTON EMPLOYMENT — Digital City Washington: Employment
 Classifieds
WASHINGTON GOLF — Digital City Washington: Golf
WASHINGTON KIDS — Digital City Washington Kids Safe
WASHINGTON KIDSSAFE — Digital City Washington: Kids Safe
WASHINGTON LOCAL NEWS — Digital City Washington: Local News
WASHINGTON NEWS — Digital City Washington: News
WASHINGTON NIGHTLIFE — Digital City Washington: Nightlife
WASHINGTON ONLINE — Digital City Washington

WASHINGTON PEOPLE — Digital City Washington: People
WASHINGTON RELIGION — Digital City Washington: Religion
WASHINGTON RELO — Digital City Washington: Relocation Guide
WASHINGTON RELOCATION — Digital City Washington: Relocation Guide
WASHINGTON RELOCATION GUIDE — Digital City Washington: Relocation Guide
WASHINGTON SPORTS — Digital City Washington: Sports
WASHINGTON TIMES — Digital City Washington: The Washington Times
WASHINGTON TRANSFER — Digital City Washington: Relocation Guide
WASHINGTON WEATHER — Digital City Washington: News
WASHINGTON WIT — Buzzsaw: The Day's News, Only Different
WASHING-TOONS — Digital City Washington: Washing-Toons from Exit Poll
WATE TV — ABC Online: WATE TV in Knoxville, TN
WATERCOOLER — AOL WorkPlace: Watercooler Conversations
WATERHOUSE — Waterhouse Investment Services
WATERS ON THE BAY — Digital City San Francisco: Waters Celebrity Chats
WAV CHAT — AOL UK: WAV Chat Room
WAV CHAT UK — AOL UK: WAV Chat Room
WAVY — Wavy Weather
WAVY WEATHER — WAVY TV Weather
WAXMAN — Access Discount Camera [Web site]
WAY TO GO — Prism Elite Software
WB — The WB Network
WB 11 — Digital City New York: WB 11
WB 17 — Digital City Philadelphia: WPHL-TV WB 17 Online
WB 17 NEWS — Digital City Philadelphia: WB 17 News
WB 17 SPORTS — Digital City Philadelphia: WB 17 Sports
WB 17 STEVE — Digital City Philadelphia: WPHL WB 17: Highland
WB 18 — Digital City Orlando: WKCF WB 18
WB 2 — Digital City Denver: WB2 News, Weather, and Sports
WB 39 — Digital City South Florida: WB39 Online [Web site]
WB 56 — Digital City Boston: WB 56 WLVI-TV
WB BOSTON — Digital City Boston: WB 56 WLVI-TV
WB CONTEST — Warner Bros Contest
WB CONTESTS — Warner Bros Contest
WB KIDS — Kids WB! Online
WB NET — The WB Network
WB NETWORK — The WB Network
WB SPORTS — Digital City Philadelphia: WB 17
WB SS — Warner Bros. Studio Store
WB STORE — Warner Bros. Studio Store
WB STUDIO STORE — Warner Bros. Studio Store

WBAY TV — ABC Online: WBAY TV in Green Bay, WI
WBRC TV — ABC Online: WBRC TV in Birmingham, AL
WBRZ TV — ABC Online: WBRZ TV in Baton Rouge, LA
WBZL — Digital City South Florida: WB39 Online [Web site]
WC — Warcraft II: Tides of Darkness
WC CHAT — The Writers Club: Chat
WC MARKET — The Writers Club: Marketplace
WC MARKETPLACE — The Writers Club: Marketplace
WC2 — Warcraft II: Tides of Darkness
WCE — AOL Computing: Windows CE Handheld PCs
WCN — World Crisis Network
WCRG — The Writers Club: Romance Group
WCVB TV — ABC Online: WCVB TV in Boston, MA
WD — Woman's Day Magazine Online
WD BETTER LIVING — Woman's Day: Ideas for Better Living
WD SPECIALS — Woman's Day: Ideas for Better Living
WDHN TV — ABC Online: WDHN TV in Dothan, AL
WDIO TV — ABC Online: WDIO TV in Duluth, MN
WDTP — AOL Computing: Desktop & Web Publishing
WDW — Walt Disney World Resorts
WDWP — AOL Computing: Desktop & Web Publishing
WDZL — Digital City South Florida: WB39 Online [Web site]
WEALTH — AOL Influence channel
WEASELS — AOL Canada: PrintWeasels
WEATHER — Today's Weather
WEATHER MALL — The WSC Weather Mall
WEATHER MAPS — Today's Weather
WEATHER NEWS — Today's Weather
WEATHER WATCH — Digital City Twin Cities: Weather
WEAVING — AOL Interests: Crafts
WEB — AOL.com [Web site]
WEB ART — AOL Computing: Web Art
WEB BROWSER — AOL.com [Web site]
WEB BUSINESS — AOL WorkPlace: Doing Business Online
WEB CLASSES — AOL Computing: On the Net
WEB DESIGN — PrimeHost
**WEB DEVELOPER — Web Developer's Virtual Library
[Web site]**
WEB ENTERTAINMENT — AOL Entertainment: Word of Mouth
WEB FIND — AOL NetFind [Web site]
WEB GUIDE LA — Digital City Los Angeles: WebGuide [Web site]
WEB HELP — AOL Member Services: Internet & World Wide Web
WEB HOSTING — AOL PrimeHost
WEB INFO — AOL Computing: On the Net
WEB LA — Digital City Los Angeles: WebGuide [Web site]
WEB PAGE — AOL Computing: On the Net [Web site]

WEB PAGE IN 60 — Create a Web Site in a Minute
WEB SEARCH — AOL NetFind [Web site]
WEB TIMESAVERS — AOL NetFind: Time Savers [Web site]
WEBB — Electra: Veronica Webb's Digital Eye
WEBB'S WORLD — Digital City Twin Cities: Webb's World
WEBMASTER INFO — AOL WebMaster Website [Web site]
WEBMETRO — WebMetro: Internet Resource Center
<u>WEBOPEDIA</u> — AOL Computing: Webopædia [Web site]
WEBSTER — Merriam-Webster Collegiate Dictionary
WEBSTER'S — Merriam-Webster Collegiate Dictionary
WEBSTERS — Merriam-Webster Collegiate Dictionary
WEDDING — The Knot: Weddings for the Real World
WEDDING DAY @ AOL — The Knot: Weddings For The Real World
WEDDING DAY — The Knot: Weddings For The Real World
WEDDING DAY AT AOL — The Knot: Weddings For The Real World
WEDDING SHOPPER — The Wedding Shopper [Web site]
WEDDINGS — The Knot: Weddings for the Real World
WEEKLIES — AOL Magazine Outlet Store
WEEKLY GOODS — Shopping Channel Newsletter
WEEKLY READER — Weekly Reader
WEIGHT LOSS — AOL Health: Dieting & Weight Loss
WEIGHTLIFTING — AOL Sports: Fitness
WEIRD FACT — AOL Research & Learn: Fact-A-Day
WEISSMANN — Travel Corner
WELCOME — Welcome Window
WELCOME AMERICA — Digital City Philadelphia: Welcome America
    Celebration
WELCOME HOME — Digital City Denver: Welcome Home Magazine
WELLNESS — AOL Health: Wellness & Disease Prevention
WELLS FARGO — Wells Fargo Bank Online
WELLS — Wells Fargo Bank Online
WELLS FARGO BANK — Wells Fargo Bank Online
WENGER — Jerry Wenger's Stock Picks
WENGER PICKS — Jerry Wenger's Stock Picks
WEST DIGC — Digital City West
WEST L.A. HOMES — Digital City Los Angeles: Ron Wynn Homes
WEST LA HOMES — Digital City Los Angeles: Ron Wynn Homes
WEST LOS ANGELES HOMES — Digital City Los Angeles: Ron Wynn
    Homes
WEST TECH EXPO — Westech Virtual Job Fair
WEST TO WEST — West to West: Devon to Oregon School Exchange
    Project
WESTCHESTER HOMES — Digital City Los Angeles: Westchester Real
    Estate
WESTSIDE HOMES — Digital City Los Angeles: Michael Greenwald
    Homes

WESTWOOD — Westwood Studios [Web site]
WESTWOOD STUDIOS — Westwood Studios [Web site]
WESTWORD — Digital City Denver: Westword News & Art Weekly
WESTWORD MAGAZINE — Digital City Denver: Westword News & Art Weekly
WF — Wells Fargo Bank Online
WFAA TV — ABC Online: WFAA TV in Dallas/Ft. Worth, TX
WFAN — Digital City New York: Sports Radio 66 AM WFAN
WFTV TV — ABC Online: WFTV TV in Orlando, FL
WGGB TV — ABC Online: WGGB TV in Springfield, MA
WGN TV — WGN-TV in Chicago, IL [Web site]
WGO — Digital City New York: What's Going On
WGST — Digital City Atlanta: News
WGST RADIO — Digital City Atlanta: News
WGTU TV — ABC Online: WGTU TB in Traverse City, MI
WHALERS — Carolina Hurricanes
WHAT IS IT — What is it? Sweepstakes Winner
WHAT IS HOT — What's New on AOL
WHAT IS IT — What is it? Sweepstakes Winner
WHAT IS NEW — What's New on AOL
WHAT TO SSEE IN LA — Los Angeles Sights
WHAT'S GOING ON — Digital City New York: What's Going On
WHATS GOING ON — Digital City New York: What's Going On
WHAT'S HOT — What's New on AOL
WHATS HOT — What's New on AOL
WHAT'S NEW — What's New on AOL
WHATS NEW — What's New on AOL
WHAT'S ON — Entertainment Asylum: What's On TV
WHATS ON — Entertainment Asylum: What's On TV
WHATS ON TV — Entertainment Asylum: What's On TV
WHEELING — Digital City Chicago: Wheeling
WHEELS — Wheels
WHEELS EXCHANGE — Wheels Exchange
WHEN SAT COMES — When Saturday Comes
WHEN SATURDAY COMES — When Saturday Comes
WHIST — Classic Card Games
WHITE HOUSE — The White House Forum
WHITE PAGES — AOL NetFind: Find a Person
WHIZ — Money Whiz
WHO KISSED WHO — Love@AOL: Who Kissed Who?
WHO KISSED WHOM — Love@AOL: Who Kissed Who?
WHOI TV — ABC Online: WHOI TV in Peoria-Bloomington, IL
WHRO — Digital City Hampton Roads: WHROLink Public Telecommunications
WHROLINK — Digital City Hampton Roads: WHROLink Public Telecommunications

WHTM TV — ABC Online: WHTM TV in Harrisburg, PA
WHY BE JEWISH — Judaism Today: Where Do I Fit?
WICCA — Religion & Beliefs: Pagan Religions & Occult Sciences
WICS — Women in Community Service
WIDE WORLD — ABC Sports: Wide World of Sports
WIDE WORLD OF SPORTS — ABC Sports: Wide World of Sports
WIFE ABUSE — Massachusetts Coalition of Battered Women Service Groups
WIN — AOL Computing: PC Windows Forum
WIN 95 — AOL Computing: Windows 98/95
WIN 98 — AOL Computing: Windows 98/95
WIN CE — AOL Computing: Windows CE Handheld PCs
WIN FORUM — AOL Computing: PC Windows
WIN MAG — Windows Magazine [Web site]
WIN MAG.COM — Windows Magazine [Web site]
WIN NT — AOL Computing: Windows NT
WIN WELL — AOL Canada: Don Cherry Online
WINDOWS — AOL Computing: PC Windows Forum
WINDOWS 95 — AOL Computing: Windows 98/95
WINDOWS 98 — AOL Computing: Windows 98/95
WINDOWS CE — AOL Computing: Windows CE Handheld PCs
WINDOWS DTP — AOL Computing: Desktop & Web Publishing
WINDOWS FORUM — AOL Computing: PC Windows Forum
WINDOWS MAG — Windows Magazine [Web site]
WINDOWS MAGAZINE — Windows Magazine [Web site]
WINDOWS NT — AOL Computing: Windows NT
WINDOWS TIPS — AOL Computing: Computing Tips
<u>WINDSOCK</u> — Winsock Central
WINDSURFING — AOL Sports: Sailing Forum
WINDY CITY — Digital City Chicago
WINE & DINE ONLINE — Food and Drink Network
WINE — AOL Interests: Food
WINE GUY — Digital City Boston: Wine Guy
WINE SPECTATOR — Wine Spectator [Web site]
WINNER — Contest Area
WINNER CARS — Winner Ford Lincoln Mercury
WINNER FORD — Winner Ford Lincoln Mercury
WINNER LINC — Winner Ford Lincoln Mercury
WINNER LINCOLN — Winner Ford Lincoln Mercury
WINNER MERCURY — Winner Ford Lincoln Mercury
WINNER'S CIRCLE — ABC Sports: At The Track
WINNERS CIRCLE — ABC Sports: At The Track
WINSOCK — Winsock Central
WINSOCK CENTRAL — Winsock Central
WINSOCK.DLL — Winsock Central
WINSTON — Winston the Wonderhound

WINSTON SALEM — Digital City Winston Salem
WINSTON THE WONDERHOUND — Winston the Wonderhound
WINSTON-SALEM — Digital City Winston Salem
WINTER GAMES — The Olympics
WIRED — Wired Magazine [Web site]
WIRED MAG — Wired Magazine [Web site]
WIRED MAGAZINE — Wired Magazine [Web site]
WIRED ONLINE — Wired Magazine [Web site]
WIRELESS — Wireless Communication
WIS — Waterhouse Investment Services
WISC — University of Wisconsin-Madison [Web site]
WIT CITY — AOL News: Daily Chuckle
WIXT TV — ABC Online: WIXT TV in Syracuse, NY
WIZARD — Wizard World
WIZARD MAGAZINE — Wizard World
WIZARD WORLD — Wizard World
WIZARDS — Washington Wizards
WIZARD'S CHEST — Digital City Denver: The Wizard's Chest
WJBF TV — ABC Online: WJBF TV in Augusta, GA
WJCL TV — ABC Online: WJCL TV in Savannah, GA
WJFK — WJFK 106.7 FM Redskins Network Online
WJFK REDSKINS NETWORK — WJFK 106.7 FM Redskins Network
    Online
WJNO — Digital City South Florida: WJNO 1040 AM
WJNO ONLINE — Digital City South Florida: WJNO 1040 AM
WKBW TV — ABC Online: WKBW TV in Buffalo, NY
WKCF — Digital City Orlando: WKCF WB 18 in Orlando, FL
WKLS — WKLS: 96 Rock in Atlanta, GA
WKRN TV — ABC Online: WKRN TV in Nashville, TN
WKYS — Radio One: The People's Expo in Washington D.C.
WLA HOMES — Digital City Los Angeles: Ron Wynn Homes
WLOS TV — ABC Online: WLOS TV in Asheville, NC
WLOX TV — ABC Online: WLOX TV in Biloxi, MS
WLS — WLS Chicago
WLVI — WB 56 in Boston, MA
WLVI 56 — WB 56 in Boston, MA
WMBB TV — ABC Online: WMBB TV in Panama, FL
WMDT TV — ABC Online: WMDT TV in Salisbury, MD
WMUR TV — ABC Online: WMUR TV in Manchester, NH
WN COMMUNITY — Women's Network: TalkWomen
WNBA — AOL Sports: Pro Basketball
WNEP TV — ABC Online: WNEP TV in Scranton/Wilkes Barre, PA
WNNX — 99X WNNX 99.7 FM in Atlanta, GA
WOJTON — Digital City Philadelphia: DjunaVerse
WOKR TV — ABC Online: WOKR TV in Rochester, NY
WOLF TRAP — Wolf Trap

WOLO TV — ABC Online: WOLO TV in Columbia, SC
WOM — AOL Entertainment: Word of Mouth
WOMAN — Women's Network
WOMAN ONQ — onQ: Women's Space
WOMAN'S — Women's Network
WOMAN'S DAY — Woman's Day Magazine Online
WOMANS DAY — Woman's Day Magazine Online
WOMEN & INVESTING — AOL Personal Finance: Women & Investing
WOMEN & MONEY — AOL Personal Finance: Women & Investing
WOMEN — Women's Network
WOMEN AND INVESTING — AOL Personal Finance: Women & Investing
WOMEN CLASS — Women's Network: Online Courses
WOMEN IN SPORTS — AOL Sports: Women's Sports
WOMEN MAIN — Women's
WOMEN ONQ — onQ: Women's Space
WOMEN SCOPES — Electra: Horoscopes
WOMEN SPORT — AOL Sports: Women's Sports
WOMEN SPORTS — AOL Sports: Women's Sports
WOMEN'S HEALTH — AOL Health: Women's Health
WOMEN'S — Women's Network
WOMENS — Women's Network
WOMENS BASKETBALL — Women's College Basketball
WOMENS B-BALL — Women's College Basketball
WOMEN'S B-BALL — Women's College Basketball
WOMENS COMMUNITY — Women's Network: TalkWomen
WOMENS HEALTH — AOL Health: Women's Health
WOMEN'S HEALTH WEB — Women's Health Internet Sites
WOMENS HOOPS — Women's College Basketball
WOMEN'S HOOPS — Women's College Basketball
WOMENS NETWORK — Women's Network
WOMENS SPACE — onQ: Women's Space
WOMEN'S SPORTS — AOL Sports: Women's Sports
WOMENS SPORTS — AOL Sports: Women's Sports
WONDERLINK — Creative Wonders [Web site]
WOOD — American Woodworker Online
WOODEN — Real Fans: Wooden Award Watch
WOODEN AWARD — Real Fans: Wooden Award Watch
WOODEN WATCH — Real Fans: Wooden Award Watch
WOODWORK — American Woodworker Online
WOODWORKER — American Woodworker Online
WOODWORKING — American Woodworker Online
WORD BOOKS — Christianity Online: Word Publishing
WORD CHALLENGE — AOL International: Language Games
WORD GAME — AOL International: Language Games
WORD GAMES — AOL International: Language Games
WORD HISTORIES — Merriam-Webster: Word Histories

WORD HISTORY — Merriam-Webster: Word Histories
WORD OF MOUTH — AOL Entertainment: Word of Mouth
WORD ORIGINS — Merriam-Webster: Word Histories
WORD PROCESSING — AOL Computing: Word Processing Applications
WORD PROCESSOR — AOL Computing: Word Processing Applications
WORD PUB — Christianity Online: Word Publishing
WORDPERFECT — WordPerfect Resource Center
WORK — AOL WorkPlace channel
WORKING WEB — AOL WorkPlace: Working the Web
WORKPLACE — AOL WorkPlace channel
WORKPLACE BENEFITS — AOL WorkPlace Benefits
WORKPLACE CHAT — AOL WorkPlace: Chats & Messages
WORKPLACE CHAT — AOL WorkPlace: Chats & Messages
WORKPLACE ETHICS — AOL WorkPlace: Ethics
WORKPLACE HEARTLAND — AOL WorkPlace: Working From The
    Heartland
WORKPLACE MESSAGES — AOL WorkPlace: Chats & Messages
WORKPLACE PRODUCTIVITY — AOL WorkPlace: Productivity
WORKPLACE RELATIONSHIPS — AOL WorkPlace: Relationships
WORKPLACE SEARCH — AOL WorkPlace: Search & Explore
WORKPLACE TRANSITIONS — AOL WorkPlace: Transitions
WORKS — AOL Computing: Word Processing Applications
WORKSTYLE — AboutWork: WorkStyle
WORLD — AOL International channel
WORLD ACCESS NETWORK — World Access Network Directory
    [Web site]
WORLD ACCESS NETWORK DIRECT — World Access Network Directory
    [Web site]
WORLD AP — AOL News: US & World News
WORLD BEAT — World Music Forum
WORLD BELIEFS — Religion & Beliefs: World Beliefs
WORLD BUSINESS — International Business
WORLD CAFE — World Cafe [Web pointer]
WORLD CRISIS — World Crisis Network
WORLD CRISIS NETWORK — World Crisis Network
WORLD CULTURE — International Cultures
WORLD CULTURES — International Cultures
WORLD CUP — AOL Sports: Soccer
WORLD FINANCE — International Business
WORLD HEADLINES — AOL News: US & World Hourly Updates
WORLD LEAGUE — Team NFL World League
WORLD MUSIC — World Music Forum
WORLD NEWS — AOL News: US & World News Front Page
WORLD NEWS TONIGHT — ABC News.com [Web site]
WORLD REUTERS — AOL News: US & World News
WORLD SPORTS — International Sports

WORLD SUMMARY — AOL News: Hourly News Summary
WORLD TRAVEL — International Travel
WORLD WIDE WEATHER — International Weather Reports
WORLD WIDE WEB — AOL.com [Web site]
WORLD WRESTLING FED — World Wrestling Federation Online
WORLDPLAY — WorldPlay Games
WORLDPLAY ACTION — WorldPlay: Action Games
WORLDPLAY ADVENTURE — WorldPlay: Adventure Games
WORLDPLAY BACKGAMMON — WorldPlay: Backgammon
WORLDPLAY BALDIES — WorldPlay: Baldies Online
WORLDPLAY BOARD — WorldPlay: Puzzle & Board Games
WORLDPLAY BRIDGE — WorldPlay: Bridge
WORLDPLAY CARDS — WorldPlay: Classic Card
WORLDPLAY CLASSIC — WorldPlay: Classic Card
WORLDPLAY CLASSIC CARD — WorldPlay: Classic Card
WORLDPLAY CRIBBAGE — WorldPlay: Cribbage
WORLDPLAY GAMES — WorldPlay Games
WORLDPLAY GIN — WorldPlay: Gin
WORLDPLAY HEARTS — WorldPlay: Hearts
WORLDPLAY MAIN — WorldPlay Games
WORLDPLAY PUZZLES — WorldPlay: Puzzle & Board Games
WORLDPLAY SPADES — WorldPlay: Spades
WORLDPLAY SPUNKY — WorldPlay: Spunky's Shuffle
WORLDPLAY STRATEGY — WorldPlay: Action Games
WORLDPLAY TIM3 — WorldPlay: The Incredible Machine 3
WORLDPLAY TODAY — WorldPlay: Top Picks
WORLDS — AOL International channel
WORLDWIDE — Digital City UK: Worldwide Links
WORTH — Worth Magazine Online
WORTH MAGAZINE — Worth Magazine Online
WORTH ONLINE — Worth Magazine Online
WORTH PORTFOLIO — Worth Magazine Online
WOTB — Digital City San Francisco: Waters Celebrity Chats
WOTV TV — ABC Online: WOTV TV in Battle Creek, MI
**WOW COM — Wow-Com: The World of Wireless
   Communications [Web site]**
WP — AOL Computing: Word Processing Applications
WP ACTION — WorldPlay: Action Games
WP ACTION GAMES — WorldPlay: Action Games
WP ADVENTURE — WorldPlay: Adventure Games
WP ADVENTURE GAMES — WorldPlay: Adventure Games
WP BACKGAMMON — WorldPlay: Backgammon
WP BALDIES — WorldPlay: Baldies Online
WP BOARD — WorldPlay: Puzzle & Board Games
WP BOARD GAMES — WorldPlay: Puzzle & Board Games
WP BRIDGE — WorldPlay: Bridge

WP BUSINESS CHAT — AOL WorkPlace: Business Talk
WP BUSINESS TALK — AOL WorkPlace: Business Talk
WP CARD GAMES — WorldPlay: Classic Card
WP CHATS & MESSAGES — AOL WorkPlace: Chats & Messages
WP CLASSIC — WorldPlay: Classic Card
WP CLASSIC CARD — WorldPlay: Classic Card
WP CRIBBAGE — WorldPlay: Cribbage
WP FANTASY GAMES — WorldPlay: Adventure Games
WP GAMES — WorldPlay Games
WP GIN — WorldPlay: Gin
WP HEARTS — WorldPlay: Hearts
WP PICKS — WorldPlay: Top Picks
WP PUZZLE — WorldPlay: Puzzle & Board Games
WP PUZZLE GAMES — WorldPlay: Puzzle & Board Games
WP PYRAMID — WorldPlay: SCHWA Pyramid
WP ROLE PLAYING GAMES — WorldPlay: Adventure Games
WP RPG'S — WorldPlay: Adventure Games
WP SEARCH & EXPLORE — WorldPlay: Search & Explore
WP SEARCH — WorldPlay: Search & Explore
WP SIMULATION — WorldPlay: Action Games
WP SPADES — WorldPlay: Spades
WP STRATEGY — WorldPlay: Action Games
WP TIM3 — WorldPlay: The Incredible Machine 3
WP TODAY — WorldPlay: Top Picks
WP TOP PICKS — WorldPlay: Top Picks
WPBF TV — ABC Online: WPBF TV in West Palm Beach, FL
WPDE TV — ABC Online: WPDE TV in Myrtle Beach, SC
WPHL — WPHL Channel WB 17 in Philadelphia, PA
WPHL NEWS — WPHL Channel WB 17: News
WPHL SPORTS — WPHL Channel WB 17: Sports
WPHL STEVE — WPHL Channel WB 17: Highland
WPHL TV — WPHL Channel WB 17 in Philadelphia, PA
WPHL-TV — WPHL Channel WB 17 in Philadelphia, PA
WPLAY BACKGAMMON — WorldPlay: Backgammon
WPLAY BALDIES — WorldPlay: Baldies Online
WPLAY BRIDGE — WorldPlay: Bridge
WPLAY CRIBBAGE — WorldPlay: Cribbage
WPLAY GIN — WorldPlay: Gin
WPLAY HEARTS — WorldPlay: Hearts
WPLAY PICKS — WorldPlay: Top Picks
WPLAY SPADES — WorldPlay: Spades
WPLAY TODAY — WorldPlay: Top Picks
WPTA TV — ABC Online: WPTA TV in Fort Wayne, IN
WQAD TV — ABC Online: WQAD TV in Moline, IL
WQOW TV — ABC Online: WQOW TV in Eau Claire, WI
WRD — Christianity Online: Word Publishing

WRESTLING — World Wrestling Federation Online
WRITE — Reading & Writing
WRITER — The Writers Club
WRITER'S — The Writers Club
WRITERS — The Writers Club
WRITER'S CLUB — The Writers Club
WRITERS CLUB — The Writers Club
WRITERS CLUB CHAT — The Writers Club: Chat
WRITERS CLUB MARKET — The Writers Club: Marketplace
WRITERS CLUB MARKETPLACE — The Writers Club: Marketplace
WRITERS RESOURCE — Grammar and Style Guide
WRITERS RESOURCES — Grammar and Style Guides
WRITING — Reading & Writing
WRITING STYLE — Grammar and Style Guides
WRTV TV — ABC Online: WRTV TV in Indianapolis, IN
WS — onQ: Women's Space
WS AOL TODAY — AOL Today
WS MOTHER — AOL Shopper's Advantage: Mother's Day Sweepstakes
 [seasonal]
WS ONQ — onQ: Women's Space
WS PART CONTROL — Parental Controls
WSB TV — ABC Online: WSB TV in Atlanta, GA
WSC — When Saturday Comes
WSF — Women's Sports World
WSI — Waterhouse Investment Services
**WSJ — The Wall Street Journal Interactive Edition [Web
 site]**
**WSJ.COM — The Wall Street Journal Interactive Edition
 [Web site]**
WSJV TV — ABC Online: WSJV TV in South Bend, IN
WSP — Grateful Dead: Widespread Panic Forum
WSVN — WSVN Channel 7 News in Miami, FL
WSVN 7 — WSVN Channel 7 News in Miami, FL
WSW — Wall Street Words
WSYX TV — ABC Online: WSYX TV in Columbus, OH
WTEN TV — ABC Online: WTEN TV in Albany, NY
WTG — Prism Elite Software
WTNH TV — ABC Online: WTNH TV in New Haven, CN
WTOK TV — ABC Online: WTOK TV in Meridian, MS
WTOP — WTOP News & Headlines in Washington D.C. [Web site]
WTOP NEWS — WTOP News & Headlines in Washington D.C.
 [Web site]
WTOP SPORTS — WTOP News & Headlines in Washington D.C.
 [Web site]
WTTW — WTTW Channel 11 in Chicago, IL
WTVC TV — ABC Online: WTVC TV in Chattanooga, TN

WTVQ TV — ABC Online: WTVQ TV in Lexington, KY
WU — Wu-Tang Forever [Web site]
WU TANG — Wu-Tang Forever [Web site]
WU TANG CLAN — Wu-Tang Forever [Web site]
WUSTL — Washington University in St. Louis [Web site]
WU-TANG — Wu-Tang Forever [Web site]
WVEC TV — ABC Online: WVEC TV in Norfolk, VA
WVII TV — ABC Online: WVII TV in Bangor, ME
WWE — Hot Education Internet Sites
WWF — World Wrestling Federation Online
WWOS — ABC Sports: Wide World of Sports
WWS — ABC Sports: Wide World of Sports
WWW — AOL.com [Web site]
WWW HELP — AOL Member Services: Internet and World Wide Web
WWW PAGE IN 60 — Create a Web Site in a Minute
WWW.ABCNEWS.COM — ABC NEWS.com [Web site]
WWW.AOL.COM — AOL.com [Web site]
WWW.PLANETOUT.COM — PlanetOut
WWWOMEN — Digital City San Francisco: Bridges for Professional Women
WXLV TV — ABC Online: WXLV TV in Winston/Salem, NC
WXOW TV — ABC Online: WXOW TV in LaCrescent, MN
WZZM TV — ABC Online: WZZM TV in Grand Rapids, MI
X COUNTRY — Cross Country Travel Tips
X COUNTRY TRAVEL — Cross Country Travel Tips
X FILES — X Files Forums
X FILES EXPO — X Files Forums
X FILES SIM — The X Files Sim Forum
X GAMES — X Games Coverage
X2 — x2 Connections
XCMD — XCMD Developers Center
XCMD SIG — XCMD Developers Center
XDSL — xDSL Information
X-FILES — X Files Forums
XMAS — Holidays @ AOL [seasonal]
X-RAY — Market News Center: X-Ray
XRAY — Market News Center: X-Ray
XTRA MAGAZINE — AOL Canada: Xtra Magazine Gay and Lesbian Bi-Weekly
XTRA WEST — AOL Canada: Xtra Magazine Lesbian and Gay Bi-Weekly
XWORDS — New York Times: Crossword Puzzles
YACHTING — Boating & Sailing
YACHTS — Boating & Sailing
YAHOO — AOL Find: Looking for Something?
YANCEY — Christianity Online: News Commentaries

YANKEE BEAT — Digital City New York: Suzyn Waldman's Yankees Beat

YANKEES — New York Yankees

YANKEES SKIPPER — Digital City New York: The Torre Story

YANKS — New York Yankees

YAO — Fishing Broadcast Network

YARD SALE — AOL Classifieds

YC — Your Church Magazine

YEAR — The Year In News

YEAST INFECTIONS — AOL Health: Yeast Infections

YELLOW PAGES — AOL NetFind: Find a Business [Web site]

YEMEN — AOL International: Yemen

YHA — Youth Hostel Association

YO — Digital City Philadelphia

YO FOOTBALL — Digital City Philadelphia: Pro Football

YOGABYTES — Digital City Denver: Yogabytes

YORK EOL — North East Events Online

YOU — All About You

YOUNG AMERICA OUTDOORS — Fishing Broadcast Network

YOUNG CHEFS — eGG: Young Chefs

YOUNG COUNTRY — Young Country

YOUNG COUNTRY DALLAS — Young Country

YOUNG COUNTRY DFW — Young Country

YOUNG COUNTRY KYNG — Young Country

YOUNG COUNTRY RADIO — Young Country

YOUR BIZ — AOL WorkPlace Channel

YOUR BUSINESS — AOL WorkPlace: Your Business

YOUR CHURCH — Your Church Magazine

YOUR FASHION STYLE — Electra: Your Fashion Style

YOUR HEALTH — Interactive Health Fair

YOUR INDUSTRIES — Professional Forums

YOUR INDUSTRY — Professional Forums

YOUR SPORTS — NESN: New England Outdoors

YOUR STYLE — Electra: Your Fashion Style

YOUR TOONS — The Cartoons Forum

YOUR WEB PAGE — Create a Web Site in a Minute

YOUTH HOSTEL — Youth Hostel Association

YOUTH NET — Youth Net

YOUTH ONQ — onQ: Youth Area

YOUTH SPORTS — Youth Sports Directory of San Diego

YOUTH TECH — Youth Tech

YOU'VE GOT MAIL — AOL Celebrity "You've Got Mail" Voice Gallery

YOUVE GOT MAIL — AOL Celebrity "You've Got Mail" Voice Gallery

YOU'VE GOT PICTURES — "You've Got Pictures!"

YP — AOL Yellow Pages [Web site]

YT — Youth Tech

YT CHAT — Youth Tech: Chat Shack
YT TOUR — Youth Tech: Slideshow Tour
YUGOSLAVIA — AOL International: Yugoslavia
YUKON — Digital Wilderness
Z — Zealot: Sci-Fi and Fantasy Fun
Z AUCTION — Z-Auction [Web site]
ZACKS — Zacks Investment Research [Web site]
ZAIRE — AOL International: Democratic Republic of Congo
ZAMBIA — AOL International: Zambia
ZEALOT — Zealot: Sci-Fi and Fantasy Fun
ZEALOT SCI-FI — Zealot: Sci-Fi and Fantasy Fun
ZEALOT TRIVIA — Zealot: Sci-Fi and Fantasy Fun
ZEALOTS — Zealot: Sci-Fi and Fantasy Fun
ZEITUNG — AOL International: Newsstand
ZEN — AOL Entertainment: Zentertainment News
ZENTERTAINMENT — AOL Entertainment: Zentertainment News
ZEO — Pangea Toy Network: Power Rangers Zeo!
ZEOS — Micron Electronics [Web site]
ZIMBABWE — AOL International: Zimbabwe
ZIP CODE — Zip Code Directory [Web site]
ZIP CODE DIRECTORY — Zip Code Directory [Web site]
ZIP CODES — Zip Code Directory [Web site]
ZIPPO — The Daily News Pointer [Web site]
ZODIAC — Horoscope Selections
ZODNAS — Sandoz Online: Research for a Better Life
ZOO PHILLY — Philadelphia Zoo
ZOOM T — Zoom Telephonics, Inc.
ZOOM TELEPHONICS — Zoom Telephonics, Inc.

APPENDIX

KEYBOARD SHORTCUTS

America Online's most frequently used commands have key combinations you can use in lieu of the standard pull-down menus. These keyboard shortcuts make navigation much easier and faster, and I highly recommend that you use them. To use a keyboard shortcut with Windows, press either the **Alt** key (located next to the **spacebar**) or the **Ctrl** key (usually located next to the **Alt** key), and then (without releasing the **Alt** or **Ctrl** key) press the appropriate letter key. On the Macintosh, do the same thing using the **Command** key, which you'll find next to the **spacebar** with either the Apple logo or the cloverleaf symbol on it. Other keys used in the keyboard shortcuts include the **function keys** (located on the topmost row of the keyboard), the **Enter** key (also called the **Return** key on the Macintosh), and the **Option** key (usually located next to the **Command** key on the Macintosh). Please note that the keyboard shortcuts are different depending on whether you access America Online from Windows or a Macintosh and may also be different based on what version of software you are using. The following keyboard shortcuts are for AOL software version 4.0 (Windows and Mac):

Function	Windows	Macintosh
File Menu	Alt+F	n/a
New	Ctrl+N	Command+N
Open . . .	Ctrl+O	Command+O
Close	Ctrl+F4	Command+W
Save	Ctrl+S	Command+S
Print . . .	Ctrl+P	Command+P

Function	Windows	Macintosh
Exit (Quit)	Alt+F4	Command+Q
Edit Menu	Alt+E	n/a
Undo	Ctrl+Z	Command+Z
Cut	Ctrl+X	Command+X
Copy	Ctrl+C	Command+C
Paste	Ctrl+V	Command+V
Paste as Quotation	n/a	Command+Option+V
Select All	Ctrl+A	Command+A
Find in Top Window	Ctrl+F	n/a
Spell Check	Ctrl+=	Command+=
Speak Text	n/a	Command+H
Stop Speaking	n/a	Command+.
Exit Free Area	Ctrl+E	Command+E
Mail Center Menu	Alt+M	n/a
Read Mail	Ctrl+R	Command+R
Write Mail	Ctrl+M	Command+M
Send Mail	Ctrl+Enter	Enter
My Files Menu	Alt+Y	n/a
My AOL Menu	Alt+A	n/a
Favorites Menu	Alt+V	n/a
Add to Favorite Places	Ctrl++	Command++
Go To Keyword…	Ctrl+K	Command+K
People Menu	Alt+P	n/a
New Instant Message	Ctrl+I	Command+I
Send an Instant Message	Ctrl+Enter	Enter
Locate AOL Member Online	Ctrl+L	Command+L
Get AOL Member Profile	Ctrl+G	Command+G
Find…	Alt+D	Command+F
Window Menu	Alt+W	n/a
Cascade Windows	Shift+F5	n/a
Tile Windows	Shift+F4	n/a

Function	Windows	Macintosh
Close Top Window	n/a	Command+W
Close All Windows	n/a	Command+ Option+W
Sign Off Menu	Alt+S	n/a
Help	Alt+H	Command+/
Abort Incoming Text	Esc	Command+.

Other keyboard navigational tips include

- **My Shortcuts:** In both Windows and the Mac, **Ctrl** (or **Command**)+**0** through **9** are do-it-yourself keyboard shortcuts, customized by selecting the **Favorites** button on the toolbar (Windows) or the **Window** menu (Mac), **My Shortcuts**, and finally **Edit Shortcuts** (see Chapter 1 for more detailed instructions on customization).

- **Alt key:** In Windows, every pull-down menu item is accessible via the keyboard. First use the listed keyboard shortcut to open the menu and then press **Alt** plus the letter underlined in the menu item you want to select. You can also use the down- and up-arrow keys to move through a menu.

- **Tab key:** You can move around some windows by pressing **Tab** to hop from field to field. The Compose Mail window is a good example.

- **Arrow keys:** The four arrow keys, usually located between your character keys and the number pad, are useful in moving through lists and menus.

VirtuaLingo
Glossary of Key
America Online
Terms

You need to know the lingo to be a true keyword connoisseur. If you can rattle off more than a dozen keywords without drawing a breath, but the semantics of cyberspace leave you speechless, read this glossary. All the terms related to using keywords, plus a few more words that make you sound good, are defined in this special version of the VirtuaLingo glossary. The complete version, with all the technical terms, jargon, and slang you could want, plus lots of useful (and trivial) information, can be found in the *AOL Companion* (MIS:Press, 1998). Credit and thanks goes to George Louie, who has been co-authoring this glossary with me since 1994.

America Online, Inc. (AOL)

> The nation's leading online service, headquartered in Virginia. Founded in 1985 and formerly known as Quantum Computer Services, America Online has grown rapidly in both size and scope, with over 12 million members and hundreds of alliances with major companies. America Online's stock exchange symbol is *AOL*. To contact America Online headquarters, call 1-703-448-8700 or use 1-800-827-6364 to speak to a Member Services representative.

alphanumeric

> Data or information consisting of the letters of the alphabet *A* through *Z* (upper- and lowercase) and the digits *0* through *9*. Keywords can be alphanumeric, but a few also contain punctuation marks.

AOLoholic

A member of America Online who begins to display any of the following behaviors: spending most of their free time online; thinking about America Online even when offline (evidenced by the addition of shorthands to non-AOL writings); attempting to bring all their friends and family online; and/or thinking America Online is the best invention since the wheel. Many, but not all AOLoholics, go on to become community leaders. If you fit this description, see keyword: LEADERS. *See also* member *and* community leader.

article

A text document that is intended to be read online, but may be printed or saved for later examination offline. Usually articles are less than 25K in size.

auditorium

Auditoriums are specially equipped online "rooms" that allow large groups of America Online members to meet in a structured setting. Visit keyword: AOL LIVE for the latest auditorium schedules.

bandwidth

A measure of the amount of information that can flow through a given point at any time. Technically, bandwidth is the difference, in *hertz* (Hz), between the highest and lowest frequencies of a transmission channel. However, as typically used, it more often refers the amount of data that can be sent through a given communications circuit. To use a popular analogy, low bandwidth is a two-lane dirt road while high bandwidth is a six-lane superhighway. How quickly a keyword works is based on bandwidth — yours and AOL's.

beta test

A period in a new product or service's development that is designed to discover problems (or "bugs") prior to its release to the general public. America

Online often invites members to beta test its new software. If you are interested in beta testing AOL software, you may be able to apply at keyword: BETA APPLY.

bug

A problem or glitch in a product, be it software or hardware. A bug may be referred to jokingly as a "feature." You can report a problem with AOL software or services by going to keyword: HELP, clicking **Error Messages**, and then clicking the **Ask The Staff** button.

channel

This is the broadest category of information into which America Online divides its material. See Chapter 1 for a list of channels or see keyword: CHANNELS or CHANNEL GUIDE.

chat

To engage in real-time communications with other members. America Online members that are online at the same time may chat with each other in a number of ways: Instant Messages (IMs), chat/conference rooms, and auditoriums. Chatting provides immediate feedback from others; detailed discussions are better suited for message boards and lengthy personal issues are best dealt with in e-mail if a member isn't currently online.

chat/conference rooms

Online areas where members may meet to communicate and interact with others. There are two kinds of chat areas: public and private. Public chat areas can be found in the People Connection area (keyword: PEOPLE) or in the many forums around America Online.

community leader

America Online members who volunteer in the various forums and areas online. They usually work from their homes, not America Online headquarters, hence they may be also known as *remotes*. They serve as guides, hosts, forum leaders/assistants/consultants, and so on. To learn more, see keyword: LEADERS.

cyberspace

An infinite world created by our computer networks. Cyberspace is no less real than the real world — people are born, grow, learn, fall in love, and die in cyberspace. These effects may or may not be carried over into the physical world. America Online is an example of cyberspace created through interaction between the energies of the members, staff, and computers.

e-mail

Short for electronic mail. One of the most popular features of online services, e-mail allows you to send private communications electronically from one person to another anywhere in the world. With America Online's e-mail system, mail can be sent directly to scores of people, carbon copied, blind carbon copied, and forwarded. You can even attach files to e-mail messages. E-mail can also be sent (and forwarded) to any other service that has an Internet address. See keyword: MAIL CENTER for more information.

Favorite Place

A feature that allows you to "mark" America Online and World Wide Web sites you'd like to return to later. These favorite places are stored in your Personal Filing Cabinet. Any World Wide Web site can be made a Favorite Place, as well as any America Online window with a little heart in the upper right-hand corner of the title bar. See Chapter 1 for more details.

Instant Message (IM)

America Online's equivalent of passing notes under the table, as opposed to speaking up in the room (chat) or writing out a letter or memo (e-mail). Instant Messages (IMs) may be exchanged between two members signed on at the same time and are useful for conducting conversations when a chat room isn't appropriate, available, or practical. Internet users can also send and receive Instant Messages if they download and install the free *AOL Instant Messenger* program (see keyword: AIM).

history

In the context of AOL software version 4.0, this refers to the last 16–25 places you visited. This history list is found under the small arrow next to the keyword entry box on the toolbar. You can clear your history list in your **Toolbar** preferences.

Internet

The mother of all networks is not an online service itself, but rather serves to interconnect worldwide computer systems and networks. The Internet, originally operated by the National Science Foundation (NSF), is now managed by private companies (one of which is AOL). America Online features the Internet Connection department, which includes access to USENET newsgroups, Gopher and WAIS databases, FTP, and the World Wide Web, plus help with understanding it all.

keyboard shortcuts

The America Online software provides us with keyboard command equivalents for menu selections. For example, rather than selecting **Send Instant Message** from the pull-down menu, you could type **Ctrl+I** in Windows or **Command+I** on the Mac. For a complete list of these keyboard shortcuts, see the Appendix.

keyword

Something you now probably know a lot more about than you ever expected. Seriously, here is our most accurate definition of a keyword: a predetermined set of characters, numbers, symbols and/or words usually based on a title or content of a page, and used to directly access that page on America Online.

member

An America Online subscriber. The term *member* is embraced because we consider ourselves members of the online community. There are currently over 12 million members accounts on America Online, each of which may be shared by up to five people.

password

The secret four-to-eight-character code word you use to secure your account. Because password security is so important, we're including a number of password-creation tips and reminders for you here. Please read these and pass these along to your friends (and enemies).

- Your password should be as long as possible (use all eight characters, if you can).

- Your password should not include any word found in your profile, any of your names (or your spouse's/kid's names), or anything commonly found in a dictionary.

- Your password should be a combination of letters and numbers.

- Try using the first letter of each word in an eight-word sentence.

- Or, use a word that is easy to remember and insert numbers into it such as SU8M3MER. (Important: Do **not** use any passwords you have ever seen used as examples.)

- Change your password often (we recommend once a month) at keyword: PASSWORD.

Personal Filing Cabinet

This is a special feature of the AOL software that organizes your mail, files, newsgroup and message board postings, and download manager information. Everything in the Personal Filing Cabinet is stored on your hard disk.

screen name

The names (actually pseudonyms more often than not) that identify America Online members online. Screen names may contain no fewer than three and no more than ten characters, and they must be unique. Any one account may have up to five screen names to accommodate family members or alter-egos, and each can (and should) have its own unique password. Either way, you cannot replace the original screen name created when you set up the account, and the person that established the original screen name and account is responsible for all charges incurred by all five screen names. To add, delete, or restore deleted screen names, sign on with your master screen name and go to keyword: NAMES.

shorthands

The collective term for the many emoticons and abbreviations used during chat, such as :) or LOL!. These devices were developed by members over time to give information on the writer's emotional state when only plain text is available. A brief list of these is available at keyword: SHORTHANDS.

surf

To cruise in search of information not readily evident in the hope of discovering something new. Usually paired with another word to describe the type of information being sought. Keyword surfing with keyword: RANDOM is an excellent example.

toolbar

The blocks of buttons usually found at the top of your screen in the AOL software,. In AOL software version 4.0, many of the buttons have menus, and portions of it are customizeable. Navigational buttons and a keyword entry box are also a part of the 4.0 toolbar.